'The best biography of the year, Axw
rescued Nader Shah from obscurity ;
human portrait of tyranny, conquest,
superb introduction to Iran itself, wh
beautifully-written, compelling worl
relevant today.'
Simon Sebag Montefiore

'a very successful [biography]. Michael Axworthy knows his Persia
… and he writes well: this is an excellent story, very ably told.'
David Morgan, *Times Literary Supplement*

'Michael Axworthy has done an outstanding job of trying to understand what moved Nadir … the result is a book that is informative and
a pleasure to read, for specialists and non-specialists alike. Thanks to
the author's deft handling of the subject, Nadir as a person becomes
real and his actions become understandable … well researched … this
is a great book and an excellent read that you can even take to the
beach.'   Willem Floor, *Middle East Journal*

'both scholarly and highly readable from start to finish … valuable for
both specialists and graduate students of history … this new volume
presents a wealth of information hitherto unknown and offers some
fresh and unique interpretations on the rise and reign of Nader Shah
Afshar.'   George Bournoutian, *American Historical Review*

'Using a vivid style, this work chronicles the rise and fall of Nadir Shah
from his early origins in northern Khurasan to his assassination by his
followers in 1747 … It draws on a variety of recent studies and a
considerable range of primary sources to create a work accessible to
both specialists and general readers … Axworthy's lively text is quite
groundbreaking … *The Sword of Persia* provides a very good overview
of Nadir's career as well as an up-to-date summary of research on him'
Ernest Tucker, *International Journal of Middle East Studies*

'I have read this book with considerable pleasure and admiration …
Axworthy has taken account of the latest research, contributed to that
himself, and produced a book that will be welcomed by specialists and
the wider history-minded public.'
Dr Charles Melville, Pembroke College, Cambridge

'Nader Shah has been too long neglected, and Michael Axworthy's *The
Sword of Persia* provides new and valued insight into his critical role in
Iran's eighteenth-century history.'
Professor Gene Garthwaite, Dartmouth College

'This is, without any doubt, a valuable book. Axworthy gives a fascinat-
ing picture of Iran in the eighteenth century and provides a key to a
better understanding of many of the issues after Nader Shah relating to
the Zand and Qajar eras.'
Professor Sadegh Zibakalam, Tehran University

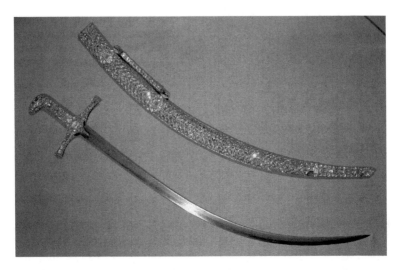

1. *Son of the Sword.*
This is the sword traditionally believed to have been carried by Nader Shah
on his campaigns. It is now in Tehran. It was inscribed and embellished in the
reign of Fath Ali Shah 50 or more years later. The scabbard is encrusted with
diamonds. Nader used the imagery of the sword to describe himself
on a number of occasions.
(Photo courtesy of the Royal Ontario Museum.)

The Sword of Persia

Nader Shah

From Tribal Warrior to Conquering Tyrant

Michael Axworthy

I.B. TAURIS

LONDON · NEW YORK

To my father

Published in 2006 by I.B.Tauris & Co Ltd
6 Salem Road, London W2 4BU
175 Fifth Avenue, New York NY 10010
www.ibtauris.com

In the United States of America and in Canada distributed by
Palgrave Macmillan, a division of St Martin's Press
175 Fifth Avenue, New York NY 10010

ISBN 10: 1 85043 706 8
ISBN 13: 978 1 85043 706 2

A full CIP record for this book is available from the British Library
A full CIP record for this book is available from the Library of Congress

Library of Congress catalog card: available

Typeset in Palatino Linotype
Printed and bound by CPI Group (UK) Ltd, Croydon, CR0 4YY

Contents

Maps and Illustrations

Acknowledgements

In writing this book I have benefited from the generous help and advice of a large number of people. Chief among these were Chris and Homa Rundle, Nargess Majd, Christos Nifadopoulos and Leo Drollas, without whose translations of source material and patient re-examination of individual points and queries the finished result would have been much inferior. Peter Avery was an encouragement and inspiration, as well as a great help on a number of specific points, and translations. Chris Rundle also read through the manuscript, as did Sandy Morton, Charles Melville, Willem Floor, Ali Ansari and Jill Bowden; and their comments and suggestions much improved the book (though they were not always accepted), as did those of Andrew Newman, who looked at parts of the manuscript at an early stage. Willem Floor allowed me sight of some of his unpublished research, which proved very important for the book. Paul Luft, along with Ali Ansari and Anoush Ehteshami, was instrumental in securing me a Research Fellowship from Durham University for the purposes of this project, and was helpful and encouraging in a variety of other ways. Ali Ansari was a stimulus and a guide at the very beginning of my interest in Nader Shah, without whom none of this would have happened.

Many others also gave me guidance, encouragement and support, whether in suggesting new lines of research or analysis, answering specific queries, or by helping me find material that was proving difficult. These included Ernie Tucker, John Appleby, Kathryn Babayan, John Gurney, Mansur Sefatgol, Heidi Hofstetter (especially), Aaron Dunne, Hannah Carter, John Carter, Sergei Tourkin, Adrian Steele, Sanjay Subrahmanyam, Michele Bernardini, Jennifer Scarce, Ian Heath, Stephen Blake, Robert Hillenbrand, Bernard O'Kane, Ian Maddock, Poppy Hampson, Bella Pringle, and Iona Molesworth-St. Aubyn. I am also grateful to my sister, Helen Axworthy, for her help with the maps and for her support generally.

Inez Lynne, Gosia Lawik, Edith Gray and the other staff of the London Library were generous and tolerant beyond normal limits in finding and lending books, equalled only in helpfulness by the staff of the Cambridge University Library, especially Claire Welford and the others in the Rare Books room, and Les Goodey.

I must also thank Iradj Bagherzade for giving me the chance to write this book in the first place, Kate Sherratt and Clare Dubois at I.B.Tauris, and my wife Sally, who happily translated one crucial Russian text for me, and without whose forbearance and support the book would never have been finished.

Note on Transliteration

Transliteration is always an awkward problem, and it is not possible to be fully consistent without producing text that will sometimes look odd. My starting point was Nader's name itself. I chose not to use the traditional transliteration (Nadir), because to modern Iranians that would read like the pronunciation of an Arabic speaker, and it seemed a mistake to present an important figure in Iranian history in a way that Iranians themselves would find alien.

From that flowed the decision generally to use a transliteration that leaned toward modern Iranian pronunciation, without diacritical marks that would distract and confuse most readers that were not philologists. But there are inconsistencies, notably over the transliteration of names and terms that have had a life of their own in western writing: Isfahan, Fatima, mullah for example. Other, less justifiable inconsistencies, of which there may be some, are in all cases my fault rather than errors by those who advised me on the manuscript in its different stages of completion.

GEORGIA

CAUCASUS MTS

Kizliar

Terek R.

AVARIA

Sulaq R.

Khunzakh • Ixan Kharab
Tiflis • Qumuq • Darband
DAGHESTAN
Qars × Baghavard • Quraish
Arpa Chay R. × Khachmaz
• Yerevan • Ganja × Deve Batan
ARMENIA Kura R. × Shamakhi
• Echmiadzin SHIRVAN Baku •
QAJARS Javad •
Araxes R. AZERBAIJAN
L. Van
Tabriz
• Ardebil Caspian Sea
L.Urmiye
• Maraghe
• Miyandoab GILAN Resht •
MAZANDERAN Sari • Ashraf
• Mosul Qazvin ALBORZ MTS
KURDISTAN DARGAZINS
• Irbil • Surdash
× Aq Darband Tehran • Damghan
• Kirkuk Sanandaj • Varamin • Semnan
× Kurijan
OTTOMAN • Hamadan
IRAQ × Kermanshah Qom •
Nahavand × DASHT-E KAVIR
• Zohab Malayer ×
• Bohriz Borujerd • Kashan
× Faluja Gulpayegan • Natanz
• Baghdad LORESTAN
Tigris R. × Murchakhor DASHT-E
Karbala • Isfahan ×
• Hilla Dezful × Golnabad
Najaf • Zayanda-Rud
• Shushtar BAKHTIARI • Yazd
KHUZESTAN • Qomishe

YOMUT AFSH
TURKMEN
Atrat R. Dastg
Khabushan
Fathabad
QAJARS
Tabas
• Astarabad Nisha
• Bastam Sabzavar
• Shahrud
× Mehmandust KHORA

PERS

Tun

DASHT-E

N

Basra • ARABS KUHGELU

× Zarqan
• Shiraz
Bushire • × Pol-e Fasa
FARS

ARABS • Lar Bandar Abbas

• Bahrain Qeys Is. Qeshm Is.
Persian Gulf
Julfar •

Sohar •

• Kerman
KERMAN

Muscat

EUROPE

PERSIA

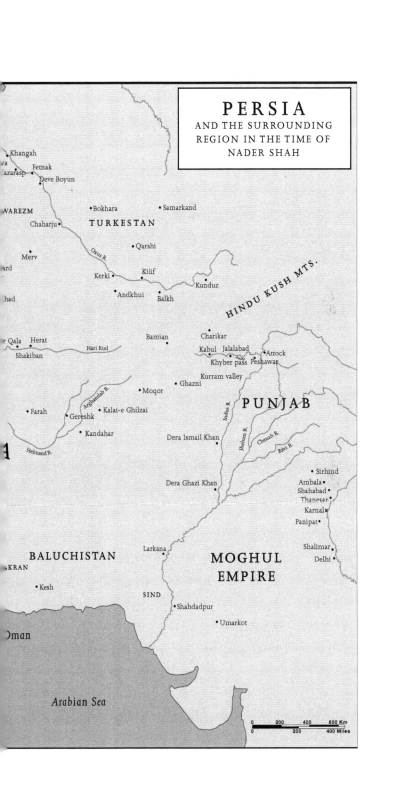

PERSIA
AND THE SURROUNDING
REGION IN THE TIME OF
NADER SHAH

Khangah
va
azarasp
Fetnak
Deve Boyun

WAREZM
Bokhara
Samarkand
Chaharju
TURKESTAN

Merv
Qarshi

Oxus R.

Kerki
Kilif
Kunduz
Andkhui
Balkh

HINDU KUSH MTS.

Qala
Herat
Bamian
Charikar
Shakiban
Hari Rud
Kabul
Jalalabad
Attock
Khyber pass
Peshawar

Kurram valley
Ghazni
Moqor
PUNJAB

Farah
Gereshk
Kalat-e Ghilzai
Indus R.

Argandab R.
Kandahar
Dera Ismail Khan
Jhelum R.
Chenab R.
Ravi R.

Helmand R.
Dera Ghazi Khan
Sirhind
Ambala
Shahabad
Thanesar
Karnal
Panipat

BALUCHISTAN
Larkana
MOGHUL
EMPIRE
Shalimar
Delhi
KRAN

Kesh
SIND

Shahdadpur
Umarkot

Oman

Arabian Sea

0   200   400   600 Km
0   200   400 Miles

In the name of God the compassionate, the merciful!

Those who possess understanding and are endowed with wisdom, know that when the times are full of troubles and confusion, when fortune favours the desires of the unjust, the supreme ruler of the universe, the arbiter of all things, brings forth an appointed one to fulfil the outpouring of his eternal mercy...

Mirza Mahdi Astarabadi, *Jahangosha-ye Naderi*

Preface

Shab-e tarik o bim-e mowj o gerdabi chenin ha'el
koja danand hal-e ma saboksaran-e sahelha

(In the dark night, with the fear of the waves, and the dreadful
whirlpool
How can they know our plight, the happy people of the shores?)

Hafez

The story of Nader Shah follows a tragic curve – from obscure
beginnings to ruthless intrigue, military success, splendour and
riches; to error, terror, frustration, ferocious cruelty, mental derangement
and death – in an historical time and place wholly unknown to most
western readers. Starting in the first quarter of the eighteenth century
as an obscure warlord of even more obscure origins, he liberated
Persia from occupation by the Afghans, ejected the Ottoman Turks,
manoeuvred the Russians out of the country, invaded Ottoman territory,
defeated the Ottomans there, made himself Shah, attacked the Afghans
in their homelands and reconquered them, then invaded India and
conquered Delhi, broke into Central Asia and pacified the Turkmen
and Uzbeks, before returning to the West and waging victorious war
against the Ottomans again. In the early 1740s the army Nader had
created was probably the single most powerful military force in the
world, and his officer cadre produced leaders who later went on to
found independent states in Afghanistan and Georgia. But after Delhi
he began to fall apart. He fell ill, lapsed into obsessive avarice, rage, and
cruelty, and in the end was murdered by his own officers.

Without Nader Shah, Iran (then known in the West as Persia) would
have suffered the same fate that befell Poland in the eighteenth century
– partial or complete partition between her neighbours: the Afghans,
the Russians and the Ottoman Turks.[1] As Nader rose to power, this

partition was already well advanced. With Persia swallowed up, power relations between the Ottoman Empire, Russia, Central Asia, Afghanistan and India would have been very different in the following decades and centuries.

Nader Shah's conquest of Delhi alerted the British East India Company to the weakness of the Moghul State in India, and the possibility of expanding Company operations there, on a grand and profitable scale, with the connivance of provincial Indian rulers. Without Nader Shah, eventual British rule would have come later and in a different form, perhaps never at all – with important global effects.[2]

The story of Nader's life is a roaring tale, but aside from the compelling interest of the story, these considerations alone make it strange that Nader Shah is not a more familiar historical figure outside Iran.* Why should this be so? From a British perspective at least, a partial explanation seems to lie in the long shadow of Victorian historiography.[3] Even where we reject or revise Victorian models, we often still work to the Victorian agenda. Items not put on that agenda then may still escape attention today.

The crude Victorian view[4] of Persia and the Orient generally was that they were incorrigibly passive, decadent and corrupt – ripe for colonisation and improvement from outside. A vigorous, ruthlessly efficient ruler like Nader did not fit into that picture, so he was sidelined.† His military successes in India might have appeared to detract from the glory of Clive and the other colonisers, and could have brought some to question the supposedly inherent superiority of western arms – all important to the myth of Empire. So he was regarded as little more than a blip in the history of India.[5]

---

* The last book on Nader Shah in English was Laurence Lockhart's study *Nadir Shah* of 1938, still invaluable, along with his later work *The Fall of the Safavi Dynasty*, for the generous range and detail of primary source material he presented (see Bibliography for further comment). Since then studies by Arunova and Reza Sha'bani, and especially Peter Avery's account in the *Cambridge History of Iran*, vol. 7, and a series of important articles by Ernest Tucker, have taken the subject further.

† By contrast, in the eighteenth century Nader was a relatively familiar figure in the West, through a variety of reports and reporters who took a variety of positive and not-so-positive views of him. Even before his conquest of Delhi there were frequent items about him in the press of the time, and afterwards there was a flurry of books in all the main European languages (see Chapter 8, note 1).

In missing out on the Victorian period of historical writing, Nader's reputation missed an opportunity. Since Stalin and Hitler, Europeans have no longer looked at what used to be called the Great Men of History with the simple admiration of our nineteenth-century ancestors.* But we cannot ignore them. It is a problem. We are repelled by their indifference to human suffering, but we cannot resist some admiration for the energy, the furious intelligence, and the sheer success of men like Alexander and Napoleon. And if we resist seduction by them, we may still be fascinated by the way in which those qualities, if we can allow them to be such, in many cases finally tore apart the Great Men themselves from the inside. The brutal events of Nader's reign, particularly towards the end, when he became a tyrannical monster, might try the strongest stomach. But harsh times breed hard men, and it would be a mistake to judge him by the standards of happier times or places, which none of his contemporaries would have recognised. As a fairer historian wrote of his assumption of power, Nader 'seized the sceptre which his valour had saved, and which a weaker hand could not have wielded'.[6]

Rousseau once wrote that to understand a book properly, it was necessary at the beginning of one's reading to suspend criticism, until one had fully grasped the argument. One could then, at the end, form a proper judgement. In writing about this extraordinary man, I have tried to follow something like that method.

New source material is still emerging on the history of Persia in the eighteenth century. Willem Floor, Mansur Sefatgol and Ernest Tucker in particular are revealing important new information and exploring its significance, in ways which will expand our understanding of events and take it in new directions. The mass of material from the records of the Dutch East India Company,† translated and published in recent years by Willem Floor, is of huge importance. Basile Vatatzes' history, once thought to be lost, some of which I have examined and exploited for this book for the first time, is a significant source worthy of more extensive examination.[7] Exploration of unpublished material in Russian archives could shift interpretation of Nader's relations with Russia and events in the Caucasus, in particular. When it comes to interpretation, my feeling

---

* Stalin read about Nader Shah and admired him, calling him a Teacher (along with Ivan the Terrible). Robert Service has shown there is an unpleasant chain of admiration between the tyrants of history. Saddam Hussein apparently had a large library of books about Stalin.

† Vereenigte Oostindische Compagnie (VOC).

is that warfare outside Europe in this period is still only imperfectly understood, and stands in need of more detailed examination, of the kind taken forward by Jos Gommans. The date of Nader's birth and the details of his early life are still uncertain and in need of further study. There must also be more material awaiting exploration in the former Ottoman archives. Unlike some other periods of history, where scholars have ploughed and reploughed the same material ever more inventively, there is scope in the history of eighteenth-century Persia (and the region more widely) for a lot of genuinely original work.

In reading the source material to establish what actually happened through the course of Nader's life, I have been as painstaking and discriminating as possible. But in addition to the material that reflects directly on the facts, there are many anecdotes and stories in the sources of more or less doubtful provenance, which it is unlikely will ever be corroborated, that nonetheless have something to contribute. Even where they are little more than fables, they show something about what contemporaries and near-contemporaries thought about Nader and his times. It would have been possible to write a dry narrative that excluded such doubtful stuff, but my preference has been rather to include it, sometimes with a warning, and allow the reader to make his or her own judgement. Every historical account has its angle, and I have been careful to look critically at what the sources have to say, but I have also been wary of overinterpreting the motivations of eighteenth-century authors. This period in Persian history is pre-colonial, and many of the attitudes and constructs that dominate our approach to the Middle East today (for better or worse) are quite anachronistic and inappropriate. My preference has been to look for the elements of value in even the dubious sources, rather than dismiss them out of hand as biased, partisan or anecdotal.

If Nader Shah had consolidated his military successes, and had passed on a strong state and army to his sons, his vigorous dynasty might not only have preserved Iran's territorial integrity, but could also have generated internal administrative and economic development, in a comparable way to that in which military competition between states stimulated long-term development in Europe in the same period.[8] More widely, it is quite conceivable that a resurgent, dynamic Persia, expanding into the vacuum left by relatively weak Moghul and Ottoman powers, under a dynasty that sought (as Nader did) to overcome the schism between Sunni and Shi'a Islam, could have averted the relative decline of the Islamic world vis-à-vis the West that has become a focus for debate and controversy recently.[9] As well as explaining how these things could have happened, this book explains why, for better or worse, they did not.

In the first years of the twenty-first century Kandahar, Kabul, Baghdad, Najaf, Basra, Mosul and Kirkuk have come to prominence again, underlining (as if it were necessary) the importance of this region and an understanding of its history. Iran is central – conceptually and geographically central – to that region today just as it was in Nader Shah's time. If this narrative does something more widely to stimulate interest in him, and in Iranian history, it will have been useful. It does not try to encompass every last item of new research relevant to the life of Nader Shah that has appeared since Laurence Lockhart's biography of 1938, though it does incorporate most of the new material and takes a fresh look at the interpretation of events; presenting new analysis at a number of important points. It is intended rather as a narrative history to bring Nader's story to a new audience. The life of Nader Shah and the history of Iran belong to us all, just as the life of Henry VIII does, or the history of Rome under the Claudian emperors. Nader Shah's story is as gripping, and as shocking, as that of Macbeth, or Richard III. It is another story that can enrich and enlarge our understanding.

It is necessary, in commenting on Nader's relevance to the modern world, to make one obvious point. Those who fear Iran as a threat today might be tempted to present this book as evidence that Iran was traditionally an aggressive power, always a threat to her neighbours. That would be entirely incorrect. Nader stands out in Iranian history precisely because the norm before and after his time was so different. Nader was exceptional, in degree and in kind. Others might point to the bloody cruelties described in the book and suggest that they are somehow unique to or characteristic of Iran, or Islam, or the Middle East, or to Oriental despotism, or whatever. That too would be an error. The ways that human beings commit atrocities, like the way they paint paintings or cook food, may differ from culture to culture, and show distinctive characteristics in each. But the propensity to cruelty is, unfortunately, more or less universal. If there is a message in this book, it should rather be about the fragility of the traditions, institutions and values that human beings have, in various times and places, established to shield themselves against such cruelty: and the importance of cherishing and protecting them.

2. *View from the East.*

Nader Shah in polite conversation with the Moghul emperor, Mohammad
Shah, by a Moghul court artist. This is probably the most accurate portrait of
Nader. The figure behind him may have been intended to represent Sa'adat
Khan. The halo-like nimbus behind Nader's head (a convention in Moghul
painting denoting royalty) is slightly larger, and Nader sits slightly higher
than Mohammad Shah, to show who is boss.

(Photo12)

PROLOGUE
Zenith

We'll lead you to the stately tent of war,
Where you shall hear the Scythian Tamburlaine
Threat'ning the world with high astounding terms
And scourging kingdoms with his conquering sword.
View but his picture in this tragic glass
And then applaud his fortunes as you please.

Marlowe

Nader Shah led the Persian army into Delhi on 20 March 1739. Persian soldiers lined either side of Nader's route from the Shalimar gardens outside the city to the great red sandstone fortress-palace of Shah Jahan, but the citizens stayed indoors. Nader was accompanied by 20,000 horsemen, and a hundred captured elephants led the procession, each bearing several veteran musketeers.* Arriving at the palace, Nader dismounted from his grey charger and entered on foot. The huge guns of the fortress fired in salute, a tremendous noise such that the city 'seemed about to collapse in on itself'.[1]

Ten years earlier, in the spring of 1729, Persia[2] had been in a desperate state, overwhelmed and humiliated. The capital, Isfahan, had been occupied by Afghan invaders for six years, and Turks and Russians had been in possession of most of the northern and western provinces. In a decade, in one of the most remarkable changes of fortune in modern history, Nader had defeated all his enemies and made Persia the dominant power from the mountains of the Caucasus to the river Yamuna. Since the beginning of their march from Isfahan two years

---

* *Jazayerchis* – foot soldiers armed with the heavy calibre *jazayer* or *jezzail* musket.

and four months earlier, Nader and his men had covered more than 1,750 miles, and had conquered most of what is now Afghanistan along the way. In 1739 he was at the prime of his life, and seemed set fair to equal if not surpass the achievements of Timur (Tamerlane), who had ridden into Delhi as a conqueror 340 years earlier. Although many of his innovations pointed to the future rather than harking backward, Nader's thoughts often turned on Timur's example. Like Timur, he had already decided to plunder the wealth of Delhi rather than attempt to annex the Empire of India.

Delhi at that date was one of the great capitals of the world. It was resplendent with monuments from all periods of its history, but particularly from the time of Shah Jahan a century earlier. The city was commonly known as Shahjahanabad, and had a population of around 400,000.[3] Of the three great empires of the Muslim world, the Ottoman, the Persian and the Moghul, the Moghul had been the richest and the most magnificent, and Delhi was the pride of its opulence.

As Nader arrived at the palace the Moghul Emperor, Mohammad Shah, received him with elaborate ceremony and pressed expensive presents on him. Mohammad Shah had been allowed back to the city with an escort of Persian cavalry the day before, so that he could make arrangements to welcome the conqueror with the necessary pomp. After his defeat at the battle of Karnal on 24 February, and the scattering of the imperial Moghul army that followed, Mohammad Shah had no choice. This first meeting in Delhi would have been in the sumptuous Hall of Special Audience,* the most elegant of the magnificent rooms constructed by Shah Jahan. The outside of the building was of white marble slung with red cloth awnings to keep off the sun. The columns, walls and ceilings inside were covered with richly decorated gold and silver leaf (which the Persians later stripped away and melted down). Mohammad Shah had spread rich carpets and cloth of gold on the floor, and had installed precious furniture of all kinds.[4] The building's centrepiece was the extravagant Peacock Throne. This was less like a chair than a kind of raised dais, about six feet long by four feet wide. It stood on four feet of gold, and every surface was studded with jewels, some of which were very large. Some of the pearls were the size of pigeon's eggs. The canopy over the throne was supported by twelve columns. It was covered on the inside with diamonds and pearls, and more pearls dangled from the fringe. The canopy bore a peacock of

---

* The *Dowlat Khane-ye khas* (or *Divan-e khas*).

gold, whose multicoloured plumage was fashioned from sapphires and other precious stones. The huge Kuh-e Nur diamond was mounted at the front of the throne, surrounded by rubies and emeralds.[5] High on the walls of the room was repeated an inscription in Persian: 'If there be a paradise on earth, it is this, it is this, it is this.'

The reception was designed to show that, as host, Mohammad Shah still held some status, but it was as if a son had been visited by his father. Nader confirmed that Mohammad Shah would continue to reign in India, with the friendship and support of the Persian monarch, because both came of the same Turcoman stock. The Emperor bowed low in gratitude, as well he might – he had been fortunate to keep his life, but now he was to keep his crown as well. In return, Mohammad Shah offered Nader all the imperial treasures – the gold, the heaps of uncut gemstones, and of course the peacock throne itself – all the enormous wealth accumulated over two centuries of Moghul rule in India. Nader demurred. Mohammad Shah insisted. Nader refused. Mohammad Shah offered again. Eventually, Nader accepted. The conquered Emperor was forced in a mocking theatre to persuade his enemy to accept his most priceless possessions.[6]

Another significant incident marked the reception. The intrigues of Sa'adat Khan, the governor of Awadh (Oudh), and the Emperor's other senior nobles, including the Nezam ol-Molk (the regent or viceroy of the Deccan) had done much to weaken the Moghul State prior to the Persian invasion. Sa'adat Khan's rashness had led directly to the disastrous Moghul defeat at the battle of Karnal on 24 February, and his own capture. Since his capture he had tried to win Nader's favour by acting as his adviser, blatantly abandoning his allegiance to Mohammad Shah. He had already been appointed to collect the tribute that was to be taken from the citizens of Delhi, and rode with Nader into the city. At the palace, Sa'adat Khan asked for a private audience, but Nader, showing contempt for his ingratiating behaviour, replied harshly, demanding why he had not begun collecting the tribute. Sa'adat Khan took this hard.[7] It seems that his sense of honour (already bruised after Karnal, and further from the impression that Nader favoured his rival, the Nezam ol-Molk) was humiliated to the extent that he despaired, took poison, and died. Nader and his personal staff took over Shah Jahan's own apartments in the fortress: Mohammad Shah moved into the women's quarters.[8]

With Persian troops firmly established in the city, the Friday prayers were read in the mosques in Nader's name as sovereign. Coins were

struck for him with a Persian inscription, which read: 'The Prince of
the Princes of the earth is Nader, King of Kings, Lord of the Fortunate
Conjunction.'* The last formula (*sahebqeran*) at least in theory signified
a ruler whose birth had been marked by an astrologically favourable
conjunction of the planets, but Nader probably valued it more as one
of the titles always associated with Timur.[9] While in Delhi, Nader was
addressed as *Shahanshah* (King of Kings) – the traditional honorific
of the Moghul emperors. Whatever his ultimate intentions, and the
ambiguity of Mohammad Shah's position, Nader made it clear from
the start of his time in Delhi that he was Emperor.

Despite the defeat at Karnal and the triumphal entry of the Persians,
the inhabitants of Delhi were not overawed by their conquerors at
first. The people of the bazaar laughed at the Qezelbash soldiers,†
who were mostly simple men from the villages and hills of Persia.[10]
Nader ordered his *nasaqchis* (who served as the army's military police)
that anyone injuring any of the citizens should have their nose or
ears cut off, or be beaten to death.[11] He was determined to avoid,
with characteristically tough discipline, any outbreaks of lawlessness
among his soldiers. Nader knew that, three and a half centuries before,
Timur's troops had run out of control in the city, looting, killing and
burning for several days. Confident in their collective strength and
security, the Persian soldiers walked through the city in small groups
at their leisure.

Only a small proportion of the Moghul army had been defeated at
Karnal, and Nader's dominant position in Delhi had been achieved
since then as much by his cunning manipulation of Mohammad Shah
and the Moghul great nobles, and by implied threat, as by the direct
use of force. The remains of the Moghul army had melted away, and the
Moghul leaders had been slowly manoeuvred into giving Nader what
he wanted. His task had been made easier by the common Turcoman/
Persian culture that the Moghuls and the invaders shared. The Moghul
dynasty was originally Turkic or Turco-Mongol, descended directly
from Timur himself, and for two centuries had enjoyed a refined Persian
court culture. To emphasise their common origin Nader insisted that he
and Mohammad Shah should speak together in the Turkic language of
the peoples of Central Asia.

* 'Hast Soltan bar salatin-e-Jahan / Shah-e-Shahan Nader-e sahebqeran'.
† At this time *Qezelbash* was a generic term for Persian soldiers. Literally it
    means 'red hats'.

The divisions at the Moghul court between factions among the nobles had weakened the Moghul State, making Nader's task easier. Many of the great Moghul nobles were adventurers who had come to India from lands to the north; another factor that had limited their loyalty to the Moghul dynasty.[12] The Nezam ol-Molk's family came from Samarkand, Sa'adat Khan from Khorasan in north-eastern Persia. The Moghul court was rarefied and artificial by comparison with the pragmatic, ruthless character of Nader's circle. The contrast was to become more apparent as the Persians' sojourn in Delhi went on. The Moghul nobles had a delicate sense of honour, for which Nader had only contempt. He disdained the sophistication of the Moghul court. On one occasion he asked how many women the Moghul vizier had in his harem. The vizier replied that he had 850. Nader derisively said he would add 150 female captives to their number, so that the vizier would be entitled to the military rank of a Min-Bashi (Commander of a Thousand).[13]

Nonetheless the common Persian-Turkic culture they shared meant that many of the great nobles probably would have felt more at home with the Persian invaders than with their Indian subjects. This explains the odd, uneasy intimacy between the Moghul nobles and the Persians in the events that followed. It made it easier for Nader to manipulate the Moghul court into docile acquiescence. Though ruthless when necessary, it was always his policy to overcome resistance by subterfuge before resorting to naked force. Securely established in the great palace of Shah Jahan, he felt confident. But events may overturn the complacency of even the subtlest princes.

The city of Delhi, beyond the courtiers in the red stone and marble Palace of Shah Jahan, was not so easily mollified. By the afternoon of 21 March it would have been common knowledge that the city and everybody in it were going to have to pay a large tribute. Many of the ordinary soldiers that died at Karnal and after had come from Delhi, and others from the defeated army had found refuge there. Most of the population were fearful and passive, but some were angry, and felt betrayed by their leaders. There were young men in the bazaar who were up for trouble of any kind. They collected together in bands, ready for exploitation by a few rash nobles who thought instability could save their fortunes, or who were simply out for revenge.[14]

The Persian New Year festival (*Nowruz*) fell on 21 March, and as usual Nader gave a party for his officers, and gave them ceremonial coats of honour (*khal'ats*). He had timed his arrival in the city so that they could celebrate Nowruz there. But that evening rumours began to circulate that Nader had been shot by one of Mohammad Shah's female Qalmaq harem guards, or that he had been poisoned, or imprisoned.[15] There had been trouble in the afternoon at the granaries in the Paharganj district of the city. Some Persian troops had gone there to fix corn prices. Some of the corn merchants, unhappy at the low price stipulated, called together a crowd towards the evening. This angry mob killed the soldiers at the granaries, then fanned out through the neighbouring parts of the city, attacking all the Persians they found. The Persian soldiers were walking about in ones and twos in the streets and markets and the Indians, rushing suddenly upon them, killed them before they knew what was happening.[16]

In the palace, Nader's servants hesitated to wake him to tell him about the rioting. Eventually 'trembling and shaking with fear' they did, but he did not believe them. Nader said 'some villain from my camp has falsely accused the men of Hindostan of this crime, so that they can kill them and plunder their property.'[17] Nader sent out a court attendant to find out the truth, then another. Both in succession were killed by the mob within a few yards of the palace gates. He then sent a thousand of his veterans to restore order, but warned them not to shoot anyone not directly involved in the rioting. These men followed his orders, but the rioters were not cowed, and began to fire muskets and shoot arrows at the Persians.[18]

It became plain that a thousand men were not enough, and that the unrest was not going to be put down by half-measures. Shots were fired and stones and other missiles thrown throughout the night. The Persians were pent up in the palace and a few other defensible buildings. On the morning of 22 March, Nader mounted his horse and rode from the palace to the Rowshan-od-Dowla mosque.* As he arrived there with his men about him, some people threw stones from balconies and windows around the mosque, and a shot was fired, killing an officer beside him.[19] He had already made up his mind, but this final insult may have added fury to Nader's frustration. He went to the roof of the mosque and stood by the golden domes, looking out over the houses, shops and roofs of the Chandni Chowk district. He ordered that no-one should be left alive in any part where any of his soldiers had been killed, and then drew his sword as a signal that the massacre should begin. Three thousand veterans were given the grim task. With drawn sword, Nader 'remained there in a deep and silent gloom that none

---

* Today known as the Sunehri or golden mosque.

dared to disturb'.[20] He had made every effort to avoid the massacre that the troops of his hero, Timur, had committed in Delhi. But events had forced his hand. His dark eyes looked out over the roofs of the city as the smoke and screams spread on all sides.[21]

The killing began at nine in the morning. The Persians broke into houses and shops, slaughtering all they came across in the specified areas. Here and there was some opposition, but in most places the people were cut down without resistance. In Paharganj men suspected of having caused the tumult were arrested, carried off and beheaded on the banks of the Yamuna (Jumna). But the bands of young bazaaris and others who had been the cause of the disturbance disappeared, and the Persians' retribution fell on minor nobles, householders, artisans and respectable heads of families. The soldiery looted and set fire to the houses as they went, and some people (mainly women and children) died in the fires rather than emerge onto the streets. Fear of rape and dishonour drove some to desperation; men killed their wives and families before committing suicide themselves, and women threw themselves into wells to escape the Persians.[22]

Two young nobles in particular seem to have helped to spread the rumours and to have encouraged the riots that had led to the massacre – Seyyed Niaz Khan and Shah Nawaz Khan. The former had shut some Persian soldiers that had been sent to protect his house in a room and burned them alive. The two then raided the stables where Nader's captured elephants were kept, killed the mahouts and carried off the animals to a fort outside the city. But after some resistance in the fort they were captured by Persian troops, brought to Nader with several hundred of their followers, and executed.[23]

To the female prisoners Nader was more merciful. Several thousand prisoners were brought before Nader, most of them women, many of whom had been raped. Nader ordered them to be taken back to their homes, 'where they retired in circumstances of the deepest distress'.[24]

The massacre went on through the morning. Thousands of houses and shops were set on fire, burning the living and the dead. The plunder of rich clothes, jewels and other goods taken by the Persian soldiers was enormous.[25] The destruction fell mainly on tradespeople in the bazaars and the jewellers' quarter. The sun reached its zenith and it continued. Heaps of bodies piled up in the streets, and the gutters ran with blood. Finally Mohammad Shah sent the Nezam ol-Molk[26] to plead for the killing to stop. According to one of the Nezam's hangers-on, he found Nader eating sweets. The Nezam apparently offered his own life to stop the killing, and boldly asked Nader whether he did not fear that God would make the building fall on his head, to avenge the innocent victims of the massacre.* At 3 o'clock in the afternoon, after six hours of slaughter, Nader issued the order 'Let their lives be spared,' which was proclaimed through the streets by the *kotwal*† and a squad of Persian *nasaqchis*.[27] Even Indian contemporaries were impressed that the tight discipline of the Persian army checked the soldiers' lust for plunder and blood so promptly:

> The Qizilbash soldiers were so much in submission and
> under such discipline and fear of their prince, that on
> hearing the sound of the word 'peace' they withdrew
> their hands from the massacre and refrained from further
> plunder and robbery. And this is the most wonderful
> thing in the world, that bloodthirsty and savage soldiers,
> who had heads of families and wealthy citizens in their
> power, at one word became submissive and obedient and
> withdrew their hands from slaughter and rapine.[28]

Estimates of the numbers killed vary widely. But Nader had set limits to the slaughter by confining it to specific quarters of the city, by halting it after six hours, and by using only a relatively small proportion of the troops available to him. It is likely that the contemporary estimate of the *kotwal*, that 20–30,000 had died, was reasonably accurate.[29] The number of Persians killed in the initial rioting is also uncertain, but it may have been as low as a few hundred.[30] The bodies were deliberately left where they fell for some days. 'For a long time the streets remained strewed with corpses as the walks of a garden with dead flowers and leaves.' [31] In Nader's terms the savage work was a success – there was no further trouble from the citizens of Delhi. When the stench of the unburied bodies began to become overpowering, they were disposed of in various ways – some dragged away to the river, others burned in heaps using the debris from the destroyed buildings.[32]

One motive for Nader's restraint in holding back from the killing, and then for limiting it, was that he wanted the best part of the wealth of the city to flow into his own hands, not to be looted by his men and

---

* One suspects that the Nezam's real words were rather more cautious than
  they were reported (Lockhart 1926 p. 238: cf also Père Saignes, p. 255).
† The chief Moghul official of the city, responsible for law and order.

dissipated. He now set about the main business of his stay in Delhi – collecting the tribute. He put guards on all the gates of the city, allowing anyone to come in, but no-one to leave.

The possessions of the great nobles that had died at Karnal or since were seized first, soon after the massacre ended. Soldiers were sent to outlying cities and territories to collect the wealth of the nobles outside the capital. The surviving nobles were then assessed, and demands made upon them individually. Since at this time these grandees were semi-independent princes, ruling great tracts of territory by virtue of their court offices but treating them effectively as their private property, the assessments were high. It seems the Nezam ol-Molk was allowed to prevaricate, claiming that his son, who was administering his territories in the Deccan in his absence and controlled all his wealth, was refusing to obey him.[33] Others were more harshly treated – modern tax collectors would no doubt love to apply similar encouragements. Mohammad Shah's vizier:

> endeavoured to elude the payment of the large contribution demanded of him; Nader therefore caused him to be exposed openly to the sun, which is reckoned a punishment contumelious as well as painful, and in that country dangerous to the health. At length, he extorted from him a whole *crore* of rupees,* besides a great value in precious stones and elephants[34]

The representative at court of the governor of Bengal, when told that province was assessed for seven crore, joked that a sum so large would need a string of wagons from Bengal to Delhi to carry it. For his sense of humour he was severely beaten, and was so devastated by the treatment he poisoned himself and his family.[35]

On the strength of the amounts collected so far, and in expectation of what was to come, on 27 March Nader sent a decree to be proclaimed in Persia that all his dominions were exempted from taxes for three years, 'to lighten the weight that oppressed them'. At the same time he settled his soldiers' arrears, paid them a year in advance, and gave them a bounty worth six months' pay in addition.[36]

---

* In India a *crore* was 100 *lakhs*, or 10 million rupees, equivalent to £1.25 million sterling at that time – so 7 *crore* would have been worth around £8.75 million sterling. A *crore* in Persia was 500,000 rather than 10 million, but in this book I use the term in the Indian sense.

At last the overall assessment for the ordinary citizens of Delhi was fixed at two crore,[37] and several of the chief Moghul nobles were ordered to collect it. For this purpose the city was divided into five parts, and a thousand Persian cavalry were assigned to help in case force were required. The taking of the money caused great distress, and many people found ways to flee the city.[38]

The total amount Nader took from Delhi, including the 'gifts' or contributions (jewels as well as cash) from Mohammad Shah and the great nobles, the money levied from the populace, the money and valuables taken from the imperial treasury and the goods confiscated (furniture, textiles, cannon and other weapons) was enormous.

A number of authoritative contemporary sources concur on a total of 70 crore (the equivalent of £87.5 million sterling at that time or perhaps £90 billion today) – some saying that Nader's soldiers took away an additional ten crore.[39] A large element in this sum consisted of the value of the jewels (perhaps as much as 34 crore), whether mounted on objects, cut or uncut; there were thousands of them. Given the difficulty of valuing gems, then as now, it is perhaps rather nugatory to debate the precise value of the haul. When assessing the worth of such a huge quantity of such precious things, standards of value themselves begin to shiver and crumble.

Most prominent among the treasures were the Peacock throne and the Kuh-e Nur diamond. The throne was later broken up, the Kuh-e Nur did not stay in Persia, and some of the other treasures were dispersed or lost after Nader's death, but the crown jewels still on display today in Tehran consist for the most part of the riches removed by Nader Shah from India in 1739. They include the Darya-ye Nur ('Sea of Light') diamond – probably the largest pink diamond in the world.* In the nineteenth century, Shahs of Persia amused themselves by devising novel settings for the gems, including jewelled swords, daggers, aigrettes, shields, thrones, cups and even a globe – but whole dishes of large emeralds, diamonds, pearls and rubies remain unmounted (and many uncut) to this day.

Delhi was devastated. In addition to the mass killing, looting and burning, the economy had collapsed, trade was at a standstill, prices for foodstuffs were at famine levels, and the value of other goods, particularly luxury goods, had fallen drastically – making it difficult, sometimes impossible, for people to put together the cash demanded of

---

* Estimated at a huge 175–195 carats.

them. Many families found that they had not only lost their money, but that they were ruined altogether; and committed suicide.[40]

While the money was being collected, Nader had his son Nasrollah married to a Moghul princess: a great-granddaughter of the Emperor Aurangzeb, and Mohammad Shah's niece. Mohammad Shah presented the bridegroom with a coat of honour, a necklace of pearls, a *jiqe*,* a dagger set with pearls and an elephant with trappings of gold. He and Nader also made lavish gifts of money and jewels to the couple, and there were fireworks along the banks of the river Yamuna.[41] According to protocol, before the wedding, court officials had to investigate the ancestry of the bridegroom and establish it back for seven generations. When Nader Shah heard this, he said:

> Tell them that he is the son of Nader Shah, the son of the
> sword, the grandson of the sword; and so on, till they
> have a descent of seventy instead of seven generations.[42]

On the night of the wedding (6 April) some Qezelbash troops broke Nader's anti-Shi'a decrees and sang part of a mourning lament for the Shi'a martyr Hosein, as was traditional in the mourning month of Moharram, which was about to begin. Aside from the breach of his instructions on religion, Nader was irritated by the soldiers' disrespect for his son's wedding, and used the incident for a demonstration of his harsh discipline. He had the soldiers arrested and executed outside one of the city gates, leaving their bodies exposed there for a month as a warning to others.[43]

With the tribute collected and the marriage concluded, Nader could relax. He was now undisputed master of Delhi and its wealth. His prestige was at an unparalleled high – no Shah of Persia had enjoyed such military success for a thousand years or more. It now remained only to settle arrangements for the future rule of the Moghul territories, and withdraw. There is no indication that he ever wavered from his early decision to plunder Delhi and leave. If he ever did consider a permanent annexation of the Moghul Empire, it was perhaps at this moment that it would have looked most attractive.[44] Mohammad Shah must have been nervous. But Delhi was a long way from the seat of

---

* The aigrette or hat-ornament denoting royalty: traditionally a bunch of black heron feathers worn by the Shah on the right of his turban. Lesser royalty wore the jiqe on the left.

Nader's power in Khorasan, in the north-east of Persia, and the Nowruz massacre would not have made an auspicious start to Persian rule. His reign was still young – he had become Shah definitively only three years before. There had been many revolts against his rule, and there were to be more. He was aware that despite his great military prestige, many Persians in their hearts regarded his rule as illegitimate, and still hoped for a restoration of the old Safavid dynasty. Nader could not afford to stay away from Persia for the length of time necessary to secure the Moghul territories. But the settlement he imposed before his departure left open his options for further intervention in India, should that prove necessary or attractive.

This settlement was promulgated at a grand *durbar* on 12 May, attended by Mohammad Shah and all the great Moghul nobles. Nader made several presents to the Moghul Emperor, including jewelled swords and other costly items. But the most significant was the jiqe, which he placed on Mohammad Shah's head himself, to show that he was once again endowed with full sovereignty. Mohammad Shah thanked Nader for his generosity, according to which he once again 'found himself to be one of the monarchs of the world', and in return begged him to accept all the Moghul lands west of the Indus, from Tibet and Kashmir to the sea.[45] This was of course, a carefully prepared deal, another of the planned pieces of political theatre spiked with ironic humour that were characteristic of Nader's career. As at the reception on Nader's arrival in Delhi, Mohammad Shah was forced into the appearance of making a free gift. The terms of the formal document ceding this territory, which we may take to have been directly dictated by Nader, referred again to the two monarchs' shared Turcoman origin. It genuflected to the memory of the earlier Asiatic conquerors Timur and Genghis Khan in its mention of the family of Gurkan.* In the document, Mohammad Shah said of Nader:

> And out of the Greatness of his Soul, and abundant
> humanity, in regard to the illustrious Family of Gourgan,

---

* 'Gurkan' (or 'Güregen') had been a title used by Timur, signifying 'son in law'. Timur had married a woman descended directly from Genghis Khan, and styled himself figuratively as Genghis' son in law to benefit from the Central Asian tribes' reverence for Genghis' memory. The Moghul dynasty descended in turn from Timur, via Babur, the Central Asian adventurer and founder of the Moghal dynasty who conquered northern India in the early sixteenth century.

and the Honour of the Original Tree of Turkan, [he] was
graciously pleased to restore to me the Crown and Gem
of Hindostan.[46]

To round off, Nader gave Mohammad Shah some advice on how to
rule his empire. He told him to confiscate the lands the Moghul nobles
enjoyed by right of their tenure of offices, and to pay them instead
with ready cash from the imperial treasury. The advice gave an insight
into Nader's own military thinking. He told Mohammad Shah that he
should retain a paid, standing army of 60,000 horsemen, and should
know the names and families of all the officers down to the lowest
level. When occasion arose, he should nominate officers for particular
tasks, and give them command of a sufficient number of men; but when
the task was accomplished, command should be terminated and the
soldiers returned to the main body. None should remain in command
for too long.[47]

Nader warned Mohammad Shah not to trust the Nezam ol-Molk and
said that if any of the nobles rebelled, he could quickly send an army or
if necessary return himself – 'upon all events don't reckon me far off.'
Prince Erekle of Georgia, who accompanied Nader to Delhi, reported
that Nader sternly warned the nobles to be faithful to Mohammad
Shah, because if not, no matter where Nader was, within six months he
would fall on them and massacre them all.[48]

The character of the settlement was paternal. Mohammad Shah
was re-established, but almost as Nader's satellite; and the possibility
of a further expedition to India was made explicit. One chronicle
says that Nader immediately afterwards contemptuously told some
of his own trusted nobles that Mohammad Shah was not competent
to rule. So why did Nader reinstate him? Re-establishing this feeble
Emperor (particularly with over-mighty subjects like the Nezam ol-
Molk still active) was to keep the Moghul State weak and give himself
the opportunity to intervene again if he pleased. Had Nader prospered
and reigned longer after he left India, it is likely that he would have
returned there, to annex what in 1739 he merely looted.[49]

Before his departure, Nader gathered a variety of useful artisans
(particularly builders, masons, carpenters and stone carvers) to
accompany him on his return journey, with the intention that they
would beautify the building projects he planned at the new Kandahar
(Naderabad), at Kalat in Khorasan, and elsewhere. Nader paid these
men expenses for their journey and retained them on the basis that they

would work for him for three years, after which they would be free
either to continue in his service or to return. But many of them defected
earlier, even before the Persian army reached Lahore.

Among the other useful people Nader found in Delhi, he took away
the chief court physician, Alavi Khan, to cure him of an illness that
apparently first appeared before he came to India; a dropsy or oedema
(an abnormal accumulation of fluid in the body tissues). Alavi Khan
was to be a significant figure in coming years, alleviating for a time
the physical and mental distress that marred the latter part of Nader's
reign, and which seemed to bring on the cruellest of his excesses.[50]

Nader forbade in the strongest terms that any women be taken
away from Delhi except of their own free will. He went to some lengths
to ensure his wishes were respected, showing the same concern he
displayed for the women taken captive by his soldiers after the massacre.
When the army halted at the Shalimar gardens after leaving Delhi, an
order was proclaimed around the camp that any captives, male or
female, should forthwith be returned to the city; and that anyone that
disobeyed would forfeit both his life and estate. Most of these captives
were women. Even wives lawfully married in Delhi and slaves bought
and sold with written proof could only remain with the army if it was
clear that they did so freely. Almost all the wives and women removed
from Delhi returned at this point. Even a few whose husbands 'by the
mildest Means and Intreaties' persuaded them to stay, were ordered
back to the city by Nader a few days later.[51]

One might look for motives other than gentle humanity for Nader's
treatment of these women; for example that he did not want his army
over-encumbered with camp-followers, or that he did not want them
to become a conduit for a flow of information between India and
Persia.[52] But the Persian army was accompanied by large numbers of
women and other non-combatants in any case; there is little evidence
elsewhere that Nader tried to constrain their numbers as a matter of
policy, and the Indian women would not have made much difference to
the total. Similarly, there were plenty of other channels for intelligence
between India and Persia – not least the craftsmen Nader himself was
bringing away. It is possible that he did not want the influence of these
women, with their knowledge of the ways of the Moghul court, to
turn his men soft. Nader's behaviour in Delhi was ruthless but, against
that savage background, his treatment of the women of Delhi showed
some compassion. There were other instances when he intervened
to show mercy to women that fell into the hands of his troops, and

some contemporaries noted this as a characteristic. But perhaps his compassion was just a kind of impatience with the consequences of his actions.[53]

One contemporary account[54] tells a story from immediately before Nader's departure, saying that once all the questions of property and territory had been resolved, the Persian officers relaxed, sent for dancers and gave themselves up to pleasure. The renowned songstress Nur Bai sang the following verse to Nader and his captains:

> What have you left of my heart
> That you should come again
> Pass the cup, clap hands and dance
> You came not to the house of pleasure to say your prayers

Nader was delighted with Nur Bai's singing, and with her beauty. He ordered his servants to give her 4,000 rupees, and said he would take her with him away from Delhi. But on hearing what the Shah intended, the singer fell sick: 'her heart died within her.' Whether real or pretended, her illness succeeded in frustrating Nader's intentions. It would be generous to think that, realising her reluctance, he forbore to take her away by force – considering the policy he was imposing on his men and officers at the same time. One of the Indian nobles apparently asked Nur Bai what would have been her feelings, had Nader Shah succeeded in consummating his desire. It seems she replied something like:

> I should feel as if my body itself[55] had been guilty of a massacre.

A huge baggage train of horses, mules and camels was prepared,* and Nader marched out of Delhi with his army on 16 May 1739. An eyewitness recalled that Nader had on his head a red cap with a white Kashmir shawl wound around it as a turban, and a jewelled jiqe. He looked young, was strongly built and held himself very erect. His beard and moustache were dyed black. He rode through the streets holding his head high and looking straight before him, and when the people acclaimed him, he flung rupees to them with both hands.[56]

---

* It took as many as 30,000 camels and 24,000 mules to carry the treasure (AAN p. 739; Floor 1998, p. 308n).

3. *A party of Turkmen slavers with their captives.*
In this case the captives are Turkmen from another tribe. This is a nineteenth-century engraving, but with bows rather than muskets the raiders would have looked little different a century earlier. Note the riding style (still to be seen in Central Asia and the Caucasus), hand on hip, firm seat in the trot, redolent of ruthless arrogance.
(Cambridge University Library)

CHAPTER ONE
The Fall of
the Safavid Dynasty

Unhappy Persia, that in former age
Hast been the seat of mighty conquerors
That in their prowess and their policies
Have triumphed over Afric and the bounds
Of Europe, where the sun dares scarce appear
For freezing meteors and congealed cold,
Now to be ruled and governed by a man
At whose birthday Cynthia with Saturn joined,
And Jove, the Sun, and Mercury denied
To shed their influence in his fickle brain!
Now Turks and Tartars shake their swords at thee,
Meaning to mangle all thy provinces.

Marlowe

The future conqueror of Delhi was born in a wild and dangerous region on the north-eastern frontier of Persia: the northern part of the province of Khorasan, far from the splendour of royal courts and palaces. There is some uncertainty about when Nader was born, but the likeliest date is 6 August 1698.[1] His father was of lowly but respectable status, a herdsman of the Afshar tribe; said also to have been a camel driver and a maker of sheepskin coats. His name was Emam Qoli. In comparison with many of the great nobles among whom he later moved, Nader's birth was obscure; but in the local context of northern Khorasan his father may have had some status among the Afshars as a village headman.[2] Nader's official historian, making no attempt to elevate his birth, wrote of his origins that 'the sword takes its merit from the natural strength of its temper, not from the mine from which its iron was taken.'[3]

The Qereqlu Afshars to whom Nader's father belonged were a semi-nomadic Turcoman tribe settled in Khorasan, in north-eastern Persia. Nader was born at Dastgerd, a fortified village on the northern side of the Allahu Akbar mountains of the Darra Gaz region, north-west of Mashhad, the capital of Khorasan. At birth he was named Nadr Qoli,[4] which means 'Slave of the wonderful' – a way of piously dedicating the child to the service of God. When years later Emam Qoli's son made himself Shah, he changed his name to Nader, meaning 'Rarity' or 'Prodigy' – it is possible that this had been a nickname earlier, as the growing boy showed his uncommon abilities.

For western readers, there might appear to be enough familiar elements here to form a picture of Nader's origins. He was born in a village, in a province, with a large city nearby that served as an administrative centre for the province. His father looked after sheep, camels and other animals. But we would be wrong to fit this picture into a contemporary Western European model, with a settled, sedentary population largely made up of peasants, a controlling elite of nobles owning the land, and a scatter of towns and cities serving as markets in a peaceful, productive countryside. There were, of course, peasants and markets; and there was settled, productive agricultural land.*

But there were large areas of less productive land in Khorasan, over which grazed the flocks of the armed nomadic or semi-nomadic tribes: Afshars, Kurds and others. Many of these peoples, including the Afshars to whom Nader's family belonged, had been moved there in earlier centuries from the western part of Persia; partly to divide over-mighty tribal confederations that might have threatened revolt, partly to help defend an exposed frontier region. Fierce Turkmen nomads† on horseback often mounted raids into the region from the steppe lands beyond to the north and east, carrying off slaves and animals for sale in the towns and cities along the old silk road of Central Asia.[5] Because the Turkmen were Sunni Muslims and their Persian victims Shi'as, religious scruples about making slaves of the hapless Persians did not apply. Their way of life, based on pastoralism and raiding, had scarcely changed since prehistory. Fear of Turkmen slavers would have been ever present in the background of Nader's childhood.

The tribes of Khorasan were for the most part ethnically distinct

---

* Some of the land, once agricultural, went permanently out of cultivation in the period of the Mongol invasions in the thirteenth century, from which rural Persia had in some ways never really recovered.

† Including the Yomut, Tekke, Salor, Ersari, Emreli and Ali Ili tribes.

from the Persian-speaking population, speaking Turkic or Kurdish languages. Nader's mother tongue was a dialect of the language group spoken by the Turkic tribes of Iran and Central Asia, and he would quickly have learned Persian, the language of high culture and the cities, as he grew older. But the Turkic language was always his preferred everyday speech, unless he was dealing with someone who only spoke Persian.[6] We know that Nader learned at some point, possibly later in life, to read and write.

Nomadic or semi-nomadic pastoralists made up about one third of the population of Persia in the early eighteenth century, numbering as many as three million people or more.[7] Their tribal groups were held together by strong bonds of kinship, and by traditions of military and economic interdependence. Culturally many of them, though assimilated into the more sophisticated, urbanised Persian culture to a greater or lesser extent, identified with the Turco-Mongol tradition handed down from the time of Timur and Genghis Khan. They regarded themselves as a cut above the settled peoples those great leaders of horsemen had conquered.

When central authority was weak, as in the early eighteenth century, the mobility, cohesion and arrogance of the tribes tended to make them the masters of the landscape. Even when central authority was strong, the Shah often appointed tribal chiefs as local and regional governors, recognising their natural authority. Even later, in peaceful times, settled peasants gave part of their crops to local tribal leaders in return for what might be called protection; and the nomads paid little or no tax to central government.[8]

Nader grew up in this paradoxical tradition: a Persian subject speaking a Turkic language, familiar with an urbanised Persian culture that was understood and revered from Istanbul to Samarkand, Delhi and beyond, yet an uncomfortable outsider in cities, disdainful of city-dwellers who could not ride a horse.[9] The life of Nader's family would have followed the ancient rhythm of moving the fat-tailed sheep (which to western eyes look more like small, dark goats) and other livestock to the cooler upland pastures around Kobkan in the spring as the snows melted and the first flush of new growth appeared, and back to the milder winter climate of Dastgerd in the autumn.

Having waited a long time for the birth of a son, Emam Qoli was affectionate toward Nader, and proud of him. In later years, perhaps remembering the early, happy phase of his childhood, Nader himself was a doting father: perhaps too indulgent, as Emam Qoli had been.

Even at the age of ten, Nader was said to have been a good horseman, hunter and racer of horses, skilled with the bow and the javelin. One of his early biographers, following the conventions common to lives of heroes in Persian literature, stressed his precociousness, saying that when Nader was one he seemed like a three-year-old and at the age of ten, riding his horse, he went hunting lions, panthers and boars.* Another story says that when he played with other children he called himself the king and let the others rule smaller parts of his kingdom. On one occasion he made these princelings fight each other and in the end, if there was a winner, he gave his clothes to that child and returned home naked. When his mother saw him, she was angry, and he ran to his father to escape her. His father took Nader home and told his mother to let the child do what he wanted.[10]

Nader's father died when Nader was still quite young, precipitating the family into friendless poverty. The years that followed were hard. It is significant for Nader's later, sympathetic conduct toward women that he saw his mother struggling as a poor widow, in a society in which a woman without male protection was highly vulnerable. Destitute and with two young sons it would have been difficult to remarry, and some in these circumstances would have moved to the nearest city and slipped into prostitution for want of other options. Nader's mother must have been a tough and strong-minded woman.

The boy must have missed Emam Qoli terribly. He grew up poor and insecure, open to jibes and sneers for his lack of a father. One might think, according to the usual wisdom in these matters, that he would have been crippled by such an experience, and lost his self-confidence. But different experiences draw out different responses in different people. In Nader's case adversity strengthened his will to survive, stimulated the restless urge to assert himself, to challenge and overcome adverse circumstances, to take control and dominate others. His response to humiliation was a burning resolve to prove himself better than his tormentors.

These hard early experiences must also have fostered a dislike of people who were soft, who had achieved status too easily, including perhaps the mullahs. He never forgot the hardships of his early years,

---

* A good parallel appears in Ferdowsi's *Shahname*, in his account of the childhood of Sohrab: *In but a single month he'd grown a year./His chest was like Rostam's, the son of Zal./At three he learned the game of polo, and/At five he mastered bow and javelin* (Trans. Jerome W. Clinton *The Tragedy of Sohrab and Rostam* p. 21).

nor his bonds with those who had shared them, especially his mother and his brother Ebrahim. Nor did he try to conceal his early life of poverty. One story says that when his father died he and his mother were so poor that he had to support them by gathering firewood in the hills, taking them to market on an ass and a camel that they could barely feed. Years later, he conferred an honour on a man that had been a companion at this time, with the words 'Do not grow proud, but remember the ass, and the picking of sticks.'[11] If some of his earliest memories included his feeling special for his intelligence and his natural dominance over other children (and for the way his father had doted on him), his later childhood marked him in a more negative way, as a social misfit and outcast. One way or another, he remained an outsider the rest of his life.

Beyond the seasonal migrations, life was unpredictable. There is a story that Nader and his mother were carried off into slavery by Turkmen raiders when he was still young. Another version suggests that he was captured with some companions by the Turkmen, but prayed for release, whereupon his fetters fell away 'like cobwebs'. He freed his friends and carried off the raiders' loot. This has been interpreted as a mythologised version of an episode in which Nader persuaded his captors to release him in exchange for a promise of future cooperation; an early showing of his ability to manipulate unpromising circumstances to his advantage.[12] Whatever the truth of it, the stories depict the sort of dangerous world in which a young boy grows up fast.

Around the age of fifteen,[13] Nader went into the service of one of the tribal leaders who represented what passed for government authority in the region. This was Baba Ali Beg Kuse Ahmadlu, the governor of the town of Abivard, an important chief among the Afshars of Khorasan. There had probably been some kind of connection between Baba Ali and Nader's father. Nader started as an ordinary musketeer* but eventually rose in Baba Ali's service to become his right-hand man. The javelin and bow he had learned to use in the Darra Gaz valley were still significant traditional weapons in tribal life and in hunting, but even in the remote north-east of Persia, the former was obsolete and the latter had been made obsolescent in warfare by the spread of gunpowder firearms. In learning to use a smooth-bore musket, Nader was learning

---

* *Tofangchi.* Baba Ali Beg's musketeers were not necessarily foot-soldiers; it is likely that they were mounted on horses, mules or camels to deal with the fast-moving Turkmen.

the dangerous trade of modern warfare. The experience taught him the relatively unexplored potential of these weapons, through the exploitation of which he was eventually to revolutionise the practice of warfare in Persia and the surrounding region. But those days were as yet far off.

As Nader made his mark among the troops of the governor of Abivard, his main responsibility would have been to pursue raiders and retrieve their loot, whether portable property, animals or human beings. No doubt there was uncertainty in many cases about what belonged to whom, and it is likely that Nader profited from such grey areas. It is easy to see how later, hostile stories of his having been himself a bandit and robber could have originated.[14]

Around the year 1714/1715 a larger than normal raid by Turkmen of the Yomut tribe broke into northern Khorasan, several thousand strong. Baba Ali's frontier force fought the Turkmen successfully, defeated them and captured 1,400 of the raiders. Nader must have distinguished himself in the fighting, because Baba Ali chose him to take the news of the victory to the Shah in the capital, Isfahan. In Isfahan Nader was presented to Shah Soltan Hosein and rewarded with a present of 100 tomans.*[15]

This was Nader's first visit to Isfahan, an encounter with a different world. Today the *meidan* of Isfahan – the central square with bazaar, mosques and palaces around it – is still one of the world's great displays of urban architecture. The soaring, blue-tiled Shah mosque,† built in the seventeenth century at the orders of Shah Abbas the Great, is breathtaking. In the early eighteenth century, Isfahan was even more impressive than it is today, with palaces, pleasure gardens and grand boulevards that have since vanished. One awestruck contemporary, who was there in 1716, was unable to look inside the royal palace but judged the interior by the exterior of the great doors, which were covered with bright glass, so that they looked like immense mirrors of crystal. He saw the Shah walk in the vast meidan in front of the palace accompanied by numbers of courtiers dressed in cloth of gold studded with jewels, by guards on foot and on horseback, and by an elephant. He wrote that one might have thought from the courtiers' love of gold that their very flesh was made of it. But he said the courtiers did not rouse themselves to valour or virtue; nothing beyond the indulgence

---

* Worth just under £190 sterling at that time; riches for a young man from Nader's background.
† Officially called the Emam mosque at the time of writing.

of pleasures.[16] An astute young man like Nader with simple provincial tastes would also have quickly realised that the Shah and his court were not as impressive as their surroundings.

While in Isfahan, Nader is said to have met an old fortune-teller in the square and asked him about his future. The man went through his usual tricks and seemed shocked. He repeated what he had done a couple of times and finally he bowed in front of Nader and said, 'You will soon be a great king, and a quarter of the kings of this world will obey you.' Nader asked, 'Have you gone mad? Or do you think you can fool me because I am a Khorasani?' The old man replied, 'I am not lying to you. I merely beg you to treat my children kindly when you become King.'

This fable belongs to a certain sort of narrative about the youth of great men, showing that their remarkable success was fated from the beginning. But it also illustrates the expectation of the rough-cut Khorasani that the citizens of the capital would try to patronise and swindle him.[17] Given his later, hostile attitude to the Safavid capital and the court, it is likely that the young provincial suffered some humiliations while in Isfahan, despite the Shah's gift. One account says that Nader was rudely treated by some court officials, and that years later, when he became Shah, he had the incident re-enacted as a piece of theatre for the amusement of his own court.[18] The story is interesting as an insight into Nader's self-image; again presenting him as an outsider, humiliated by sophisticates too foolish to see his superior qualities.

What were Nader's impressions of the Safavid court, and what was the nature of the Safavid regime? We know from later incidents that Nader was impatient with vain pomp and courtly sophistication. However superior and patronising the court officials may have been towards him, he disdained the vain ostentation, the pettiness, the laziness and dithering of their circle. He always preferred austerity in dress and conduct. Some of this was personal to Nader, but there was a deeper, culturally resonant aspect to this confrontation between provincial warrior and court protocol.

Over three centuries earlier the great Arab historian and theoretician Ibn Khaldun developed a compelling theory of the cyclical rise and fall of ruling dynasties in the Islamic world, based on an analysis of the shifting relationship between nomad tribes and urban authority.[19] He had travelled widely, from Spain to Syria, where he met the great Timur. Although Nader may never even have heard of him, Ibn Khaldun's theories convey something of attitudes and prejudices that would have been familiar to Nader and his contemporaries, bringing us closer to an understanding of the way he and they thought about their world.

Central to Ibn Khaldun's analysis was the concept of 'group feeling' (*asabiyah* in Arabic). It was this quality of strong mutual support and fellowship, fostered by the hardships of life in the mountain and desert margins, which gave tribal nomads cohesion in battle and in politics, and made them such a potent force. The natural tendency was for warlike nomad tribes to progress from dominating the countryside to conquer the cities, found a dynasty and rule the urban population. But once established in the city, the ruler of the new dynasty had to distance himself from his former nomad supporters, to secure himself from rivals among the tribes and broaden his support in the towns.

Once fully secure, Ibn Khaldun observed that the dynasty would relax and enhance its prestige, for example by erecting splendid buildings, as the Safavids did above all in Isfahan under the reign of Shah Abbas the Great, at the beginning of the seventeenth century. But by this stage the tough, austere values that established the dynasty were being lost. Deluded by its own prestige, the dynasty followed new courtly traditions of display and magnificence as ends in themselves. In its last stage the monarchs of the dynasty gave themselves up to pleasure and waste. Inherited treasures that should have paid the State's soldiers and other servants were squandered, and faction divided the dynasty from its most powerful supporters: 'the dynasty is seized by senility and the chronic disease from which it can hardly ever rid itself, for which it can find no cure.'[20] This process was cyclical, and the dynasty was destroyed by conquering nomads like those that set it up, supported by city-dwellers disillusioned by the corruption and decadence of the dynasty in its last stages.

The theory has its weaknesses when applied to the early eighteenth century,[21] but there are a number of striking parallels with the history of the Safavid state. The Safavids first appeared in the late fifteenth century as the leaders of a confederation of Turcoman tribes in eastern Anatolia. The 'group feeling' of this confederation was strengthened by a radical version of Shi'a Islam, which had drawn the tribesmen into religious/ military brotherhoods. The members of these fighting brotherhoods were known as Qezelbash ('red hats'), and accorded their leader, Esmail, quasi-divine status.[22] They conquered Azerbaijan by 1501, and Esmail had himself crowned Shah in Tabriz. Within a few years they took the rest of western Persia, and Fars and Khorasan, but were prevented from breaking back into their old homelands in Anatolia when an Ottoman army defeated Esmail at the battle of Chaldiran in 1514. This failure limited the new regime to borders corresponding closely to those of ancient Persia. The rivalry between the Ottoman and Safavid empires was given extra bitterness by the Sunni/Shi'a religious schism.

Before the Safavid conquest the Persian territories were little more disposed to Shi'ism than any other part of the Islamic world, apart from centres of strong Shi'a belief like the shrine cities of Qom and Mashhad. Sunni Muslims were probably in a majority; and outside Persia there were large numbers of Shi'as in Anatolia, the Lebanon and elsewhere. But once the Safavids and their Qezelbash followers were established in Persia, they pursued a religious policy that was to turn the country into a predominantly Shi'a State. The Safavids imported Shi'a scholars from the Lebanon and Arabia, and enforced Shi'a religious practice in mosques and schools. Sunni theologians left Persia for more favourable lands. At the same time Shi'as were persecuted in the Ottoman territories, where they were regarded as traitors and potentially as spies for the Qezelbash enemy. To understand Persia in the early eighteenth century it is necessary to understand the Shi'ism that underpinned the Safavid State.

The origins of the division within Islam go back to the era of the Prophet himself. Shi'a Muslims believe that Mohammad chose his cousin Ali as his successor.* But despite this, others were elected as caliph or temporal leader after the Prophet's death in AD 632: in succession, Abu Bakr, Omar, and Osman ibn Affan, the last of whom was assassinated in 656. These first three caliphs were occupied with wars of conquest, and the administration of newly conquered territories, but Ali held himself aloof, devoting himself to a life of prayer and preaching. By the time Osman died Ali had gained a large following, partly by the contrast between his holiness and the perceived worldliness of the first three caliphs. Ali was elected as the fourth caliph, but some Muslims rejected his caliphate and made war. The war was indecisive, and Ali was murdered in 661, possibly by extremists from among his own followers who felt betrayed when he attempted a compromise.

After Ali's death the division in Islam persisted. A dynasty of caliphs succeeded him, the Ommayads, based on the party that had resisted Ali in his lifetime. Ali's followers† regarded his son Hasan as his true

---

* His marriage to Mohammad's daughter Fatima also made Ali the Prophet's son-in-law.

† Called Shi'as from *Shi'a Ali* – 'partisans of Ali'.

successor and their Emam or leader, and Hasan became the second
Shi'a Emam, after Ali. When Hasan died Hosein, Ali's second son and
the grandson of Mohammad himself, became the third Emam. Hosein
refused allegiance to the Ommayad caliph and attempted an armed
revolt, but he, his family and his few troops were overwhelmed and
mostly massacred at Karbala in AD 680.

This martyrdom of Hosein and others of the Prophet's closest
descendants at Karbala was the defining moment in the early history
of Shi'a Islam. Ever since, the death of Hosein has been commemorated
by Shi'a Muslims each year, and they have nursed a sense of injustice
and betrayal. Thereafter the Shi'a Emams, as descendants of Ali
and Hosein, were spiritual leaders for a dissident faction within the
political and religious structure of the caliphate. At the death of the
sixth Emam, Ja'far (in AD 765) there was a further schism, with some
following Ja'far's first son, Esmail (these becoming known as 'seveners'
or Ismailis) and the majority his second son, Kazem. In 873 the twelfth
Emam, Mohammad, disappeared. Since then he has been venerated by
'twelver' Shi'as as a Messiah who will one day reappear.

The early Safavid rulers ordered that all their subjects should
publicly demonstrate their adherence to Shi'ism by cursing the first
three caliphs, Abu Bakr, Omar and Osman. This was extreme Shi'ism
and it provoked an extreme response from the Ottoman Sultans, who
by the early sixteenth century had taken over the caliphate, with
the authority over Sunni Muslims that entailed. But the religious
enthusiasm of the Qezelbash did not prevent their leaders intriguing
and fighting each other for influence over the ruling dynasty. From the
mid-sixteenth century onwards, as Ibn Khaldun's theories predicted,
the Safavid dynasty distanced itself from the Qezelbash, relying
instead increasingly on gholams – slaves, many of them recruited from
the Christians of Georgia and Armenia – for soldiers and bureaucrats
(a characteristic strategy of what have been called the 'gunpowder
empires' – Ottoman Turkey, Safavid Persia and Moghul India).[23] Under
Shah Abbas the Great (1587–1628) Persia recovered lost territory, and
the prestige and solidity of the State were consolidated. But despite
a revival under Shah Abbas II (1642–1666) the quality of Safavid rule
slumped thereafter into indolence and decay, cushioned by a lengthy
period of external peace.

Nader would have recognised Ibn Khaldun's picture of a senile
dynasty in the spectacle of Shah Soltan Hosein's court; and from his tough
provincial background he would have concurred with Ibn Khaldun's

moralising judgement on it. Even in a senile monarchy, whatever the exterior conditions, one might have hoped for an exceptional individual to be thrown up by genetic chance, someone with the strength of personality to overcome obstacles and make reforms. In the Safavid monarchy this was made less likely by the tradition of confining heirs to the throne in the ruling Shah's harem. This arrangement made it difficult for royal princes to become political rivals to the Shah, but meant they could receive little serious training in the arts of politics, war or government, or establish relationships with the leading men of the state. Within the harem the princes lived separately and frugally with special tutors. But they grew up isolated and what we would call institutionalised, developing a fear of the noise and complexity of the outside world, and a lack of self-confidence. When their turn to rule eventually came, the royal princes were often unfit for the task.[24]

The Safavid system in its heyday was designed for an autocrat, a strong Shah like Shah Abbas I. There were other poles of power, and provincial governors enjoyed some independence of action. But the state system centred on the Shah, and needed a firm, relentless, inquisitorial personality at the centre to keep it functioning properly. In the latter part of the seventeenth century, with no serious external threats or internal challenges to his authority, the ruling Shah[*] let things slip. He gave less and less attention to government, leaving responsibility to the chief vizier and others. No doubt there were efficient, energetic men among these officials, but when they saw their efforts disregarded by the Shah, and others profiting for themselves and ignoring the interests of the state, they became discouraged. Gradually a miasma of inefficiency and neglect descended on the system.

The causes of the downfall of the Safavid dynasty[†] are still disputed,

---

[*] Shah Soleiman, Shah Soltan Hosein's father; ruled from the 1660s to 1694.

[†] No modern theory of the end of the Safavids has yet proved as inventive as that of Rostam ol-Hokama, who blamed it on an outbreak of ungovernable sexual promiscuity. According to him, the fatal series of events began with the impromptu seduction of a respectable young wife of Isfahan, and ended with the anal rape of all the diplomatic representatives from foreign courts present in Isfahan. This naturally led to difficulties in Persia's overseas relations, so that when the Afghans invaded, the Safavid dynasty found itself without allies. The only aspect of the story which rings entirely true is the account of Shah Soltan Hosein's response to these crimes: he did not know what to do, was advised that the situation was entirely normal, and so did nothing. *Rustam at-Tawarikh*, vol. 1, pp. 243–52.

but the dramatic failure of a previously powerful State like Safavid
Persia does not just happen out of the blue. It used to be thought that
an economic decline in Persia set in from the mid-seventeenth century,
caused by the expansion of European-dominated maritime trade and
the slackening of commerce along the old land routes through Persia.
But recent research suggests that trade along the old routes of the
interior retained much of its former vigour throughout this period.[25]
There is a view that a period of tribal resurgence in Iran[26] corresponded
to a general 'breakout' among such peoples in the region generally,
producing the Afghan incursions into Persia and northern India as well
as the rise of Nader Shah himself. But although complex economic and
social changes may have enriched and strengthened some well-placed
tribes, there is good reason to think that the tribes took advantage of the
weakness of traditional dynasties, rather than causing it.[27]

The silk industry, based primarily in Gilan and other parts of the
north-west, was of great significance for the Persian economy and royal
revenues; it was the country's most important export commodity. It
seems that the silk trade fell off in the latter part of the seventeenth
century as the main export market, India, began to produce its own
silk, and Bengali silk pushed the poorer-quality Persian product out
of trade with Europe too. At the same time Indian cotton began to
export to Persia, worsening what today would be called a balance of
payments crisis that the other main export to India, horses, could not
assuage; and accelerating a net outflow of silver currency from the
country, which could not but weaken the Safavid State.[28] Yet the silk
trade continued, particularly through the Levant, and also reorientated
itself toward Russia. The bulk of the trade westwards had been and
remained in the hands of the Armenians, not the Dutch and English
East India companies. The falling-off of the government's silk revenue
was as much a result of governmental feebleness in collecting it as a
slump in taxable profits.

The picture of overall economic decline in Persia at this time may
be overdrawn. The rise to economic dominance of European trade in
Asia was yet to happen in 1700, and throughout this period the volume
of Persian trade with India was always significantly greater (even if
declining) than the volume of trade with Europe. It seems more likely
that the Safavid State failed to adjust to a shift in economic and social
structures. The ultimate test of any state, European or Asian, in the
eighteenth century was war; the successes of the large, well-equipped
armies of Nader Shah in the 1730s and 1740s would not have been

possible if Persia's economic base had become as decrepit as used to be suggested (successes all the more remarkable for the fact that Persia's population was a mere 9 million or less, set against 30 million in the Ottoman territories and 150 million in the Moghul).[29] We should resist the impulse to expect a simple economic cause for the failure of the Safavid dynasty. When the hands on the levers of State were feeble, the levers and the State itself also looked weak; but the levers worked well enough again when returned to firm hands.[30]

When Shah Soltan Hosein's father Shah Soleiman lay dying in 1694, he left it undecided which of his sons should succeed him. Calling his courtiers and officials, he told them, 'If you desire ease, elevate Hosein Mirza.* If the glory of your country be the object of your wishes, raise Abbas Mirza to the throne.'[31] Once Soleiman was dead, the eunuch officials who guarded and supervised the harem decided for Soltan Hosein, judging that he would be easier for them to control. Soltan Hosein was also the favourite of his great-aunt, Maryam Begum, the dominant personality in the harem; and he duly became Shah. Shah Soleiman had been a great drinker; consumption of wine damaged his health and brought him to a premature death. Contemporary accounts tell us the eunuchs chose the same means to neutralise and control Shah Soltan Hosein.

Initially the prospects for this scheme did not look good. Soltan Hosein Mirza, though rather passive and weak-willed, had been a devoted and pious Muslim and began his reign as Shah with a series of dramatic religious actions, under the influence of the great Shi'a mojtahed (jurist and cleric) Mohammad Baqer Majlesi. These included measures against the Sufi religious order,† the destruction of the former Shah's wine cellar (the bottles were carried out of the palace and broken

---

* The Persian word *Mirza* signified 'Prince' when placed after the name, as here. When placed before the name it denoted a senior official or bureaucrat – Nader's secretary and official historian Mirza Mahdi Astarabadi for example.

† Sufism was a mystical movement within Islam that emphasised direct personal experience of God through contemplation rather than the scholarly, legalistic tradition of *shari'a* and Qur'anic studies followed in the theological schools (*madrases*). Several of the most important Persian poets had been influenced by Sufism, as had previous Safavid Shahs and the Qezelbash phenomenon as a whole. Sufism preserved popular pre-Islamic religious elements and was regarded with suspicion by the *shari'a*-minded scholars.

in public) and a decree against the consumption of alcohol generally. Provisional governors and other officials were to enforce shari'a law and any who had failed to do so in the past were to be punished. Music and dancing in mixed company were banned, as were coffee-houses, gambling, prostitution and sodomy, and opium and other 'colourful herbs'. The decree was carved in stone in many mosques across the country, though that is not to say it was universally enforced. At the same time orders went out that women should not go walking in gardens without their husbands, linger in the streets without good reason, or leave the harem without permission. By attempting to outlaw the Sufis and arrogating all religious authority to the mojtaheds, Mohammad Baqer attempted a kind of Islamic revolution.[32]

But the supple minds of the eunuchs and court officials rose to the challenge, and on this occasion they had a powerful ally, Maryam Begum. This formidable woman is a striking exception in the story of the last years of the Safavid dynasty, both as the only woman to appear as a significant actor in the events of the time, and (often at least) as a rare voice of penetrating good sense. But more research is needed to bring out the circumstances of her life and her influence on events. We know the dates neither of her birth nor her death, but in 1694 she was already an elderly lady by contemporary standards, and she was to live at least a further 25 years. She was the daughter of Shah Safi, who had reigned from 1629 to 1642. She had lived on in the royal harem as the sister, aunt and great-aunt of successive shahs. Over the years she became the dominant personality in the royal family, a matriarch. But as a woman confined to the harem her power was limited; she could only act through her influence on the Shah and others.

Maryam Begum was unhappy at the new dominance of Mohammad Baqer Majlesi. His constraints on women would have made her uneasy at least, and the ban on alcohol meant she could no longer enjoy her wine, but the threat to her position at court was much more serious. As passed down to us the story goes that, working with the eunuchs and others, Maryam Begum feigned a serious illness. She then plaintively told Shah Soltan Hosein that the physicians had said there was only one remedy – a little wine. The Shah sent urgently to the Armenians for some, but they were suspicious of a trick, and claimed that, obedient to the Shah's decree, they had none. They referred the Shah's messenger to the Polish ambassador, who found some wine at last, thereby fulfilling one of the traditional functions of diplomatic missions. But when it was poured for Maryam Begum, she would not take it until the Shah himself did the same – claiming that he too, and his courtiers, needed its solace, being weighed down with so many responsibilities. The Shah drank some wine, and was hooked:

> The King could not stand against so pressing a
> Solicitation, and drank a large Cup of it, which inspired
> him with a certain Briskness that he had no notion of
> before; and he took such a Fancy to it afterwards, that it
> was rare to find him sober, and capable of attending to
> the minutest Affair of Government.[33]

The story may have been embroidered, and it is typical of the time that Maryam Begum's successful reassertion of influence over her great-nephew should have been portrayed as feminine deviousness. But it is clear that from being pious and abstemious, Shah Soltan Hosein became a heavy drinker after his accession. This exacerbated his tendency to indolence, and his desire to be left alone.* He disliked being given bad news, so his officials kept information from him. He developed little interest in affairs of State, which as in his father's latter years were left to the chief vizier† and others. Instead he devoted himself to the construction of pleasure-gardens, notably at Farahabad outside Isfahan; and the expansion of his harem, taking pretty girls from all over his dominions.

When it comes to discussion of the harem and its influence, one might suspect western travellers and observers of prurient fascination, and exaggeration on flimsy evidence. There certainly were some highly coloured stories about Shah Soltan Hosein's harem in circulation:

> Anyone that had a particularly beautiful daughter took
> pains that the Shah's harem officials should come to
> hear of it. Then the maiden, with her face like the moon
> and all her other more than splendid qualities, would
> be married to the prince according to the shari'a and

---

* His upbringing probably damaged Shah Soltan Hosein more than the alcohol, and it was a convention to blame drunkenness for the failings of a weak Shah, where a stronger ruler might drink as much and retain a reputation for pious temperance. But it would be perverse to set aside the evidence of contemporaries like Krusinski just because we are suspicious of such conventions. He was there; we were not.

† *E'temad od-dowle* – the Shah's chief minister of state.

the laws of religion. With accomplished politeness and
gallantry, with exceedingly pleasant techniques and
tempting movements he then stormed her tightly sealed
fortress like a Rostam,* broke her into his possession,
and opened her secret ruby lock with his diamond key.
Both fell in this way into desire and a tumult of the
senses, were blessed and enraptured to such a degree,
that neither an oral nor a written account can do justice to
it; for before the act he applied an ointment to his penis,
so that it immediately began to tingle, and the woman's
vulva, once he was engaged with her, similarly began to
tickle from this embrocation… his couplings were very
long drawn out and accompanied by unusually vigorous
movements. It went so far, that both partners were near
to losing consciousness from excessive desire.

This author goes on to say that the Shah deflowered no fewer than three
thousand 'rose-featured, almond-eyed, sugar-lipped maidens' in this
manner, and slept with two thousand more women 'slim as cypresses…
coquettish and charming' that presumably had not been maidens. The
women were then divorced from the Shah and returned whence they
came, pregnant and laden with presents. Many of them were given in
marriage to Persian noblemen, whose apparent heirs by this procedure
were in fact sons of Shah Soltan Hosein. The same source says that the
women that stayed in the harem secretly hated the Shah and would
have preferred a bathhouse-stoker or the man who cleaned out the
privies. They longed for the Shah's overthrow, so they could find a
proper husband.

But this is not a western writer exaggerating oriental wickedness
for a credulous far-away readership; it is a Persian source.[34] One might
think the account a little overwritten (not to say overheated) but it
helps to put the reports of western writers in context, and to show what
kind of stories were in circulation. All these commentators, Persian or
foreign, were only human. They were fascinated to know the secrets of
the royal harem, took scandalous stories from eunuchs and others, and
decided for themselves what they wanted to pass on.

The combination of secrets and sex will always act as a strong
stimulus to the imagination. Life in Shah Soltan Hosein's harem was

---

* The legendary Persian hero, celebrated in Ferdowsi's *Shahname*.

certainly more mundane than it was depicted. Rather than a brightly coloured bordello, it was simply the place where the women of the royal family and the palace lived out all the various ordinary activities of their constricted lives. But there is good evidence that Shah Soltan Hosein's enjoyment of and expenditure on his harem was regarded as excessive.[35] His use of his position to gratify a near-indefatigable sexual appetite should be no surprise: it has plenty of parallels both in his time and in our own.* The excess of the harem and its bad influence on government were a stock feature of western commentary on the Persian monarchy in this period. But many of the Shah's own subjects would have agreed: the western commentators disapproved,[36] but their comments reflected the disapproval of their Persian contacts and informers.

Shah Soltan Hosein maintained his religion, and a praiseworthy aversion to the shedding of blood, though the latter quality did not enhance his reputation as a strong monarch. His weakness encouraged intrigue and faction at court, where eunuchs, officials, nobles and servants bickered and strove for influence.[37] When asked for a decision, Shah Soltan Hosein would tend to agree with whoever approached him last – usually with the words *Yakhshi dir* ('It is good' in the Turkic court language). One story says that this became such a regular phrase with him that the eunuchs and courtiers nicknamed him *Yakhshi dir* behind his back.[38]

The early Greek philosopher Heraclitus, emphasising the contingent and changing nature of existence, is supposed to have said that no-one ever steps into the same river twice, because new waters are always flowing down. Others have taken this as an image for human personality – that the notion of a fixed personality is an illusion.[39] Perhaps, despite the enervating effect of his upbringing, if Shah Soltan Hosein had been challenged by a serious crisis early in his reign, some otherwise concealed part of his nature might have been stimulated to vigorous action. If successful, he could have continued in that vein and made a strong Shah.

But Persia, blessed with strong natural frontiers and protected by the great distances of the Iranian plateau, would only infrequently be

---

* In Europe, Louis XIV and Augustus the Strong were contemporaries. Although priests may have pursed their lips at those princes' harems, many seem to have been prepared to indulge a manly vigour that they would have condemned as decadence in weaker rulers.

threatened by serious crises from external causes, and the early years of
Shah Soltan Hosein's reign were tranquil. In the security of his palaces
in Isfahan, the Shah lapsed into a pleasant life of indolence, drinking,
beautiful women and garden improvements. He slotted lazily into the
place allotted for him in the court culture that had developed under his
father. With a vacuum at the very top of this highly centralised system,
courtiers and officials intrigued among each other to secure advantage,
and to prevent any rival achieving any kind of dominance. Neglect
of the interest of the state became the norm, in favour of the private
interest of individual courtiers. Such was the Shah and the court Nader
encountered on his visit to Isfahan – a far cry from the barren hills and
hard realities of Khorasan.

By sending the young Nader to Isfahan with the news of their
victory over the Turkmen, Baba Ali had made a public demonstration
of his esteem, elevating Nader above the level of his other officers. After
his return from Isfahan in about 1715 this was reinforced by Nader's
marriage to Baba Ali's daughter, and Nader's first son, Reza Qoli, was
born of this marriage on 15 April 1719.[40] The name Reza Qoli, like the
birth-names of Nader's other sons and his father's name (Emam Qoli),
is a strong indication that Nader was brought up and remained in his
youth a Shi'a Muslim, as one would expect from his Afshar, Qezelbash
background.

Baba Ali was an important man in Khorasan and these signs of favour
to such a young upstart incited jealousy among other local chiefs, Afshars
and others. Before the marriage could take place there was fighting
and some of the jealous chiefs were killed. In facing down opposition
in this way, Baba Ali would have been motivated by something more
than just approval of an able young man. There may have been a pre-
existing bond of kinship, or a strong friendship or obligation between
Baba Ali and Nader's dead father.[41] However the marriage came about,
it established Nader as a coming figure in the politics of Khorasan, and
set him on the path to dominate them as the state of the country as a
whole descended into anarchy. But it also created enduring bitterness
within the Afshar tribe, and Nader's unpopularity with some elements
in northern Khorasan was deepened later by feuds with the Kurds. His
success won him followers, but made him an outsider and enemy even
to some of his own tribe, sowing the seeds of later betrayal.

By 1710 Shah Soltan Hosein's pleasant life at court in Isfahan was
increasingly troubled by conflict and rebellion in the provinces. As early

as 1699 Baluchi tribesmen from the south-east raided into the province of Kerman on a large scale. Shah Soltan Hosein sent against them a Georgian prince, known as Gorgin Khan to the Persians. In war he was bold and determined, but the finer arts of politics and diplomacy were not his style. He was arrogant, and saw force as the solution to any problem. Gorgin pacified the Baluchi tribesmen, and stayed in Kerman to keep an eye on them. In 1704 he moved against them again when they made an attack on Kandahar.[42] What is today Afghanistan was then divided between the Persian and Moghul empires: the border lay between Kandahar and Kabul, which had a Moghul governor. Kandahar was the capital of a Persian province, as was Herat.

When Gorgin arrived in Kandahar the Baluchis quickly submitted. Gorgin Khan had been made governor of Kandahar before he left Kerman, and now set about enforcing his authority in the frontier territory. He did this in a characteristically bullying way, and his Georgian troops soon became unpopular with the Afghans, who had resented them from the start for their Christian origins.

In the summer of 1706 Shah Soltan Hosein set out with an enormous retinue of 60,000 people including courtiers, harem and escort troops, on a pilgrimage to the holy cities of Qom and Mashhad, where they stayed for almost a year.* The cost was ruinous, both for the State treasury and for the provinces through which the cavalcade passed.[43] Extra disturbance of ordinary life was caused by the *qoroq* – the institution whereby the Shah travelled with the women of his harem and the eunuchs in a kind of bubble two or more miles long, within which anyone found in the open was liable to suffer a severe beating, or death. In towns warning was given ahead of the qoroq, so that houses looking onto the Shah's route could be emptied, and others closed up. Eunuchs marched a mile or more ahead and a mile or so behind the Shah with swords drawn, to enforce the qoroq. The Shah amused himself along the way by whipping the mules on which the women rode, so that they kicked and threw their riders.[44]

While the Shah made his leisurely way to Mashhad, there was a severe food shortage in Isfahan – possibly caused by profiteering grain merchants, taking advantage of the court's absence; and the people revolted. They gathered in the great square, threw stones at the doors of the Ali Qapu palace, shouted insults against Shah Soltan Hosein, and

---

* These cities were and are sacred to Shi'a Muslims as the burial places of the eighth Emam, Emam Reza (at Mashhad) and his sister Fatima (in Qom).

called for his brother instead, demanding that he be brought to them out of the harem. Shah Soltan Hosein sent one of Gorgin's nephews, Kei Khusrau, from Mashhad, and he successfully put down the revolt.[45]

It is hard to imagine such a demonstration taking place in the capital of a true autocrat, as Shah Abbas had been. A sharper administration would never have allowed the famine to get so serious. The stone-throwing was a sign that Shah Soltan Hosein's prestige, and that of the monarchy as a whole, had already fallen to a dangerously low level. Any form of government is a conjuring trick to some extent; even a despotism depends ultimately on the consent of subjects to be ruled, and the respect in which the rulers are held. Once the prestige and respect begin to crumble, the compliance of subjects (particularly the more unruly ones) starts to erode too, and a slide toward anarchy gathers pace.

At the same time there was trouble with the warlike Lazgi tribes from the mountains of Daghestan in the far north-west. The Lazgis played a similar role as a persistent and dangerous irritant to the Persian monarchy as they and the Chechens, their near neighbours in the Caucasus, did in later centuries to the Russian State. Like the Turkmen, the Afghans, the Baluchis and the Kurds,* the Lazgis were Sunni Muslims and their depredations carried the extra animosity of religious schism. In 1706 they raided into Georgia, partly because the subsidies normally paid them to keep the peace had been embezzled by corrupt Persian officials. Lack of grip at the centre of the State was causing other problems too. As the Shah's reign went on merchants and travellers were less and less safe on the roads and caravan routes. Sometimes they were robbed by the very officials that were supposed to protect them, and banditry became commonplace.[46]

Established as Governor in Kandahar, Gorgin intended to strengthen Persian authority in this wild region, and did so with an iron hand. The leading personality in Kandahar was Mir Veis, an Afghan noble of the Ghilzai tribe. Mir Veis was a wealthy man, from a well-known family. He was generous to his partisans and the needy, and became a focus for the resentment of the ordinary people toward the oppressive rule of the Georgians. Gorgin distrusted Mir Veis. One of the main measures taken by Gorgin to guard against Moghul interference was to prevent Afghan

---

* There were a variety of religious groups among the Kurds, including Sufis, Yazidis, some Shi'as and members of the Ahl-e haqq sect; but the majority tended to Sunnism.

raids into Moghul territory that might have served as a provocation. This would have ranked high among the actions the warlike Afghans of Kandahar found oppressive in their new governor.[47]

The Afghans are important in Nader's story. From contemporary descriptions of them one gets a strong sense of asabiyah, the group feeling central to the theories of Ibn Khaldun. They lived on a simple diet, mainly of bread, grilled meat and raw vegetables, being unused to spices – 'In their greatest Entertainments they have nothing more, and their only Drink is Water, there being scarce any Nation perhaps that is more averse to Wine.' They dressed simply, shaved their heads, leaving a tuft of hair by each ear, and wore a turban made of a single piece of cloth wound around the head, with one end left dangling down to the shoulder. Only the wealthy wore shoes: the others went barefoot, and most of their soldiers wore no body armour.

The Afghans were warlike and proud, brought up to fighting and raiding against their neighbours; and their discipline in war was harsh. They generally fought on horseback with the traditional lance, bow, sword and shield. Their attacks were led by picked men* who after the first skirmishes would filter back round the flanks of the main body to take up positions in the rear. From there, while the main force engaged, they would beat back to the fight or if necessary kill any faint-hearts that might try to make away.[48] At this time the Ghilzai Afghans were based on Kandahar, and the other main tribe, the Abdali Afghans, on Herat. The Abdalis and the Ghilzais were great rivals and often fought each other. Both tribes were Sunni Muslims, and tended to be austere and devout.

As his governorship of Kandahar wore on, Gorgin's suspicions of Mir Veis reached such a pitch that he had him arrested and sent to Isfahan.[49] He did so with advice to Shah Soltan Hosein that Mir Veis was a dangerous, influential man of doubtful loyalty; and that Persian rule in Kandahar would be best secured by keeping him in the capital. Sending Mir Veis to Isfahan, where he could see for himself the weakness of the regime, was a mistake that was to prove fatal not only for Gorgin, but for Persian rule in the Afghan territories as a whole. Like Nader later, Mir Veis quickly saw the nature of court life, and the potential advantage to him of the factional strife there. He ingratiated himself widely, and established some influence even over Shah Soltan Hosein.

Soon Mir Veis achieved a position as one of the Shah's most favoured courtiers.[50] He got permission to make a pilgrimage to Mecca, and

---

* *Nasaqchis* – they served as both a kind of military police and executioners.

while there he secured a fatwa* from the religious authorities allowing the Sunni Muslims of Kandahar to free themselves from the rule of the heretical Persians. Mir Veis returned to Isfahan from Mecca in the summer of 1708, and thence to Kandahar, heaped with honours. Gorgin was furious. Back home, Mir Veis prepared his followers for a revolt against the arrogant Georgians, and the chance came in April 1709. One story says that Mir Veis himself went into Gorgin's tent and collapsed it from the inside, preventing Gorgin from making any resistance, and then killed him. Many of the Georgians died with Gorgin, and the remainder only fought their way out of the province with difficulty.

In Isfahan the Ghilzai revolt failed to galvanise the Safavid government. Shah Soltan Hosein only slowly realised his mistake in trusting Mir Veis. He sent two envoys in succession to remonstrate – both were imprisoned. Eventually a force was sent under Kei Khusrau, Gorgin's nephew, to restore the province. But despite gaining the help of the Abdalis of Herat, and some successes, Kei Khusrau moved very slowly and in October 1711 he was forced to withdraw after a lengthy and unsuccessful siege of Kandahar. As the Persians pulled out, Mir Veis attacked. The Georgians and Abdalis fought bravely, but were caught at a disadvantage, and Kei Khusrau himself was killed when his horse threw him as he tried to cross a stream. Most of the army managed to escape, but it was a serious defeat, and the Safavid monarchy had lost Kandahar for good. A further expedition sent from Isfahan never reached Kandahar; the forces dispersed when the elderly commander died on the way, at Herat.[51]

Mir Veis extended his control over the whole of the province of Kandahar, but was content with the title of vakil or regent. He died in 1715. One story said that as he lay dying he was asked how the Ghilzais should handle the threat from Persia in the future. Mir Veis said that if the Persians attacked, the Ghilzais should make peace; but if the Persians showed themselves less bellicose, they should attack them 'even to the Gates of Isfahan'.[52] Mir Veis was succeeded as ruler by his brother; but the brother was less belligerent and less popular with the Ghilzai chiefs. They encouraged Mahmud, the eldest son of Mir Veis, to take over as their leader. Mahmud did so, murdering his uncle in 1717 – the first of a grim cycle of bloody deeds. In these latter years the Persians made no further attempts to resume control of Kandahar because they were taken up with the revolt of the Abdalis in Herat,

---

* A formal religious ruling.

which was the next domino to fall.

The Abdali tribe were the great rivals of the Ghilzais at this time, and may have been more numerous. Having witnessed at first hand the debacle of Kei Khusrau's expedition to subdue the Ghilzais, the Abdalis saw the opportunity to rid themselves of the feeble Persians. The Safavid Governor of Herat saw trouble coming and arrested some principal chiefs, but was then locked up by his own troops, who mutinied. A new governor sent from Isfahan was defeated by the Abdali tribesmen, and an attempt by the governor of Mashhad to break the rebellion met the same fate in 1716.

Among the troops sent from Mashhad against the Abdalis were 500 under Baba Ali, Nader's father-in law. Nader was left behind as Baba Ali's deputy in Abivard. But Baba Ali was shot and killed in the fighting,[53] and was replaced as governor of Abivard by his brother, Qorban Ali, under whom Nader campaigned again successfully against Turkmen raiders of the Tekke tribe. Qorban Ali died, ostensibly of illness, after only a short time.[54] It is possible that Qorban Ali did not in fact die of natural causes, and that his death was the origin of later stories that Nader murdered his father-in-law (the stories confusing Baba Ali with his brother). At any rate Qorban Ali's death brought a step up for Nader; he was formally made deputy governor of Abivard under the new governor appointed from Isfahan, Hasan Ali Khan. As time went on Nader became increasingly the dominant partner in the relationship: an exercise in the assertion of the realities of power over the formalities that was to be repeated later in Nader's career.

The Safavid regime still struggled ineffectually to overcome the revolts in the eastern part of its dominions, but each failure, instead of remedying the situation, weakened the prestige of the government further. There were further expeditions from Isfahan to reconquer Herat: all failed. Nader himself took part in one of them, accompanied by troops from Abivard. But when it came to battle the Persian cannon were turned on their own troops in error, the Abdalis penetrated the Persian formation, and the Persian commander broke down and blew himself to pieces on a powder barrel.[55] Nader and his men managed to escape from the scene of disaster. In each episode Nader learned more about war and the command of men.

Having survived the danger of repression from Isfahan, the Abdalis were free to attack their traditional Ghilzai enemies, but were defeated by Mir Veis's son Mahmud in battle in 1720, and thereafter fell into conflict among themselves, different chiefs struggling for supremacy. Mahmud sent the heads of some of the Abdalis to Shah Soltan Hosein as a gesture of loyalty. Shah Soltan Hosein, showing his usual simplicity and wishful thinking, accepted this ruse at face value, made Mahmud Governor of Kandahar and gave him the title Hosein Qoli Khan.[56] This meant 'slave (or servant) of Hosein' – to be named after the Shah himself in this way was a great honour.

As the government in Isfahan lamented the dismal events in the east, news reached the court that several islands in the Persian Gulf, important Persian possessions for the safe passage of trading vessels, had been seized by Arab pirates from Muscat. The elderly matriarch of the harem, Maryam Begum, seems to have been the only one to understand the need for firm action in the face of these manifold troubles. At her urging, and with a gift of her money for the purpose, the Shah she had elevated as her protégé moved with his court to Qazvin in the north-west to raise troops. But once there the leading courtiers did nothing, postponing action, quarrelling among themselves and attending only to the usual round of pleasant pastimes – 'each one by reason of his vain personal interests and hypocrisy against the others, veiled his eyes to what was expedient for the state.'[57]

In the years 1717–1720 there was plague in the north-western provinces, and revolts broke out again in Kurdistan, and in Shirvan. The Sunni Muslims of Shirvan and possibly Kurdistan too seem to have been driven to rebel at least partly by the religious intolerance of their governors – under the influence of the Shi'a religious revival that had taken place in the early years of Shah Soltan Hosein's reign. The central figure in this movement, the scholar and cleric* Mohammad Baqer Majlesi, died in 1699. He had been a vigorous and determined character, a strong advocate of traditional Shi'ism and of firm adherence to shari'a law; determined to reassert the dominance of Shi'ism over Sunnism, Sufi mysticism, and the religious minorities in the country. His plentiful writings in Persian as well as Arabic gave his views a wide circulation and stimulated new scholarship, aside from his influence with Shah Soltan Hosein and at court, where the setback inflicted by the eunuchs and Maryam Begum over the drinking of wine did not overthrow his position. His written collections of Shi'a traditions have remained influential to the present day.

In Persia and other Muslim countries minority groups of Christians

---

* *Mojtahed.*

and Jews were traditionally given privileged status as 'people of the book' above other non-Muslims, on the basis that the Bible both held sacred was also revered in the Muslim tradition. Despite the protection they should have enjoyed in theory, Mohammad Baqer's example, carried forward after his death by his grandson, the chief mullah,* Mohammad Hosein, led to persecution of Jews and Armenians, and the Shah passed a decree for the forced conversion of Zoroastrians, fire-worshippers whose ancient religion dated back long before the arrival of Islam.[58] Hindu merchants from India also suffered, as did the Sufis, whose mysticism had done much in previous centuries to assimilate diverse religious impulses, including popular pre-Islamic elements, and soften the edges of Islam. Sunni Muslims were also persecuted. The resurgence of strict Shi'ism, with the tacit approval of the court if not always the formal support of the State, created tensions among the Shah's non-Shi'a subjects, and added to the monarchy's political difficulties. The spirit of the times narrowed and soured.[59]

A story about Mohammad Baqer was current among later generations, of a dream someone had about him after the great scholar had died. In the dream they asked Mohammad Baqer about the afterlife, and how he had been treated in the other world. Mohammad Baqer replied 'None of my actions profited me at all, except that on one day I gave an apple to a Jew, and that saved me.'[60] One should be wary of building too much on this sort of tale, but the idea that such a stern and learned mojtahed might have profited more in heaven from a simple gesture of humanity than from his lifelong insistence on orthodoxy suggests a natural reaction against religious extremism.†

---

* *Mullah-bashi.* The origins of this title are obscure, and Sandy Morton has pointed out to me that there is even a facetiousness about it, but it seems to have originated toward the end of the reign of Shah Soltan Hosein. See Minorsky 1943, p. 41.

† It is right to doubt contemporary or later western writers that castigated so-called Islamic bigotry, but the religious movement in the time of Shah Soltan Hosein drew criticism within Persia – one example being the *Rustam at-tawarikh*, whose author squarely blamed the bad influence of religious extremism for leading Shah Soltan Hosein onto the 'crooked path of error' (vol. 1, pp. 220–223). The fact that this account (based largely on conversations with the author's father, uncle and others, who were contemporaries) was not put together until the early 1780s (vol. 1, p. 20) and was not finished until the nineteenth century is balanced by the fact that no author would have been as frank about the errors of a regime that was still in power.

Nader himself may represent a more violent reaction – at some point he turned against the contemporary forms of Shi'ism, and possibly against religion altogether.* Nader may have been an early example of the phenomenon warned of by some modern Islamic thinkers and Shi'a theologians; that when religious zeal becomes too political, it may risk discrediting religion itself.[61]

The Shah's personal inclinations were less rigid, more humane and relaxed than those of his chief mullah – but he went along with his advisers, as usual. The tense religious atmosphere was a significant factor in the revolts on the Sunni periphery, especially unfortunate at a time when the monarchy was weak. The clearest example was the revolt in Shirvan, where Sunni religious men had been killed, religious books destroyed and Sunni mosques turned into stables;[62] but there were outbreaks in Kurdistan and it may have had some effect in the revolt of the Ghilzais and Abdalis too. The rebels in Shirvan appealed to their co-religionists, the Ottoman Turks – an ominous development. When eventually the Sunni inhabitants of Shamakhi, the main town of Shirvan, opened one of the gates to Lazgi tribesmen in August 1721, thousands of the Shi'a population were massacred (foreigners and Christians were only robbed). The Shi'a governor, his nephew and other relatives were cut to pieces by the mob, and their bodies thrown to dogs.[63] The province passed into Ottoman control.

The next great blow to the rule of Shah Soltan Hosein came from the east in the autumn of 1719 when Mahmud Ghilzai of Kandahar, the son of Mir Veis, raided Kerman with about 10,000 Ghilzais, Sistanis and others. The governor of Kerman fled and Mahmud entered almost unopposed. The city was thoroughly sacked.

In Kerman Mahmud showed some of the unpredictability that was later to deepen into insanity. He ordered forced conversions to Sunnism, then rescinded the orders; he punished troops that committed crimes, and then allowed terrible atrocities to go ahead. The Zoroastrians, bitter at the persecution of previous years, took advantage of the chaos to attack the Shi'a citizens; but themselves suffered further from the Afghans. As time went on there were more and more killings, and

---

* One wonders what the attitude of local mullahs was to Nader's mother in her poverty. There is no evidence to bear upon this at all, to my knowledge, but a humiliating rejection of an appeal for charity from Nader's mother, for example, would explain a lot in Nader's later attitudes and behaviour. As a poor widow, Nader's mother would also have been sexually vulnerable.

more and more damage was done until when the Ghilzais finally left in the summer of the following year, most of the buildings of the city had been burned and the bazaar was strewn with bodies. Mahmud returned to Kandahar with his loot.[64] It was a terrible warning of what was to follow, on a much larger scale.

As Mahmud withdrew Fath Ali Khan Daghestani, the chief vizier, encouraged the Shah to move with the court to the north-east, to bring the extra prestige necessary for a successful campaign against Kandahar. There seemed at last some hope that a forceful personality might be taking control at the centre of the State. But the Shah moved no further than Tehran. The problem again was faction within the court, where Mohammad Hosein, the chief mullah, along with the Shah's physician, were intriguing with others against Fath Ali Khan. Aside from simple dislike of a rival who seemed temporarily to have the upper hand, they disliked the vizier for his Lazgi origins and Sunni religion.[65] Someone forged a letter to a Kurdish chief, purporting to have come from Fath Ali Khan. It urged the chief to send troops to assassinate the Shah and his family. The letter was shown to the Shah, and Fath Ali Khan was arrested. He was blinded, and tortured to tell where his valuables were hidden.[66]

The operation of court politics under Shah Soltan Hosein in this last stage seems to have worked in an almost diabolical way to subvert the true interests of the monarchy. Any individual among the court officials that appeared to be about to take decisive action against the various threats to the State immediately brought upon him the hostility of the other court factions, who feared loss of their own influence should he succeed.[67] The united efforts of the rest of the court could always turn the Shah against such a figure, or his advice. Rather than see a rival become dominant by defeating the enemies of the State, the eunuchs and courtiers systematically crippled any serious effort to deal with Persia's growing mass of problems. In the end, Safavid Persia fell because those entrusted with its security failed to understand the nature of their responsibility, the true basis of the power they exercised, or the reality of the threats to it. The court lived in a parallel universe in which the continuation of the dynasty was an unassailable certainty, and any form of misgovernment could be indulged in, because there would be no consequences.

A new man was appointed as chief vizier, Mohammad Qoli Khan Shamlu, and the Shah returned with his court to Isfahan in the spring of 1721. In his absence there had again been rumours (at least) of plots to replace him on the throne with his brother Abbas. Maryam Begum had kept affairs in order in Isfahan, and when she saw how he was wasting his time in Qazvin, had urged the Shah to return earlier. But he had ignored her, and from the absence of further mention of her in the sources after 1719, it seems likely that by the time he came back in 1721 Maryam Begum was dead, and that last voice for good sense was gone.

The people of Isfahan rejoiced at the Shah's return (the presence of the court was the stock in trade of the bazaari artisans and traders) and the Shah retired to his usual residence in the gardens of Farahabad, to the south-west of the city. The army that had assembled marched to Mashhad, but many of the soldiers deserted. Instead of the planned campaign against the Afghans, the remaining troops were eventually used against another rebel: Malek Mahmud Sistani, the former governor of Tun and Tabas. But Malek Mahmud prevailed, and thereafter was able to expand his power in the north-east with little interference.

At Farahabad, Shah Soltan Hosein again tasted the best food his cooks could supply. He enjoyed the loveliest women his officials could find in his territories, and through an alcoholic haze, he surveyed and planned improvements to his favourite buildings and gardens. Though most of these have disappeared, the beautiful Madar-e Shah madrase* and its neighbouring caravansarai (now a hotel) survive to show the architectural achievement of his reign. But delicate arches and blue-glazed tiles could not uphold the security of a sprawling empire and its inhabitants. Harsh correction was on its way. Shah Soltan Hosein's detached life at Farahabad may have been a kind of aesthetic and sensual paradise, but it was about to descend into an abyss of horrors.

Encouraged by the success of his raid against Kerman, Mahmud left Kandahar on his second expedition into Persia in the high summer of 1721. Baluchis and other adventurers joined him along the way. But this time they met tougher resistance in Kerman. The new governor had refortified the citadel and most of the population (about 50,000) took refuge there. They suffered terribly, packed together without adequate food, and exposed to the Afghans' gunfire.

Having no heavy siege cannon to break down the walls, the Afghans blockaded the citadel and by February 1722 only about 3,000 of those who had taken refuge there were still alive. Some of them were resorting to cannibalism for want of food, and the original brave governor had

---

* Today officially called the madrase Chahar Bagh.

died. His successor paid the Afghans 1,700 tomans* in gold and silver to end the siege.[68] Mahmud was glad to leave. He had lost many men in the fighting, and others were deserting. He marched on to Yazd, but that city too was resolute and strongly held. Boldly raising the stakes rather than quitting the game, Mahmud bypassed Yazd and drove on towards Isfahan. By early March he halted his men just short of the village of Golnabad, about 18 miles north-east of the capital.

The courtiers in Isfahan had been alarmed at the news that Mahmud was again at Kerman, but when they heard that he was marching on towards the capital they were close to panic. The new vizier, Mohammad Qoli Khan, cautiously advised the Shah to keep his troops within the city and bide his time while a large army could be raised in other parts of the realm. Given the Afghans' failure to take Kerman or Yazd, this was good advice. If the vizier's plan had been followed, the small Afghan army would have been progressively weakened by another siege, and the royal forces could have chosen their moment to attack, with overwhelming numbers.

But as ever, there were two factions. Seyyed Abdollah, the governor of Arabistan, pressed for an immediate attack on the Afghans. He was in special favour with the Shah (to the displeasure of the vizier) and his advice prevailed. Troops were recruited in Isfahan and the surrounding countryside to augment the standing army, and on 3rd March 1722 they marched out to do battle with the Afghans. They were joined on the way by 12,000 Arab cavalry under Seyyed Abdollah. The total Persian force probably numbered about 42,000, but of mixed quality. Many of the infantry were untrained recruits, some only armed with sticks. On the other hand there was a strong force of Persian cavalry, the royal guard troops, commanded by another of the late Gorgin Khan's nephews, Rostam Khan; and a body of warlike horsemen of various Lori tribes under Ali Mardan Khan, the governor of Loristan. These men were both experienced, able commanders. There were also 24 cannon under the Master of Artillery,† Ahmad Khan, assisted by a French gunner, Philippe Colombe. But the feud between Seyyed Abdollah and Mohammad Qoli Khan, the vizier, meant that there was no unity of purpose at the highest level of command.[69] On the day the various Persian commanders each fought their own battle without support from the others.

On 7 March the Persian army marched past Golnabad and

* Worth about £900 sterling at the time.
† *Tupchi-bashi.*

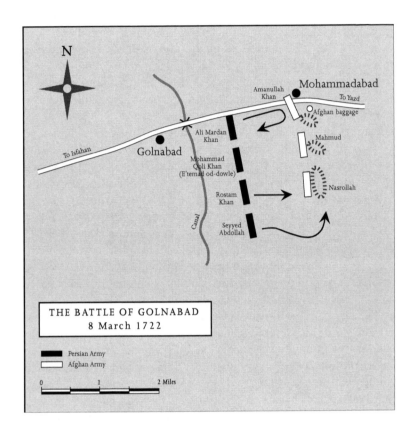

N

Mohammadabad

Amanullah
Khan

To Yazd

Afghan baggage

Ali Mardan
Khan

Mahmud

To Isfahan

Golnabad

Mohammad
Qoli Khan
(E'temad od-dowle)

Rostam
Khan

Nasrollah

Canal

Seyyed
Abdollah

THE BATTLE OF GOLNABAD
8 March 1722

Persian Army
Afghan Army

0   1   2 Miles

approached the Afghan camp, just south of the Isfahan-Yazd road. To do so they had to cross a canal. There was a brief skirmish there with some Afghans, who were beaten off. The Shah's astrologers had pronounced that the Persians should not give battle before 8 March, and the Afghans showed no immediate inclination to attack, so the two armies settled down for the night about a mile apart.

The following morning the Afghans, facing west, were drawn up on three small hills, in three bodies. Mahmud himself commanded the centre, Amanullah Khan the right, and a Zoroastrian from Sistan called Nasrollah, a former bandit, the left wing. The Persians drew up opposite in four bodies: Ali Mardan Khan on the left (with another Lori chief), the Shah's vizier Mohammad Qoli Khan commanding the centre, Rostam Khan to his right and Seyyed Abdollah with the Arab tribesmen on the right wing. The cannon were placed in front of the vizier and most of the Persian infantry in the centre. Both armies fielded a high proportion of cavalry, armed with lance, bow and shield, and the Afghans may have been all or almost all mounted.

The Afghans were many fewer than the Persians and after their losses at Kerman may have numbered as few as 11,000,[70] which meant that Seyyed Abdollah's Arabs were able to overlap the outnumbered Afghans to the south. As on the previous day, the Afghans held their ground. This has been attributed to their awe of the size and magnificence of the Persian army; but in holding back they also kept the advantage of the rising ground. They may also have calculated that the size of the Persian army would make coordination and control difficult. With their smaller numbers and strong position it made sense for the Afghans to let the Persians take the initiative, in the hope that they would make mistakes.

Time passed, and the two armies watched each other uneasily across the open plain. There was a great contrast in their appearance: the Afghans simply and shabbily dressed, down at heel after eight months on campaign; the Persians multifarious, Lors in bright tribal colours, Arabs in white robes, the Persian guards in sumptuous uniforms and shining mail and plate armour, polished helmets and lance-points glittering in the sun.

In overall command in theory, but reluctant to be in the field at all, the vizier was no more anxious than the Afghans to attack. As time went on Rostam Khan and Seyyed Abdollah grew impatient. Eventually, at about four in the afternoon, Rostam Khan took his men forward and charged. As the royal guards crashed into Nasrollah's men, Seyyed Abdollah also advanced, taking his men round the Afghan left flank.

Seeing Nasrollah's men giving ground, and the Arabs swinging round toward his rear, Mahmud thought his luck had run out – 'he ordered the swiftest Dromedary to be got ready for his escape, if a Change did not happen.'[71] If the Persian centre had advanced too, the Afghans might have broken. But the vizier still did not budge, and events were already taking a different turn. Seyyed Abdollah, rather than using his flanking movement to intervene in the main battle, took his men to loot the Afghan camp. As Ali Mardan Khan advanced on the left, Amanullah's Ghilzais retreated before him, but then cantered aside to reveal a mass of about 100 kneeling camels. Each of these carried a small cannon on its back, on a swivel mounting, loading a ball of one or two pounds' weight. They were called *zanburak*,* and made up for the Afghans' lack of other artillery. They fired a crashing volley into the advancing Lori horsemen at close range, doing terrible damage. Ali Mardan Khan himself was wounded, his brother was killed, and when the Afghans followed the zanburak volley with a cavalry charge the Lors fled from the battlefield.

Some of Amanullah's men followed up their defeat of the Lors by overrunning the Persian cannon. Mohammad Qoli Khan's men had not been deployed close enough to protect them. The Afghan assault was so rapid that only three of the guns had time to fire, and most of the gunners, including the Frenchman and the Tupchi-bashi Ahmad Khan, were run down and killed.

With the Persian centre still immobile, Mahmud summoned up his courage and took the bulk of his own men forward to support the Afghan left under Nasrullah, thereby surrounding the best of the Persian troops under Rostam Khan. These brave men, having pushed their enemies back, were now attacked on all sides and outnumbered. Rostam Khan tried to fight his way out, but still got no support from the vizier, who may already have begun to retreat with the troops of the Persian centre. Rostam Khan fell when his horse stumbled as it tried to clear the canal to the rear of the Persian positions. Floundering in the mud, a Ghilzai hit him with a mace before he could remount, and others speared him with their lances, killing him. The Persian army as a whole was now in full flight. Pulling away from their plunder of the Afghan camp, Seyyed Abdollah's Arabs followed at a safe distance.[72]

Mohammad Qoli Khan, the vizier, took most of the blame for this disaster, for failing to support Rostam Khan's attack on the Afghans,

* 'Little wasp'.

and for (according to the general view) having been the first to retreat, without having struck a blow. Seyyed Abdollah's behaviour was also regarded with suspicion. The rivalry between the two had been fatal; some speculated that (in the true spirit of Shah Soltan Hosein's court) the vizier had held back simply because he feared that Seyyed Abdollah would get credit for a victory.[73] Some of the Afghans said after the battle that they would have lost if the Persian centre under the vizier had held position a quarter of an hour longer. But the Afghans' resilience deserved credit too, and Amanullah Khan's intelligent use of the zanburaks was an innovation in the use of mobile firepower that was to prove significant later.[74] Aside from the zanburaks and the brief splutter of the Persian artillery before it was overrun, firearms played little part in the battle. For the most part the Afghans fought without them, and the troops on the Persian side that fought hardest did so mainly with lance and sword. In that sense too the battle marked the end of an era.[75]

This was no minor setback in a frontier skirmish – it was headlong rout of the main royal army, in the centre of the realm, almost within sight of the capital, inflicted by what would months previously have been dismissed as a smallish band of ragged tribesmen. It was a terrible defeat, a great blow to the tottering prestige of the monarchy; all the more so for the palpable incompetence that had brought it about. It made possible a further round of betrayals and disasters.

It is a natural tendency when examining this sort of event to pile in every trend, every bit of evidence of decline, to explain it. It was because of the economic decline, it was the divisive religious extremism, it was the court politics, it was the long period of peace, it was the decline of the army… and so on. Had the army as an institution declined? What exactly was the Safavid army, as an institution? One thing is plain: the Safavid army was not a single permanently constituted institution like that of a modern nation-state. There were elements that resembled that sort of institution to some extent – the royal guards were paid and uniformed, and were maintained at full strength even in peacetime. Likewise the artillery, though perhaps not at full strength. At Golnabad there were a large number of rapidly recruited militia-style infantry armed with muskets, who in the event played little part in the fighting.

But the bulk of the Safavid army was always made up of tribal or other troops from the regions – as had been the case in the armies of Persia since the days of Darius and Xerxes. They were good troops. Most of them, the trusted companions of provincial governors and tribal chiefs, were excellent, experienced, tough, disciplined cavalry accustomed to manoeuvre and fight together in a body. They did not fight like western cavalry, but this was not Europe – and they were not subject to the same influences that might have caused a decline in the fighting efficiency of the soldiers based in Isfahan.

The case for the decline of the Safavid army may be at least partially correct, but it has not been proved.[76] The standing elements of the army may not have been kept properly paid or equipped.[77] The series of defeats in the east must have had a bad effect on morale. But there was no obvious sign of these factors on the day of battle at Golnabad. The size of the army might have been greater if more provincial governors had sent troops more quickly, but as it stood the numbers were more than adequate to beat the Afghans. The elements that could have won the battle, notably the guards, were well-equipped and in good fettle. There was no lack of aggression, except in the command of the vizier, and the sources seem to agree that this was down to his personal conduct rather than that of his men. In general the Persians, including the provincial and tribal troops, fought hard.* But an army of disparate elements needed firm central control and a strong sense of unified purpose to be effective. That is what was missing. The Shah was missing, and in his absence no one personality was dominant. The battle was lost for the same reason that the Safavid state had decayed – lack of central control in a highly centralised system designed for a strong Shah.

Perhaps shocked by the experience, and unable to believe his luck, Mahmud lingered near the battlefield. He did not let his men pursue far, for fear of an ambush. This meant that the Persian losses were relatively light – perhaps 5,000 – but they left behind all their cannon and many of the Persian infantry threw away their muskets as they fled. There was panic in Isfahan when the first of the fugitives arrived, and women ran screaming for the safety of the citadel. The court deliberated whether the Shah should stay in Isfahan, or leave to raise new forces in the provinces. It is probable that after Golnabad, only the Shah's presence could have brought together the provincial forces necessary to relieve

---

* One could claim that the failure of the artillery corps was down to poor training and readiness, but hard evidence for this is wanting. Mohammad Mohsen (fol. 207a) was clear why the Persians were beaten: 'Because of their lack of unity, the Shi'a suffered a serious defeat. Had they remained united, they might have beaten the Afghans.'

Isfahan. He would have been safer, and of more use, outside the capital. But as usual the worst counsel prevailed and he stayed in the city.[78]

After three days Mahmud resumed his march and occupied the Farahabad palace complex on the south-western side of Isfahan, along with Julfa, the Armenian quarter. Mahmud quickly set about stripping the leading Armenians of their wealth (beating them on the soles of their feet until they gave it up)* and their young women. The heads of the Armenian community paraded their families before the Afghans, and about 50 girls were taken. Mahmud kept the most beautiful for himself, and shared the rest out among his officers. But their tears and anguish were such that the burly Afghans, discovering perhaps a gap between the idea and the reality of machismo, took pity on them. Some of the girls were allowed back to their homes straight away, and others were ransomed. Within a few days only a few remained with the Afghans, and they too were returned eventually. According to one account this was because Mahmud came to believe that their impious abduction had incurred divine disapproval, slowing the progress of his siege of the city of Isfahan. The Armenian priests rebaptised the girls, telling them and their parents that this would restore their former purity.[79] This gave them some chance of finding husbands; otherwise they would have been likely to end up as prostitutes.

The siege of Isfahan lasted from March to October 1722. Inside the city, the usual bickering and folly prevented determined action even in this extremity. The Shah brought two of his sons in succession out of the harem to share his rule, but when the boys spoke harshly of the Shah's physician, the chief mullah and the defeated commanders from Golnabad and their mismanagement of affairs those courtiers took offence, and got the Shah to send the princes back. The Shah was advised again to go into the provinces to raise troops, but he did not do so and when the Afghan grip closed around Isfahan, this chance was lost. It would have been possible early on to move some of the people out of the city, to reduce the demand for food, but nothing was done and the population was actually swollen by the arrival of refugees from nearby villages. Some extra troops and provisions were brought in too, but the Shah's appeals to provincial governors to send new troops to his relief got a mixed reception.

By now, in consternation at the Shah's mismanagement, the

---

* This form of beating, called the *falake* in Persian, was known in the West as the bastinado. It caused terrible pain and if prolonged could end in death.

provincial grandees were in doubt between loyalty and the need to look to their own interests. The single most powerful source of potential help was Vakhtang of Georgia,* but he was seriously disillusioned with the incompetence and debility of the regime.[80] There was another factor too – Vakhtang knew that Tsar Peter the Great of Russia was planning an intervention in the Caucasus. The Christian Russian monarchy, fresh from crushing military success against the Swedes in the Great Northern War, looked much more attractive than the collapsing Safavid State. Contemporaries believed the mere approach of a Georgian army would have saved Isfahan, but Vakhtang made no effort to intervene against the Afghans.

In Khorasan, as elsewhere in the country, the siege of Isfahan meant a lapse of State authority, and the leading personalities of the region eyed each other up to gauge who would emerge on top if the province were permanently cast adrift. In Abivard Shah Soltan Hosein's appointee as governor prudently withdrew and Nader, in command of the small but battle-hardened frontier force known as the Atak army, took control.

Mahmud's army of Ghilzai Afghans and others was small for the siege of a city the size of Isfahan, and lacked heavy artillery. Afghan assaults failed, though killing many on both sides. The besiegers were forced to settle down to a blockade, to starve the citizens into submission, but initially Mahmud had trouble closing off the city to supplies from outside. The Persians made some successful sallies, but most of their attempts to hit back at the Afghans came to nothing. Some of these were led by Seyyed Abdollah, commander of the Arab wing at Golnabad, and his half-hearted leadership led the citizenry to suspect his loyalty. He was, in fact, secretly in league with the Afghans. But he was still a favourite with the Shah, who suspected nothing.

The cost of provisions steadily rose, and there were more demonstrations against the Shah's government in the square in front of the royal palace, calling for him to be replaced by his brother. Spirited refugees from the villages around Isfahan broke into the houses of the Shah's physician and the chief mullah, loudly blaming them for the country's disasters. Loyal forces from Qazvin and Loristan tried unsuccessfully to relieve the city in May.[81]

After the Shah's courtiers had vetoed his two eldest sons, the third, Tahmasp, was allowed to take their place at his father's side. Tahmasp

---

* Another of Gorgin Khan's nephews, appointed regent in Georgia at Gorgin's request in 1704.

was as malleable as his father, and presented no threat to the Shah's incompetent advisers. The Shah eventually decided that Tahmasp should leave the city to raise troops for its relief, and he broke out successfully with 1,000 men on the night of 7/8 June. But rather than join up with one of the loyal provincial governors, or make a determined effort to put together a relieving force, Tahmasp went to Qazvin and wasted time there. His messages to provincial chiefs asking for soldiers got even less attention than his father's had done.[82]

By now there was a serious shortage of food in Isfahan. A force of 8,000 Bakhtiari tribesmen attempted to break through with a large convoy of provisions in late June, but they were blocked by the Afghans after some hard fighting. In July there were rumours that a large relieving force under Malek Mahmud Sistani, the rebel former governor of Tun and Tabas, was approaching from the north-east, but this force took a long time to materialise.

In early August the Shah refused an Afghan offer to negotiate, and by this time even the richer people were eating horseflesh, the poorer were catching dogs and cats for meat, and anything that could possibly have given nourishment was taken as food:

> The City of Isfahan being so full of Trees… Part of them was felled… and the Leaves and Bark sold by the Pound. The Roots of Herbs made into Meal were eaten. Shoe-Leather being boiled was for a time the common Food; at last they came to eat human Flesh, and the streets being full of Carcasses, some had their Thighs cut off privately… several Children were stolen and eaten, half dead as they were of Famine…[83]

As time went on more and more bodies lay unburied in the streets, and money ceased to have value. The only commodity of any worth was food.

Around the end of September Malek Mahmud Sistani at last arrived at Golnabad with a long-awaited relieving force of several thousand men. The Afghans, knowing this was Isfahan's last chance, sent Nasrollah (Rostam Khan's opponent at the battle of Golnabad, and a native of Sistan like Malek Mahmud) to negotiate with him. Nasrollah sweetened his arguments with seven splendidly harnessed horses, and two camel-loads of silk, cash and jewels. He explained that Isfahan was on the point of falling, and that when that happened Shah Soltan

Hosein would be finished. The Ghilzais would be the new masters. In return for his cooperation, Malek Mahmud could be the new ruler of Khorasan, with the help of the Afghans. Malek Mahmud had probably never intended to follow through the relief of the city. He let Nasrollah persuade him, and turned back toward the north-east. Having recruited more troops, he headed for Mashhad, the capital of Khorasan.[84]

After the cruel disappointment of this last hope, some Isfahanis tried a mass breakout, but only a few got past the Ghilzai patrols. Thousands were dying of starvation and the garrison were so enfeebled that the Afghans could have broken into the city at any time, but Mahmud held off in order that the riches of the city and its palaces should not be lost to him in the sack that would have followed a successful assault.

In early October 1722 Shah Soltan Hosein finally offered Mahmud his surrender, but the Afghans spun out the negotiations. There is a tradition that on his last day in the city the Shah went through the streets dressed in black, abjectly lamenting his misfortunes.[85] At last, on 23 October the Shah rode out to give himself up, on a horse borrowed from the Afghans. Riding toward the river, he passed bodies on every side. The people watched in silence. When he arrived at Farahabad, his former paradise, he was told that Mahmud was asleep, and he would have to wait. After this further humiliating delay, the Shah was taken to Mahmud, and they greeted each other. Mahmud lolled on a gold cushion. The Shah said:

> My son, since the Supreme Being does not wish me to
> reign, and the moment has come which he has decreed
> for you to ascend the throne, I cede my empire to you
> with all my heart, and I wish that you may rule it in all
> prosperity.[86]

He was made to remove the symbol of royalty, the jiqe, from his own turban, to take it to Mahmud, and fasten it personally on the turban of the new Shah. The old Shah and the new Shah then drank tea and coffee together, and Mahmud undertook to treat his dismal predecessor kindly. So ended over two centuries of Safavid rule in Persia.

A little later, Amanullah Khan took 3,000 Afghans into the city, sealed the palace doors, and replaced the Persian guards with Afghans. Bodies were cleared from the streets in preparation for Mahmud's triumphal entry. It was estimated that over the eight months of the siege as many as 80,000 people had died from starvation and disease (the fighting caused relatively few casualties).[87] In 1710 the Dutch had reckoned the population of Isfahan at around 550,000, based on a government census. By the end of the siege there may have been as few as 100,000 left – the majority having fled.[88] The great, glittering city would never be the same again.

4. *Not Enough to be Nice.*
Shah Soltan Hosein was well meaning but weak and self-indulgent: he was
punished by the loss and destruction of everything he most loved.
(From Cornelis de Bruyn's *Voyages*, Cambridge University Library)

CHAPTER TWO
Tahmasp Qoli Khan

Nature has left this tincture in the blood,
That all men would be tyrants if they could

Daniel Defoe

South of Abivard, between that town and Mashhad, the terrain rose above the plain known in the eighteenth century as the Atak to sheer cliffs, at the top of which there was a large plateau twenty miles long. This plateau was known before Nader's time as Kalat (meaning 'fortress') and afterwards as Kalat-e Naderi. It was a prime natural defensive position, and dominated the landscape for miles around. Nader took it over as his stronghold some time around the year 1720.[1] Kalat had been one of Timur's fortresses; he captured it after a long siege in 1382. The connection of Kalat with Timur may have been one of the first coincidences that turned Nader's mind toward Timur as a model.

One tale says that Nader discovered a cavern full of Timur's treasure and an inscription at Kalat. In the story the inscription was effectively a direct message from Timur to Nader: 'The man who comes to this place shall become the rarity of the age [*nader-e dowran*] and lord of the conjunction [*sahebqeran*]…' It went on to warn him not to become over-reliant on the size and prowess of his army, since Timur himself had only conquered Kalat, after a long siege, once he had turned to rely on the grace of God: 'Do not be proud when your army wins a victory, but thank God.' The story may tell us more about the man that wrote it and his views on Nader's life than about Nader himself, but it is possible that the legend is a version of a story Nader himself told, suggesting a kind of supernatural connection with Timur, and a legitimacy derived from it.[2]

When the news of the Afghan conquest of Isfahan arrived in Mashhad in November 1722, the people of the city revolted. Anarchy spread in the province of Khorasan and throughout Persia, and dozens of petty warlords and princelings set themselves up as independent rulers. Nader was still consolidating his hold on Abivard and was careful not to overreach himself. He was not yet dominant outside his own corner of northern Khorasan, and there were many tribal leaders and others competing for influence – 'chiefs and warlords who had been ants became snakes and those who were foxes turned into lions.'[3] Some allied themselves to Nader, others looked elsewhere or bided their time, waiting for a favourable moment.

When Malek Mahmud Sistani reached Mashhad with his army, fresh from his deal with the Afghans outside Isfahan, he quickly dealt with the rebels who had taken power there, blasting their leader from his hideout with cannon and executing him. With Malek Mahmud Sistani established in Mashhad, Nader had a formidable rival in Khorasan.

Nader's possession of the secure base at Kalat gave him an advantage over the other local contenders for power. Even Malek Mahmud, with an army of several thousand men and with Mashhad under his control, could not effectively impose his authority on the province as a whole. Some of the tribal chiefs who had resentfully acquiesced in Nader's supremacy in the Abivard area before the new ruler of Mashhad entered on the scene, saw a chance now to use Malek Mahmud's presence to slip out of Nader's grip. They appealed to Malek Mahmud to get rid of the upstart of Abivard.

Malek Mahmud and Nader were worthy rivals, equal in cunning, and wary of each other. Both sought to avoid a damaging direct confrontation, while trying to strengthen their own position. The chiefs' appeal to him over Nader's head strengthened Malek Mahmud's prestige and his authority as arbitrator in northern Khorasan, but instead of sending an army to deal with Nader, he merely sent a new governor to Abivard (although Nader had been in control there, the formal post of governor had been vacant since Hasan Ali Khan left earlier in 1722). The governor had instructions not to depose or insult Nader, but to give him authority as deputy governor, with enhanced powers: notably over the administration of justice, with all the symbolic importance of that function. Concealing his irritation, Nader cordially accepted the appointment: the appellant chiefs who had wanted to get rid of him ground their teeth in disappointment.

Now nominally working under the authority of Malek Mahmud,

Nader started to use his position to work off some old scores and extend his power – after all, avowed enemies of Nader were necessarily now enemies of Malek Mahmud too. One by one the recalcitrant chiefs were either brought to accept Nader's authority, or were killed off. Several retreated to fortified strongholds, where Nader besieged them. Those that surrendered were usually taken back into his favour, even if the previous fighting had cost Nader many men – so long as they served him faithfully thereafter with the troops at their disposal. But those that remained obdurate or feigned submission were harshly dealt with. One, Allahverdi Beg, made a truce with Nader after some fighting, and came to Nader's camp under safe conduct. The two men celebrated the truce together, with their followers. But Allahverdi then made the mistake of going to bed early. Nader cross-questioned his companions, and found that the man intended to kill Nader if a chance arose. Despite the safe conduct, Nader had Allahverdi Beg pulled out of his bed, and beheaded.[4]

Each time a man like Allahverdi was overcome, Nader took over his armed followers. These tactics of benevolence to those that submitted, combined with harshness to prevaricators and traitors, proved success-ful: Nader followed the same principle throughout his career. He was quite ruthless, but not pointlessly vindictive. He would rather take even a man of dubious loyalty into his service than destroy him unnecessar-ily. His prestige grew, and attracted new chiefs and armed followers into his service, eager for a share in the proceeds of future successes.

One of the groups of recruits attracted to Nader's band at this time was a large contingent of Jalayer* tribesmen, led by Tahmasp Khan Jalayer, 'a brusque man... like a buffalo',[5] who in time became Nader's friend and trusted lieutenant. Many years later someone who had seen them both together drew the contrast between Nader and Tahmasp Khan. Nader was tall and handsome, with a fine, animated face; Tahmasp Khan was short in stature, corpulent and ill-formed, with 'a most detestable countenance'; his skin hung in folds 'like the hide of a rhinoceros': his head and neck 'were fit only to be cut asunder'.[6] Whatever his appearance, Tahmasp Khan was a perfect subordinate. He was loyal, intelligent and capable, with a natural authority over men; but without Nader's strong drive for supremacy, or his imaginative vision. Nader showed his confidence in Tahmasp Khan by making

---

* The Jalayer tribe were Mongol in origin, and had produced a dynasty that had ruled Baghdad before Timur's time.

him responsible for Kalat. By now Nader had a force of around 1,200 cavalry at his disposal.

By 1724 Nader felt strong enough to oppose Malek Mahmud. The immediate cause of the breach between them was that Malek Mahmud had shown signs of taking royal authority. He claimed descent from the legendary Kayanid kings of Persia, and made the most of this ancestry in his propaganda. Nader could not tolerate this – if his rival had succeeded in getting himself recognised as king, he would have lifted himself entirely out of Nader's league. One account says that Nader made the break by striking at the man Malek Mahmud had appointed as governor of Abivard.

According to this story, Malek Mahmud, Nader and the governor had spent a day hunting and passing the time smoking in the country outside Mashhad. In the evening Malek Mahmud set off back to the city, but Nader kept the governor talking. As dusk fell, they finally prepared to go. Nader mounted first, but as the governor grabbed his horse's mane ready to mount, and put his foot in the stirrup, Nader suddenly raised his sword and brought it down on his neck, severing his head. This was the signal for Nader's men to attack the governor's followers, killing some and scattering the rest.[7]

It is likely that Nader committed many crimes and betrayals in his rise to prominence, and that some of them went unrecorded. To be successful, he had to be quite ruthless, and his actions created a profound well of feud and bitterness with some of the Kurds and Afshars among whom he had grown up.

Having secured Abivard, Nader made a substantial raid to Mashhad with his main force, encountering Malek Mahmud's troops, beating them off and devastating the area around the city. When Malek Mahmud put on the royal jiqe and had coins minted in his name Nader did not go to Mashhad to do him homage – but many others did, including the leaders of the warlike Chameshgazak* Kurds, Nader's near neighbours at Khabushan.† Nader now had a large, well-equipped force – a small army, including artillery and zanburak camel-guns.[8]

In the confused period that followed there was little fighting between Nader and Malek Mahmud directly. Nader's main opponents were the Chameshgazak Kurds. But ever the outsider even within his own tribe,

---

* The Chameshgazak, Qarachorlu and Shadellu Kurds were the main Kurdish tribes of northern Khorasan at this time.
† Now called Quchan.

he also continued to have trouble with a number of Afshar chiefs. Nader was called to help the city of Merv against attack by nomad tribesmen, and to intervene in a war between different Turkmen tribes. Each appeal enhanced his prestige as an authority in the region, whether he took action or not; and each time he did, he emerged successful, taking more warriors into his band in the aftermath. Around this time a new element entered the Khorasan equation – the forces of the new Safavid Shah, Tahmasp II, the son of the former Shah Soltan Hosein.

In 1725/1726 Tahmasp and his meagre forces were no more than a minor element in the greater game being played over the territory of Persia. Tahmasp had announced himself as the new Shah within a few days of the fall of Isfahan and his father's deposition. But he won little significant support, and in December 1722 the Afghans ejected him from Qazvin. From there he went to Azerbaijan,[9] only to flee from there when the Ottoman Turks invaded. Tahmasp escaped to Mazanderan, on the southern shore of the Caspian Sea, to the area controlled by the powerful Qajar tribe from their capital at Astarabad.* There, finally, with the help of a faction among the Qajars, he was able to start putting together an army.

By this time large parts of the north and west had been taken over by the Ottomans and Russians. In the years leading up to the Afghan invasion the Russian and Ottoman Turkish governments both sent special diplomatic missions to the court of Shah Soltan Hosein, and they reported back in detail about the Shah, his court, the Persian government and the state of the country generally. Both drew similar conclusions – that the Shah himself was weak, and that he was surrounded by third-rate advisers. They judged that the troubles of the monarchy were mounting, and there was no sign either of their being taken seriously or of anyone coming forward with the strength of will to tackle them.[10]

Both the Russians and the Turks saw this situation as an opportunity, and when the Afghans invaded each was spurred on by the concern that they might get left behind in the grab for Persian territory. Like the Russians, who had defeated the Swedes in the north, the Ottomans had recently concluded a war: but less successfully. Under the treaty of Passarowitz in 1718,[11] the Ottomans lost Belgrade and other Balkan lands to Austria. The Ottoman grand vizier Damad Ebrahim and the

* Now called Gorgan.

Sultan Ahmad III were both personally disinclined to war, being more interested in conserving the state finances, in encouraging literature and in building projects. The Sultan built extravagant gardens and enthusiastically encouraged the cultivation of tulips, stimulating a craze for those flowers like that in Holland in the previous century. His reign was later known as the *lale devri*, the Tulip Era. But as the Safavid collapse accelerated, the chance to make compensating gains in the east, with little risk, looked attractive to the Ottoman government. Since the Treaty of Zohab with Persia in 1639 the Ottoman/Persian border had been stable and peaceful (on almost exactly the same line it follows today between Iran and Iraq) but earlier the Ottoman Turks had held lands to the east of that line at different times. The Shi'a religious revival and the persecution it engendered had brought appeals to the Ottomans from Sunni Muslims in parts of western Persia, reviving the religious antagonism that had embittered the old wars between the Ottomans and the Persians.

While the Ottomans were encouraged to intervene in Persia by the Lazgis and the Sunni inhabitants of Shirvan, Peter the Great of Russia was encouraged by the Christian Georgians. The Russians were also able to claim the necessity of protecting their interests within Persia against the increasing disorder there, citing losses by Russian merchants in the sack of Shamakhi by the Lazgis in 1721. Peter had his eye on the Gilan silk industry, and wanted to take full control of the Caspian littoral.* In 1722 Peter was at the peak of his success. Having defeated Sweden in the Great Northern War, he had established Russia as the dominant power in northern and eastern Europe and had built a new capital on the Baltic – St Petersburg, symbolically looking west. Sweeping reforms had modernised and westernised Russia, at least superficially. But these achievements had only been possible through the use of brutal methods that were going out of fashion in western Europe. The settlement of St Petersburg was achieved largely by force, and large numbers of serf labourers died in its construction. Peter's own son died under torture in 1718, suspected by his father of conspiring against him. Nader and Peter never met, but Peter was the only ruler to swim within the ambit of Nader's story to match him for determination, intelligence and ruthlessness.

---

* This was despite the disastrous outcome of his expedition of 1716 against Khiva, on the eastern side of the Caspian. This had ended with the death or captivity of all the Russian troops, and with the stuffed body of the Russian commander swinging in the breeze outside the palace of the Khan of Khiva.

Tsar Peter personally led an invasion force by sea and land from Astrakhan to Darband in the summer of 1722, while the siege of Isfahan was still going on. He met little serious opposition, but his army and the forts they built were harried by Lazgi tribesmen and suffered badly from the heat and from disease. Finally, a large number of supply ships from Astrakhan were lost in a gale, making further progress that season impossible. Peter garrisoned the territory he had gained along the coast of Daghestan and left with most of his troops at the end of the year.[12]

Throughout Persia regional governors looked to their own interests after the collapse of Safavid authority. Georgia had been one of the bulwarks of the Safavid state, supplying large numbers of soldiers, courtiers and bureaucrats, but Vakhtang of Georgia had been sending messages to the Russians all through the autumn of 1722, urging Tsar Peter to march into Georgia. When the Russians did not come, conflict broke out between Vakhtang and rival Georgian princes, and in the summer of 1723 Ebrahim Pasha, the Ottoman governor of Erzerum, invaded. Eminent Georgians fell over each other to win Ebrahim Pasha's favour, but the Ottoman was determined to keep all real power in his own hands. Some of the leading Georgians retreated to the mountains and forests to harry the Ottoman occupying forces with guerrilla raids.

Vakhtang and his son both eventually ended up in exile in Russia, and despite brave resistance by Persian garrisons in the sieges of Yerevan and Tabriz, the Ottoman Turks occupied almost all of Georgia, Armenia, Shirvan and Azerbaijan by the end of the campaigning season of 1725. Further south, Ottoman forces under the Pasha of Baghdad had already taken Kermanshah, Hamadan and the surrounding provinces in 1724 (though Hamadan fell only after a lengthy siege in which the inhabitants also resisted fiercely). The Ottoman Sultan controlled the entire western part of Persia.

The Ottoman/Russian land grab caused tension between the two empires, and it seemed for a time that it might lead to war. Neither was quite sure of the intentions of the other, nor where eventual lines of demarcation might be drawn. However little they had done to help them, the Russians also felt obliged to strike postures on behalf of their fellow Christians in Georgia and Armenia. There were lengthy negotiations between the Ottoman grand vizier and the Russian ambassador in Istanbul, with French mediation, and in June 1724 they signed a treaty for the partition of Persia.[13]

For the most part the Ottoman/Russian partition treaty recognised the accomplished fact of the military occupation the two powers had achieved, and a previous treaty Tsar Peter had made with the cowed representatives of Tahmasp after the Russians had captured Baku in 1723. According to that treaty Russia had acquired Darband, Gilan, Mazanderan and Astarabad (though Tahmasp never ratified it, and in practice the Russians were to be little present east of Resht, leaving local Khans in power in the remaining parts). The Ottoman/Russian treaty stated that both powers would recognise Tahmasp in the remainder of Persia if Tahmasp accepted the partition. The treaty agreed in principle a frontier through the provinces of Daghestan and Shirvan, giving Russia the coastal strip. But after Peter the Great's death in February 1725 Russian interest in Persia waned and their troops were left to moulder in their unhealthy forts along the western part of the Caspian coast.

Meanwhile in Isfahan the new Afghan Shah, Mahmud, had been consolidating his rule. He locked up the former Shah Hosein and his large family in the palace, and treated them gently to start with; but apart from the ex-Shah's lawful wives he gave most of the women of the royal harem to his officers. Mahmud himself married one of the former Shah's daughters. He began his rule with grand gestures worthy of a benevolent monarch. He brought food into the starving city, and executed all those Persians who had betrayed Shah Soltan Hosein. In this he followed the wise principle that men who had betrayed one monarch, were likely to serve another the same way, given the chance.[14] He made an exception for Seyyed Abdollah, the most notable and damaging traitor, merely confiscating his property, and imprisoning him. Not trusting the Persian State officials, but knowing his own men would not be competent on their own, he appointed an Afghan to shadow each senior Persian.[15] This arrangement proved effective.

But before long Mahmud was showing his harsher side. More large demands for money were made of the Armenians of Jolfa, and there was some looting in the main part of the city. After Tahmasp declared himself Shah in November 1722, Mahmud sent Amanullah Khan with an army against Qazvin. Tahmasp escaped, and the town submitted, but the population of that city became enraged at the brutal and rapacious behaviour of the Afghans, and in January 1723 they revolted. The revolt was entirely successful, and many of the Afghans were killed.[16] The remainder fought their way out and trailed in defeat back to Isfahan.

Mahmud was worried that the arrival of the defeated Afghans would encourage the Isfahanis to follow the example of their brothers in Qazvin, and decided on a bloody show of strength. He invited the senior Persian ministers and nobles to a meeting on the evening of 24

January 1723, tempting them with promises of gifts and titles, and ordering them to wear their best clothes. When they arrived they were brought to him one by one, stripped of their jewellery and valuables, and beheaded – with the exception of the former chief vizier, on whose behalf some Afghan officers interceded. The bodies were thrown naked into the meidan in front of the royal palace for the populace to see.[17] Not content with this, Mahmud had the murdered men's sons killed too, and then as many as 3,000 of the Persian royal guards.

In 1723 and 1724 Mahmud successfully expanded the sphere of his rule, capturing the towns of Kashan and Golpeyegan, and finally Shiraz. But he still controlled only a relatively small part of the territory of the former Safavid realm. He was short of soldiers, and there were disputes and rivalries among his own people. Amanullah Khan and Mahmud's cousin Ashraf were particularly turbulent. Dissent among the Afghans grew after the failure of an expedition against the Kuhgelu tribesmen of the Zagros mountains south of Isfahan; and a further failure against the city of Yazd, which continued bravely to hold out across the Afghans' lines of communication back to Kandahar.

These setbacks made Mahmud more gloomy, suspicious and anxious than before. He knew that the Afghans' position in Persia was precarious; far from their base in Kandahar, exposed to threats on all sides and unpopular with the Persian people. Some of the Afghans, sensing a change in the wind, had already slipped away home; and to dissuade the remainder of his troops from disappearing likewise Mahmud had brought many of their wives and families to Isfahan. The soldiers were disillusioned and mutinous, and Mahmud could not trust even his highest officers. He was particularly antagonistic toward his cousin Ashraf, who seemed to gain favour with the troops as Mahmud's popularity waned. Mahmud decided that his bad luck was a sign of divine disapproval, and that he should undertake a religious exercise to restore himself to favour. This entailed a period of forty days of self-imposed solitary confinement, a practice called *tapasya,* taken up by the Afghans from an Indian custom. Mahmud had himself shut up in an underground cistern or cell with no light and only a very little bread and water. After the prescribed term he emerged, 'reduc'd almost to a Spectre'. Perhaps this treatment might have brought spiritual enlightenment to a man of strong mind; but its effect on Mahmud, always of a mercurial and unstable temperament, was to tip him over into paranoia and insanity.[18]

Shortly afterwards, in February 1725, Mahmud was told a rumour that Safi Mirza, one of the sons of the former Shah, had escaped.* This put him into an insane rage, in which he swore to kill all the surviving Safavid princes, leaving only the former Shah Soltan Hosein alive. The miserable princes, including Hosein's brothers and uncles as well as his many sons by various women, were brought into a courtyard of the palace, where their hands were tied behind their backs with their own waist-sashes. Then one by one they were cut down and killed by Mahmud himself and two helpers, who slashed at them with their sabres. Soltan Hosein, hearing the screams and groans of the victims from his part of the palace, ran into the courtyard, to find it running with blood and most of his male relatives dead or dying. Two of his youngest sons ran into his arms to escape the killers. Mahmud rushed on him and the children in a frenzy, cutting at them with his sword. Hosein was wounded in the hand protecting the children, and the sight of his blood seemed to bring Mahmud up short. He allowed the two little boys to live, but they were the only survivors.[19] It may be that over a hundred of the royal family died in the massacre. This was cruel punishment for Soltan Hosein's weakness and failure as Shah, but his suffering was not yet at an end.

The last victim of the massacre was Mahmud himself, whose mental disorders now overcame him. His career had been marked by murder and massacre ever since he killed his own uncle to take supremacy over the Ghilzai Afghans in 1717, and it seems that his madness, like that of Lady Macbeth, had its origin at least partly in guilt. He raged and raved. All sorts of remedies were tried until finally some Armenian priests were brought in to pass a special manuscript of the Gospel (written in red ink) over the head of the deranged Shah. This odd recourse to Christian religious symbolism *in extremis* is perhaps explained by a superstitious faith in the efficacy of the alien and the exotic. It was believed to be an effective cure for madness. Perhaps believing too in some part of his troubled mind, Mahmud recovered long enough to send the Armenian priests two thousand tomans in thanks; but then fell back into insanity, made the more horrible by new, physical afflictions:

> Mahmud's lucid Interval lasted not long; and the Palsy, or
> as others pretend, the Leprosy, joyning to the Delirium,
> one half of his body rotted, and his Bowels became so
> disorder'd, that he voided his excrements at his Mouth;

* Although there were later pretenders who claimed to be Safi Mirza, it is unlikely that any escapes were made.

and in the horrid Torments he endur'd, he turn'd his Fury
against himself, and tore his Hands with his Teeth. [20]

It became plain to the Ghilzais that Mahmud was on the way out. Mahmud had earlier imprisoned his cousin Ashraf in Ishahan under suspicion of treachery, but Amanullah Khan and some others freed him on 22 April 1725, went with several hundred followers to the royal palace, overwhelmed Mahmud's guards and took control. Three days later Mahmud was dead – he may have died of his diseases, but he was probably just quietly suffocated.[21] On 26 April Ashraf was declared Shah.

The would-be Safavid Shah, Tahmasp, wanted to move against Isfahan as soon as possible, but the warlike Qajars who were his main support counselled caution, believing that the Afghans were still too strong. Fath Ali Khan Qajar,* Tahmasp's general, also saw advantage for himself and his followers in pursuing conquests nearer their base in Astarabad. He coerced Shah Tahmasp to campaign in Khorasan and take Mashhad from Malek Mahmud before any attempt was made on Isfahan. The fluid situation in Khorasan promised also to yield more armed followers for the eventual attack on the Afghans. All these calculations proved correct – except the one that the Qajars would benefit.

In Khorasan, Nader had by the end of 1726 confronted and subdued the Chameshgazak Kurds (at least temporarily) by fighting them in the open field and besieging their base at Khabushan. This hard-fought success enabled him again to expand his area of influence and draw in new tribes further west. He also sent troops raiding in the direction of Herat, demonstrating the broad range of his power over Khorasan, and Malek Mahmud Sistani's relative impotence outside Mashhad.

Early in 1726 Shah Tahmasp had sent a senior courtier to sound out Nader's willingness to cooperate with Shah Tahmasp and the Qajars against Malek Mahmud in Mashhad.† Nader had reacted positively,

---

* Fath Ali Khan was chief of the Qoyunlu clan of the Ashaqabash branch of the Astarabad Qajars. There is a tradition among later Qajar writers that Fath Ali Khan had been in Isfahan during the siege of 1722, but left in disgust when Shah Soltan Hosein's courtiers offended him. Lockhart, 1958 (p. 280) discounted this story, but the VOC records state (Floor, *Afghan Occupation*, p. 148) that a group of 50 Qajars deserted from Isfahan on 17 July.

† Some sources suggest that Tahmasp's forces had already made an attempt to break into Khorasan and unseat Malek Mahmud Sistani but, without Nader's help, had failed.

urging Tahmasp to come to Khorasan soon, and in return the official had confirmed Nader's nominal office as deputy governor of Abivard. In September 1726 Shah Tahmasp and Fath Ali Khan Qajar marched into Khorasan from Astarabad and established a base for themselves at Khabushan. On 19 September, Nader joined them there with an impressive force of around 2,000 cavalry and infantry, mainly Afshars and Kurds, with some cannon and zanburak camel-guns.[22] According to one account, Tahmasp met Nader on the road, and Nader ordered his men to divide and line either side of the road as Tahmasp approached 'with the composure and pride that befits a tribute to a king', kneeling and bowing as he passed. Then Nader ran up, knelt and embraced Tahmasp's leg, saying 'Here I am, your highness, by God and my ancestors, I am all yours and so are they who stand by me, and many others who are not here – we are all your faithful servants, being ready to sacrifice ourselves as needed.' Tahmasp dismounted and embraced Nader, and immediately gave him the title of Khan, signifying leadership and nobility.

This date marks Nader's transition from a provincial to a figure of national importance. With Nader present in Tahmasp's counsels, the army quickly moved from Khabushan to a position threatening Mashhad, and new recruits flowed in.

Tahmasp's relationship with Fath Ali Khan Qajar had been a stormy one long before Nader came upon the scene. Tahmasp had arrived in Fath Ali Khan's territory at a desperate time, in flight after a defeat by the Afghans near Tehran, in the course of which he had very nearly been captured.[23] At an early stage Fath Ali Khan had disobeyed him, and the dispute had come to a fight, in which Tahmasp's men had been defeated and his baggage taken. But Fath Ali Khan had sought a reconciliation. Tahmasp was valuable as a symbol. The loyalty of many Persians to the Safavid cause – a familiar rock in a period of turmoil – meant that there would be a constant dribble of armed men to join the young Shah. Gains of territory and power that the Qajar might make in his service would have a legitimacy they would otherwise have lacked. By early 1726 Fath Ali Khan had virtually made Tahmasp his prisoner; but in entering Khorasan and allowing Nader to join forces, he made a fatal error.[24]

In Khorasan, Fath Ali Khan was off his usual territory. Even his position among his fellow Qajar tribesmen of Astarabad was far from secure. Nader on the other hand was on his home ground, at the peak of his prestige. Nader quickly made his way in Shah Tahmasp's affections, and Tahmasp was keen to escape the humiliations that Fath Ali Khan had imposed on him. His courtiers, in keeping with the contrary spirit that had ruled the Safavid court in his father's time, welcomed a chance to humble the personality that had up to then been dominant. In his arrogance Fath Ali Khan had worn in Tahmasp's presence some of the Shah's own clothes, looted from his baggage after the battle they had fought. This was foolish – Tahmasp could be irascible and unlike his mild father, tended to bear a grudge.

Before long Fath Ali Khan realised that Nader was fast encroaching on his position as generalissimo of Tahmasp's forces.[25] Fath Ali Khan had not expected this – the intervention in Khorasan had been his idea, after all. Within a few days, exhilarated by the command of more troops than he had ever previously controlled, Nader showed his prowess in several probing attacks against the defences of Mashhad. These actions would have appeared to advantage against Fath Ali Khan's previous delays. Away from Astarabad, even some of Fath Ali Khan's own Qajar followers showed signs of being willing to betray him. He began to make doubtful noises about the siege, disputing strategy with Nader and the young Shah. Casting around for ways out of his predicament, Fath Ali Khan considered withdrawing to Astarabad, and then opened a treasonable correspondence with Malek Mahmud.

On 10 October one of Nader's scouts intercepted a message from Fath Ali Khan to Malek Mahmud. Nader's degree of responsibility for what followed has been disputed, but in passing on the intercepted letter to Tahmasp, he effectively sealed Fath Ali Khan's fate, and he cannot have much regretted the outcome. When Tahmasp read the letter he was furious and summoned Fath Ali Khan to give an account of his actions. This proved unconvincing, and Tahmasp ordered Nader and his men to seize him. Nader removed the shawl from his own waist and tied Fath Ali Khan's hands with it. Nader's soldiers took Fath Ali Khan into custody. Perhaps dissembling to avoid responsibility, perhaps fearing the loss of the Qajar troops if Fath Ali Khan were executed, Nader suggested that he be held at Kalat until Mashhad had been captured and Malek Mahmud dealt with. It was typical of Nader to act cautiously against a rival, rather than seek to eliminate him at the first opportunity, as others might have done. But Nader's forbearance was not to save the unfortunate Qajar. Tahmasp feigned agreement with Nader's advice, but the following day he sent two men to kill Fath Ali Khan while Nader was occupied with other business. The guards were told that Nader himself had sent the murderers, who in this way gained access to the tent where Fath Ali Khan was being held, and beheaded him. They took the bloody head and laid it at Shah Tahmasp's feet.[26]

Shah Tahmasp, pleased at the removal of his bugbear, appointed Nader as his *Qurchi-Bashi* (the equivalent in Tahmasp's reduced circumstances of commander-in-chief).[27] At this time or earlier he also gave Nader the new name and title of Tahmasp Qoli Khan ('Slave of Tahmasp'). This might sound demeaning, but it was regarded as a great honour to be allowed to use the Shah's name: 'The greatest Honour a Persian King can confer on any Subject, is giving him Liberty to make use of his own Name, altho' it is only to signify, he is his Slave.'[28]

If Tahmasp and his ministers thought the new generalissimo was going to be a softer touch than Fath Ali Khan Qajar, they were about to learn a new variation on the master/slave relationship – the boot was to be on the other foot. Some of the Qajar leaders were arrested temporarily to prevent trouble, but a rival Qajar from another clan* was happy to take over as their chief and serve under Nader, and the storm blew over.

Nader's task now was to cement his new authority by defeating Malek Mahmud and taking Mashhad. Restless and impatient, every day he made a new attempt against the defences. When Malek Mahmud heard that Fath Ali Khan was dead, he assumed this would weaken the royal army, and made a sortie against their camp with a large force, including artillery. But Nader met this attack with his own men, and defeated it, forcing the enemy back into the city. They never attempted another breakout. Several of Malek Mahmud's officers were killed, including his master of artillery, which may have had a significant effect in the events that followed. Malek Mahmud's possession of powerful artillery had been one of his main assets; but the guns were of no use if not properly handled.[29]

Early in November 1726, in the last stages of the siege, a minor incident took place in the royal camp that showed how far Shah Tahmasp's courtiers had succeeded in their traditional policy of turning their head of state into an alcoholic; and why it was relatively easy for others to achieve dominance over him. One day Tahmasp, who had probably already been drinking, demanded that one of his Georgian courtiers

---

* This was Mohammad Hosein Khan Qajar, of the Develu clan of the Yokharibash branch of the Astarabad Qajars, who had been a rival to Fath Ali Khan and his clan in Astarabad, and was later believed by the Qajars to have been instrumental in Fath Ali Khan's arrest (Hanway, vol. 1, p. 197). He was to play a sinister role in the future of both Tahmasp and Nader.

bring him some *chikhir* (a strong spirit traditionally distilled by the people of the Caucasus). The Georgian said he had none – the Russian emissary at Tahmasp's court, Avramov, kept some, but the Georgian doubted he would part with it. Tahmasp set off for the Russian camp in a fury, threatening to have all the Russians beheaded if he did not get his drink. Arriving there, some of his servants pulled Avramov before him, dressed only in a shirt. Avramov, familiar already with Tahmasp's extremes of temper, prostrated himself and begged for mercy. Tahmasp jeered at him and demanded the chikhir. After some more undignified toing and froing, Avramov went to fetch the spirit. At one point, on his way back to his own quarters, the Shah fell in a ditch and emerged covered in mud – this made his mood even worse. He told Avramov that he had got very dirty, and it had all been Avramov's fault.

Eventually Avramov returned with the chikhir, and the Shah's mood brightened. He ordered food, and told his musicians to play. He clapped his hands to the rhythm and told some risqué stories, but then his temper dipped again, and he blamed Avramov for the loss of his kingdom. Terrified, the Russian began to stutter some kind of defence, but Tahmasp interrupted, saying that there should be no more business and they should all make merry instead. Apples and light food were passed around with the bottles, and when they were empty Avramov supplied some more. Tahmasp slipped gradually into a pleasant oblivion. Avramov agreed to keep a supply of chikhir and vodka for the Shah in future.[30] The Russian diplomat Avramov, who recorded these events, was plainly not an unbiased source for the Shah's character, but Tahmasp's petulance, inconstancy and drunkenness are well corroborated by others, and the story rings true. One of his more honest courtiers told Avramov that the Shah would never make a success of his reign because he was always drunk and no-one was in a position to correct him.

As time went on, as Tahmasp's forces grew more powerful, and as the Russians wearied of their occupation of the Caspian coast, contacts intensified between Tahmasp's court and the Russian commander there, Levashov.[31] The Russians were not happy at the large gains made by the Ottomans in the Caucasus and western Persia, but were unwilling to commit further military forces to the region, when the men already there, guarding their Caspian forts, were dying of disease at a horrifying rate. It seems likely that the Russians agreed not to intervene against Tahmasp's interests while he and Nader fought to restore the Safavid monarchy to dominance in Persia. In the longer term, the Russians saw

Tahmasp and Nader as proxies against their traditional enemies, the Ottomans. They promised to withdraw from Persian territory (without specifying timings), and may have sent some military support.

Nader himself was always more sceptical than Tahmasp about the Russians. He was perhaps wary that they might one day support Tahmasp against him. Avramov says that, when told that there was a possibility of a treaty with the Russians, Nader said to Tahmasp 'Who are these Russians – give me the order and I will go and cut them all down.' According to Avramov, this was one of the rare occasions on which Tahmasp faced Nader down, telling him that the matter was not his affair.[32] In practice, seeing its strategic value, Nader accepted the de facto alliance with the Russians.

In the autumn of 1726 some of these grand prospects were still far off, but after nearly two months of siege things were going well for Tahmasp's forces and the outlook for Malek Mahmud was poor. Supplies were running short in Mashhad and there was no hope of relief from outside. His associates began to desert him, and eventually his commander-in-chief, Pir Mohammad – 'seeing that the fortune of his master was like an image painted on water or on the waves of the sea'[33] – decided enough was enough. Pir Mohammad let Nader know secretly that on the night of 10/11 November he would open one of the city gates and let in the royal forces. On the appointed night the guards in that sector were killed and thrown over the walls, and the gate opened.

Nader and his men streamed into the holy city. Malek Mahmud attempted a desperate counter-attack within the city the following morning, but this was defeated, and he retreated to the citadel. There he quickly saw the hopelessness of his position, went to Nader and gave up the royal jiqe for the humble robe of a religious devotee. Nader generously allowed him to retire to the precincts of the shrine of Emam Reza in the centre of Mashhad, but discovered a few months later that Malek Mahmud had been in contact with some Turkmen in Merv, inciting them to attack the new rulers of the sacred city. Following his usual rule of harshness to those that abused his clemency, Nader had Malek Mahmud, his brother and his nephew all executed on 10 March 1727.[34]

As soon as his troops were established in the city, before Malek Mahmud surrendered, Nader had gone to the shrine of Emam Reza and kissed the ground in thanks. In obedience to a public vow he had made before the city was taken, he later had the dome of the shrine regilded, and a new minaret built next to it,[35] which still stands today. From this one might assume that he still regarded himself as a pious Shi'a, but these could equally have been acts purely for public consumption; to please his army's Qezelbash troops, and the religious authorities of the newly captured city.[36] Nader's deeper scepticism toward the ostentatious display of religious faith emerges from a later story about his treatment of one of the beggars at the shrine of Emam Reza:

> Many of these believed that the holy Imam Reza, who
> is interred at Mashed, continued to work miracles;
> and this belief gave rise to a number of impositions.
> Persons, pretending to be blind, went to his tomb; and,
> after a long period of prayer, opened their eyes, and
> declared that their sight had been restored by the holy
> Imam. One of these was seated at the gate of the sacred
> mausoleum when Nadir passed. 'How long have you
> been blind?' said the monarch 'Two years' answered the
> man. 'A proof' replied Nadir 'that you have no faith. If
> you had been a true believer you would have been cured
> long ago. Recollect, my friend, if I come back and find
> you as you now are, I will strike your head off.' When
> Nadir returned, the frightened fellow pretended to pray
> violently, and all at once found his sight. 'A miracle!
> A miracle!' The populace exclaimed, and tore off his
> coat in small pieces, as relics. The monarch smiled, and
> observed, 'that faith was everything.'[37]

By the end of 1726, in the space of a few remarkable weeks, having been an obscure provincial warlord, Nader had risen to become the bright hope of the reviving Safavid cause in Persia. Like Fath Ali Khan Qajar before him, Nader was well aware of the importance for his personal fortunes of his allegiance to Shah Tahmasp. Possibly the young Shah and his ministers thought Nader would be easier to control than the arrogant Fath Ali Khan had been; the title of *Qurchi-Bashi* given to Nader was a lesser one than the title of *Wakil** that Fath Ali Khan had extracted. If so, they were perhaps deceived by the fact that Nader's manner was less blatantly domineering. But Tahmasp and his courtiers were going be given a lesson in the realities of power, and to be put firmly in their places.

* Deputy or regent.

5. *Zanburak.*

This weapon, in the V & A collection, comes from Moghul India, but those used by Nader's camel-gun corps would have been similar. Zanburaks usually fired a ball between 1/2lb and 2lb in weight, and their portability suited the rugged Persian terrain.

(Photo courtesy of Tower Armouries)

CHAPTER THREE
War with
the Afghans

War is the father of all and king of all; and some he has made
gods and some humans, some bond and some free.

Heraclitus

From the capture of Mashhad at the end of 1726, friction worsened between Nader and Shah Tahmasp. The courtiers, resenting the newcomer, did their best to poison Tahmasp's mind against Nader, and some local Kurds, remembering their bitter clashes with Nader in earlier years, may have encouraged them. Like his father, Tahmasp followed where his advisers led, and in February 1727 he slipped away from Mashhad and set himself up in the Kurdish town of Khabushan. From there he denounced Nader as a traitor[1] and sent letters all over the kingdom demanding military help against him. His ministers urged the Kurds and others to rise against Nader, which some of them did.

Nader acted swiftly. He confiscated all Tahmasp's property in Mashhad, and that of his ministers, and put his brother Ebrahim Khan in control there. Nader himself went with his troops to Khabushan, skirmishing with the Kurds along the way. He put Khabushan under siege, defeated an attempt by some Kurds of the Qarachorlu tribe to relieve the town, and took them prisoner. It seems Nader had a ditch dug, and the Kurds thrown into it, threatening to bury them alive – but released them after giving them a scare.[2]

Soon Tahmasp, defeated and short of provisions, decided to come to terms. He sent the chief mullah Mohammad Hosein to negotiate with Nader. Nader talked with him, but expressed concern that Shah Tahmasp might at some time try to have him killed. Mohammad Hosein protested that Tahmasp had sworn not to harm him. Nader replied ironically, 'I know the Shah, how constant and truthful he is: he swore to [protect] Fath Ali Khan in the morning and in the evening he ordered his head to be cut off.'[3] But a settlement was made, Nader returned to Mashhad, and Tahmasp followed resentfully a little later, making his entry to the city at the festival of the Persian New Year (Nowruz) on 21 March, amid great celebrations. These were extended to two full weeks by Nader's marriage to the daughter of one of the Kurdish chiefs.

According to Nader's official historian, on the night of Tahmasp's return to Mashhad, Nader had a dream, in which he saw a large water bird. He shot it with a musket, wounded it and captured it. Then he saw a pool with a fountain, and in the pool a large white fish, with four prominent horns on its head. He ordered his attendants to take the fish, but none of them were able to do so; whereupon he himself reached into the water and was able to seize it. When he told his friends about the dream the next day, they told him that to dream of capturing a bird and a fish was an infallible sign that he would rule an empire. The four horns on the fish were interpreted to signify Persia, India, Turkestan and Khwarezm.[4]

There are a number of intriguing aspects to this story. Whether or not Nader had a dream, whether his historian recorded it correctly, or whether he dreamed it on this or another occasion, the imagery of the story the historian chose to report, particularly that of the white fish with four horns, is significant. The most obvious connection is to the red four-pointed hat that Nader later ordered to be worn throughout his dominions, and which he can be seen wearing himself in his portraits. It was known variously as the *taj-e Tahmasi* and the *kulah-e Naderi*. The fact that the Qezelbash had traditionally worn a hat with twelve sections or scallops (the number corresponding to the twelve Shi'a Emams)[5] has led some to believe that the four points of Nader's version had a religious meaning, but it seems more likely that like the horns of the fish, they signified the four corners of the territories he aspired to conquer. When he became Shah, Nader commonly styled himself as the ruler of four domains in proclamations and on coins. The dream and the hat became part of the paraphernalia of his rule; the dream was presented as indicating divine sanction for his ambitions, and the hat made the symbolism manifest in the dress of his subjects.[6]

Neither Tahmasp's submission nor the marriage brought an end to Nader's troubles with the Shah and his court. Nader insisted that the Abdali Afghans of Herat must be pacified before any attempt on Isfahan be made. Although the Abdalis had been crippled by internal conflicts for most of the previous decade, they were powerful and warlike. They had besieged Mashhad in 1716, and again in 1722/1723.[7] Traditional antipathy made it unlikely that the Abdalis would ally with the Ghilzai Afghan regime in Isfahan, but even on their own they were a sufficient threat to the power base Nader and Tahmasp had established in Mashhad for it to be absolutely necessary to neutralise them before the royal forces attempted to campaign outside Khorasan. But Tahmasp's courtiers would have murmured that Nader was seeking only his own aggrandizement; and Tahmasp was impatient as ever to regain the Safavid capital. His ministers did not slacken in their machinations against Nader, and a series of further insurrections broke out among the Kurds of Khorasan. The Tartars of Merv also rose, and some Turkmen tribes joined in.[8] No sooner was order restored in one part than trouble broke out anew in another. Nader might not have survived these manifold revolts had it not been for the staunch faithfulness of his brother, Ebrahim Khan, and Tahmasp Khan Jalayer, who could always be relied upon to keep important strongpoints like Mashhad and Kalat while Nader rode out to deal with the rebels.

Nader's concern to secure Khorasan rather than launch a premature campaign to reconquer the old Safavid capital was prudent, but it also showed a divergence of outlook. Nader's Turkic origins in Khorasan inclined him to look east, toward Bokhara, where a descendant of Genghis Khan still ruled, and Samarkand, Timur's old capital. Mashhad and Abivard might have looked like dubious border country from Isfahan, or to those who hankered after Isfahan,* but to Nader they were central to a region with a different identity. Old Khorasan included Herat; Timur's descendants had crossed the Afghan mountains and conquered India. Mashhad and Khorasan remained central to his world.

In the summer of 1727 Nader made an initial, probing attack on the Abdali Afghans, despite difficulties with the heat and thirst and with his cannon, which sank in the soft sand en route. Nader himself directed the retrieval of the guns by a group of strong men mounted on camels.[9] This incident illustrates one of the reasons why siege warfare was undeveloped in Persia at this time. Heavy artillery had to move by road, on wheels; or preferably by water. There were few navigable waterways in Persia, and not many roads in the country were good enough for heavy, wheeled transport over long distances. For the most part goods were transported by pack animals. Without siege artillery, sieges were long and difficult.[10]

---

* Or to someone looking at a map of modern Iran.

The army settled down to a siege of Sangan in September. One day Nader was with the engineers, watching the slow process by which the artillery was battering a breach in the walls of the besieged town, in preparation for an assault. One of the big siege cannon had just fired, and a gunner went forward to insert the charge for the next shot. At the same time, Nader fortuitously stepped back a few paces. Made nervous by the presence of his chief, the man perhaps forgot properly to extinguish the sparks left in the gun barrel by the previous discharge; perhaps he put two charges of powder in the gun by mistake. The new charge went off prematurely, splitting the gun and scattering lethal shards of metal in all directions. The gunner and several other bystanders were killed, but Nader was unhurt.[11] The town was taken by assault on 1 October, and all the inhabitants were slaughtered for having feigned submission earlier and then broken their word.

Shortly afterwards, news arrived that a relief force of 7,000–8,000 Abdali Afghans were approaching. Nader met them in battle near Sangan with his army, which was about the same size. Nader's official historian observed of the Afghans on this occasion that a cat may be a tiger when it fights a mouse, but is as a mouse itself when faced with a tiger. In truth, the Persians were neither tigers nor mice. They were proud and keen for revenge, encouraged by the confidence of their leader and their recent successes; but many of them were still relatively inexperienced in serious warfare, and deep down were unsure of themselves against the Afghans, who had defeated the Persian armies so many times. Nader, 'reading the hearts of his soldiers',[12] intended to build up their confidence by degrees, and would not risk too much in an early encounter. He ordered the infantry to stay in trenches, from which they could fire at the enemy while remaining protected. Meanwhile Nader himself took 500 of his best cavalry and manoeuvred against the attacks of the Afghan horsemen from outside the entrenchments. After four days of fighting and skirmishing, the Abdalis retreated towards Herat.

Nader ordered his men not to pursue. He may have heard about further trouble behind him in Mashhad; more likely he never intended a full-scale attack on the Abdalis at this stage. He returned to Mashhad, and there his disagreements with Tahmasp continued, with Nader insisting on the need to subdue the Abdalis. A little later, while Nader was out of the city, he was told that Tahmasp was attacking his allies and again issuing orders that Nader's commands should not be obeyed. Nader immediately marched on Tahmasp, who shut himself up in the town of Sabzavar. When Nader arrived, Tahmasp had the gates closed against him, so Nader brought up his artillery and lobbed cannon balls into the town until, on 23 October 1727, Tahmasp surrendered.

Tahmasp was now abject and desperate. That night he left his tent, with the excuse that he wanted to wash his hands, and escaped. He got some distance away from the camp before Nader found he had gone, and was about a mile away when Nader caught up with him. Tahmasp drew a knife and made to kill himself, but Nader disarmed him and took him back to the camp. From there he had Tahmasp escorted to Mashhad, with only two attendants. After this, Nader kept Tahmasp's seal himself and issued decrees in the Shah's name.[13]

From now on, Tahmasp made no serious attempt to break free from Nader's domination. The next few months were taken up with further punitive expeditions against the ever-truculent Kurds, and the Yomut Turkmen, and there may have been another probing expedition against the Abdalis in the summer of 1728.[14] Some of Tahmasp's followers, deserting him after the debacle at Sabzavar, nonetheless continued action against Nader's interests. This time one of Tahmasp's former generals, Mohammad Ali Khan, and a relative, Zolfeqar, declared themselves masters of Mazanderan and Astarabad in Tahmasp's name (though their sway over the region seemed only to permit riot and robbery). Tahmasp claimed to be innocent of any involvement, but Nader told him contemptuously that he knew he had been in communication with Zolfeqar.[15] Nader marched into Mazanderan in November 1728, with Tahmasp in train. Mohammad Ali submitted to him almost immediately, but Zolfeqar remained defiant. Eventually he was captured. Nader would have spared him even then, but Zolfeqar continued to rail against him even in captivity, and eventually 'the just conqueror delivered his rebel neck from the weight of a foolish head.[16] Having established control over Mazanderan by the end of December, Nader sent an envoy to the Russians demanding the restitution of Gilan.

In March 1729 Nader celebrated Nowruz in Mashhad, and was finally able to make his preparations for the decisive campaign against Herat. He feasted his officers, and made generous gifts of money, horses and weapons to them, as was to be his custom before most of his campaigns. This was to be a crucial venture, pitting his small army against the most formidable enemy they had yet encountered. An eyewitness account from this time, from the Greek merchant and traveller Basile Vatatzes, gives a vivid impression of the daily exercises Nader had imposed on the army, to prepare them for battle. We know that he made these routine for his troops throughout his career, and the practice may have dated as far back as his time with Baba Ali in Abivard, but no other source describes the exercises in such detail.

Vatatzes wrote that Nader would enter the exercise area on his horse, and would nod in greeting to the officers, the commanders of 1,000 and the commanders of 100.* His physical presence was powerful, handsome and manly. He would halt his horse and sit silently for some time, looking at and examining the assembled troops, and as he did so Vatatzes noticed that in his concentration his larynx would be moving constantly, as if he were trying to swallow some phlegm in his throat. Finally he would turn to the officers with a playful look, and say 'What are your orders, my lords?' – to ask what battle formations or weapons the troops would practise with that day. Then the exercises would begin:

> And they would attack from various positions, and they
> would do wheels and counter-wheels, and close up
> formation, and charges, and disperse formation, and then
> close up again on the same spot; and flights; and in these
> flights they would make counter-attacks, quickly rallying
> together the dispersed troops... And they exercised all
> sorts of military manoeuvres on horseback, and they
> would use real weapons, but with great care so as not to
> wound their companions.[17]

As well as practising movement in formation, the horsemen also showed their skill with individual weapons: lance, sword, shield and bow. As a target for their arrows a glass ball was put at the top of a pole, and the men would ride toward it at the gallop, and try to hit it. Few could, but when Nader performed the exercise he would hit the target two or three times in three or four attempts. Vatatzes says that as he galloped with his bow, he would open his arms out from his body like wings, take an arrow from his quiver, aim it and shoot it all in one smooth movement, looking 'like an eagle'.

The cavalry exercises lasted three hours. The infantry also exercised together:

> ... the infantry – I mean those that carried muskets

---

* In his Greek text Vatatzes uses the terms *chiliarchos* and *hekatontarchos,* which correspond to the Turco-Mongol terms *min-bashi* and *yuz-bashi* used in Persia at the time.

– would get together in their own units* and they would
shoot their guns at a target and exercise continuously. If
Takmaz Kuli Khan saw an ordinary soldier consistently
on top form he would promote him to be a leader of 100
men or a leader of 50 men. He encouraged all the soldiers
toward bravery, ability and experience, and in simple
words he himself gave an example of strong character
and military virtue.[18]

Vatatzes' description dwells on cavalry manoeuvres and the display
of individual weapon skills because these were dramatic, but his
description of infantry training and the expenditure of costly powder
and ball in exercises is significant, showing Nader's concern to maximise
the firepower of his troops, which was to prove crucial. This passage
also makes plain the care he took with the selection of good officers,
and their promotion by merit. For the army to act quickly, intelligently
and flexibly under his orders, it was essential to have good officers to
transmit them. Three hours a day of manoeuvres, over time, brought
Nader's men to a high standard of control and discipline, so that on
the battlefield they moved and fought almost as extensions of his own
mind. Vatatzes shows the way Nader impressed on the men what they
had to do by personal example: a principle he followed in battle too,
often leading from the front, without any apparent care for danger.
Training, firepower, discipline, control and personal example were part
of the key to his success in war. Nader's transformation of the army was
already well advanced.[19]

Nader set out from Mashhad in early May, accompanied by Tahmasp,
marching for Herat. Having realised for some time the seriousness of
the preparations going forward in Mashhad, the Abdalis set aside their
differences and united under the leadership of Allah Yar Khan, making
him governor of Herat. He led an army from Herat against Nader. The
two forces met at Kafer Qal'a, about 50 miles west of Herat.

Nader again deployed his men cautiously, not using entrenchments
this time, but surrounding his infantry with artillery and holding them
back. As at Sangan, he put himself at the head of a picked troop of
cavalry as a reserve separate from the main body. He also sent some
cavalry forward to skirmish with the enemy, hoping to wear down their
strength. But the ferocity of the initial Afghan attack nearly upset all his

* *Tagma.*

plans; the Abdalis fell on the left wing of the Persian infantry and broke into their formation. The Persian musketeers started to give way. Seeing this, Nader led his reserve in a furious countercharge, killing the first of the Afghans with his own sword, and forcing the enemy cavalry to pull back. In doing so, he was wounded in the foot. With night coming on, he ordered a retreat, and both armies withdrew.[20]

This was a hard-fought engagement, and the Persians must have been rather shaken. But the following day it was the Abdalis who withdrew further, pulling back over the nearby river, the Hari Rud. Nader moved forward, drawing closer to Herat. He fought two more battles with the Abdalis in the following days, and in both Allah Yar Khan's men came off worse. After the second Nader's men camped on the battlefield, and a dust storm prevented further fighting for two days. Messengers brought an offer of peace from Allah Yar Khan, but Nader was sceptical, and demanded that the Abdali leaders should come to him in person if they expected to be taken seriously. At that point Allah Yar Khan got word of reinforcements, and was encouraged to renew the struggle. After another tough battle over two days at Shakiban, the Persians again had the victory, despite the Abdali reinforcements attempting an ambush.

Allah Yar Khan again sent messengers offering submission. But Nader replied that, as long as the Afghan chiefs refused to enter Persian service and as long as his troops still drew breath, his army would not desist from war or abandon their intentions[21] – revealing that this campaign was, as usual, as much about recruitment as reconquest. After this message, several Abdali chiefs came to Nader and, bowing in submission, protested their loyalty to Persia, their long-standing opposition to the Ghilzais, and their preparedness to serve against them in the future. The Abdalis had got the message. Nader received them favourably, despite the disgruntlement of Tahmasp and his ministers, who no doubt wanted a triumphal entry into Herat, and were probably uneasy at a further augmentation of Nader's military strength. Rightly so – the Abdalis were to become some of Nader's most dependable and hard-fighting troops. The discussions continued; the Abdali chiefs brought presents, and were rewarded with *khal'ats*. Many Abdalis entered Tahmasp's service, and some Persian-speaking clans were transplanted to the area around Mashhad. Allah Yar Khan was confirmed as governor of Herat in Tahmasp's name, and Abdali prisoners were freed. Nader and Tahmasp returned with the army to Mashhad, where they arrived on 1 July 1729.

The campaign against the Abdalis had not ended in their utter defeat and subjection, but in their submission and a kind of alliance. They would revolt again, but this was enough for the time being. The campaign had strengthened the confidence of the Persian army, showing them and the rest of Persia that the Afghans could be beaten; and this was as important as a preparation for the trial of strength with the Ghilzai enemy in Isfahan as the strategic neutralisation of the threat from Herat. It is worth considering how Nader had achieved this effect.

The conditions of warfare in the Middle East and Asia at this time are imperfectly documented by comparison with the knowledge we have of European warfare in this period. For Europe we have contemporary drill-books, manuals of tactics and military theory, and detailed memoirs written by soldiers themselves. For the wars of Nader Shah none of these things exist, or if any do, they have yet to come to light. The chroniclers who wrote the records of Nader's campaigns were not soldiers, and tended to write of the doings of the military in formulaic terms. It is quite possible that Nader wanted it that way, and did not want people spreading abroad the secrets of his success.[22] The bureaucrats and scholars who wrote the chronicles would have regarded the soldiers' trade as dirty and thuggish, and the soldiers, most of whom would have been illiterate, would have tended to regard the business of clerks and literary men as unmanly and effete. This division did not help the easy flow of accurate information. We know the outlines of the ethnic composition of Nader's army, the overall numbers at different times, the commanders and the rank structure, but we know frustratingly little about their drill or the way they fought.

Conditions and traditions of warfare in the east were different. For example, we know that unlike their counterparts in Europe, Nader's infantry did not use the bayonet.[23] In Europe the bayonet had been introduced in large numbers 40–50 years earlier to enable infantry to hold off attacks by cavalry. But where the cultural memory of mounted warfare in the west revolved around the crushing knightly charge, in the east it was the horse archer. Horses made a big target for muskets, and horsemen in the east were reluctant to risk their horses, which generally they paid for themselves (it may be significant that Nader supplied horses to his cavalry at his own expense, probably to avoid this problem).[24] The cavalry manoeuvred and fought in looser formations than in Europe, which would have made it more difficult to get the horses to charge home against dense masses of infantry with muskets that spat fire and made a lot of noise.

There were other differences. In the east commanders often formed
up their artillery in front of their infantry, to serve as an extra deterrent
and barrier to cavalry, and Nader's order to his men to dig entrenchments
when first facing the Afghans would have been a means to the same end.
We know that the Austrian cavalry in the eighteenth century adapted
their tactics when fighting the Ottomans to emphasise the use of firearms
on horseback rather than the full-tilt cavalry charge; this echoes some
recent research about the use of firearms on horseback by Afghan troops
in Moghul India later in the century.[25] There is a general impression that
Ottoman and Persian soldiers took greater pride in their marksmanship[26]
and their individual fighting prowess than European troops, who the
Ottomans regarded as unmanly automata, drilled en masse to fire and
reload and move in time as if they were parts of a single organism. One
illustration of this is that whereas the European soldiers at this time
carried paper cartridges, each containing a charge of powder and a
bullet to speed up reloading, the Persians loaded from a powder horn,
enabling them to measure the appropriate charge for the range of the
target. This made each shot more accurate, but took longer.* The eastern
muskets tended also to be heavier than the European equivalent, firing
a larger ball, and carrying to a longer range (better marksmanship and
longer range would also have helped to keep cavalry away). The *jazayer*
muskets Nader favoured for his elite troops were heavier still, needing
to be supported on a rest when firing.† The interpretation that eastern
warfare was just different, not somehow more primitive, is reinforced
by the fact that European warfare became in a sense easternised through
the eighteenth century (largely by the influence of the Austrians' use of
eastern-style light cavalry and light infantry) and particularly at the turn
of the century (under French influence), as light troops and skirmishing
tactics proliferated, and drill simplified.

Nader's innovations from before the time of his Afghan campaigns
centred primarily on the introduction of firearms as standard equipment,
and training the infantry to use their weapons for devastating mass
effect. Before Nader's time the Safavid Shahs had maintained bodies
of musketeers, often mounted, but the artillery corps had come and
gone over the years, and there had been a general reluctance among
the military classes to take up firearms. For many, many centuries the

---

* American colonial frontiersmen in the eighteenth century used a powder
  horn too, and had similar attitudes both to European troops and their own
  marksmanship.
† See plate 7, p.210.

classic mode of warfare in Persia and Central Asia had centred on the horse archer, and firearms were adopted slowly and reluctantly. This was partly for practical reasons: firearms were awkward to load and fire on horseback. But there were deeper cultural reasons: firearms were regarded as a dirty innovation and many, thinking in the mode of the heroic poetry of the *Shahname,* would have regarded the lance and bow as more noble and manly. The subject needs further research,[27] but Nader's reign was significant as the period in which Persian armies for the first time exploited the full potential of gunpowder weapons to defeat their enemies, bringing about (albeit briefly) the beginnings of what in Europe has been called a military revolution.[28]

Nader's emphasis on drill and firepower gave his men a decisive advantage in battle, but there was a price. The soldiers had to be retained and motivated in a different way. They could not just be called together for a campaign, paid off with plunder and then packed off back to their tribal homelands, as had been the practice for most of the provincial troops under the Safavids. They needed to be permanently with the army to get the benefit of the new training and equipment – Nader could not allow them to disappear with their new muskets and never come back. They had to be paid well and promptly so that they would not desert. The men had to be supplied with food, and clothing, with ammunition and replacements for equipment that got broken, lost or worn out, and with pack animals to carry them and their belongings over the great distances of the Iranian plateau. The cavalry had to be supplied with good quality horses, strong enough to carry the men and their equipment in battle. And to get the benefits of mass firepower, there had to be a mass of men to fire the muskets. Nader's armies grew and grew, constantly.

The upshot of all this was that the army was ruinously expensive. Nader was always looking for new sources of cash to maintain it, and this meant a heavy burden of tax and forced contributions in the territories his army controlled. The growth in the army, the transition to a large standing army, the new emphasis on drill and firepower, and on the logistics necessary to keep them supplied, and the great increase in cost, all directly paralleled developments that had begun in Europe in the preceding 150 years.* In Europe the financial strain

---

* Lest the argument be thought unduly Eurocentric, Parker points out the parallel with the growth in armies and bureaucratic state structures in China in the Warring States period, 770–221 BC (Parker 1988, pp. 2–3). Some historians place the beginnings of the European military revolution earlier.

of these developments led on, in time, to reforms in government, and economic expansion. Nader Shah brought about a military revolution in Persia, adapted to discrete eastern conditions, but it did not survive long enough to produce these more deep-seated effects.

The sources do not give us great detail about the clashes at Sangan and in the valley of the Hari Rud, but it is clear that the attacks of the Abdali cavalry were unusually determined and aggressive (probably because the Abdalis had not before encountered firearm infantry in large numbers). They were gradually worn down in successive defeats by the superior firepower of an advancing Persian army strong in disciplined musketeers and artillery. The Abdalis were defeated by a new, unexpected form of warfare, against which they had no viable answer, and by the determination of an innovative and talented commander. Nader had found a military formula that gave his men a decisive advantage over their opponents: at least over these opponents.*

In his campaign against the Abdalis Nader had shown considerable caution in the direction of his troops; he could not have known at the outset how successful the effect of his innovations would be. But at the end of the campaign he must have felt a surge of confidence, and a sense of new possibilities opening up. The victorious royal forces were at last ready for the move against Ashraf Ghilzai in Isfahan.

Having deposed his cousin Mahmud in April 1725 and made himself Shah in Isfahan, Ashraf had endeavoured to make himself secure with a characteristic mixture of ruthlessness and subtlety. He commiserated with the former Shah Hosein, affecting regret for Mahmud's slaughter of his family, and had the bodies that still littered the palace precincts removed and decently buried. In return for this small outlay of sympathy, the former Shah gave Ashraf one of his daughters in marriage. Ashraf by these means also probably won the good will of the Persians in Isfahan to some extent. But to remove any possible rivals (and to gather to himself the wealth they had looted) he executed most of the men who

---

* Nader's contact with the Russians through Avramov and the Greek traveller Vatatzes prior to his campaign against Herat raises the possibility that he had some Russian military assistance. The Russians certainly gave help later, and further investigation in Russian archives may shed more light on the matter, but at present there is no direct evidence to support the idea that Nader's military successes were due to Russian assistance to any significant extent. Nader was quite capable of developing his military innovations on his own, just as military pioneers in Europe had.

had helped with the coup to depose Mahmud, including the old soldier Amanullah Khan. Ashraf blinded his own brother and had him shut up in the harem in order to prevent any conspiracy from that quarter.[29] He also put to death some Persians who, before the coup, had been in touch with Tahmasp on Ashraf's own behalf. Ashraf was as brutal and ruthless as Mahmud, but more calculating, less impulsive, and less prone to self-doubt. He had need of these political skills, because the position of the Afghans in Persia was growing more precarious, and his coup in Isfahan had alienated the Ghilzai leadership in Kandahar, who had supported Mahmud.

The most pressing threat to Ashraf's rule in Isfahan and his pretensions to rule all Persia seemed to be the Ottoman Turks, who by the summer of 1725 had completed their conquest of most of western and north-western Persia. Ashraf sent an embassy to Istanbul in the summer of 1725 with a letter demanding the restitution of these provinces. The letter ended with a sinister snatch of verse in Persian, which translates 'God takes the vessel where He wills / No matter how the captain may tear his clothes.' This was taken to mean that God favoured the Ghilzai cause, no matter how it might upset the Sultan. The message did not please the Ottoman authorities, who had expected something more submissive and conciliatory. They were also uneasy at the popularity of the Afghans in Istanbul, as fellow Sunnis and victors over the heretic Shi'a Persians. For many ordinary Muslims the simple, austere piety of the Afghans represented one kind of ideal of militant Islam.

Asked for a religious judgement on the status of Ashraf's rule, and what response should be made to his letter, the Ottoman *ulema** decided that the Afghans had taken power in Isfahan unjustly, and that there could be no peace between two rival Muslim powers that pretended to the same authority unless some natural obstacle, like a sea, divided them. It was beyond question that the Ottoman Sultan enjoyed that legitimate authority as the shadow of God on Earth: therefore the only possible answer was that Ashraf was a rebel, and the Sultan should wage war on him until he submitted. This answer, convenient enough for the purposes of Ottoman imperialism, was duly given to the Afghan emissary, who started back for Isfahan in March 1726.[30]

War began between the Ottomans and the Afghans in May 1726. For the most part this merely meant that local guerrillas who had been

* The ulema were the class of religious scholars and elders, who came together to make religious judgements.

resisting the Ottomans fought on, with some help from the Afghans (there were also clashes between the Russians and the Afghans in Gilan). But in the autumn of 1726 the governor of Baghdad, Ahmad Pasha, advanced toward Isfahan from Hamadan with an army of 70–80,000 men. He sent ahead an insulting message to Ashraf that he was coming to reinstate the rightful ruler of Persia.

Ashraf moved to meet the Ottomans with a much smaller force, perhaps as few as 12,000. He decided on an unforgettable reply. He sent three men galloping back to the palace in Isfahan. They made the deposed Shah Soltan Hosein kneel in the Hall of Mirrors of the palace, cut off his head, and returned swiftly to the Afghan army with it. Ashraf sent the head of the unhappy Safavid to the Ottomans with the words that he expected to give Ahmad Pasha a fuller reply with the points of his sword and his lance. In this way Shah Soltan Hosein gave in death a sharper answer than he ever gave in life.[31]

Ahmad Pasha continued his advance, and the two armies halted about 12 miles apart. But then there was a delay, which worked to the Afghans' advantage. Ashraf sent men with bribes to the Kurds in the Ottoman army, encouraging them to change sides. When Ahmad Pasha sent out a reconnaissance in force, the 6,000-strong body was taken astray by their guides, ambushed, surrounded and massacred by the Afghans.[32]

But there was worse to come for Ahmad Pasha. Four Afghan holy men appeared in the Ottoman camp, and made their way to his tent unharmed, by reason of their aged and distinguished appearance. Once there the leader of the four harangued Ahmad Pasha in Ashraf's name, berating the Ottomans for allying with the Christian Russians, and exhorting him to end his attacks on the Afghans, their fellow Sunnis. Ahmad Pasha should instead join with the Afghans in holy war on the heretical Persians. Such words from such men made a great impression on all the bystanders: Ahmad Pasha tried to argue with them, but was interrupted by the call to prayer, which the four Afghans obeyed along with the Ottomans. After that, the four left, calling on Ahmad Pasha to refrain from further bloodshed.

Ahmad Pasha decided he had now waited too long, and ordered an immediate attack with a signal of ten cannon-shots. But the Ottoman troops' lack of enthusiasm was now made manifest. Most of the army refused to move forward, and a large number of Kurds deserted to the Afghans. Ahmad Pasha reorganised his forces and managed to lead forward his right wing to attack the enemy, but they were repulsed, and the remainder of his army stayed put. Mounted on an elephant in the manner of an Indian prince, Ashraf showed his sangfroid and his confidence in the outcome by playing a flute. Two more Ottoman attacks were equally unsuccessful, and eventually Ahmad Pasha withdrew, leaving 12,000 dead. That night the remaining Kurds in the Ottoman camp set up a disturbance, causing panic and confusion. The Kurds began pillaging the camp, and Ahmad Pasha pulled out, leaving behind all the baggage and artillery. The Ottomans retreated first to Hamadan, then all the way back to Baghdad.[33]

Ahmad Pasha attempted to renew hostilities in the summer of 1727, but by then the war was thoroughly unpopular in Istanbul and with ordinary Muslims throughout the Ottoman territories, who admired the Afghans and believed their successes were a mark of divine favour. When Ashraf suggested peace, negotiations were taken up by the Ottoman side, and yielded a treaty that recognised the Ottomans in possession of the Persian territory they had occupied, and Ashraf as the legitimate Shah of Persia in the remainder.[34] This recognition of his right to rule, by the prime authority in the Muslim world, added immeasurably to Ashraf's prestige and authority. It was a triumph for him. The inconsistency with the previous Ottoman/Russian treaty of partition, which recognised Tahmasp as Shah, was glossed over.[35] But in any case, the Afghan/Ottoman treaty was not to signify very much for very long.

When an Ottoman envoy visited Isfahan to confirm the treaty in the spring of 1729, Ashraf's courtiers accommodated him outside the city and did their best to conceal from him the state of the citizens. But it was plain to him that they were miserable, that many were starving, and all lived in fear of wanton robbery, murder and arson by their Afghan overlords. The condition of the population of Persia generally was grim at this time. In the Ottoman sector, women and children had routinely been sold into slavery until an edict ended the practice at the end of 1725. Elsewhere trade was at a standstill, discouraged by the political instability, general brigandage and uncertainty; and the economy was collapsing. Deaths due to war, famine and disease, along with emigration, are estimated to have caused a drop in population by up to a third. Ashraf had issued an edict giving a list of races, in order of the treatment they should expect. First came the Afghans themselves, then Armenians, then the Dargazins (Sunnis from an area of western Persia near Hamadan who had joined forces with the Afghans), then the Indian merchants (known as banyans), then the Zoroastrians, then the Jews, and finally – 'The Seventh and Last Rank is to the Natural Persians, who are treated like Slaves by the six other Nations.'[36] The occupiers (whether Afghan, Ottoman or Russian) were generally hated. The resentment gave rise to a number of revolts in different parts of the country, led by a variety of personalities, many of whom claimed to be sons of the former Shah Soltan Hosein, or to be descended from earlier Safavid monarchs.

None of the revolts achieved any significant success, because they were not coordinated. Their enemies could bring overwhelming force to crush them one by one. But like the dogged resistance of several villages around Isfahan in the months of the siege of Isfahan, the rebellion of Qazvin against the Afghans and the bitter defence of Tabriz and Hamadan past all hope of relief, the revolts show a stubborn popular resistance to the oppressors; something of a leitmotif in Persian history. The centrality of concepts of martyrdom and injustice in Iranian Shi'ism has led some to speculate that these give unusual force in Iranian political culture to the 'lower hand' – that the *mostaz'afin** strongly see themselves as more virtuous, and spiritually more powerful, than their oppressors.[37] Ashraf's arrogant decrees and the Ghilzai atrocities stoked the fires of eventual destruction for the Afghans.

For a long time Ashraf did not believe that there was any serious threat to his rule from Tahmasp. But it seems that Nader's campaign against Herat changed his mind. In August 1729 he set out from Isfahan with an army of 30,000 men to attack Tahmasp's forces in Mashhad. He may have thought he could take the city by surprise while the royal forces were grappling with the Abdalis – if so, he was disappointed by the rapidity with which Nader achieved his victory. The relatively large size of Ashraf's army (compared to those fielded earlier by the Ghilzais) reflected an inflow of recruits after his success against the Ottomans. Ashraf took his men north to Tehran, gathering more troops from scattered detachments and garrisons along the way, and then led them east towards Khorasan, along the southern slopes of the Alborz mountains. By early September he was besieging Semnan, with an army 40,000 strong or more.[38]

Nader rapidly put his men and supplies in order, and on 12 September 1729 set out with Tahmasp to meet the Afghans, via Nishapur and Sabzavar. His army was smaller than the Afghan; one estimate put the

* The dispossessed, the oppressed.

Persian strength at 25,000.[39] After more than a week of marching, the Persians camped in the fields around Bastam, about 50 miles north-east of Damghan. Nader sent forward a message to the garrison of Semnan, urging them to hold out until he arrived. Ashraf, getting word from his scouts of Nader's approach, detached a force to cover Semnan, and advanced to meet him. When Nader learned of these movements, he moved his men forward to Shahrud, and there was a sharp skirmish south-west of the town with Ashraf's advance guard, who had been sent under Mohammad Seidal Khan to attack Nader's artillery. The Persians got the better of the fight, and took 14 prisoners, who were given over to Nader for questioning. Nader then took the army forward again, along the valley of the Shahrud river, with steep hills on either side. They came up against the main Afghan force a little way to the east of the village of Mehmandost, and the two armies camped for the night a few miles apart. According to one account, in the course of a drinking party that night, Tahmasp promised Nader his sister in marriage if the coming battle were won.[40]

The following morning, 29 September 1729, the Persians formed up in four bodies, the Afghans in three.* Ashraf was confident; he had the advantage of numbers. From his command in the centre, he ordered the two strong wings of his army to envelop and surround the Persian flanks. He gave orders to a group of two or three thousand men to ready themselves to pursue the Persians after they were beaten, and to capture Nader and Tahmasp. That done, the way would have been clear for him to advance and conquer Khorasan. The armies moved forward, closing the distance between them.

Before the latter part of the nineteenth century, warfare was different. In a terrible way it was more human, more intimate than modern warfare. Men closed up together for support, to avoid being cut off and killed in the open by bands of the enemy – much as herd

---

* As elsewhere in this book, the labels Persian and Afghan are plainly inadequate to describe armies that included a great variety of different ethnic groups, some united only temporarily to their leaders' causes. Adle in his article on Mehmandost rejects these labels (p. 236n), preferring 'les Qezelbas' 'l'arriere-garde naderie' and 'Les escadrons d'Asraf', for example. 'Qezelbash' for Nader's army is at least as misleading as 'Persian'. 'Safavid' and 'Naderite' beg questions that are better dealt with by the narrative, and the latter looks foolish in English anyway (implying that Ashraf's men were formed up in squadrons is also misleading).'Persian' and 'Afghan' are at least simple and clear, once the background is understood.

animals gather in groups for security from predators. In this way the conditions of warfare were adapted to some of mankind's most basic instincts. Modern soldiers have to be trained to scatter rather than bunch together when suddenly threatened by shellfire, for instance. When soldiers arrived on the battlefield, in the tense moments before combat began, they had the asabiyah of their comrades around them, and they could see their enemy. There is something very deep about this situation. In all probability, human beings – male human beings – had been doing something like it for not just thousands, but tens and perhaps hundreds of thousands of years.[41]

In the Song of Songs, a beautiful bride is described as *terribilis ut acies ordinata* – terrible as an army ordered for battle. The two armies sought each other out. They might try to find a position that gave their side an advantage, but if it were too strong the enemy would withdraw, rebuffed. Once they were past a certain point of proximity, withdrawal became more dangerous than battle – both were committed. But before the killing began there was a moment of vision, a moment for fear, but also awe and perhaps even admiration. The commanders consented to the killing, to sacrifice and loss on their own side, for the chance of victory. The soldiers consented too, even though they might be killed or maimed – why? Most of these men were young, full of the abandon of youth. For fear of discipline, for the hope of plunder, perhaps. But the most important thing was that they belonged; they were surrounded by companions, many of them tribal kin and relatives, the closest friends they had ever had. They were fearful, but feared above all that they might let down their friends. They wanted to excel in their eyes. They were ready to kill, and die, for them. They, the young ones at least, went to battle as to a bride.

Among the Persians on this occasion there was little of the colourful panoply the royal army had displayed at Golnabad seven years before, nor the disunity – instead a united, steely determination and a will to retribution. Nor was there a long delay this time, but something unexpected instead. The Persians did not hold their ground, or move forward to the attack, but before they got too close, began instead to withdraw over to the left, toward the side of the valley where the Tal hills rose up. The withdrawal was covered by a rearguard of horsemen several thousand strong. The Afghan left, under Mohammad Seidal Khan, immediately swung to attack them. The Afghans thought the Persians were trying to escape, and that the battle was already won. The Persian rearguard kept them at a distance with firearms and arrows, circling and skirmishing in the dust, while still slowly withdrawing.

Nader used the time bought for him by the delaying tactics of the rearguard to position his cannon and camel-mounted light artillery (zanburaks) on the slopes of the Tal, above the valley floor. He brought the rest of his men into one compact body below the guns, and ordered them strictly to remain silent, to hold their fire until the Afghans were at close range, to keep to their ground and not to budge without his command. The Afghan troops thundered forward 'with that impetuosity, which [they] had generally found successful'.[42] As they had been ordered, the Afghans attempted an envelopment, to overwhelm their enemy on all sides; attacking in the centre and on the flanks simultaneously. As they closed in, the Persian artillery crashed out from the hill, their balls targeted on the Afghan centre, where their impact on the packed Afghan formation 'sliced three or four hundred soldiers in two pieces like cucumbers'.[43] This was where Ashraf was with his bodyguard: several of his spare horses, in rich harnesses studded with gems, were killed close by him. Then, as the charging Afghan cavalry on the flanks closed in, the Persian muskets fired all together. The first volley, carefully aimed by each man before clouds of powder smoke obscured the lines of sight and the confusion of reloading could disorientate, was always the most effective. Hundreds of horses and riders went down, and those behind blundered into them in the dust and smoke as they struggled on the ground. The force of the Afghan charge was lost: they failed to break into the Persian ranks.

The incessant crashes and bangs of the cannon and muskets echoed and blended in the valley into one numbing noise as the Persians fired again and again into the enemy mass. The Afghan commanders tried to restore order, but one by one Ashraf's zanburaks were picked off by Nader's cannon, and his standard-bearer was blown to bits by a cannon-shot. Then the Persians themselves, with new confidence, began to advance. A group of Persian *jazayerchis* and musketeers charged forward at what was left of Ashraf's artillery, and pressed on into the heart of the Afghan centre, pushing aside and cutting down all opposition. The shattered Afghans fled, with the loss of perhaps 12,000 of their comrades. By midday it was all over. A group of Afshars followed the Afghans a couple of miles but Nader restrained the main army from pursuit, not wanting to risk an ambush.[44] The Persians had retrieved their self-respect. The Afghans' arrogance was in pieces, and their adventure in Persia, so recently in the ascendant after Ashraf's successes against the Ottomans, was on the skids.

If there had been anything awe-inspiring about the spectacle of the armies before the battle, there was nothing beautiful about the battlefield afterwards, littered with heaps of dead and dying men and animals, and splashes of blood soaking into the dust. On the Persian side, wounded soldiers with loyal servants among the camp followers may have received help, but there is no indication at this time or later of any organised medical provision for the wounded. As in other times and places, they would have dragged themselves to the shelter of rocks or bushes, as dying animals do.[45] Those Afghans too badly wounded to make their escape would simply have been plundered and killed, or left to die. It was a harsh age.

The Persians rested, and moved forward to Damghan. On the way Nader, always thinking a few moves ahead, sent an ambassador to the Ottoman Turks, demanding the restitution of Azerbaijan. There was also another quarrel between Nader and Tahmasp – 'as the truth is bitter, his words displeased Shah Tahmasp' – and the Shah withdrew from the army in a huff, taking his guards with him. Nader sent trusted men after him, with soft words, and after a few days' delay Tahmasp returned – 'cleaning the dust of anger from the mirror of his soul'.[46]

It seems the quarrel arose over Tahmasp's eagerness to push on to Isfahan. Nader argued that it would be prudent to return to Mashhad, to prepare for a march on Isfahan the following year, but Tahmasp insisted they should press on immediately. It may be that Nader prevaricated partly in order to extract further promises from Tahmasp, but it was typical of him to want to avoid unnecessary risks. The dispute was resolved, and for once Tahmasp got his way. As the army marched on westward, 'the citizens of each place flocked in thousands to give a respectful reception to the Shah's cavalcade, as it approached them; and raised shouts of joy and thanksgiving to Saturn upward. From all parts reinforcements joined the victorious army.'[47]

Ashraf pulled back to Varamin, where he assembled more men from Tehran and the environs. Judging that Nader's continued advance must take him through a narrow valley to the east of Varamin, he laid an ambush there; putting sharpshooters in the hills, placing artillery to sweep the road, and blocking it with fortifications. A force of cavalry lay in concealment to complete the defeat of the Persians. Unfortunately for Ashraf, Nader's scouts spotted and informed him of these preparations. Nader infiltrated his men round the Afghan rear, and attacked the valley from two directions with strong forces of musketeers, supported by artillery. He led the assault personally, and the ambushers became the ambushed. The Afghans ran, leaving behind their artillery and baggage, and headed for Isfahan.

In all these battles the firearm infantry and the artillery were the battle-winning element in the Persian army. Nader had discerned that firepower was the decisive factor, and was deploying it to great effect; but it is also significant that the infantry were the most 'Persian' part of the army. Nader's troops, though of disparate origins, were not just a collection of mercenaries. The cavalry were predominantly tribal and already included a variety of non-Iranian (and some non-Shi'a) elements – Turcoman Afshars and Qajars, Kurds, steppe Turkmen, Abdali Afghans and others. But the infantry would mainly have been recruited from among the Iranian peasantry of the settled agricultural areas, and young town-dwellers. It is reasonable to see their aggression and resilience in battle as another expression of a general spirit of resentment against the Afghans.

In Isfahan, Ashraf had 3,000 of the leading citizens and clerics massacred to forestall a rising, and his troops set to plundering and burning the bazaar district. A desperate appeal to Ahmad Pasha brought Ashraf some Turkish artillery to replace that he had lost,[48] and some other troops. By now the Ottomans too had begun to fear the resurgent Persian cause. His army strengthened by these allies, Ashraf marched out of Isfahan to face the royal army a third time on 31 October, taking up positions near the village of Murchakhor and strengthening them with entrenchments.

Nader meanwhile had parked Tahmasp in Tehran. This time, for the decisive battle to liberate Isfahan, there would be no dispute about who deserved the glory.[49] Having ensured that any deficiencies in equipment among his men were made good, Nader took the army south – by a longer route than usual, so that the artillery would not get stuck along the difficult but more direct route through the mountains. As the Persians approached, an advance guard of Qarachorlu Kurds fell upon an Afghan scouting force at night and overwhelmed them, taking 100 prisoners.[50]

The Persian army was already near Murchakhor when Ashraf arrived there. On the morning of 13 November 1729, rather than attack the Afghans in the defensive positions Ashraf had set up, Nader instead attempted to draw them out into the open plain by marching across their flank, direct for Isfahan:

Nader commanded the kettledrums of his august army to

tear the air with their warlike sound, and the banners to
pierce the sky with their billowing peaks.[51]

Military standards and military music had played an important part
in Muslim armies for hundreds of years, making up a large ensemble
that accompanied the ruler to war as a symbol of authority – known in
the writings of Ibn Khaldun as the *alah** – 'the display of banners and
flags and the beating of drums and the blowing of trumpets and horns.'
They were believed to hearten friends and to dismay the enemy. Ibn
Khaldun wrote further – '… listening to music and sounds no doubt
causes emotion and pleasure in the soul. The spiritual temper of man is
thereby affected by a kind of drunkenness, which causes him to make
light of difficulties and to be willing to die…'[†52]

Ashraf would not be drawn out, but held to his positions.[53] He had
arranged his men in a compact body, in imitation of Nader's earlier
tactics, with large numbers of cannon on all sides, infantry in the centre
and bodies of horsemen outside the main formation for freedom of
manoeuvre.[‡] Ashraf was attempting, from his experience so far, to find
an effective counter to the new warfare Nader had introduced; trying
to augment the firepower of his troops by adding artillery, and fighting
more defensively. In vain: the superiority of Nader's tactical system had
taken years in the making, and an effective counter could not be found
in a few weeks.

Nader told his men to obey their commanders dutifully, and warned
the cavalry not to dismount to loot, lest they be taken unawares by
surprise attacks. Then the Persians advanced, musketeers and artillery
in the lead. Having taken the enemy fire, they closed in, and delivered
a concerted volley at point-blank range into the Afghan trenches before
rushing forward to fight hand-to-hand. The Afghan cavalry made

---

* 'The outfit' or 'the kit'.

† Many of the characteristic Muslim instruments were taken into European
military bands via the Turkish and Austrian military – including kettledrums
and a pyramid of bells on a pole that was later known in the British army as
the 'jingling johnny'. The latter even found its way into the final movement
of Beethoven's Ninth Symphony – 'Freudig, wie ein Held zum Siegen'. Many
other eastern fashions and items of equipment were taken westward in this
period – notably the curved Persian sabre.

‡ Both armies probably numbered somewhere between 16,000 and 20,000 men;
the VOC report that the Afghans had 40,000 and Nader 5,000–6,000 (Floor,
Afghan Occupation, p. 262) cannot be correct.

desperate attacks against the Persian flanks and rear, but could make no impression. The day became dark by the great clouds of dust thrown up by the pounding hooves of the horses, and the powder smoke. The Persians overran Ashraf's artillery, and after some savage fighting the Afghans as a whole broke and fled. Arriving in haste back in Isfahan that same evening, Ashraf rapidly threw together all the valuables he could, and put them on all the baggage animals he could find, along with the women of the Safavid royal family. He rode out of the city for Shiraz the following morning, an hour before dawn.[54]

Nader captured a number of Ottoman Turks among the other prisoners after the battle, but treated them humanely, released them and allowed them to return to Baghdad. He had to discipline some of his own men, who had plundered the Afghan baggage against his orders, and entered Isfahan with his army on 16 November. Looting and disorder had broken out in the city, but this quickly came to an end as Nader's troops took control. He had the remaining Afghans hiding in the city rounded up and executed, with the exception of a few who had behaved humanely during the occupation, who were set free. Valuables left behind by the Afghans were distributed among the soldiers. The vengeful populace were allowed to demolish and desecrate Mahmud Ghilzai's tomb, and they later built a public latrine on the site.

Nader met Shah Tahmasp outside the city on 9 December 1729,[55] with a formal ceremony of greeting (the *esteqbal*). When Tahmasp saw Nader:

> he alighted from his horse, as if he meant to pay him homage: the general dismounted also, and ran to him in a respectful manner, to prevent this great mark of condescension; but the Shah insisted upon walking a few paces with him, declaring that he could not show too great a distinction to the person who had delivered his country, and driven his enemies from Isfahan. After a short conversation he mounted again, preceded by his running footmen; the Khan following just behind him at the head of his troops.[56]

The people of the city welcomed Tahmasp joyously, but his happiness turned to tears when he saw the damage done by the Afghans. It is said that when he arrived in the royal palace an old woman threw her arms round his neck – and he realised it was his mother, who had disguised herself for years as a servant, performing menial tasks in the harem.[57] The Afghan occupation of Isfahan was over, but celebrations for the restoration of Safavid rule were to prove premature.

6. Isfahan.
This is a nineteenth-century engraving, but this view of the southern end of the great meidan of Isfahan would have been identical in Nader's time, and is very little changed today. On the right is the Ali Qapu palace, where crowds threw stones and asked in vain for Shah Soltan Hosein to be deposed.
(Author's collection)

CHAPTER FOUR
War with
the Ottomans

*Wer mit Ungeheuern Kaempft, mag zusehn, dass er nicht dabei
zum Ungeheuer wird.*

*(He who fights with monsters should look to it that he does not
become a monster.)*

Nietzsche

Shah Tahmasp and the people of Isfahan were united in their joy at the removal of the Afghans and the restoration of the Safavid monarchy. But their expectations did not coincide with Nader's; and whatever the outward appearances, he was the one in the position of strength. Nader seldom put anything above the need to keep his army paid and content, and it soon became clear that his memories of Isfahan had made him vindictive rather than sentimental. The remnants of Persia's riches left behind by the Afghans were not enough to satisfy the troops for long, and the rejoicings of ordinary Isfahanis were soon cut short.[1] Nader's soldiers, who were short of food and clothing after their hard campaign, beat the citizens to extract money from them. They plundered homes, and sold whole families of poorer people into slavery if they could not find the money demanded.

According to one story a soldier raped the wife of a prominent noble, and her husband went to Nader to complain. Full of self-importance, he said he could not live after so great an insult to his honour. 'No,' said Nader, 'I think you cannot,' and gave the order for him to be strangled. Nader excused his cruelty by telling his officers that if he were to follow up every complaint of that kind, he would spend all his time punishing his own army rather than the country's enemies. Later he changed his mind, and enforced tighter discipline on his troops.[2]

This story is significant in illustrating the attitude of men to women in Persia at this time. Among tribal nomads and the labouring classes, economic necessity ensured a less restricted role for women: most women had to work, and work hard, in the fields or elsewhere. But any man with a claim to social status kept his wives and other female family members out of sight, in a part of his house only visited by other females and by himself. Even what might seem a minor infringement of this rule would expose him to derision and dishonour. Women of the artisan, merchant and upper classes lived radically restricted lives. Some might read into Nader's reaction to the affronted husband a disgust at a man who can only think of his own amour propre when his wife is raped. Nader was untypical among his contemporaries in his attitude to women, but we should be wary of projecting modern sensibilities onto him. Nonetheless, if the story is true, there was plainly something about this man that Nader did not like.

The representatives of the Dutch and English trading companies in Isfahan must initially have been among those most pleased to see Nader's soldiers arrive in Isfahan. The European traders had been rivals in Isfahan for years and had squabbled between themselves over small points of favour from both Safavid and Afghan rulers. They vented their enmity for each other in their reports back home. For a while after Murchakhor the English feared that the Dutch had won Nader's favour, but soon both companies were being pressured for more and more cash by Nader's officials. Both soon took a negative view of his rule, which mingled together a sense of their own damaged interests and their indignation at Nader's oppressive methods.[3]

Now he was restored to the familiar surroundings of his family's palaces and gardens in Isfahan, Tahmasp was keen that Nader should pursue Ashraf eastwards, to finish him off and rescue the Safavid princesses he had taken with him, Tahmasp's sisters and relatives. But Nader prevaricated. He said his men were tired, that the season was late for another campaign, and that anyway it was time he returned to Khorasan. This was theatre: Nader's true aim was to extract in full his reward for reconquering Isfahan. The arguments went to and fro. Tahmasp called a grand council of army officers and courtiers in an attempt to apply pressure, but the soldiers supported Nader, and Nader still demurred. At the end of a day spent arguing in this assembly, Tahmasp lost his temper and threw his jiqe, the symbol of royalty, to the floor.

Finally, Nader agreed to pursue Ashraf, but in return he secured the personal rule of Khorasan, Kerman and Mazanderan for himself

(Tahmasp had promised him these territories before they left Mashhad). In addition, Nader got the right to levy taxes throughout the country to pay the army, and the right to wear the jiqe. To establish the permanence of the arrangement, it was agreed that he and his son, Reza Qoli, would each marry one of Shah Tahmasp's sisters,[4] and Nader married one of them, Razia Begum, shortly afterwards. By these concessions Nader enjoyed almost full sovereignty over a great swathe of northern and eastern Persia and, for the time being, satisfied two of his prime concerns: cash, and legitimacy. He declared he would defeat the Shah's enemies for good, and then return to Khorasan.[5]

The granting of the right to levy taxation was the vital element in the deal. It gave Nader authority not only over the provinces assigned to his personal rule, but over the most important parts of state administration in the rest of the country too. As in any state, the raising of taxes was the key to power. In Nader's state it was vital to maximise revenue in order to pay his ever-expanding armies. He paid close attention to money matters, and over the succeeding years built up a complex network of officials, inspectors and spies to control and monitor taxation, changing and strengthening the structures that had served the Safavids. Each province had to submit regular accounts. After the laxity of the later Safavids and the chaos of the period of Afghan dominance, a strong central authority with real administrative grip returned. But Nader's tax demands were high. They were sometimes doubled without warning, and the penalties for evasion were harsh.

Nader gained a reputation for having eyes everywhere. According to one story, a citizen of Isfahan had to pay Nader a fine, and Nader nominated a local tax collector to collect the money. But without any attempt at concealment, the tax collector spent all the money on wine, women, music and roasted meats. When the man who had paid the fine reproached him for this, asking him how he would now pay Nader, the tax collector drunkenly bragged that he had nothing to worry about, because he would never see Nader again. A few weeks later one of Nader's *nasaqchis** appeared in the bazaar, smacked the tax collector over the head with his battleaxe, and carried him off to Nader's court. There Nader said, 'Look, we have met again after all,' and had him strangled.[6]

This story illustrates the reputation Nader acquired for close attention to financial matters. But, like the earlier story of the wronged husband, it is also typical of a certain kind of story about Nader. Whether these

* Military police.

incidents really happened, and to what extent he became a figure about whom people liked to tell such stories, sending a shiver down the spine of their listeners, is difficult to judge. But the stories were told by contemporaries and near-contemporaries, and though they may have been embroidered, people who lived at the time would not have repeated them if they had not thought there was some kind of truth at the core.

We do not know the date of Nader's marriage to Razia Begum, Tahmasp's sister; nor anything else much about it, beyond that it took place at this time. Somehow she had avoided being taken away by Ashraf with the other royal princesses, but she must have led a traumatic life over the previous eight years under Afghan rule, living through if not witnessing directly the violent deaths of her father and most of her other male relatives. Almost her whole life had been lived in the harem apartments of the royal palaces of Isfahan. Now it was about to change completely, so that she would spend most of the next 20 years on the move, on horseback, in camel-litters, or in camps; following Nader on his campaigns. Whether she welcomed the change, or resented it, remembering happier days in Isfahan before the arrival of the Afghans, we do not know. Nader was already married, to Gowhar Shad, the younger daughter of his early patron, Baba Ali Beg of Abivard. It is likely there was some tension in the harem between the two women, but we know nothing of that either.

Even if the lives of Razia Begum and Nader's other wives remain largely unknown, the lives of Isfahani women generally in the last years of Safavid rule, thanks to recent research, are no longer so obscure as they once were. A satirical text from the 1680s portrays a complex life of customs and practices within what we might otherwise have thought of as the deadening world of the harem. The clerical author seeks to scandalise his audience by telling them that women routinely broke social and religious custom; by disobeying their husbands, failing to behave modestly before men outside the family circle and misbehaving with other women in bathhouses. The satire goes on to give a lot of detail about friendships between women, which the author clearly regarded as a threat to the menfolk. Women sent one another tokens in the form of small wax dolls to declare their commitment to each other, and sometimes exchanged other items, that signified sexual desire. So for example, a clove meant that the sender was burning with longing, and a salted hazelnut signified 'I continue to desire you all over.'

The purpose of the satire was to encourage the sort of harsh measures to constrain women that duly followed, at the beginning of Shah Soltan

Hosein's reign. The author may have exaggerated the sexual side of the rituals of friendship he described, the better to achieve that end. But if he had made it all up, he would not have been believed. Despite the narrow limitations placed on them by the harem, women developed strong relationships with each other that had nothing to do with their husbands. This reaction to constraint is entirely plausible. Ruled out of broad swathes of contemporary life, women's emotional lives expanded to fill the spaces that were available, pushing the limits as far as they could get away with.

Despite the religious crackdown of the 1690s and the appalling trauma of the Afghan revolt, it is pretty certain that the women of Nader's time would have maintained these strong friendships and harem customs, though some things may have changed and shifted over time. Another text, from the later 1690s, gives an account of a widow's pilgrimage from Isfahan to Mecca, in the form of a long poem written by the woman herself. Her husband had been one of Shah Soltan Hosein's chief scribes but, although she had only lost him quite recently and was still grieving, her thoughts on the Hajj were preoccupied as much with a female friend she had been separated from some years before. So much so that despite the difficulties of the journey, she diverted from her pilgrimage to visit the friend, north of Tabriz. The idea of a literate woman, able to travel alone, is in itself a surprising corrective to the usual view of women in Persia in this period.[7]

With the marriage, the territories and the right to levy taxes, Nader had got what he wanted from Tahmasp. On 24 December 1729 he marched out of Isfahan, heading for Shiraz with an army 20,000–25,000 strong. Ashraf advanced to meet him at Zarqan, north-east of Shiraz, having strengthened his depleted forces with Arabs and other tribal troops. Yet again, the Afghans attacked furiously, only to be brought up short by the disciplined musketry of the Persian infantry, to which they had no answer. Nader led a counter-attack, smashing into the Afghans, and their army broke.[8] Ashraf escaped to Shiraz; many other Afghans were captured.

Ashraf attempted to negotiate surrender with Nader from Shiraz, and sent him the royal princesses. But then, rather than put himself in the power of his enemies he fled, heading for Kandahar via Lar. At the bridge of Pol-e Fasa 500 Afshars and Kurds of Nader's advance guard caught up with the Afghan rearguard at dusk, and fell on them. The Afghans resisted bravely, but were overwhelmed. Many fled into the river and drowned in the panic. Large numbers of women and children that had been trailing in the rear of the Afghan column scattered into the night – 'on this day a man fled, abandoning his brothers, his mother, his father, his friends and his children.'[9]

Nader's men captured several important Ghilzais at Pol-e Fasa, including some religious leaders: most of them were later executed. But when he came up with his advance guard Nader was angry. His commanders had attacked without first sending back a report. This incident is a sidelight on Nader's expectations of his officers, and the tight rules of command he expected them to uphold. Despite their victory over the Afghan rearguard, he had the Kurdish commander's eyes torn out, and the Afshar's ears cut off as punishment. Such was the harsh price of thoughtlessness under Nader's command. It was vital for Nader that his officers should keep him informed of what was happening. They were his eyes and ears in the field – the point was made with brutal clarity. Time and again in his later campaigns the Persians secured an advantage because Nader's scouts told him of some development early, enabling him to respond swiftly and take the initiative. Prompt intelligence was the raw material of victory. There is no indication that Nader had to repeat the lesson to his officers.

Nader had the surrounding area searched for the Afghan women and children who had scattered, and sent the captured wives and children of Mahmud Ghilzai and Ashraf under escort to Mashhad. Ashraf himself had already been across the river when the Persians appeared, and he escaped again, but from this point on the much-depleted Afghan army disintegrated. Nader carried on the pursuit a little way beyond the river, but then returned to Shiraz, issuing orders that all the frontiers and ports should be guarded to prevent the Afghan fugitives from escaping. Bodies littered the road to Lar. Some of the Ghilzais were killed by peasants and tribesmen along the way,[10] others committed suicide or killed their families rather than see them captured.

Ashraf and the other Afghan survivors took refuge briefly at Lar, and pondered their predicament. They were a long way from home, and the landscape around them was hostile. They knew the route back to Kandahar through Baluchistan and the harsh Makran desert was going to be tough and dangerous. Ashraf could no longer control the dwindling band, and some broke away, heading south, for the coast. Many were ambushed and killed along the way; those that made it boarded ships heading for the southern shore of the Persian Gulf, but some of the ships sank. A few Afghans landed safely on the coast of

Oman, only to be enslaved by the Arabs of Muscat and put to work at menial tasks. One of Ashraf's brothers was later seen there carrying water, and others ended up working in clay-pits.[11]

Ashraf himself, after a delay, resumed his eastward flight from Lar toward Kandahar with a few followers. There are various accounts of how he met his end; the most authoritative says that Mahmud Ghilzai's brother Hosein, who ruled in Kandahar, eventually hunted him down some months later. Ashraf had made it to Kandahar province. He had avoided the city for fear of Hosein, knowing Hosein would kill him for the deposition and murder of Mahmud. But Hosein heard of Ashraf's return, and set off after him. Getting closer, he sent his son Ebrahim ahead with a small detachment. They finally found Ashraf and his men after dark in a small village. Ashraf tried to escape on his horse, but Ebrahim followed and caught up with him. As their horses galloped on, Ashraf stabbed Ebrahim in the side with a dagger, but Ebrahim managed to shoot and kill him.[12]

Ashraf had faced many threats to his position when he came to power in Isfahan. Some historians have regarded his defeat as inevitable; but he outwitted the Ottomans, fought them to a standstill, got their recognition for his rule, and showed ruthless skill in his conduct of government generally. He was beaten by something that neither he nor any contemporary could have foreseen; a resurgent Safavid cause led by a military genius, leading an army that had been trained and equipped to outclass any rival in the region.

Having destroyed the remaining threat from Ashraf, Nader rested awhile with his men in Shiraz. He sent an envoy to Delhi to inform the Moghul Emperor of the successful campaigns against the Afghans, and of his intention to restore Kandahar to Persian sovereignty. He also asked the Moghul Emperor to prevent any Afghan fugitives from taking refuge in his territories,[13] a request that was to acquire greater significance later on, when it was used as an excuse for war. He also sent an envoy to the Ottoman court, demanding the restitution of the Persian territories the Ottomans had occupied.

Nader appointed a new governor in Shiraz, who set about repairing the damage done by the Afghan occupation. Nader himself gave money for the embellishment of a mosque, and the new governor gave orders for thousands of trees to be planted in the famous gardens of the city, which had been ruined. Shiraz is also famous for her poets, most notably Hafez and Sa'di. One account says that while they were in the

city, Nader spent a day in the gardens by the tomb of Hafez, and one
of Nader's companions opened a volume of Hafez as an oracle, to see
what the future held for Nader. The verse on the page where the book
fell open spoke of tribute, and a crown, and declared:

> Your languishing eyes have reduced all of Turkestan to
> confusion; China and India pay tribute to your curly hair…

Making allowance for the odd effects that might be expected to result
from seeking auguries for a warrior in a book of love poetry, this was
taken to bode well.

It is likely that it was during this stay in Shiraz that Nader met Taqi
Khan Shirazi, who was the son of an official that had been responsible
for the city's water supply. Taqi Khan was devious, highly intelligent
and skilful in financial matters. For some reason that is difficult to
recover across the centuries, but which may have had something to do
with a shared sense of humour, the two men hit it off, and Taqi Khan
became one of Nader's favourite companions. It is likely that he helped
Nader through the complexities of the tax system.

While in Shiraz, Nader talked about returning to Khorasan, but
he can have been no more serious than when he had aired the same
possibility on previous occasions. The purpose of the idea of retirement
to Khorasan was to suggest that, left to himself, he would have preferred
a quiet life; that the campaigns and wars were forced on him by others
or by circumstances. The truth was exactly the contrary. He was not
the man for a life of ease, and a few weeks relaxing in Shiraz would
have been quite enough to remind him of that, had it been necessary.
Stuck in one place for any length of time he soon became restless and
irritable. He belonged in the saddle, and in tented encampments, with
the wind of the Iranian plateau blowing through his battle-standards,
not in towns. He lived for activity, conflict, the overcoming of obstacles
and enemies, and the expansion of his personal dominion.

And his work was not finished. Having dealt with the Afghans,
the obvious next step was the removal of the power that had occupied
most of western Persia: the Ottomans. One account says that petitioners
from Hamadan and Azerbaijan came to see him in Shiraz, telling him
of their sufferings under the Ottomans. The liberation of captives and
other Shi'a Persians under Sunni Ottoman rule was a recurring theme
of Nader's justification for his campaigns in the years to come. As
the weeks passed and no answer came from the Ottoman court, he

resolved on a campaign in the west. There is no sign that he discussed the decision with Tahmasp, though they probably exchanged letters. Nader marched his men out of Shiraz westwards on 8 March 1730.[14]

As before his campaign against Herat the previous year, Nader halted his men along the way for a lavish Nowruz celebration. The purpose was to thank them for their efforts against the Afghans and prepare them mentally for the new campaign against the Ottoman Turks. Nowruz, the Persian New Year, is celebrated at the vernal equinox each spring, on 21 March. It is in origin a Zoroastrian festival that was celebrated in Persia under the Sassanian and Achaemenid empires long before the Prophet Mohammad. It is still the main festival of the year in Iran, and lasts for several days. Falling in the spring, at the beginning of the new campaigning season, it was the right time for Nader to renew his contract of loyalty and trust with his soldiers.

Nader gave superb clothes to his commanders as part of the celebrations. In addition, Shah Tahmasp sent 300 robes of honour* for the officers of the army from Isfahan, in gratitude for the victory over Ashraf. The Shah's messenger confirmed Nader's authority over Khorasan and the other north-eastern provinces, but Nader forbore to wear the jiqe[15] – a typical touch. He had won the right to wear the aigrette of heron feathers, establishing his princely status; but had not taken it up – why not? It may be that he wanted people to gossip, to create an undercurrent of speculation. Some already believed that he intended to displace Tahmasp and make himself Shah.[16] They would have asked why did he not wear the jiqe – because, out of laudable humility, he felt he was not worthy? Or was the time not yet right? Popular speculation about Nader and the jiqe helped to spread doubt about Tahmasp's future as Shah.

The Ottoman government had not formally replied to the Persian demand for return of the lands the Turkish armies had occupied. In Istanbul a Persian envoy negotiated with the unwarlike Turkish vizier, Damad Ebrahim Pasha, for withdrawal of the Ottoman forces. These negotiations may have made some progress, but Nader did not wait for their outcome, and continued his march to the north-west. The great distances and the difficulty of travel in those days meant that diplomacy was often overtaken by events. At Dezful Nader met on the road the ambassador that Ashraf had sent to Istanbul, Mohammad Khan Baluch. Mohammad Khan prudently gave Nader the letters the

* Khal'ats.

Ottoman Sultan had intended for Ashraf, and was rewarded with the governorship of a province (an appointment Nader was to regret).[17]

Impatient to confront the enemy, Nader marched on to Borujerd, and by night to Nahavand, surprising the Ottoman commander there. Trusting to their previous success in battle with the Persians, the Ottomans came forward to fight. But Nader's Persians were troops of a different calibre to those they had previously encountered. The Ottomans were defeated after a short struggle and fled towards Hamadan.

After the Persians had taken Nahavand, Nader's scouts warned him that an Ottoman army of 30,000 men was approaching. The two armies faced each other in the plain of Malayer, separated by a small stream. Facing an army strong in firearm infantry, composed more like his own than that of the Afghans he had fought before, Nader deployed his troops into a looser formation of three bodies and held back the centre, which he commanded himself, as a reserve. The Ottomans and Persians closed to musket range, and exchanged fire for some time across the stream. But then Nader broke the impasse by ordering his right wing to cross the stream and charge the Ottoman left. After a lengthy struggle, the Ottoman standard-bearer was killed, his banner fell and the dismayed Turkish troops retreated from the field. They tried to escape into the mountains, but Nader's cavalry pursued, killing many, capturing some senior Ottoman officers and much plunder. One account says that the Ottoman troops, shocked at their unexpected defeat by the Persians, were heard calling out to each other as they fled 'What shall I do?' and 'Escape! Escape!'[18]

This battle broke Ottoman control over this part of western Persia. The Ottoman governor of Hamadan quit the city and withdrew to Baghdad. Nader was able to march into Hamadan unopposed. He freed 10,000 Persian captives and took over quantities of artillery and supplies that the Turks had abandoned in their haste.[19] Shortly afterwards, after some more fighting, Nader's troops marched into Kermanshah and secured the entire province. Nader gave orders for new fortifications to be built at Kermanshah against future Ottoman invasions. He rested his men for a month in Hamadan but, impatient to finish the job, set out northwards on 17 July 1730 to eject the Ottomans from Azerbaijan and reconquer Tabriz.

Affronted by Nader's attacks on their forces of occupation, the Ottoman government in Istanbul formally declared war and imprisoned the Persian ambassador (as was their custom) – but nonetheless continued, via a special envoy to Isfahan and their governor in Baghdad, to press Tahmasp to make peace. Sultan Ahmad and his vizier Damad Ebrahim still hoped for a treaty with the Persians that would enable them to keep Georgia, Shirvan and Yerevan, but were worried about unrest in Istanbul, where the people were increasingly angry at rumours of defeat in the east.

Indifferent to discussions going on elsewhere, which his actions tended anyway to make irrelevant, Nader marched north via Sanandaj, and ran into another Ottoman army at Miyandoab, south of Lake Urmiye. As the Persians approached, the Turks drew up in battle formation, but the news of Nader's earlier victories must have shaken their confidence. When the Persians charged forward, and the dust from the Persian horses' hooves blew in their faces, blinding them, the Ottoman soldiers fled before the Persians made contact.

Nader continued his advance northward. Mutiny was breaking out among the demoralised Ottomans. After some further minor clashes, Nader's men defeated Mostafa Pasha, the Ottoman governor of Tabriz, near Soheylan. After each of these battles the Persians killed many of the Ottomans in flight, captured much artillery and booty, and many prisoners. After Soheylan many of the Ottoman women too fell into their hands – 'beautiful as the houris of paradise'. Following his usual practice toward women, Nader gave orders that they should be escorted safely home, forbidding severely that anyone should lay hands on them.[20]

The Persians entered Tabriz on 12 August, and shortly afterwards defeated yet another force of Ottomans sent to reinforce the city. Nader treated kindly the Turks he captured, released a number of the more senior Pashas and sent peace proposals with one of them to Damad Ebrahim in Istanbul. In less than a year, in rapid, bold campaigns, Nader had comprehensively defeated the Afghans and Ottomans, and had regained all the major cities of the Persian heartland.

The Ottoman vizier, Damad Ebrahim, with great ceremony and ballyhoo, had crossed the Bosphorus with an army ten days before Nader took Tabriz, ostensibly with the intention of marching to humble the Persians. But he advanced no further toward Nader than the Asian side of the Bosphorus and lingered there with his army, fearing to risk the uncertainties of battle, and still hoping for a negotiated peace. Meanwhile mutinous troops and refugees from Tabriz and elsewhere made their way west, adding to the dangerous blend of chagrin, frustration and anger in Istanbul.

On 28 September a revolt broke out in the bazaar area of the Ottoman capital. Trouble had been building for some time. There was dissatisfaction with the high level of taxation imposed to pay for the wars with Persia. There had been outbreaks of plague and cholera in the overcrowded city, and fires caused by arson. Many of the people of Istanbul had long resented what they regarded as a westernising policy by the government: notably the treaty with Russia of 1724 and the war against the Sunni Afghans that followed it. The Sultan and his grand vizier were perceived as luxurious and incompetent; enjoying their tulip gardens and entertainments while poor Muslims starved and provinces were lost. Damad Ebrahim was personally unpopular with many eminent Ottoman courtiers for his lack of respect. He alienated a number of them by tossing gold coins down their wives' dresses at public receptions; a trick at which he apparently became quite adept, to the dismay of his victims and their husbands.[21]

The factor that turned the revolt of 1730 in Istanbul into something more serious was the decision by some of the Ottoman ulema to support the rebels. When the revolt began some of the ulema refused to back the Sultan and this contributed to a fatal delay in government action to crush the unrest. The rebels took the initiative, and recruited many janissaries to their cause. They murdered Damad Ebrahim and many others, and in the fluid situation that followed, Sultan Ahmad was deposed in favour of his nephew Mahmud. It was some time before the new Sultan could make himself secure enough to expel the rebels from his capital and take full control of his government. Early in 1731, when Istanbul had calmed down, he appointed a new grand vizier, Topal Osman Pasha.

Nader was unable to take advantage of this disarray among the Ottomans. He had intended to follow up his success in Tabriz by a campaign further north, toward Yerevan. But he had been in Tabriz only five days when he got news that the Abdalis of Herat were in revolt and had defeated a Persian force outside Mashhad.[22]

Hosein Soltan of Kandahar was the only Afghan leader Nader had not yet subdued. Contemporaries believed that, fearing that Nader sooner or later would turn the victorious Persian army on him, Hosein Soltan encouraged the Abdalis to revolt to strengthen his otherwise dangerously isolated position. The faction-ridden Abdalis were open to sedition. Allah Yar Khan, the governor Nader had appointed at the end of his campaign against Herat in 1729, remained loyal. But his rival Zolfeqar Khan took control of the revolt and forced Allah Yar Khan to retire to Mashhad. After taking Herat, Zolfeqar Khan marched on

Mashhad, where Nader's brother Ebrahim Khan was in command.

Mashhad was Nader's power base and he could not risk losing the city. Fearing trouble, he had already sent reinforcements and supplies. He had ordered his brother to sit tight within the city in the event of an attack, but when the Afghans arrived Ebrahim, keen to achieve a success and prove his worth to his victorious brother, found it impossible to obey. After hesitating for a couple of weeks, he led his troops out of the city around the beginning of August to attack the Abdalis, and was soundly beaten. In his shame he fell into a deep, debilitating melancholy.[23] It was Reza Qoli, Nader's twelve-year-old son, who sent the news of the defeat outside Mashhad to Nader in Tabriz.

Nader replied immediately, telling his son to hold on within the city, and that he was on his way to relieve him. He also sent a harsh rebuke to his brother, telling him he should go to Abivard, lest Nader execute him for his foolish disobedience when he arrived in Mashhad.[24] Nader set out on 16 August, but before long received another message from Reza Qoli telling him that the Abdalis, having devastated the countryside around the city, had pulled back from Mashhad. Without heavy artillery to batter breaches in the walls, the Abdalis could not take the city.

Nader marched on eastward with his army. The attack on Mashhad was an insult to his newly won prestige that could not be allowed to pass, and it was important to secure Khorasan for good. But now he could afford to take his time. Another courier brought him a letter from Allah Yar Khan, begging him to forgive Ebrahim for his disobedience and defeat outside Mashhad. Nader replied that he would forgive his brother, since he had shown his deep remorse, and because the defeat had been the will of God. But he added '… he must put right his error by more prudent conduct, and seek our favour by more judicious behaviour in future'.[25] There is a striking contrast here with other examples of Nader's harsh treatment of disobedience. But Nader did not rule his subordinates simply by terror, and was prepared to forgive honest mistakes, especially by members of his family or those within his inner circle who had proved their loyalty repeatedly in the past.

Nader finally arrived in Mashhad on 11 November, and ordered the cannon of the city to thunder out a welcome. Once there, he still took his time. Three days after his arrival, he had some of the tribes that he had resettled in Khorasan pass before him in review. These included some 50–60,000 Kurds, Afshars and others he had ordered east after his latest campaigns in Hamadan province and in Azerbaijan. He chose

from among them some of the strongest and fittest young men, and
gave orders that they should be trained up for war.

As time went on, the policy of resettlement became a motif of Nader's
rule. The concentration of warlike tribesmen in Khorasan served a
variety of purposes. It divided and weakened tribes elsewhere in Persia
that might otherwise have caused serious trouble. It helped to make
Khorasan itself, Nader's power base, more secure against threats from
Turkmen raiders, revolts by the Kurds and attacks from the Afghans.
The selection of young men from among the settlers to serve in Nader's
personal guard not only gave him a reserve of superb, disciplined
cavalry; their presence close to him made them hostages for the good
behaviour of their relatives in Khorasan and elsewhere. The tribes were
always unruly, and the chaos of recent years had encouraged their
instinct to raid, to plunder, to extend their independence and attempt
local hegemony. Within the tribes the young men would always be
the most turbulent element. Resettlement and the recruitment of these
young men into some of the most prestigious units of his well-paid
army gave them and their relatives an interest in Nader's state and
its success. The policy also strengthened the non-Persian, non-Shi'a
element in the army, the faction among the troops that owed loyalty to
him alone rather than the Safavid cause.

But Nader's resettlement policy caused great resentment among the
tribes and contributed to the persistent rebellions that plagued the latter
part of his reign. Forced movement of large numbers of people was
always bound to cause great suffering, and many of the poorer people
would have died on the journey. Different accounts give contrasting
impressions of Nader's attitude to the settlers. Nader gave 300 Armenian
families sent to Khorasan in 1736 two bullocks each to help them carry
their belongings on the journey, but this may have been a sign of special
favour, and the resettlement of the Armenians was in any case not a
success.[26] Sometimes, resettlement was intended as a punishment, as
when 6,000 Georgians who had supported the Ottomans were sent to
Khorasan from Tiflis in 1735. At other times it was purely a matter of
policy, as appears to have been the case with the Afshars of Urmiye.

One example of the resentment caused by resettlement was that of
the great Bakhtiari tribe. After Nader captured Hamadan in 1730 he sent
orders to the local governor in the Bakhtiari country for 200 families
to resettle to the immediate neighbourhood of Isfahan, probably in an
attempt to make good some of the depopulation caused by the Afghan
siege and occupation. But with Nader's army at some distance and unable

to apply direct pressure, the Bakhtiaris refused to move. When he heard of this disobedience, Nader had all the Bakhtiaris in his army disarmed, and their chiefs put in chains. He ordered the local governor to punish the disobedient tribesmen, and to send 400 families to Isfahan instead of 200.[27] But that was not the end of Nader's trouble with the Bakhtiari.

Nader spent the winter of 1730/1731 in Mashhad, preparing a campaign to crush the Abdali revolt and take Herat. He sent Allah Yar Khan back to Herat province to agitate against the Zolfeqar faction. But there was time for lighter business. Nader must have been proud of the prompt and intelligent response of his son Reza Qoli Mirza to Ebrahim's defeat. It was the first sign of a precocious talent that was to make Nader particularly devoted to his eldest son. In January 1731 Reza Qoli married Shah Tahmasp's sister, Fatima Soltan Begum. There were magnificent celebrations in the Chaharbagh gardens outside Mashhad, which lasted a week and ended with a particularly propitious conjunction of the planets. This was followed by a great hunting expedition in the area around Kalat and Abivard, Nader's old home ground. Perhaps as part of a process of rehabilitation in this time of family celebration and goodwill, Nader sent his brother Ebrahim on a punitive expedition against the Turkmen, in which he was successful and must have regained some of his former confidence.[28] A few weeks later the festival of Nowruz was celebrated with great gusto and splendour, as the mountain snows melted, the spring flowers appeared and the season of heat and bloodshed again arrived. Within a few days of the spring solstice, Nader took his army out of Mashhad, heading for Herat.

Over this period Hosein of Kandahar had been negotiating both with Nader and with Zolfeqar. With Nader he agreed the exchange of two Safavid princesses for Mahmud Ghilzai's widows and children. With Zolfeqar, Hosein played hard to get (despite his encouragement of the revolt earlier in the year), but eventually sent several thousand Ghilzais under Mohammad Seidal Khan to support Herat.

Nader arrived at Noqra, a few miles west of Herat, early in April 1731. Persian troops fanned out over the surrounding countryside, pillaging and taking possession of minor forts and towers. Only three days after the Persians' arrival, Mohammad Seidal Khan and several thousand men attempted to surprise the Persians with a night attack. In the confusion Nader himself was left behind in a small tower with only eight musketeers, and was surrounded by a much larger force of Afghans. Nader and his small party fought for their lives in the darkness, killing many of the enemy, until a detachment of Persian infantry arrived to rescue them.[29]

Herat was symbolically as well as strategically important. It was one of the great cities of Asia, and was ringed with strong fortifications from the time of Shahrokh, Timur's son, who had made it the capital of his empire. On 4 May Nader moved to encircle the city on all sides. He left a garrison of 10,000 men in entrenchments at Noqra, and defeating another major sortie along the way, took the rest of the army over the Hari Rud river at a bridge south of Herat. He set up camp there, and made the place his headquarters. He had a small pleasure-house built for himself at a little distance – 'where he could relax from the continual fatigues to which his great heart was exposed'. But he was nearly killed in the midst of his relaxations when the Afghans succeeded in dropping a heavy cannon ball right into it at long range. The ball tore through the roof, fell close by his couch and rolled several paces before coming to rest. Nader's companions took the happy outcome of this rude interruption as another sign of the special favour of Providence.[30]

Making progress by slow stages as was necessary in siege warfare, Nader completed the encirclement of the city with another fortified camp to the east. On 22 July Zolfeqar led another force against the besiegers, crossing the Hari Rud, but Nader was able to assess the line of attack from a hill, and sent a force to outflank them while he led a force of cavalry against them frontally. This action disrupted Zolfeqar's attack, and his men fled. Many were killed. By now many of Mohammad Seidal Khan's Ghilzais were dead, and this defeat was the last straw for him. He left the city, and the Abdalis, further demoralised by his departure, sent messages to Nader's camp that they were ready to submit.

There was still dissent among them, but eventually the Abdalis submitted properly, leaving the city, putting themselves at the mercy of Nader's cannon and asking him to appoint Allah Yar Khan as their governor. Nader agreed, Allah Yar Khan took office in the city and Zolfeqar was banished to Farah with his brother. Nader showed forbearance in not occupying Herat in person, but only a few days later the Abdalis' courage was reignited by a rumour that 40,000 men were coming to their assistance at Farah. Allah Yar Khan tried to calm things down, but Nader lost his patience and took some Abdali chiefs under guard in his camp, which antagonised some of the Abdalis further. In early September Allah Yar Khan himself revolted, carrying out raids and attacking Nader's troops. Nader intensified the siege, drew the blockade ever tighter and gave orders that any Afghans taken prisoner should be killed. He was grimly determined that in this contest between his will and the indomitable spirit of the Abdalis, his will would prevail.

Despite further overtures, ruptures and reversals of intent, the Abdalis under Allah Yar Khan finally surrendered on 27 February 1732, and the joyful shouts of the Persians echoed through the hills around Herat. Nader's brother Ebrahim occupied Farah, completing his personal rehabilitation in Nader's favour. Zolfeqar and his brother fled, seeking refuge with Hosein in Kandahar, but Hosein threw them into prison. This time Nader took no chances with Herat. Parties of his soldiers marched in to man the gates and towers, and enforced an evacuation. Allah Yar Khan was exiled, but there was no massacre or sack, and contemporaries were generally struck by Nader's leniency.[31] Nader installed Pir Mohammad Khan as governor, a man he had trusted with tricky duties since 1726, when Pir Mohammad had transferred his allegiance to Nader from Malek Mahmud Sistani. 60,000 more Abdalis were sent to various parts of Khorasan,[32] adding to those resettled after the campaign of 1729. Their fighting qualities were an important addition to Nader's military strength, and again reinforced the non-Persian element in the army. Nader was on his way to join Ebrahim at Farah when he got disturbing news from the other end of the country.

Nader's departure for Khorasan in the summer of 1730 had given Shah Tahmasp his big chance. In the absence of his overbearing generalissimo, Tahmasp could try to boost his personal prestige and establish himself as worthy of his throne in his own right. But although some of his courtiers urged him to do so by a new campaign against the Ottomans in the north-west, to recover Yerevan and Georgia as Nader had planned, Tahmasp spent five months drinking and enjoying himself in Isfahan, showing little sign of urgency.[33]

Meanwhile the Ottoman state slowly recovered from the period of chaos that followed the revolt of September 1730 and the deposition of Sultan Ahmed. When Tahmasp eventually left Isfahan for Tabriz in January 1731 the new Ottoman Sultan, Mahmud, was ready for him. In Tabriz Tahmasp replaced the governor Nader had appointed with one of his own partisans, and moved north-west with 18,000 men. Approaching Yerevan, his army encountered a force of Ottoman Turks and defeated them after a short engagement.[34] The Ottomans retreated to Yerevan, and Shah Tahmasp's men settled down to a siege of the city.

But this early success was not to last. Tahmasp had advanced rashly, without considering the danger from enemy forces on his flanks. Other Ottoman troops, operating to the south of Yerevan, were able to interrupt the flow of supplies to Tahmasp's army, and after only eighteen days he was forced to withdraw again to Tabriz. While there, he heard that the Ottoman governor of Baghdad, Ahmad Pasha, had invaded Persian territory, heading for Kermanshah and Hamadan. Tahmasp hurried south to meet the new threat; leaving Tabriz exposed to the Ottoman forces, who regained their courage and advanced again from Yerevan.

By the time Tahmasp arrived near Hamadan, Ahmad Pasha had occupied Kermanshah. Tahmasp halted at Kurijan, north-east of Hamadan, and the Ottoman army advanced to meet him. Ahmad Pasha sent messengers with peace proposals, and Tahmasp responded, but by this time the two armies were too close, within cannon shot. The Persians were organised into three bodies, with cavalry on the wings and musket infantry in the centre. Whereas the Persian musketeers were mainly new recruits (Nader's veterans being with him in the east), the Ottoman infantry were experienced janissaries. The ancestors of these janissaries had, in previous centuries, been taken as children from the Christian population of the Sultan's European provinces and raised as soldiers, but by this time most of the janissaries in the Ottoman provinces were the sons and grandsons of the original troops from the Balkans. Their training and discipline was not up to the standard of the janissaries of the main Ottoman army, based in Istanbul, but they were still good troops, better than Tahmasp's levies.

Fearing that the Ottomans were about to make a surprise attack despite the peace negotiations, Tahmasp ordered his cannon to fire, and soon the battle became general. The Persian cavalry outclassed the Ottoman horse and charged through them three times. But the Ottoman janissaries ground slowly forward despite the Persian horsemen and opened fire on the Persian musketeers, who fled almost immediately. Then the janissaries turned on the Persian cavalry. Before long Tahmasp himself was almost surrounded. He managed to escape, but by now the Persians were irretrievably beaten. Those of the infantry that were not killed were rounded up by the Ottomans and put in chains, and most of the rest of the survivors, demoralised, went straight home.[35]

Tahmasp, escorted by just a few nobles and guards, likewise made a hurried departure from the field. But unlike many of his companions in the campaign against the Ottomans, the immediate consequences of the defeat did not seem for him to be too serious. He returned to his palace in Isfahan to party on as if the disaster had never happened.[36]

CHAPTER FIVE
Coup d'État

Within a few weeks of Tahmasp's disastrous defeat at the battle of Kurijan the Ottomans had occupied Hamadan, Tabriz and all the other territories the Persians had taken from them in 1730, wiping out all Nader's successes in the west. Eager to fix the swinging balance of war at this advantageous point, Ottoman envoys pressed for a peace settlement. They were prepared to evacuate Kermanshah, Hamadan and Tabriz, in exchange for confirmation of their possession of Georgia, Armenia and other territories north of the Araxes river. In January 1732 Tahmasp agreed a treaty with the Ottomans along these lines.

It was a copy of Tahmasp's treaty with the Ottoman Turks that had caught up with Nader on his way from Herat to Farah. He may have intended to follow up his success against Herat by marching on Kandahar, but now those plans had to wait. If Nader had thought previously that, by his absence, he would give the incompetent Tahmasp enough rope to do himself great damage, if not hang himself, he could not have imagined that even Tahmasp would make quite such a hash of things. Tahmasp had spoiled his chance: now it was Nader's turn.

Nader went back to Herat, and from there sent two pungent messages
to the Ottomans. The first, addressed to Sultan Mahmud, demanded
that he should return all the territories of Azerbaijan, or prepare for
war. The second, sent to Ahmad Pasha in Baghdad, simply told him to
expect a visit.[1] He also sent a trusted companion to Tahmasp's court to
reproach the Shah's ministers for their errors, and published a manifesto
denouncing the pernicious treaty.

In the manifesto Nader declared that, through the favour of God, he
had achieved victories over the Afghans, but that he had then received
word of a treaty with the Ottomans, ceding to them the territories north
of the Araxes. This treaty was an empty and fruitless one, above all
because the important question of Persian captives* in Ottoman hands
was nowhere even mentioned in it. The manifesto stated that as a leader
of men, Nader remembered the precept that shepherds should look
after their flocks. The empire should be rid of the seeds of corruption;
and since the treaty's provisions for new borders were contrary to the
wishes of the Almighty, he had rejected them. Furthermore, since the
angels themselves desired the liberation of Muslim prisoners, he had
resolved to leave Mashhad toward the end of March, and lead forward
his army of valiant lions; and any who opposed him would be deprived
of their nobility, honour and happiness, would be subject to the curses
of heaven, become a stranger to the true faith, and confounded among
the crowd of rebels.[2]

Nader wrote to the governor of Fars and perhaps others in similar
terms, except that the appeal to Shi'a sentiment was even more explicit.[3]
Like the manifesto, the letter was intended to be widely read and
repeated. Nader exploited religion and the outstanding question of the
Persian captives to discredit Tahmasp's ministers and gather support
for the renewal of hostilities against the Ottomans – a policy which
otherwise might not have been particularly popular. Given the exhausted
condition of the country after years of war, the depredations of the
Afghans, and the Ottoman occupation of most of the western and north-
western provinces, many might have looked on the treaty as welcome
and moderate – indeed, in Istanbul the treaty's restitution of Tabriz to
the Persians was widely criticised as much too generous. Nader took his
time, put out his propaganda, sounded opinion. He moved cautiously:
this was his moment to seize power, and he had to get it right.

---

* i.e. both the Persian civilians enslaved by the Ottomans in the previous
  decade, and the soldiers captured at Kurijan and elsewhere.

As well as being a pivotal moment in Nader's career, this was also a pivotal and revealing moment in Iranian history. A man from nowhere, with nothing to recommend him but his 'crescent-formed and all-subduing scimitar',[4] was challenging the authority of a royal government whose dynasty had ruled for over two hundred years with unquestioned authority. His challenge was made not by brute force or assassination: the force was there, but he was seeking the support of what one would call, in anything but a highly centralised absolute monarchy, the political class.* It was unheard of that the people of Persia should support such a man against the will of the hereditary ruler – even more unheard of than their being asked. But hereditary authority was weakened by failure. The new man knew better than to challenge Safavid rule directly, but when they read the letters or heard the manifesto, most must have realised, uneasily or with enthusiasm, what was happening. The language was revolutionary: 'Such of the tribe of Shi'as, as are backward on this great occasion, and are reconciled to this shameful peace, should be expelled from the faithful seat; and for ever counted among its enemies. To slaughter them will be meritorious; to permit their existence, impious.'[5] It was a modern moment, which argues against those who deny the existence of any but local and dynastic loyalties in this period. The significance of Nader's pronouncements and their implications for Tahmasp's future would have been avidly discussed outside the mosques and in the bazaars of the cities of Persia, and in private when the great chiefs, governors, bureaucrats and nobles met each other. This had been Nader's intention precisely.

Over the next couple of months a number of Tahmasp's courtiers visited Nader, urging him to press home his opposition to the treaty. These included Hasan Ali Khan, who had first met Nader in Khorasan in 1726, and Mirza Zaki Khan. Both were high officials at Tahmasp's court, and were to become Nader's close companions.

To win over men like these to his side, Nader would have included them in his regular evening drinking sessions. Nader's fondness for drinking parties in the evening was well known, and from early on they became part of his daily routine. This might seem surprising, but despite the pious tradition that rejected wine, typical for example of the Afghans and the followers of the mullahs in the Persian cities, there was a heroic, Turkic and Persian warrior tradition of heavy drinking that

* 'The peace… neither meets the *approbation of the nobles* nor the *commonalty of the empire*' (my italics). Malcolm, *Two Letters*, p. 539.

went back to Timur and beyond.* Nader never allowed his drinking
to take over, as Tahmasp and Shah Soltan Hosein had. Business and
pleasure were normally kept separate. The purpose of Nader's drinking
parties was relaxation at the end of the day, and asabiyah. Business was
not normally discussed. The sessions served to create bonds of fellow
feeling and trust – though there were still rules to be observed, and
traps for the foolish:

> He never indulges himself in any kind of Pleasure in the
> Day-time, but constantly at Sun-set retires to a private
> Apartment; where, unbending himself at once from
> Business, he sups with three or four Favourites, and
> drinks a Quart, or at most three Pints of Wine,† behaving
> all the Time in the freest and most facetious Manner.
> In this private Conversation no Person is allowed to
> mention any Thing relating to public Business; nor, at
> other Times, must they presume, upon this intimacy to
> behave with more Familiarity than their Equals… He
> has been very kind to those who please him in private
> Conversation, and behave with a becoming Decency and
> Deference in Public, where they are taken no more notice
> of, nor have they any more Influence over him than
> others of the same rank.⁶

Conversation at the drinking parties ran freely, and Nader allowed
liberties he would not have permitted at other times. But it did not do
to relax too much. One man spoke too readily when Nader asked:

> during a wine-drinking get-together … what kind of
> children would be born to the women who had been
> loved by ten soldiers. He then had answered: "Ones, just
> like you a Nader dourou" (*nader-e do-ru* – 'a rare two-
> faced one' – i.e. a crook, rascal or bastard).⁷

---

* The euphonious Persian term for this was *razm o bazm* (fighting and
  boozing).
† Cockell, the EIC representative who wrote this account in about 1741,
  intended his description of Nader's drinking to sound moderate, which by
  comparison with Cockell's familiars in London at the time, it probably was.

The smiles froze. Nader was perhaps reminded of jibes thrown at him when he and his mother had lived in poverty in Khorasan, after his father died. He had the man strangled.

While Nader entertained important courtiers, sounded out their opposition to the treaty with the Ottomans and prepared his next move, in Isfahan the pleasant round of court life was disrupted by a strange, ineffectual plot to overthrow Tahmasp. There is no indication that Nader or his supporters had anything to do with it. The plot turned on a man called Esmail Mirza, who had arrived in Isfahan around the time Tahmasp returned after his defeat at Kurijan. Esmail claimed to be one of Tahmasp's brothers, and that he had been saved from Mahmud Ghilzai's massacre of the Safavid royal family by a faithful guardsman. Arriving back in Isfahan after various adventures, Esmail was questioned by Tahmasp's courtiers and eventually was given an audience with Tahmasp himself, who recognised him as his brother. But shortly afterwards some of the courtiers, perhaps hoping to forestall action by Nader, developed a plot to replace Tahmasp with Esmail. Tahmasp was told of the plot, and reacted savagely. Esmail protested his innocence, but was executed anyway, along with the courtiers who had dreamed up the idea. They were publicly beheaded, and their bodies burned or fed to the animals of the royal menagerie. Tahmasp even had the wives of the conspirators killed: they were bricked up in the chimneys of their houses and left there to die.[8]

Nader spent Nowruz in Herat, and then went to Mashhad. From there he sent a message to Isfahan, asking Shah Tahmasp to meet him in Tehran or Qom. With the message he sent back the court officials that had carried the copy of the Ottoman/Persian treaty to him, with instructions to explain again his reasons for repudiating it. He issued orders that replaced a number of provincial governors with his own men, strengthening his position in the country for the coming political upheaval.

While in Mashhad he also received an envoy from the Russians, telling him that they were ready to evacuate Gilan. Nader sent two of his officers to Gilan to observe the Russian withdrawal. Then, as promised in the manifesto, he left Mashhad; but he took his time, visiting Kalat and Abivard, and going on hunting expeditions. By the end of May Nader was at Semnan with 80,000 horsemen and 40,000 foot.[9] Arriving in Tehran, he reviewed the army, and distributed generous payments, ostensibly for the repair and renewal of their

equipment, which in truth were inducements to ensure the loyalty of
the troops in what was to follow. Shah Tahmasp had not come to meet
Nader as he had been bidden. He may have considered fleeing Isfahan:
even flight from the country altogether, to Ottoman territory or beyond.
But if so, his companions dissuaded him. Nader went to Tahmasp in
Isfahan, marching by stages at night to avoid the intense heat of high
summer. He arrived on 25 August.[10] The cannon of the city blasted out
a welcome, and Nader set up his camp in the Hazarjarib gardens. He
had brought 32,000 men south with him; more than enough to overawe
any opposition in the capital.

Two days later Nader paid a courtesy visit to the Shah at the
Sa'adatabad gardens, accompanied by 3,000 of his troops – but stayed
only 15 minutes, which was taken as a snub. According to one version,
he gave Tahmasp a package of letters sent to him by various ministers
and courtiers, showing their disloyalty. Nader removed most of the
Shah's ministers from office, confiscated their possessions and had them
imprisoned (they were released a few days later, but were exiled from the
capital). Having prepared the ground, Nader then invited Tahmasp to
the Hazarjarib gardens for a return visit. Tahmasp had little choice but to
accept. He went to the gardens, and according to one account reviewed
the troops there. As he rode along the ranks, some of the junior officers
and ordinary soldiers called out, 'If your Majesty has any Commands,
we are ready to execute them.' Momentarily taken aback at this sign of
pro-Safavid feeling among his men, Nader coolly made Tahmasp tell
them that as the command of the army was given to Nader, the proof of
their obedience to their sovereign was to obey their general.[11]

The review over, Nader treated Tahmasp to a sumptuous meal. Both
men drank wine, and musicians played to ease the tense atmosphere.
Nader encouraged Tahmasp to drink heavily, and Tahmasp was not
loath. Nader told him he had ordered an end to all state business for
several days, so that they could enjoy themselves. Tahmasp began
to relax. It all went according to plan. Tahmasp's weaknesses made
him all too easy to manipulate, and perhaps by this time he was
accustomed simply to abandon himself to Nader's stronger will, when
in his presence. After lengthy jollifications under Nader's grim eye,
Tahmasp fell into a stupor. Nader's men jeered at the state he was in.
One account says that a loyal servant, Bijan Beg, had earlier warned
Tahmasp of treachery, accompanied him to the Hazarjarib gardens and
stood behind Nader throughout, waiting for the Shah's signal to kill the
over-mighty generalissimo. But Tahmasp waved his entreaties away.[12]

Once the Shah fell unconscious, Nader had him confined, his men shouldering aside Tahmasp's personal servants and guards. Following his pre-planned stage directions, Nader called together the officers of the army, the nobility, courtiers and ministers. He showed them the condition Tahmasp was in. One account says that he personally carried Tahmasp out of the pavilion in which he had been lying and put him down on the lawn of the gardens outside, roaring drunk. The assembled notables saw that Tahmasp's crown* had fallen to one side, his trousers were stained, and the top of his head was dirty as he lolled on the grass.[†13]

Nader feigned anger, and accused the Shah's courtiers of having corrupted him by leading him into the pleasures of wine-drinking. The courtiers, fearful of the outcome, declared that they were not responsible for the Shah's weaknesses, and that it had proved impossible to stop him. They said no-one had been to blame for his carousing but Tahmasp himself. In this way Tahmasp was condemned by his own closest partisans, who became complicit in Nader's seizure of power. Nader said the Shah was plainly no longer fit to rule, and sent a group of the courtiers to tell him so. They returned with the royal jiqe, and Nader proposed to the assembly that Tahmasp's infant son should be made Shah as Abbas III. Some of them pressed Nader to ascend the throne himself, but he refused, protesting the inviolability of the hereditary principle.

A few days later, on 7 September 1732,[14] the new Shah had his formal investiture. Nader laid the fateful jiqe by the little boy's head (he was only a few months old), the assembly made their obeisances, and quantities of sweets were handed around. Drums rumbled in celebration through the city for seven days. The child-Shah had his name read in the Friday prayers (the *khutba*), a new royal seal was made, and new coinage was issued.[15] Nader took the titles of regent and chief minister.[‡] Tahmasp

---

* Probably the turban to which the royal *jiqe* was attached.

† The *Rustam at-Tawarikh* gives a racier version of these events, saying that the notables hid behind a curtain and spied through holes in it while the drunken Tahmasp undressed and ordered his 'beardless pages' to undress too and go down on all fours. He had a courtier daub their bottoms with spittle from a golden cup, and then 'bent with perfect grace over each one' (*Rustam at-Tawarikh*, vol. 1, p. 371). But Mohsen (fol. 215b) also mentions 'debauchery', and it is likely that Tahmasp was bisexual (cf. GD 3/14 October; Avramov, p. 96).

‡ *naib* and *wakil od-dowla*.

had been packed off to Mashhad with his harem, servants and a strong escort a couple of days before.

One account says that the little boy began to cry during the crowning ceremony. Nader asked those nearby whether they knew why he was crying. Prudently, they said Nader surely knew best himself. Nader said Abbas was crying because he wanted to rule over the Afghans of Kandahar and the Ottoman Sultan, and declared to general acclaim that to gratify this wish, he would throw reins around the necks of the rulers not only of Ottoman Turkey and Kandahar, but also Turkestan and India.[16]

To all appearances, there had been little to stop Nader making himself Shah, but it was never his way to take unnecessary risks. As regent for a child king, with the army behind him, no-one could challenge his supremacy. He could afford to wait, allow opinion in the country to adjust itself to his rule, and choose his moment. He knew that sentiment for the Safavid dynasty was still strong, and he preferred to humour it for the time being, and build further the strength of his position, rather than confront it too early. In taking power as regent he had easily outmanoeuvred his opponents. His handling of the episode shows a confidence born of a certainty that he would always be two or three steps ahead of them. It is also worth noting that Nader was more merciful to Tahmasp than Tahmasp had been to Esmail a few weeks earlier. Nader's seizure of power was not followed by wholesale massacre after the example of Mahmud Ghilzai or Ashraf. In fact, it seems there was no bloodshed at all.[17] Nader was not shy of bloody cruelty if it was necessary, but unlike other usurpers and monarchs that had used it routinely in order to impress others and perhaps themselves with their ruthlessness, he employed his butchers selectively. He did not need piles of bodies and streams of blood to boost his self-confidence.

Nader spent the next few weeks in Isfahan. Tahmasp Khan Jalayer, who had earlier been his agent in the city, was made governor. A familiar figure had returned: the Russian, Semeon Avramov. He had been sent to Isfahan as ambassador to Tahmasp's court, and instead found himself on arrival the envoy to Abbas III's powerful regent.[18] Nader's deposition of Tahmasp was welcomed in St Petersburg, where Nader was regarded as a valuable ally against the Ottomans.

Others also recorded their impressions of Nader at this time. The English East India Company representative wrote later that he had been over six feet tall, handsome and well-proportioned, with a strong constitution that might have been inclined to fat but for his constant exercise in travelling on horseback. His complexion was sunburned and weather-beaten, but this only gave him 'a more manly aspect'. His voice was unusually powerful, enabling him to bellow orders to his troops at over 100 yards' distance. He ate frugally and simply, mainly rice pilaf and other plain food, never taking more than half an hour over a meal. If prevented by business from eating, he would eat a few dried peas he carried among his clothes, with some water. He always preferred to be travelling and in the field, resenting the time he had to spend in cities. Another contemporary wrote later that he had no fixed home to return to; his court was his camp, and his tent was his palace.[19] Nader spent the largest portion of his life on the move, in the saddle. Nothing is more expressive of his restless, relentless energy: perhaps his single most characteristic trait. When on campaign he ate, drank and slept like one of the ordinary soldiers, and expected his officers to do likewise. Sometimes, as when he made forced marches to catch the enemy by surprise, he would sleep in the open covered by a cloak, with a saddle for a pillow – even when there was a heavy frost on the ground.[20]

The Englishman also recorded that Nader was 'extremely addicted to women', but that he only ever went to his harem late in the evening, never during the day. Another Englishman, Jonas Hanway, wrote later more moderately that he 'was remarkable for his love of women',[21] meaning perhaps to echo the remarks he made elsewhere about Nader's generous treatment of women captives as much as to comment on his sexual appetite. As with his consumption of wine, many contemporaries praised Nader's sexual continence, tacitly contrasting his behaviour with that of Shah Soltan Hosein and Tahmasp, who neglected the business of government to pass days and weeks in the pursuit of pleasures. Nader may in fact have drunk excessively, such that he gave himself liver trouble, or at least exacerbated thereby an ailment that had other causes. But his contemporaries did not give him the character of a drunkard, because he drank discreetly and did not let his drinking interfere with official business. Similarly with his sex life – Nader did not retire to the harem during the day. There are indications from the latter part of his life, when Nader gave up his evening drinking parties and spent increasing amounts of time with his women when on the move and in camp, that he simply liked the company of women. Given the plots and betrayals of his latter years, and his difficulties with ambitious and arrogant male relatives and courtiers, that is perhaps understandable.

In Isfahan Nader's officials continually harassed the merchants, the English and Dutch trading posts, the Armenians, the Indian *banyan* merchants, the nobles and the ordinary citizens for money, using the bastinado to encourage those that were reluctant to pay. Prominent among these predatory officials was Mohammad Taqi Khan Shirazi, who was particularly valued by Nader for his subtlety in money matters. The Dutch regarded Taqi Khan as Nader's principal adviser at this time, and the two men were close companions both publicly and in Nader's private drinking parties.

Nader had the royal palaces ransacked for valuables and some were partially dismantled, with even doors and windows stored away for sale. In October he married off the last three of Shah Soltan Hosein's sisters to his supporters (one of them was married to his brother Ebrahim, marking his restoration to full favour), and ordered the rest of the Safavid royal family, the harem, the nobles of the court and servants to remove themselves to Qazvin. The infant Shah was to follow. All but 15 of the royal eunuchs were removed from their duties, with the suggestion that they should devote the rest of their lives to prayer.[22]

Isfahan's long history as the capital of the Safavid dynasty was over. After the devastation of the siege and the Afghan occupation, the removal of the court was the last blow, which prevented the city ever recovering its previous position. A large part of Isfahan's economic life had depended on the presence of the court, the nobility, the court officials, the harem and its women, the administration and its scribes and bureaucrats. For generations the merchants and artisans of the city had grown fat on the demand for necessities and luxuries that derived from its function as the capital. Under Nader that was all gone, replaced by never-ending and exorbitant demands for cash. No wonder that Nader was deeply unpopular with many in Isfahan, including the representative of the Dutch East India Company, van Leijpsigh, whose reports over the next seven years (drawing on his contacts in the city) were a catalogue of woes. He suggested to his masters in March 1733 that the Dutch trading post in Isfahan should be closed down, but he was kept there until he died in November 1739.[23]

Despite Nader's unpopularity with some, for others he appeared as a saviour, a military leader with the ability to defeat Persia's enemies and restore internal order. In these early years he acquired a reputation for justice that was widely held and reported on by a number of contemporaries. One recounted an incident from one of Nader's campaigns against the Ottoman Turks, when his advance guard of Qarachorlu Kurds ran into an unexpected cannonade from the Turkish artillery, which killed many. Nader sent reinforcements, but by the time they came up the original force, despite their losses, had all but overcome the Ottomans. The newcomers, who belonged to Nader's own Afshar tribe, fell to plundering what the Ottomans had left behind. This enraged the men of the original advance guard and their commander, who saw the spoils of their hard-won success falling into the hands of men who had not fought for it. The Kurds and Afshars came to blows, and several men were wounded before calm was restored. Nader ordered an investigation, and when he had established what had happened, praised the Kurds and their commander for their defeat of the Ottomans, and ordered several of the Afshars to be beaten. This action, rewarding bravery and forbearing to favour men of his own tribe unfairly, showed Nader's commitment to firm and impartial justice.[24]

Another account, from the Greek Basile Vatatzes, illustrates the way that Nader's reputation for severe but fair judgement had spread among ordinary people. While in Mashhad, Vatatzes saw some children playing by a small stream. The children had an argument about the rules of the game, became angry, and one of them cursed another and hit him. The one who had been hit shouted, 'How dare you curse me and hit me? Do you not know that Tahmasp Qoli Khan is in Mashhad?' The eyewitness, who met Nader himself, said this incident was indicative of the general view of Nader shared by most of the population; that he 'had a great ability to judge with care and intelligently, and to trace with accuracy the truth, and to judge without any prejudice the richest, the poorest and the weakest alike':

> To such an extent was his reputation for justice known,
> that not only did the powerful culprits become afraid and
> ceased their injustices, but also the weakest held him as
> their champion, as he allowed them to live without fear
> and in safety through his safe judgments.[25]

Allowing for a degree of hyperbole, fair administration of justice was the prime attribute expected of a good leader: all the more so of a monarch.

On 19 October 1732 Nader marched out of Isfahan with a small force on a punitive expedition against the Bakhtiari tribe, who had murdered the governor Nader had appointed over them. The guilty tribesmen retreated to a mountain fortress in their home territory in the Zagros range, south-west of Isfahan, but after 21 days came out fighting desperately, only to die at the hands of Nader's troops. Nader gave orders that 3,000 families of the Bakhtiari should resettle in Khorasan. A further punitive action was carried out against the small Zand tribe, who had been raiding and plundering in the area south of Kermanshah since the time of the Afghan invasion. Their punishment was more severe, and was never forgotten; 500 or more heads of families were put to the sword, and their wives and children were sold as slaves.

Continuing westward, Nader joined up with the main body of his army at Ottoman-held Kermanshah,* which opened to the Persians after a short resistance. He marched out of Kermanshah on 10 December with around 80,000 men, heading for the Ottoman frontier and his promised rendezvous with Ahmad Pasha in Baghdad – his first venture beyond the traditional borders of Persia.[26]

In doing so Nader was attempting something rather different from his earlier campaign against the Ottomans, in which he had regained Persian territory straightforwardly by attacking the Ottoman forces that were occupying it. This time his intention was to force the Ottomans to restore the Persian territories in Azerbaijan and north of the Araxes by attacking them further south, and threatening Baghdad. If he were successful, he could trade Baghdad for the Persian territories the Ottomans had occupied; or the fall of Baghdad might precipitate a wider collapse in Ottoman power, permitting more extensive gains. At any rate he could hope to avoid a difficult campaign in the mountainous and thickly wooded territories of the Caucasus. It was an ambitious plan, but Nader had a larger army than he had ever commanded before, with an unblemished record of victory; and the performance of the Ottoman troops against him had not, up to then, been impressive.

The Ottomans were prepared for Nader's invasion, and had reinforced their posts in the border mountains, at Zohab and elsewhere. Looking at the lie of the land around the strongpoint at Zohab, and disregarding the protests of local guides who declared what he intended to be impossible, Nader led his men through hills and valleys full of snow, along a mountain path 'as narrow as the heart of a miser', where the Persians went at first on horseback, then on foot, and finally clinging to the rocks. Most of his men fell behind in these difficult conditions,

* The Ottomans had evacuated Hamadan in accordance with their treaty with Tahmasp, but not Kermanshah.

but after the long, arduous march he emerged behind the defences of Zohab with 600 men. Without waiting for the stragglers, Nader attacked immediately while it was still dark, and the Ottomans awoke to the drumming hooves of the Persian horses. Taken completely by surprise, they fled. Many were killed, and their commander was captured. Nader gave orders for new fortifications at Zohab, and marched on into the plain, where more troops met him from Hamadan.[27]

Knowing that a siege of Baghdad would be lengthy and difficult, Nader tried to draw Ahmad Pasha out of the city by moving on Kirkuk and plundering the area round about, but Ahmad Pasha did not respond. Nader left 7,000 men to besiege Kirkuk, and marched south again, defeating more Ottomans as he neared Baghdad, and establishing the Persians' dominance in the region around the city. Nader set about encircling Baghdad with his forces, with the aim of imposing a blockade that would either force a battle or starve the defenders into submission.

Ahmad Pasha was an energetic and resourceful character, who regarded Baghdad more as his personal possession than a passing appointment. He was determined to resist Nader at every point. He tried to prevent Nader completing this ring of steel round his city by opposing him at river crossings, and fortified the western bank of the Tigris opposite Nader's camp with artillery. Nader decided to outflank this obstacle. Moving at night to conceal his intentions, he crossed the Tigris further upstream with the help of a German engineer[28] who rapidly constructed a bridge for the troops made out of the long trunks of local palm trees, resting on inflated animal skins.

Nader crossed the great river with an advance guard of 2,500 picked men on 15 February 1733 and moved south with them. But Teutonic design was not equal to the weight of Persian horses. 1,500 more Persians crossed the next day; but then the bridge collapsed and was swept away. Nader's advance was slowed by poor roads and difficult terrain, which enabled enemy scouts to warn that he had crossed the river. The Ottomans set up opposite the Persian camp withdrew, but when Ahmad Pasha heard that the failure of the bridge had left Nader stranded with relatively few troops, he assembled a much stronger force (including cavalry, artillery and janissary infantry)[29] and sent them out against him.

Nader ordered forward bodies of Kurds, Turkmen and Abdali Afghans against the advancing Ottomans in succession. The Kurds and Turkmen were forced back, but the Afghans held, and when a dust cloud appeared to the north, signifying the arrival of the 1,500-strong

second force of Persians, Nader renewed his attacks on the flanks of
the Ottoman column (which may have been impeded by the terrain
from bringing its superior numbers to bear). At length the Ottomans
escaped in disorder, abandoning their artillery and many dead.[30] Nader
executed some of the Kurds and Turkmen that had turned aside from
the battle, and rewarded the Afghans.

Having come through this dangerous moment, Nader was now free
to proceed with the blockade without further interference. He pressed
the siege right up to the walls of Baghdad, and built a great ring of 2,700
towers around the city, each within musket-shot of the next, to enforce
the blockade. Boats crewed by Persian soldiers patrolled the rivers,
and a huge camp was built upstream of Baghdad around two large
forts on either side of the Tigris, with shops and comfortable quarters
for the soldiers and their women. It was estimated that there were
300,000 people in the Persian siege lines around Baghdad at this time,
but only a third of these were soldiers. The remainder were servants,
traders, artisans of various kinds, and slaves. Of the soldiers, 80,000
were cavalry, and 20,000 were foot soldiers. But Nader did not have
enough of the heavy cannon needed to breach the thick walls of the city,
and one account says that when he tried, Ottoman cannon returned
fire with such intensity that the Persian battery was forced to pull back
out of range.[31] Without a breach, Nader could not attempt an assault.
He had to rely instead on hunger to force the defenders to submit. His
men took possession of Samarra, Najaf, Karbala, Hilla and other towns
around Baghdad. More troops were sent against Basra, on the Persian
Gulf to the south, supported by Arab tribesmen who were rebelling
against the Ottomans.

The Persians celebrated Nowruz in their camp north of Baghdad on
21st March with great magnificence. Seven thousand robes of honour
were issued to the officers of the army, and those lucky enough to be
invited to the grand banquet were given silver vases, each filled with
a pound of gold. There were no such jollifications in Baghdad. As the
weeks passed, the situation in the city became more desperate, and the
people (many of whom were Shi'as sympathetic to the Persians) more
restive. Food was short. People ate horses, asses, cats, dogs and even
mice, and many were dying of hunger and disease. Some escaped to
the Persians; others killed themselves.

It was later estimated that 60,000 people died in Baghdad during
the siege.[32] The citizens saw the Persians living comfortably in a camp
that looked worryingly permanent, and large bodies of troops arriving

regularly to reinforce the Persian army. In fact, this was an illusion. Nader had devised a stratagem to dismay the Ottoman garrison, whereby he secretly sent large bodies of men out of the siege lines by night, for them to march back from a different direction the next day, in full view, with banners flying and trumpets blaring. Nader was partial to watermelons and did his best always to have a good supply sent to him, wherever his campaigns took him. He derisively sent some cartloads of these watermelons into the city for Ahmad Pasha, to assuage his hunger; the Ottoman governor in return sent back some fine loaves of bread, with a message that these were the daily food of the people in the city.[33]

Despite this bravado, the Ottoman garrison were at the end of their resistance, and on 13 July Ahmad Pasha opened negotiations for the surrender of Baghdad, on the basis that he would give up the city on 11 August if no relief had arrived by then. But the drawn-out game was not yet over. Only a few days later the Ottoman garrison got word that the former grand vizier, Topal Osman Pasha, had been made *Serasker* or supreme commander of the Ottoman forces, and was advancing to the relief of Baghdad with 80,000 men and 60 cannon. These troops were not the low-grade provincial forces, militia and tribesmen that Nader had been fighting up to that point. They were drawn from the main strike force of the Ottoman state, including janissaries and cavalrymen normally based in Istanbul.

The Ottomans regarded Topal Osman as their empire's greatest soldier. He was an old man in 1733. He had led a long and adventurous life, and had at one time been a prisoner of the Knights of St John in Malta. Sultan Mahmud had made him Grand Vizier after the revolt of September 1730, but he fell into disfavour for returning Tabriz to the Persians under the treaty that followed the battle of Kurijan and in March 1732 the Sultan removed Topal Osman from office. But the latest crisis had forced the Sultan to call upon him again.

Topal Osman passed Kirkuk and advanced toward Baghdad along the banks of the Tigris. His servants carried him in a litter because of the infirmity caused by the many wounds he bore from his campaigns, and a French physician attended him.* Nader sent a defiant message urging him on to fight, but Topal Osman put the messenger under guard, continued his advance, and did not reply, grimly telling his companions that he would take his answer in person.[34]

---

* This was Jean Nicodeme, who gave an eyewitness account of the battle for Baghdad.

When the Ottoman army reached Samarra, Nader began to detach troops from the siege lines around Baghdad surreptitiously, by night, to avoid Ahmad Pasha realising that they were on the move. Nader had a difficult choice to make. Baghdad was close to surrender. If he removed all his men from the siege lines, supplies might get through that would permit the city to hold out for several months more, and the garrison might attack his rear when he gave battle against Topal Osman's army. On the other hand, leaving men to guard Baghdad would divide his forces, and might rob him of the vital extra reserve he needed to defeat Topal Osman. If Nader's main force were beaten, Baghdad would be lost anyway.

All his experience encouraged Nader to believe in the superiority of his Persian troops, and perhaps he could not bear, after so many months, to abandon the siege completely. He left a minimum force of 12,000 men under Mohammad Khan Baluch to keep up the siege, while the main army advanced to meet Topal Osman.[35] Nader joined them at the last minute, to face the Ottomans some way north of the city with about 70,000 men.

Dawn on 19 July promised searing heat by the time the sun reached its zenith. As his troops fell into their battle order, Nader would have sniffed the wind confidently, looking forward to a day of victory, and a victory that would bring him great rewards; the keys of Baghdad, restitution of Persian lands in the Caucasus, possibly even the collapse of Ottoman power across the whole eastern part of their empire.

But this time Nader was opposed by an experienced commander, equal to him in cunning. Topal Osman had positioned his men to take advantage of the uneven ground on the bank of the Tigris, with the river behind them and the wind too, so that the dust and smoke of battle would be blown in the Persians' faces. He encouraged his men by spreading rumours that food and reinforcements were about to arrive. On the morning of battle Topal Osman waved away his litter, mounted a horse despite his old wounds, and inspected his troops 'like a young man, sabre in hand, with eyes and face radiant'.[36]

Topal Osman had deliberately kept the advance guard and the rearguard of the Ottoman army weak, to tempt the Persians to attack them; but he strengthened them overnight. Early in the morning of 19 July Nader ordered his large vanguard of cavalry to make a move round the Ottoman left flank, but the Persians found much stronger forces to oppose them than they had expected, and were beaten off by cannon fire. Rather than attempt another stratagem after this setback, Nader took forward the main body of his army, about 50,000 men, in a frontal assault. These included his infantry, Persians and Afghans in three divisions, who after a sharp struggle forced the troops of the Ottoman centre to retire, pushing them back as far as the tents of their camp. The Persians captured a number of cannon, and the Turks seemed to be wavering when 2,000 of their Kurdish troops fled; but then Topal Osman brought forward the 20,000 men of his reserve, recapturing the guns.[37] As the fighting went on toward midday, rolling savagely backward and forward, the heat became intense and the northerly wind blew dense clouds of dust in the Persians' faces.

Fighting like this bore little relation to the orderly rectangles and fronts in the diagrams drawn by military historians. Each man fought in his own narrow world of confusion, smoke, dust and fear, with little idea of anything more than a few yards away, and little sense of anything beyond survival and keeping faith with his closest comrades. The Turks could draw water from the river behind them but the Persians had no relief for their thirst. According to some accounts the Arab tribesmen in Nader's army changed sides and attacked one wing of the Persian cavalry. Nader's horse was shot from under him in the thick of the fighting, and he quickly mounted another. The struggle was fierce:

> The Turks, seeing him pass like a salamander through
> fire, shot at him from all sides; but their shots (deflected
> by Providence) could not touch him.[38]

The Persians were wavering, and Nader rode up and down through the struggling men, encouraging them to one last effort. One authority says that in battle he was always quick to see the balance of advantage on either side, and to send reinforcements where they were needed; but if one of his commanders gave ground unnecessarily, he would ride up, kill him with a blow of the battle-axe he always carried, and reassign command to the next officer in rank.[39]

The crucial moment came when, in the thick of the fighting, Nader wounded a Turk with his lance, and the man fell along with his horse. But Nader's own horse shied, fell on its head and threw him. Before Nader could remount, the Persians, already weakened by heat, thirst and fatigue, believing their commander had been killed, panicked. In many battles the deciding moment arrived in this way: the pressure built up over a long period of minutes and hours, men saw men killed, confusion and disorientation spread, but they continued to fight on until some incident, or the rumour of an incident, broke the psychological tension. One group of men would surge back away from the enemy: others around them, seeing this, would panic in turn. After nine hours of fighting the Persian army began to fall back, and no threats or exhortations would stop them. Nader was forced to order a withdrawal to Bohriz, leaving his artillery and baggage behind.* The Ottomans followed them for five hours before calling off the pursuit. Many Persians were killed as, disregarding danger in their desperate thirst, they tried to get a drink of water at the banks of the Tigris.

Nader may have lost as many as 30,000 men killed in this hard-fought battle. The Ottomans massacred 500 Persian prisoners in cold blood, and 3,000 more were taken into captivity.[40] Even the Ottoman victors lost 20,000 men. As the main Persian army pulled back in disorder, Ahmad Pasha's garrison attacked the Persians that had been left to guard the siege lines. Their commander, Mohammad Khan Baluch, got away with some horsemen, but most of the foot soldiers were either killed or captured before they could escape. Few of the camp followers would have got away either. The starving citizens of Baghdad seized with joy the provisions abandoned in large quantities by the Persians in the towers and camps.

Topal Osman's army entered the city in triumph on 24 July, but he was forced to withdraw most of his men to Kirkuk within a few days, because the city and surrounding area had been left so poor and devastated that they were incapable of supporting such a large number of men and animals. Ahmad Pasha's men, picking over the battlefield, cut the heads off the dead bodies of the Persians, threw the bodies in the Tigris, and piled the heads in heaps as ugly memorials to the Ottoman victory.[41]

It was a catastrophe, wiping out the previous successes of the campaign in Ottoman Iraq. Nader's men paid the price for his overconfidence in dividing his forces before the battle, and in attacking Topal Osman's army frontally on unfavourable ground. Caught between Baghdad and the advancing Ottoman army, his position had been awkward. His men had fought hard in appalling conditions, but the bloody day showed that his new Persian army was not invincible,

---

* The captured artillery included four 30–pounders, six 15–pounders, eight 9–pounders and 500 *zanburak* camel guns. The Persians also buried some cannon. (Perhaps some of them still lie there, awaiting discovery along with more recent weapons of mass destruction – eyewitness account of Jean Nicodeme, in von Hammer, p. 523.)

as previously its soldiers might have thought after their remarkable run of successes. The defeat before Baghdad was the worst setback of Nader's military career up to that point, but what was to follow was even more extraordinary.

CHAPTER SIX
Nader Shah

Nader's first thought after the crushing defeat outside Baghdad was for the morale and loyalty of his surviving troops, many of whom had lost all their possessions and weapons. Having reached a safe distance from the Ottomans, retreating past Bohriz toward the traditional Persian border, he halted and spoke to his officers. He told them that the soldiers had fought well. Their defeat had been out of their hands, being the will of Providence. He admitted that he had made mistakes:

> He made his own and that of the army one common
> cause; and by reminding them of their valour on so many
> occasions, he assured them they should have such an op-

137

portunity of revenging themselves, as should entirely ef-
face the remembrance of an accident, for which they were
in no way to blame. Thus he ingratiated himself with the
common soldiers, as well as the officers, in such a manner, that he kept the army in good spirits, and without
the least reluctance to try their fortune in another battle.[1]

For that was his intention: to return to fight Topal Osman again, and
defeat him quickly, before the repercussions of the defeat at Baghdad
could spread. It was a dangerous moment. The momentum of his
previous successes had faltered, and his enemies within Persia had an
opportunity to take back the initiative. But in this crisis Nader showed
no hesitation, just a burning drive to regain supremacy. Whatever his
plans for war in Ottoman Iraq previously, he now needed a victory over
Topal Osman just to stay in power.

Nader gave instructions for a complete refit of the army, and for the
governors of Loristan, Kermanshah and Hamadan to supply everything
necessary – horses, draught animals, tents and so on. He sent orders to
the governors of Khorasan, Herat, Sistan, Fars and Kuhgelu to send
reinforcements. The men who had just returned from Ottoman Iraq
were allowed to go home, but were ordered to return to the colours in
Hamadan in two months' time. Cannon were to be replaced at a higher
standard than previously, and there were to be more of them. Each
soldier was to have his losses made up to double the value of what had
gone, whether it be horses, camels, armour, tents or other goods.[2]

This episode gives an idea of why the soldiers apparently spoke
of Nader using the nickname *baba bozorg* ('big daddy').[3] There is no
evidence that there were any signs of dissent or mutiny. Indeed there
appear to have been no mutinies in the army at any time in Nader's
career (except at the very end, in extreme circumstances), despite
many hardships and setbacks: a testament to his understanding of and
attention to the needs of his soldiers, the discipline he maintained, and
the loyalty with which they repaid him.

But the measures taken to supply these needs at such short notice, in
high summer, imposed great suffering on the inhabitants of the western
provinces of Persia. Already, before Nader's defeat in July 1733, people
were running away from towns and villages to seek refuge in the
hills rather than receive new tax demands and the beatings that often
accompanied them. Now the pressure intensified. On one occasion some
officials drew his attention to the poverty of the people in one village

and said they would not be able to pay what had been demanded from them. Nader said, 'If they are not able to pay I want you to get it from them willy nilly. If not, I'll send 500 horsemen to sell them with their wives and children to get my money.' He justified this to one courtier as follows:

> How is it that they talk so much about me, for I have not
> come to leave the country in peace and quiet, but to turn
> everything upside down, since I am not a human being,
> but I am God's wrath and punishment.[4]

Nader arrived in Hamadan on 4 August, reviewed the troops and supervised the preparations. He distributed 200,000 tomans to the men for their expenses – an enormous amount.* By the end of September all was ready, and the army was reassembled. On 2 October 1733 they marched out of Hamadan again, heading for Kirkuk.

Meanwhile Topal Osman Pasha had been begging the Ottoman court in Istanbul to send him the reinforcements he needed to bring his forces back up to strength. He had also been asking them in vain for provisions and other supplies, and that they replace him with a younger man, because his health was failing. His army had been badly beaten up in the battle with the Persians, and Topal Osman was aware of Nader's preparations to renew the struggle. But in Istanbul they were blasé: the Ottoman armies had won a glorious victory over the heretical Persians, and had relieved Baghdad. Some of the troops that defeated Nader at Baghdad may have returned to Istanbul.[5] The Sultan heaped Topal Osman and his family with honours (which he did not want). From Istanbul all seemed well on the eastern frontier, and little was done to strengthen the battered Ottoman army in Kirkuk.

As Nader crossed back over the Ottoman border, he was given bad news about a revolt in the south of Persia. Mohammad Khan Baluch, the governor of Kuhgilu, had commanded the troops left behind to guard the siege lines outside Baghdad when Nader had gone to attack the army of Topal Osman. But returning to his province after the battle, he had taken advantage of the confusion and uncertainty after the defeat to revolt against Nader. In doing so he had joined forces with the Sunni Arab tribesmen of Sheykh Ahmad Madani, who had already been in revolt for some time, in the area south and west of Lar.[6] Mohammad

---

* Equivalent to about £375,000 sterling at that time.

Khan's rebellion exploited pro-Safavid feeling after the deposition of Tahmasp, and dissent among Arab tribesmen and others in the south-west, exacerbated by the heavy tax demands. His union with Sheykh Madani meant that a large area of the Persian Gulf coast from its northern tip to the island of Qeys was in revolt.

There were rumours flying at this time that Tahmasp had escaped, and was recruiting troops in Khorasan; or that if the army were successful against the Ottomans, Nader had said he would restore Tahmasp. It is possible that Nader made some kind of promise along the latter lines to assuage pro-Safavid feeling in the army, and that Tahmasp was briefly moved out of Khorasan; but if so, Nader soon changed his mind, and had him taken to Mazanderan.[7] It may have been around this time that Nader's own mother spoke to him about Tahmasp, at the prompting of others:

> [She] intreated Nadir Shah, some Time after he had
> seized the King, to restore him, not doubting but his
> Majesty would make him sufficient Amends, by creating
> him Generalissimo for Life. He ask'd her 'whether she
> really thought so?' She told him, 'She did.' Upon which
> he smil'd and said, 'If I was an old Woman, perhaps I
> might be inclined to think so too,' and desired her to give
> herself no Trouble about State Affairs.[8]

It is perhaps significant that people who feared to approach Nader directly might try to do so through his mother. It suggests that Nader's respect and consideration for his mother were well known. Nader was close to all his family, and his relationship with his mother, drawing its strength from the hardships shared and overcome in his childhood, was particularly strong. But no-one, not even his mother, was allowed to presume upon private affection to try to influence his public policy.

Poised to descend into Ottoman Iraq, Nader decided he would leave his provincial governors to deal with Mohammad Khan Baluch's revolt for the time being. It was a difficult and risky decision, to attack the Ottomans again while a serious revolt festered in his home territories, but he must have reasoned that the danger of the revolt spreading was best averted by a prestigious victory over the Ottomans. It was a bold move; another man would have tackled the lesser enemy first, securing his rear before attacking Topal Osman again. Nader marched on into Ottoman Iraq. On 24 October elements of both armies skirmished with each other south of Kirkuk, at Leilan. The outcome was indecisive, and Topal Osman's men withdrew within the walls of Kirkuk. Nader, trying as usual to draw the Ottoman army out for a decisive battle, marched round to the north-east, against the fortress of Surdash, which he captured. Shortly afterward, his scouts told him that 12,000 Ottomans were marching toward him through the Aq Darband valley.

Nader manoeuvred his men into a strong position above the Ottoman troops in the valley, and sent a group of several thousand jazayerchi infantry* to cover the line of the Turks' retreat. That done, on 9 November he led his men into the attack. Shortly after the two bodies of troops engaged, Topal Osman marched out with the main Ottoman army in support. The Ottoman Turks numbered perhaps 100,000 men in total; but their losses in July had been made up with troops of inferior quality from Syria and elsewhere. Nader's army would again have been a little smaller.

The two armies kept up a furious duel of musketry on each other for two hours, in which the heavy calibre weapons used by both Turks and Persians would, at close range, have torn terrible wounds in the bodies of the soldiers. Then the Persians charged forward, keen to avenge their defeat earlier in the year, and broke into the Ottoman centre. Topal Osman left the litter in which he had been carried and mounted a horse to steady his troops, but a flank attack by Nader's Abdalis threw the Ottomans into disarray. At this point Topal Osman was hit by two musket balls and fell dead from his horse. The Turks ran, abandoning their artillery, their camp and its contents.

A man named Allah Yar cut off Topal Osman's head and took it to Nader on a lance point. The jazayerchis poured heavy fire into the fugitives from their prepared positions, and Nader sent his Afghans after the Arab tribesmen that had betrayed the Persians in July, killing many of them. The Ottomans lost perhaps 20,000 men killed and taken prisoner. Having ordered that Topal Osman's body be found and brought to him, Nader mused over the great soldier's remains for some time before sending them to the Ottomans in Baghdad for burial.[9]

After the battle, Nader made arrangements for the blockade of Baghdad to be resumed, and for the towns around to be occupied as before. He intended then to take his main army north to eject the

* These were veteran infantry, armed with an unusually heavy calibre musket (jazayer or jezzail) and often mounted on horses when on the march. Nader used them for specially dangerous or crucial tasks, and sometimes led them in battle himself.

Ottomans from Tabriz, but the Turkish garrison withdrew before he could get there, and another force of Persians marched in to secure the city. Despite increasingly serious reports about the progress of Mohammad Khan Baluch's rebellion, Nader returned to Baghdad, and before long Ahmad Pasha sent word that he wanted to negotiate. On 19 December 1733 the two men agreed a treaty whereby the Ottomans would restore all territory occupied since 1722, both sides would return all captives and cannon, and provision would be made for the correct treatment of Persian pilgrims visiting holy places in Ottoman Iraq.

But the truth was that Nader had been forced to raise the siege of Baghdad prematurely, by the need to march east to deal with the rebellion that was spreading through Khuzestan and Fars. Once again revolt robbed him of the full benefits of his success in battle. Ahmad Pasha told his superiors in Istanbul that but for the treaty he could not have withstood the Persian siege more than a month – Nader himself had told the Russians that his hopes were high, because the Ottoman commander and a number of others had sent their families out of the city.[10] The treaty yielded little benefit to the Persians. Ahmad Pasha sent orders for Ganja, Tiflis, Yerevan and Shirvan to be evacuated,[11] but Istanbul countermanded them. Instead of ratifying the treaty the Ottoman government appointed a new Serasker,* Abdollah Koprulu, and sent reinforcements to him at his base in Diarbekir in eastern Anatolia.

Before leaving Ottoman Iraq to deal with the revolt, Nader briefly visited the Shi'a shrines at Najaf and Karbala, and then rode rapidly south-east. He joined forces with Tahmasp Khan Jalayer and the new governor of Kuhgilu along the way. Mohammad Khan Baluch was camped in the Shulestan valley, north-west of Shiraz, and was aware of the approach of the two governors, but did not know that Nader was with them. One account says the sound of Nader's thundering voice giving orders for the attack was enough on its own to demoralise the rebels. Many of them fled rather than face Nader's charge, and the rebel army fell apart.[12] Mohammad Khan tried desperately to ride at Nader with a few companions, and kill him with his lance, but failed. He fought his way out, and escaped with 300 men.

Mohammad Khan Baluch fled first to Shiraz, then to the coast, and escaped to the island of Qeys. But eventually he was captured there and brought back in chains to Isfahan. He was blinded, and died of the treatment shortly afterwards.[13] Sheykh Ahmad Madani was also

* Commander-in-chief.

captured, and executed. Nader gave orders for punitive actions against the Arabs of Khuzestan and along the coast of the Persian Gulf; all the areas that had supported the revolt. As usual, large numbers of the rebels were resettled in Khorasan.

Nader went to Shiraz, where he celebrated Nowruz in March 1734. While there he appointed his friend and adviser Taqi Khan as governor of Shiraz and the province of Fars. Nader and Taqi Khan had a strange relationship, difficult to characterise. They were very different. As a city-dweller, a fixer and a financial juggler, not a warrior, Taqi Khan was far removed from the kind of men Nader normally favoured. But it seems that one of his prime talents was the ability to make Nader laugh. Later, in 1736, the Dutch in Isfahan referred to Taqi Khan in a report home as Nader's buffoon or jester.[14] Taqi Khan's skill in financial matters emerged later in the reformed tax assessments, pioneered in the province of Fars, that Nader instituted from 1736 onwards. Nader normally avoided appointing governors that were natives of the provinces or towns they were to govern. Taqi Khan's appointment to his home province was a sign of special favour and affection; but in the long run it was to show the unwisdom of departing from Nader's usual practice.

After Nowruz Nader went to Isfahan, arriving at the end of April to magnificent celebrations, music and fireworks that lasted several days.[15] On the way to Isfahan Nader had received word by courier that at Nowruz Reza Qoli's wife, Fatima Begum, had given birth to a son. This boy, Nader's first grandson, was named Shahrokh. Timur's son had been given the same name, and this was the first overt sign of Nader's wish to portray himself publicly as a conqueror on the scale of Timur.

As was the custom, one of Nader's officials* opened the Qur'an to divine the destiny of his new grandson, and the book fell open at the following lines from the Surah of Joseph: 'Thus we established Joseph in the land, and taught him to interpret dreams. God has power over all things, though most men may not know it.'[16]

Nader was given a copy of the text and put it away carefully. Had he been given a less vague prophecy, one closer to the truth, he would have been more worried for his grandson's future.

More than 60 years later, in 1796, Agha Mohammad Shah† arrived

---

* The official was Mirza Mahdi Astarabadi, who recorded the prophecy in his history (vol. 1, p. 191). Mohammad Kazem, whose account is often more fanciful, says that astrologers at the time of Shahrokh's birth accurately predicted his blinding, and Nader asked who was going to do it, so that he could kill them (pp. 238–9).

in Mashhad, ending the rule of Nader's grandson Shahrokh there and imprisoning him. The Shah, vicious and vindictive, with an obsession for jewels, had the old, blind man tortured to reveal the hiding places of the last gems he had inherited from his grandfather, but for some time Shahrokh would not tell. Stricken with grief for their former master, some of Shahrokh's attendants sent a respected mullah of the city to plead with Agha Mohammad Shah on his behalf. They sent a message with the mullah, saying that the helpless old man had nothing and that, had there been anything left of the jewels and money, and had he been reluctant to give them up, to obtain his deliverance they themselves would have revealed the treasure.

The mullah later reported that he went to see the Shah in the evening. On opening a curtain he entered the room where the Shah was and saw that a cloth had been spread on the floor. In the middle of the cloth lay heaped up a large number of mounted and unmounted gems, which competed in brilliance with the flames in the stove. Seated at the edge of the cloth the Shah had collected a few large rubies by his side and was busy examining them in the candlelight. The mullah sat down next to the Shah. Despite the poor light in the room, the Shah spotted a small ruby ring on the holy man's finger. He asked 'What is your ring?' The mullah replied, 'A little ruby of no worth.' He took it off and gave it to the Shah to inspect. Like a professional gem-dealer the Shah compared the ring with his rubies one by one and remarked, 'Your stone well merits being a touchstone and evaluator of other gems of the same colour.' It occurred to the mullah that this comment was made to prompt him to make a gift of the ring, but instead he conveyed to the Shah the message from Shahrokh's people. The Shah asked him what he thought of the message: were they speaking the truth? The mullah answered that he had no evidence to the contrary. Agha Mohammad replied, pointing to the gems on the cloth – 'What evidence is clearer than these? Today this lot have been brought to light and tonight the rest will be revealed.'

His message having been superseded by events, the mullah was dejected. He sat silently as if he had forgotten the ring, but the Shah,

† Agha Mohammad Shah was a Qajar, and had eventually come to power in the long civil wars that followed Nader's death. He hated the Afsharids; as a boy he had been castrated by Nader's nephew, Ali Qoli (who had also blinded Shahrokh after Nader's death). When Agha Mohammad Shah took the throne he had Nader's remains exhumed and reburied under the steps of his palace in Tehran (along with those of some of his other least favourite people), so that he could tread on them every time he entered or left.

thinking he was waiting for a decision about it, took a poker from the stove, skilfully removed the small ruby stone from its mount and threw it onto his heap of gems. He handed the ring back and said the mullah should find a cornelian of good hue and fit that into the ring instead, adding, 'A cornelian ring is more appropriate for you.' This remark was the mullah's dismissal. The next day he heard that Shahrokh had broken completely, telling the torturers where the remaining jewels were, to the very last item.[17]

Another account says the last gem Shahrokh gave up (after having had boiling lead poured on his head) was a large ruby that Agha Mohammad Shah had long coveted, which had once decorated the crown of the great Moghul Emperor Aurangzeb.[18] Shahrokh was sent to Mazanderan with his family but died on the way of the injuries inflicted by his torturers, at Damghan. Such was the ultimate fate of the little boy born in Mashhad at Nowruz in 1734.

Having defeated his external and internal enemies, Topal Osman and Mohammad Khan Baluch, Nader had restored his prestige and stabilised his position, both strategically, and politically within Persia. Now it was time to clear the remaining Ottoman forces from Persian territory for good. In Isfahan an envoy arrived from the Ottoman Sultan, with the message that Abdollah Koprulu, the new Serasker, had full authority to make peace with Persia. Nader treated this overture with scorn, and sent Abdollah Koprulu a message insisting on the restitution of the provinces north of the Araxes.

Nader also received a mission from the Russian court, under Prince Golitsin, whose object was to get Nader to renew the Turkish war, using promises to evacuate the Russian forts still lingering on the Caspian littoral as an inducement. Nader was suspicious, and unwilling to be used as a cat's-paw by the Russians. He intended to attack the Ottomans anyway. He may have become more sceptical when he heard that the Russians had sent Vakhtang of Georgia to Darband, with instructions to conquer Shamakhi and Tiflis for Russia.

Nonetheless, the uneasy informal alliance with the Russians continued, and Golitsin accompanied Nader when he left Isfahan on 14 June, heading north-west. Arriving in Ardabil on 10 August,[19] he was handed a further message from Abdollah Koprulu, suggesting that the restitution of the Caucasus territories be deferred for two years, which Nader took as final proof that the Ottomans would not keep the terms of the peace he had made with Ahmad Pasha the previous December.

The war must be renewed; he would have to attempt a campaign in the difficult territory of the Caucasus, something he had so far avoided. He resolved to march first on Shamakhi, held for the Ottomans by Sorkhai, Khan of Shirvan.

Nader sent ahead a message to Sorkhai, reminding him of Ahmad Pasha's order that Shamakhi be evacuated. Sorkhai responded defiantly – 'I conquered Shirvan with the scimitars of my warlike Lazgi lions – by what right does Ahmad of Baghdad meddle in what concerns me?'[20] but as Nader approached, Sorkhai pulled back northward into the hills of Daghestan. The Persians occupied Shamakhi, and on 15 September Nader set off again for Sorkhai's stronghold of Qumuq, with half the army (about 12,000 men). A second column, under Tahmasp Khan Jalayer, headed in a more easterly direction, and encountered Sorkhai at Deve Batan.

In addition to Ottoman troops, Sorkhai's army also included some Tartars from the Crimea, whose long march to Daghestan round the northern and eastern coast of the Black Sea at the orders of their overlords in Istanbul had severely strained the peace between the Ottoman Empire and Russia. Tahmasp Khan attacked his enemies boldly, defeated them and took Sorkhai's newly built fortress of Khachmaz.[21] Nader caught up with Sorkhai a little later, and defeated him a second time. Sorkhai fled further north, into Avaria, and Nader took Qumuq. Meanwhile, the attention of the Ottomans had been diverted by the Georgian King Taimuraz of Kakheti, who had revolted against the Ottomans in support of the Persians. Nader decided it was too late in the season to campaign in the mountain snows of Avaria, and took his men south to besiege Ganja, where he arrived on 3 November 1734.

In Ganja, Prince Golitsin gave Nader some welcome news. Nader's success so far had impressed the Russians, who were edging closer to war with the Ottoman Empire on their own account. The Russian government now formally notified Nader that their troops would evacuate Persian territory, asking only for a continuation of the alliance against the Ottomans in return. In October the Russian commander in the Caspian region,[22] Levashov, was ordered to evacuate all his outlying positions and withdraw to Darband, preparatory to a total withdrawal. In these circumstances, any pretence that the Russians would or could help Vakhtang of Georgia recover that province became absurd, and he retired to Astrakhan.

The siege of Ganja went forward in fits and starts, but Nader pursued it more aggressively than he had the siege of Baghdad. The

Ottoman garrison withdrew to the citadel, and Nader moved guns up
to bombard the walls, setting them up on the roof of a mosque in the
town – but the Turks flattened the mosque with their own guns before
the Persian cannonade could make much impression. As at Baghdad,
the Ottoman siege artillery outgunned the Persian; by numbers, weight
of shot or range, or all three.

The Persians dug several mines, with the aim of placing charges of
gunpowder at the ends of the galleries, under the walls of the citadel.
But the defenders discovered some of the workings, and dug their own
counter-mines. When the opposing miners met underground, there
was confused, murderous fighting with daggers, tools and whatever
else came to hand. The Persians succeeded in exploding six of their
mines together, killing 700 Turks, but they were still unable to make a
successful assault on the walls, and a Turkish counter-mine killed 30 or
40 Persians.[23]

Nader himself, determined as ever to oversee the work, however
dangerous, had several narrow escapes: on one occasion a mortar
shell fell in the middle of his entourage while he was resting in one of
the mosques of the town, and killed one of his guards. Another time
a cannon ball took off the head of a man next to him, spattering his
coat with blood and brains. Nader's master of artillery was killed by a
mortar bomb. Seeing Nader's men in difficulties, the Russians sent an
officer of engineers and four gunners in Persian dress to assist, with
some heavy siege guns.

Baghdad was a major regional city: it was not surprising that the
Persians might have had difficulty besieging it, and be reduced to
starving the garrison into surrender. But Ganja was an altogether smaller
place, and the failure of Persian siege technique was more glaring:
particularly when highlighted by the necessity of accepting Russian
help. In Europe at this time a sophisticated science of siege warfare had
developed, codified by the great French engineer and military architect
Vauban. The Ottomans too had been acknowledged masters of siege
warfare for centuries, and had trained engineers and large quantities of
big siege guns at their disposal.

Nader had equipped a large army with gunpowder weapons for
the first time in Persia, and had trained them to use muskets and
light artillery to devastating effect on the battlefield. That was a great
achievement, but with the men, the materials, the money and the
discipline it had been a relatively straightforward matter. To build up
an efficient siege capability was altogether more difficult, and Nader

had barely begun the process. To manufacture the siege cannon was just the first step. To move the heavy siege guns to where they were needed in a huge country where most goods were transported on the backs of mules or camels was an almost insuperable problem. In Europe they were moved by water wherever possible, along navigable rivers, and later in his career Nader tried to do the same, but there were not enough big rivers, and very few at all on the central Iranian plateau. A decade later, by the mid-1740s, Nader put together a respectable train of siege artillery. But he always had problems with siege warfare, not least because the sedentary, slow, patient style of successful siege fighting did not suit his restless temperament.

Despite the Russian help, the siege of Ganja dragged on, and once again, as at Baghdad, Nader decided that the town would only fall by blockade. Leaving sufficient men for that purpose, and seeing that Abdollah Koprulu was reluctant to emerge from his base at Qars, Nader went to Tiflis, setting up a blockade of the Ottoman garrison there with the ready help of the Georgians.

Satisfied with the way the war was going, at Nowruz (21 March 1735) the Russians signed a treaty with Nader at Ganja by which the Persian/Russian frontier was established at the river Sulaq, and all Russian troops were to be gone from Persian territory within two months. The parties agreed a perpetual alliance, and each undertook not to make a separate peace with Ottoman Turkey without the consent of the other. The Russians had lost an estimated 130,000 men in Persia since 1722, mainly to malaria and other sickness in the hot and humid climate of Gilan, and were not reluctant to be gone. Since the death of Peter the Great, the impetus for Russian imperialist expansion had disappeared, replaced by the less ambitious concern to protect the Caspian region from the Ottomans. With Nader now in the ascendant, the Russians could be confident on that point. Had matters turned out differently, they might have been happy to see Vakhtang of Georgia set himself up in the Caucasus as a Russian surrogate; but they had sent no additional troops to the region to support such a bid. They were quite content to let Nader fight their battles for them in the Caucasus instead.

Having agreed the treaty of Ganja, Nader renewed his efforts to bring Abdollah Koprulu and his army to battle, sending troops to trail their coats before Qars. The hills were still thick with snow and movement was difficult. On one occasion the Persians had to use their swords to cut their way through a ravine full of drifted snow. There were skirmishes, but the main Ottoman army would not come out to fight.[24] Abdollah Koprulu was plainly unwilling to risk the defeat that Topal Osman and other Ottoman commanders had suffered, but it is not clear what his plan was. He may have been expecting reinforcements. At length Nader withdrew.

At Aparan Nader met the head of the Armenian church, the Catholicos Abraham of Crete. In the subservient position the Armenians found themselves in at this time, caught between the Persians and the Ottomans, treated as second-class citizens by both and with no political power of their own, the Catholicos served as the leading representative and advocate for his people, as well as religious patriarch. He saw a lot of Nader in the next few months and later wrote a valuable account of his impressions, which opens a window of almost modern reportage into a short but important episode of Nader's life. Tellingly, one of his first observations was that Nader insisted on speed and urgency in everything he did:

> I appeared before him and welcomed him. He said,
> 'Welcome caliph! How are you? Are you well? Get on
> a horse caliph, we are moving forward!'* Right then
> he mounted his horse and left with his entourage. His
> army followed him. He gave me soldiers from among his
> bodyguard and I followed them...[25]

After a few days, Nader told the Catholicos to return to Echmiadzin, the monastery that served as the seat of the patriarch and the centre of Armenian Christianity, a little to the west of Yerevan. Nader went to visit the Catholicos there, arriving outside the monastery on Monday 13 June 1735. But at this point a misunderstanding blew up between them that could have derailed the whole relationship at the outset. The Catholicos failed to meet Nader when he arrived, sending his deputy instead, a day later. Nader took this as an insult. The deputy returned to the patriarch, grief-stricken, perplexed and deathly pale, saying that Nader had been angry and had demanded why the Catholicos had not come in person to greet him.

Realising his error, the Catholicos was seized with terror and despair. Aside from the danger he believed he had exposed himself to personally, the success of this visit was important for the Armenian people as a whole. He prostrated himself on the floor of the cathedral in

---

* *De atlan khalifay, kedek ileri.*

prayer, and entrusted his fate to God. Then, 'with a sinking heart and at death's door' he went to Nader's camp. Nader asked him why he had not come before, and the patriarch 'shaking and tearful' pleaded ignorance of Persian court customs, saying that if anyone were to be executed in punishment, it should be him alone. Nader turned angrily to his chief secretary, Mirza Mahdi* and said, 'Why didn't you tell the caliph? He is a foreigner and does not know our ways' Fortunately, Nader had already decided that he would forgive the Catholicos. He calmed down and said, 'The caliph speaks honestly, he does not know the custom of our land. We shall, therefore, honour him with a khal'at.'[26]

The khal'at Nader gave to the Catholicos Abraham was a velvet mantle embroidered with gold and trimmed with fur. More importantly, Nader granted the Catholicos *raqams* (writs or royal orders) confirming him as patriarch and putting Echmiadzin under his protection. Mirza Mahdi was there to note down the content of the documents that he and his staff would have to write out. The Catholicos later described Mirza Mahdi as a 'wise, humble, polite, attentive, and respectable man'.[27]

At the same audience Nader decreed that Armenians who converted to Islam would lose their inheritance. This might appear a harsh measure, but the purpose was to relieve the Armenians, by reversing the oppressive practice under Shah Soltan Hosein and earlier monarchs according to which converts had appropriated all the inheritances of their Armenian relatives (which had been a powerful incentive to embrace Islam, and had been used to oppress the Armenians). Nader had taken a liking to the Catholicos, but he must have decided before he visited Echmiadzin that he would lighten the burdens of the Armenians and make their lives more predictable, as a matter of policy. Securing the goodwill of the large and prosperous Armenian nation was an important part of Nader's emerging policy of cementing his political position by drawing support from non-Shi'a elements in Persia.

After this first audience Nader allowed the Catholicos to return to the monastery and make preparations. Later the same day, Nader went there himself, accompanied by a great procession, with chasubles, banners, candles and other impressive flummeries. The Catholicos took him on a tour of the cathedral, explaining the significance of various features. Nader asked about the paintings, and the construction of the building.

---

* This was Mirza Mahdi Astarabadi, Nader's chief secretary (*Monshi ol-Mamalek*); later his official historian. Nader called the Catholicos 'caliph' (as was customary) by analogy with the traditional head of the (Sunni) Muslim faith. They spoke in Turkish.

He then took a seat, and commanded that the service should begin. It was vespers. He stayed through the service with approval, and afterwards allowed his female relatives and the women of his harem to visit.

The next morning he came at dawn and again passed some time in the church, explaining the building to his companions as the Catholicos had told him, eating sweets, drinking sherbet and smoking a water-pipe. When he left, he summoned the Catholicos, thanked him and said, 'Don't worry, don't be sad and don't be scared, this house is ours* and you are a venerable old man. Your house will be bountiful [which means something like "may you be healthy and may your house be plentiful"].' He told the Catholicos that he would compensate him for the fodder his horses had eaten, then whipped up his horse and rode off to set up a new camp, a little further away.[28]

After this interlude at Echmiadzin, Nader moved his army to Ottoman-held Yerevan, putting that city under blockade too. Nader was working on the principle that if Ganja, Tiflis and Yerevan all threatened to fall into his hands like ripe apples, the Ottoman Serasker would be forced to leave Qars and attempt to intervene.[29] Before long word finally came that Abdollah Koprulu was marching toward Yerevan with 50,000 cavalry, 30,000 janissaries and 40 cannon, and had crossed the Arpa Chay river.† According to the Catholicos Abraham, Nader said, 'Thank God, I have been waiting for this for a long time.'[30] He marched rapidly with his advance guard of 15,000 or 18,000 picked troops to intercept the Ottomans, the main army of 40,000 Persians following up behind. Koprulu had camped with his army near Baghavard,‡ north of Yerevan.

On Sunday 19 June the Ottomans, alerted to the presence of Nader and his advance guard, and being superior in numbers, advanced to the attack. In words reminiscent of the Dauphin in Shakespeare's Henry V, one of the Ottoman cavalry commanders had boasted the night before, 'Where can the Persians hide from my cavalry, which will trample them?'[31] But Koprulu was not a commander of the calibre of Topal Osman, and Nader had learned some of the dead Serasker's tricks.

The fighting began at two o'clock in the afternoon. Nader posted some men in ambush (in a wood and a valley), and charged down on the Ottomans with only 3,000 men§ from the hill on which the Persians

---

* i.e. under Nader's protection. The parenthesis is the Catholicos' own explanation.
† Today the Akhuryan river, the border between Turkey and Armenia.
‡ Known by the Armenians as Eghvard, and by others as Murad-Tappa.
§ Three units of 1,000, each under a min-bashi or commander of a thousand.

had camped overnight, tempting the Ottomans to think this small force was all they had to deal with. With these troops engaged, Nader led a group of his tough, reliable jazayerchis (perhaps 2,000–3,000 men) to capture some Ottoman artillery that Abdollah Pasha had deployed on a small hill. Surprised by this bold move, the Ottomans on the hill were overrun. The cannon were of totemic as well as practical significance in the Ottoman armies and their loss caused dismay. At the same time another group of Persians moved against the other main concentration of artillery, on the Turkish left wing, and the centres of the two armies engaged. With the Turkish artillery neutralised or distracted, the Persian cannon, supported by 500 or more zanburaks, delivered a punishing fire into the Turkish centre, which fell into disorder and began to retreat. Nader chose this moment for the remaining Persian cavalry, as well as the troops in ambush, to attack and turn the retreat into headlong flight. Nader pursued, cutting down the fleeing Turks with a force of 1,000 light cavalry.

In flight, Abdollah Pasha Koprulu was followed by a Persian called Rostam, who grabbed the Serasker's reins as he tried to descend a rocky path into a steep river valley. In the struggle, Koprulu fell from his horse and wounded his head against a stone. Rostam dismounted, beheaded him and took the head to Nader. Several other senior Turkish commanders were killed, and the fleeing Ottomans were pursued and hunted down for several miles, all the way back to the Arpa Chay river. The local Armenians joined in, blocking the escape of the Ottomans and enabling the Persians to catch up.

Some contemporaries put the total number of Turks killed or captured at 40,000–50,000. This may be exaggerated, but Nader himself reported that the Persians 'cut all the janissaries to pieces, so that not one soul of them escaped' as well as 'a great number' of the Ottoman cavalry, and that, 'by the Grace of the Most High, Almost their whole Army is kill'd.' The Catholicos Abraham, who was also present, wrote that he saw thousands of bodies strewn over the countryside; and that many wounded fugitives sought refuge at Echmiadzin the next day. The Catholicos ordered that the Greeks and Armenians among them be looked after by the monks. Some of them died, but most eventually recovered and moved on. The Muslims among them were sent on to the Ottoman garrison in Yerevan by night.[32] The Persians, whose own losses were negligible, captured 32 cannon as well as the usual large quantities of baggage, valuables and animals. Nader had the bodies of the Turkish commanders reunited with their heads and sent them to the Ottoman garrisons in Qars and Yerevan for burial.

Writing to Prince Golitsin afterwards (Golitsin had left for Darband shortly before, on his way back to St Petersburg) Nader himself said, 'Since I began to make War, I never was so fortunate.'[33] But his skill, and the Ottomans' ineptitude, had been at least as important as luck. He had defeated the Ottomans with a much smaller force: it seems the main Persian army never made contact. The numbers of the Ottoman army were as much an impediment as a strength (Koprulu succeeded in bringing only a relatively small proportion of his own army to bear). Their unwieldy bodies of troops were slow to manoeuvre and the small, trained, cohesive bands of Persians always had the initiative. Once again, the key had been firepower. The Catholicos wrote afterwards that the Ottoman guns had fired only two or three times, but the Persian cannon* had fired 300 balls or more. Nader had achieved superiority in artillery by his pre-emptive action against the Turkish cannon; enabling him thereafter to gun down the Ottomans with his own artillery and zanburaks without opposition.[†]

Nader owed his success to the toughness and bravery of his troops, but also to the care with which he had equipped and trained them. Shortly afterwards the Catholicos Abraham praised their hardiness – they could gallop all day, and cover rocky mountain slopes 'like a partridge'. They did not know tiredness, and never grumbled. They would break rocks to make a track, dig earth and snow, and then meet the enemy bravely, give battle and be victorious. They carried large guns, and each man had two powder-flasks to make sure they did not run short. Many of them wore armour – some chain mail, others just a plate on back and breast, others four plates, with one under each arm in addition.[‡] There were constant strict drills for both cavalry and infantry, and if a man killed his horse by riding it too hard, he would immediately be given a replacement without quibble.[34]

The battle of Baghavard was decisive, transforming the situation in the Caucasus. Nader afterwards ordered that a monument be erected

---

* Not including the zanburaks.

† The zanburaks were an effective weapon in large numbers because their bigger calibre enabled them to shoot up the enemy with impunity, from beyond normal musket range. They were highly mobile, and could cope with rough roads and tracks on campaign that would have halted or disabled heavier cannon. But in battle the camels made a large target and were vulnerable to cannon-fire, if the enemy artillery had not been put out of action first.

‡ The traditional 'char aine' (four mirrors) armour.

on top of the hill on which the Persians had camped the night before the battle, in the shape of the tent in which he had slept. In Istanbul another grand vizier fell from office when the news of the disaster became known. With all hope of relief gone, the Ottoman garrison of Ganja surrendered on 9 July, and that of Tiflis on 12 August. Nader installed governors in each city, and later visited Tiflis in person. Yerevan continued to hold out, but Nader laid siege to Qars, cutting off the town's water supply and intensifying pressure on the Ottoman government to make peace.

In addition to producing these effects, Nader's victory at Baghavard also neutralised a serious additional threat; the arrival of over 50,000 Crimean Tartars in Daghestan under the Tartar Khan of the Crimea. It had perhaps been the expectation of these troops that had encouraged Koprulu to play a waiting game in the spring campaign. Their march also served to precipitate war between the Ottomans and Russia. The Russians strongly resented the movement of the Tartars through what they regarded as their territory on the northern and eastern shores of the Black Sea. A Russian force raided into the Crimea, and a larger army invaded Ottoman territory in the spring of 1736 and took Azov.

In his negotiations with the Ottomans, Nader initially insisted that they cede Qars, but agreed eventually to trade Qars for Yerevan, which surrendered to the Persians on 3 October 1735. Anxious to placate Nader and under pressure from the Russians, the Ottomans also agreed to order the Tartar Khan to withdraw. Nader made a show of moving into Daghestan to attack the Tartars, ejecting en route a detachment of Lazgis who had fortified themselves on the frozen summit of one of the highest mountains,[35] but the Tartar descendants of the Mongol Golden Horde showed no fight, and began their long return journey home before Nader got close. They had achieved little by their round trip of over 1,500 miles.

Nader had achieved a decisive victory over the Ottomans in the Caucasus in the summer of 1735, but it seems that another enemy that summer inflicted a small, but damaging wound. It is likely that Nader was bitten by a malarial mosquito around this time. Initially he would have disguised the effects of the illness, but its effects began to be noticed within a few years.

Despite the arrival of severe winter weather and the difficulty of movement through the mountain snows, Nader continued his campaign to subdue the Lazgis, exploiting the momentum of his successes and the demoralisation of his enemies. He pursued Sorkhai and his tribesmen, using his Afghans and jazayerchis as assault troops to throw the Lazgis out of one mountain redoubt after another. Finally, in January 1736 he defeated Sorkhai in the Ghazi Qumuq valley, and the leader of the Lazgis fled again into Avaria. The other Lazgi chiefs gave up the fight, one of them (Ahmad Khan) sending Nader two of his daughters and his son as a gesture of submission.[36] But Sorkhai was still at large. Nader never quite succeeded in crushing the resistance of the Lazgis completely: there was always a loose thread left. From the hills of Daghestan Nader set out for the Moghan plain.

By the end of 1735 Nader had triumphantly overcome the effects of his defeat outside Baghdad in the summer of 1733, and had completed the reconquest of western and north-western Persia. As his historian later put it, he had 'taken the keys of victory from the hands of his enemies, and had pulled the Persians from under the heavy foot of shame and slavery'.[37] He had quelled the rebellion of Mohammad Khan Baluch, and had restored the borders of Persia to their position prior to the Afghan rebellions and invasions, with the exception of Kandahar. His supremacy, if not his legitimacy, was undisputed within those borders, and his army was feared throughout the region. Now was the time to reach for the position of supreme majesty that corresponded with his achievements. But as usual, Nader approached his goal indirectly.

In the summer of 1735 Nader had sent raqams all over Persia, telling nobles, senior clerics and officials to prepare themselves to travel to a great assembly in Tabriz or Qazvin, once Yerevan had been restored to Persian rule. The assembly was to discuss and decide upon a regular form of government for the country, something Nader claimed he had been prevented from doing up to then by the necessity of recovering the lost provinces. Later on he sent more precise orders, stipulating just who should attend, and the location: the Moghan plain.[38] Divided today between Iran and Azerbaijan, the Moghan is a huge expanse of flat, lush grassland:

> If one puts an apple on the ground, it can be seen from
> far away, for there is not a single stone or even evidence
> of stone, on this flat plain. However, plenty of grass and
> rush grows on it and it is full of wild fowl and boars,
> which, like sheep, move in herds.[39]

Nader chose the Moghan for the space, for the fresh water, and for the grass, which would provide fodder for the large numbers of horses and other animals that would accompany the delegates to the assembly. But the Moghan was short of shelter for the human visitors; as many as 20,000 were expected. Nader ordered the building of 12,000 huts made of reeds. Some of the more important buildings (including a palace, with courts and *iwans*)* were made of wood. There were also mosques, rest houses, baths and a bazaar, everything necessary for the function of a small city. The site was near Javad, with the Araxes to the south and the Kura to the north, just to the west of the confluence of the two rivers. Two temporary bridges were built, one above (on the Araxes) and one below the confluence. The army camped separately, around the bridge on the Araxes. The bridge below the confluence, to the east, had artillery forts at either end to protect against raiders.[40] Nader was taking no chances.

The assembly was called a *qoroltai* – a Mongol term. Its use was another attempt by Nader to connect himself and his rule with earlier conquerors in Asia – Genghis Khan and Timur. Genghis Khan had used the qoroltai to demonstrate his power over his nobles, and to make a show of their consent, but there was no real participation. The qoroltai had been for acclamation, not election.[41] Nader's qoroltai on the Moghan was to prove similar. The most detailed and vivid account of it comes from the Catholicos Abraham.

Anxious not to risk another lapse of etiquette, the Catholicos arrived at the Moghan early for the qoroltai, on 14 January 1736, and celebrated the Armenian Christmas there.† But after the Christmas ceremonies snow began to fall, it became very cold and the reed shelters proved inadequate. The Patriarch went to ask the *nasaqchi-bashi* (the chief of Nader's military police, who was in charge of the preparations) for permission to withdraw somewhere more comfortable until Nader arrived. Everyone was nervous that Nader would react badly if the people he had called to the qoroltai were not there when he arrived. The *nasaqchi-bashi* was worried in addition that he would be found at fault for not providing adequate accommodation. But he gave the Catholicos permission to withdraw, saying that he should not be forced to stay, because he was old and ill. When Nader came the Catholicos would return, and would not be punished – 'for the Khan loves him and therefore will not harm him in any way'.[42]

---

* The *iwan* had been one of the main characteristic features of Persian architecture since the time of the Sassanids. It was a large arched portico, closed at the back and open at the front.

† On the feast of the Epiphany, 17 January New Style, 6 January Old Style.

The hapless Patriarch had no sooner left than he had to return to the camp, because Nader himself arrived on 22 January. The Catholicos hurried back, and went to see Nader on the morning of 24 January, but he need not have worried this time. Of all the notables presented that morning, he was given precedence. Nader was pleased with the gifts he brought, and glad to see the Catholicos. He said, 'Welcome caliph! How are you? Do you feel well? Are you sound and healthy? Did you meet with any injuries on your journey due to the winter and snow? You are after all an old man. Have you been here long?' Thinking quickly, the Catholicos decided not to mention his brief departure, and replied, 'My Khan, may Allah grant you a long life. Now that I have seen your perpetually mighty and blessed face, the winter has turned into spring. Thank God that I see your majesty unharmed, healthy, and bright.' Nader laughed and told the *nasaqchi-bashi* to find him good lodgings, saying, 'Take care of him, for he is a venerable old man.'[43]

The impression is that Nader knew exactly what had been going on. He wanted his subordinates to know he was aware of the comings and goings, and the doubts about the quality of the lodgings. Later on, Nader asked the Catholicos some questions about the conduct of the officials in charge in Yerevan, and about the ploughing and sowing. The Catholicos knew, or found out later, that Nader had already sent an official into the villages in secret, to look into preparations for next year's crops.

The Patriarch was unsure whether Nader was testing his truthfulness, or whether he was genuinely concerned about the land, the Armenian peasants and the prospects for the harvest (there was a shortage of seed and animals for ploughing). But he gave truthful answers, and Nader reassured him, saying, 'Don't worry, I know that is so. God is kind and you shall not have any need.'[44] He then allowed the Catholicos to go back to his lodging, and the following day had a lamb sent him to eat, as a present. A few days later he sent the Catholicos two magnificent vestments, embroidered with scenes from the life of Christ. They had probably been looted in Georgia.

This brief section of reportage shows how different was the nature of Nader's administration to the lax style that had been normal under Shah Soltan Hosein and Tahmasp. Nader was renowned for his memory, and his attention to detail. It was said that he knew the names of all the officers in his army down to the lowest level, and many of the ordinary soldiers too, along with details of their service and pay. If they complained to him about their pay, he would make calculations with the prayer beads he carried, and would usually be able to catch them out if they tried to deceive him. He kept spies in every city, and appointed an official to shadow the governor in every town and province, to keep track of the governor's actions and report back. These officials were expected to be particularly attentive to money matters, and any signs of disloyalty. But the purpose of this administrative efficiency was aimed less at the well-being and prosperity of the country than at the single, narrow goal of supplying the necessary revenue to keep the army paid on time. Whatever the suffering of the people, the soldiers were always paid on time.[45]

The Catholicos' account gives another example of Nader's implacable attention to detail in his administration, and shows the abuses that his subjects could suffer from local officials. While at the qoroltai, the Catholicos made a complaint against Mirza Razi, the revenue collector* of the province of Nakhichevan, who had put Armenian villages there under duress (in one village a man had been killed with an axe) and had taken bribes from them. He had also allowed one of his servants to abduct, forcibly convert to Islam and marry a Christian girl, against the wishes of her father.

Mirza Razi, the servant and the girl were all at the qoroltai, and the father had followed them there to seek redress. They all went before Nader to argue their case, and the Catholicos made his accusation against Mirza Razi. Nader immediately ordered the tax collector to be beaten, and six men hit him savagely with sticks, from his neck to his feet. He tried to speak up in his defence, but in vain. Nader ordered them to give Mirza Razi the bastinado (*falake*), and accordingly they began to beat the soles of his feet. Appalled at the man's suffering, the Catholicos regretted making the complaint. He began to implore Nader to stop the beating, not in words, but by meekly raising his hands, shedding tears with a bent head.

Seeing that the Catholicos wanted the beating to stop but feared to ask it, Nader ordered the thugs to cease. They dragged Mirza Razi before him. He told him to make an account of the bribes he had taken, and return with it. Nader also ordered that the abducted girl be delivered up to the Catholicos. The latter took no chances. He made the man who had forcibly married her sign and seal a divorce decree before witnesses, and got Nader's secretaries to write a raqam saying that the girl was to remain a Christian and should marry a Christian, and that

* *Zabet.*

the abductor should not be allowed to bring litigation over the case. Then he gave the girl and the raqam to the father, and she was rushed off to marry 'some young man'. No one seems to have asked the girl herself what she wanted.

The Catholicos went back to Mirza Razi, who had been wrapped in a sheepskin to ease his pain, and helped him draw up his account. When it was delivered to Nader he spotted a discrepancy, and gave the man three days to yield up the full sum. Only then was Mirza Razi forgiven, but he lost all his appointments, and would have lost his life but for the intervention of the Catholicos.[46] Beatings of this kind at Nader's court were routine, particularly over tax matters.

Over the following days a stream of grandees from all over the realm arrived at the camp in the Moghan, including Nader's brother Ebrahim, Tahmasp Khan Jalayer from Mashhad, Pir Mohammad Khan from Herat, and Taqi Khan Shirazi. Each day all the leading notables, the provincial governors, the city officials, the army officers, nobles, tribal chiefs and mullahs would get up at sunrise and go to the audience hall.* Nader would appear two or three hours later, there would be prayers, and then his guard of 3,000 jazayerchis would march into the fenced area around his quarters, lining up in close order, two or three ranks deep, each holding a huge jazayer musket ornamented with gold and silver bands.

As if the silent jazayerchis were not intimidating enough, there were normally 300 *nasaqchis* present, 300 *chandavols*,† 300 *khanzadegan*,‡ and a number of *keshikchis*.§ Once all the guards and troops were settled in their ranks, everyone would file past Nader in strict protocol order. After this, the gathering might be entertained by wrestlers, or fighting camels, and would then disperse. Nader would retire to relax and drink wine with his closest companions, including Tahmasp Khan Jalayer, Hasan Ali Khan of Isfahan and Mirza Zaki. These men, along with Nader's brother Ebrahim, had advised Nader on the conduct of the qoroltai. Hasan Ali Khan and Mirza Zaki had advised him earlier too, before the deposition of Tahmasp.

---

* *Divankhane.*

† Men of the rearguard, who carried silver axes and served inter alia as executioners.

‡ Sons of khans; they administered beatings on the spot when ordered by Nader.

§ Watch-guard or sentinels; several thousand strong and armed with muskets, they guarded Nader's quarters day and night in shifts.

As the days went on, Nader had a number of private meetings with other delegates in the evenings, to ply them with wine, assess their views and shape them to his plans – rather different from Nader's usual drinking parties, including khans that were not normally part of his inner circle.[47] When they went away, spies followed them in the darkness to listen outside their tents to what they said.

After a few days a huge tent 220 feet long or more arrived from Qazvin. Nader's servants erected it in the fenced area set aside for him and his immediate court. It was reddish-purple in colour, supported on 20 columns, each of which had a silver ball at the top, the size of a watermelon.[48] On 14 February, to celebrate the end of the month of Ramadan, everyone went to a special audience in the great tent, with sherbet, singing, music and dancing. Nader sat on a costly carpet that had been specially ordered from Isfahan, worked with gold and pearls from Bahrain in the Persian Gulf.[49] This was not just idle show. The display and the ceremony served to impress and cow the delegates to the qoroltai in advance of the serious business, reminding them that Nader was Shah already in all but name.

The next day, instead of the usual audience, the assembly were invited to a field at some distance from Nader's quarters. Seven of Nader's closest advisers, including Tahmasp Khan Jalayer and Mirza Mahdi, had the nasaqchis bring groups of the delegates to them in succession. Each group was told that Nader wanted them to confer among themselves and decide who they wanted to rule the country. They said Nader had, with the help of God, rid the country of its enemies. The land was now pacified, but he himself was tired, and wished for nothing but to retire to Kalat in Khorasan. The delegates should choose one of the Safavid princes,* or some other, great and virtuous, for their sovereign.† The seven told them to confer and give their answer later in the day.[50]

There had been rumours before the qoroltai that a restoration of Safavid rule might be in the wind.[51] It may be that some less astute delegates at the assembly, some of those traditionalists who still wanted a return to the old dynasty, felt a brief thrill at Nader's message, and began to wonder which among the available Safavid princes might be the one to choose. But many, after the horrors and disasters of the Afghan invasions, saw Nader as a saviour, a strong man who despite, or

---

* Some of the Safavid princes, descendants in the female line, had been called to the qoroltai (Floor, *Nader Shah*).

† The obvious answer, that Persia already had a Shah (the young Abbas III), was plainly unsayable.

perhaps because of the harshness of his rule, was the obvious choice.

For all that it had not yet been offered, there was really only one choice on offer. Once again, it was political theatre, and the tent, the fierce jazayerchis, the prayers and the speeches, were the backdrop, the painted scenery. Except – the jazayerchis, the nasaqchis and the other thugs were real. The words were false, but the long muskets, sabres, axes and cudgels were not props. Nader had not wasted the first three weeks of the qoroltai. He had carefully prepared what was to follow, not just with his inner circle, but also with many of the most important among the other delegates. He must have been enjoying himself enormously.

For fear of being thought reluctant, some of the notables hurried to give their answers before the appointed time. The seven went diligently through all the groups of delegates, carefully taking their replies. It took a while, and they were still moving through the delegates after sunset. But the replies made little demand on the memory – they were all the same. As one, the delegates declared they would have no other Shah but Nader. They were told to disperse.

It may have been at this point that one of Nader's spies overheard the chief mullah, Mirza Abol-Hasan, through the side of a tent, saying that despite what was being said in the assembly everyone was still for the Safavids; and foretelling evil for any family that should usurp their throne. Nader had the chief mullah brought to him the next day with a rope round his neck, and had him strangled.[52] Had any of the delegates still been in any doubt about the true purpose of the qoroltai, this must have removed it.

The next day the notables appeared at Nader's quarters, and were escorted out into the open plain again, where they divided into smaller groups as before, and sat on the grass. After a while they were called together in a great circle, and the seven, standing in the middle, gave them another message from Nader. This told them that since the assembly would not let him retire, he would have to make three conditions for his continued rule.

The first condition was that they would not support a son or other relative of the former Shah should such a figure appear at some future date as a rival for the throne. The second was that the Persians should refrain from cursing Omar and Osman, and from beating themselves to draw blood at the Ashura festival.* The division between Sunni and

---

* The commemoration of the martyrdom of Hosein each year, in the mourning month of Moharram.

Shi'a, inflamed by the first Safavid monarch, Shah Esmail, had caused much bloodshed between Persia and Ottoman Turkey. The Persians should accept Sunni religious practices, and take the Emam Ja'far (the sixth Emam) as the symbolic head of their sect. Thirdly, they must agree to obey Nader's relatives and children after his death, to commit no treason against them, and accept their succession. This last condition showed that Nader was not taking power just as a dictator for life; he was founding a dynasty. His family were to become the centre of the state. The Safavids were not merely being sidelined for a while; they were finished. The delegates were told to consider these conditions, and were again dismissed for the day.[53]

On 17 February the delegates assembled again at the *divankhane* and the ceremonial audience went ahead as on earlier days. Then Nader invited the most senior notables to lunch with him. As they ate he repeated his various reasons for refusing the crown, and asked them to elect someone else, so that he could retire to Khorasan. The khans insisted he become Shah; begging, imploring and flattering him. Nader said that despite what they said, he knew that many of the khans were dissatisfied with him – rightly, because he had robbed many of their gold and silver. He had killed and destroyed. He had turned many places into ruins, and had terrorised and ravaged the land. He said these evils should end, and the people should be free from oppression in future:

> The khans responded by saying, 'That which you state is
> true, but it was necessary to do so to achieve your lofty
> position and to command the troops. If you were not
> so steadfast in all things, how could you accomplish so
> many great deeds? We, therefore, ask you once more, to
> do as you have done, for God has given you the power
> to rule over the land. Everyone is indebted to you and
> shall obey your every command. Those who dare to defy
> you deserve to be judged and condemned. Let those who
> obey your orders be honoured and given khal'ats. For
> otherwise it will not be possible to rule the country.'[54]

This was the decisive moment. Nader approved the truth of what they had said, and agreed to accept the royal jiqe. It was a great moment for him – a characteristic moment, in which again his enemies found they had no option but to insist on giving him, as if of their own free will, the prize he wanted but had never openly asked for. But there were also many, probably a majority, who were genuinely enthusiastic; who were delighted with Nader's stunning victories over Persia's enemies, who saw opportunities for themselves under his regime, and for whom it was plain that he was the best possible choice for Shah, as well as the only choice. Among those present there was at least one who felt the full gravity of what had happened. The Catholicos Abraham wrote later: 'I whispered the prayer, "Father, I have sinned." Then they let us go to our quarters.'[55]

An agreement was drawn up, setting out the conditions, and it took three days for all the delegates to sign and seal it. The daily audiences continued as before. On 21 February Nader called the Catholicos to him, along with the officials entrusted with governing the province of Yerevan. He told them to look after the Catholicos, his people and the monastery of Echmiadzin, saying that they were under his protection. The Catholicos was a good, honourable, loyal man: they must respect him and take his advice. Nader did not want to hear any complaints from him about them.

Nader liked the old priest, perhaps for his honesty, emotional piety and simplicity. In this Nader showed a different side to his own character, which but for the Catholicos' account, we might not have seen. Whatever the state of his own soul, he could still recognise virtue in others, and apply the charm he had used to beguile Baba Ali Khan and Tahmasp.

After the signature of the agreement, Nader distributed gifts. He gave each of the senior delegates a khal'at, graded in value according to the significance of his office or position. The outfit he gave the Catholicos included a heavy coat of gold cloth, and a fine black kerchief for his head. Nader had given some thought to this, for when he next saw the Catholicos:

> [he] smiled and said to his grandees, 'I doubted whether the caliph would tie the kerchief to his head, for he never removes his black cowl from his head.' When he saw that I had tied the kerchief to my cowl he was very pleased and said, 'How beautiful! How it suits the black on the head.'[56]

The religious conditions were an important part of the compact between Nader and the delegates at the qoroltai. The implications of the demands Nader made went deep – deeper than was immediately apparent. It was explicit from the start that Nader was determined to confront the religious support the Safavid dynasty had enjoyed from Shi'a Islam, and enforce an end to important Shi'a religious practices. His regime was to bring a clean sweep of both dynastic and religious traditions. The realignment of Persia toward Sunni Islam would have significant implications outside Persia too, and Nader intended the acceptance of the religious conditions at the qoroltai as a demonstration for the benefit of the Ottoman ambassador, Ganj Ali Pasha. This became clear a little later, when Nader had the delegates approve a series of further conditions, this time for a peace treaty with the Ottomans as follows:

> 1) The Persians, having given up their former beliefs and chosen the Sunni religion, should be recognised as a fifth sect,* the Ja'fari;
> 2) Since each of the Emams of the four existing sects had a column in the Ka'ba assigned to them, a fifth column should be provided for the Emam Ja'far;
> 3) A Persian Amir ol-Hajj (leader of the pilgrimage) with a position equivalent to that of the Amirs of the Syrian and Egyptian pilgrims, should be appointed, and allowed to conduct the Persian pilgrims to Mecca;
> 4) Prisoners on both sides would be exchanged, and none of them should be bought or sold;
> 5) Each country should send an ambassador to the court of the other, to regulate the affairs of the two empires, and to cement the peace between them.[57]

Because Ganj Ali Pasha had no authority from his masters to negotiate any agreements beyond recognition of the traditional borders between the two states, he suggested that Nader send an envoy to Istanbul to present these new proposals. Nader agreed, and Ganj Ali Pasha returned to his capital on 6 March, accompanied by a group of Persians nominated for the negotiations, including the new chief mullah. Nader seems to have decided that the main business of the gathering was over – his son Reza Qoli was also allowed to leave, to take up new

---

* Sunni Islam recognised four sects (mazhabs): the Shafi'i, Hanifi, Maliki and the Hanbali, named after four principal early interpreters of doctrine.

responsibilities as the governor of Khorasan, as was the Catholicos Abraham.[58] Among other new appointments, Nader's brother Ebrahim was put in overall charge of the reconquered territories of Azerbaijan, and Mirza Mahdi was made Nader's official historian. The coronation took place on 8 March 1736, on the day and at the time the astrologers had chosen as the most propitious.[59]

On the day of the coronation Nader received the remaining delegates in the usual way. He sat flanked by his brother Ebrahim, his younger son Mortaza Qoli, his nephew Ali Qoli, Tahmasp Khan Jalayer, Mirza Zaki and his other companions. Mirza Zaki took up a large golden crown shaped like a helmet, studded with jewels and pearls, and placed it on Nader's head. Then there were prayers, and after that servants brought rosewater and sherbet in golden cups and vessels on golden trays. Finally the notables prostrated themselves before the new Shah in the traditional way. Most of them left, and young girls and boys performed music, singing and dancing. After half an hour the remainder of the guests departed, and two hours after that Nader, perhaps embarrassed by its magnificence, took the crown off and replaced it with his usual four-pointed hat, bound with a white shawl. Drums and trumpets played non-stop for three days.[60] Typically, the ceremony had been businesslike rather than sumptuous. Rumours circulated that the young Shah Abbas had been murdered, but in fact he was sent to join his father Tahmasp in custody in Khorasan.[61]

There was no precedent for the religious measures Nader inaugurated with his coronation.[62] They were as revolutionary as they were unexpected. Faced with the problem of legitimacy posed by his supplanting the Safavid dynasty, Nader boldly overturned the conventions of legitimacy themselves, by outlawing important elements of the Shi'ism that the Safavids had introduced, and which had at one time been their prime support. The strangling of the chief mullah was not just the removal of a dissident – there must have been others that Nader could have executed had he so wished. The killing of the leading cleric in Persia marked a break with the old order, standing out the more starkly by the absence of other bloodshed at the qoroltai.

The religious conditions for Nader's accession and the death of the old chief mullah showed that Nader was not prepared to compete with the Safavids for the approval of Persia's Shi'a population. He was their master, not their supplicant. Instead he relied on his army, which was increasingly recruited from Sunni Afghans, Kurds, Turkmen, Baluchis and others (who naturally were gratified by the new religious policy), and on the legitimacy accorded to successful military leaders, whose victories were traditionally held to show the favour of God.[63] Once again, as at the deposition of Tahmasp, Nader had achieved an elegant political triumph, almost without violence. But this time, having ruled the country for several years already as regent, he did not need to canvass support or issue manifestos. He was in control; his position was unassailable.

Despite the more autocratic style of Nader's conduct at the Moghan, his religious policy gave pious Shi'as within Persia an escape route. Ja'far was after all an important Shi'a Emam. The Persians were not simply ordered to adopt Sunnism as practised elsewhere in the Muslim world; they were to retain their own discrete religious identity. Internally, Nader banned certain Shi'a practices; the more extreme ones, typical of the early Safavid period. He issued instructions to the ulema that the Emam Ali should be venerated as before, but that the formula naming him as the deputy of God should no longer be spoken, because it had caused enmity between Shi'as and Sunnis.[64] Externally, he presented the policy as a wholesale conversion to Sunnism. There was a difference. Within Shi'ism there was a doctrine well adapted to this kind of situation – *taqiye* or ritual dissimulation. *Taqiye* had evolved as a means to allow Shi'as to survive persecution – they were allowed outwardly to conform to what their persecutors demanded while privately continuing in their Shi'a beliefs.* One of the prime exponents of the theory of *taqiye* had been the Emam Ja'far. In the later religious negotiations with the Ottomans, one of the Ottoman negotiators came to believe that the whole process could have been a grand exercise in dissimulation.[65] In general, Nader's religious policy did not provoke popular opposition within Persia. People adapted. His removal of the Safavids was more unpopular.

Nader was determined in other ways to break with the old norms of Safavid rule. Some contemporaries recorded that he even rejected the title of Shah itself, telling people instead to address him as *'Valine'mat'* ('Lord of Beneficence').[66] Another example was his choice of red as the usual colour for his clothing, as can be seen from his portraits. Under the Safavids, the Shah never wore red, save when pronouncing a sentence of death on a wrongdoer. This would have been generally known, and it seems likely that Nader wore red deliberately, to emphasise his

---

* The idea, and the circumstances of its origin, shows similarities to the doctrine of mental reservation associated with the Jesuits.

reputation for firm justice.[67] Nader also, building on the arrangements he had set up during his regency, developed administrative practices that differed significantly from those of the Safavids. The changes were directed at efficiency and maximising tax revenue.[68] But some were symbolic too: the office of grand vizier* was left unfilled.

A further example may be found in his attitude to women. Shah Soltan Hosein's extravagant enthusiasm for new sexual partners had been notorious, and one account suggests that, as might be expected, other nobles imitated his practice. But Nader acted against this tendency:

> On his coming to the crown he published an ordinance, which made it present death to any person whomsoever, who should attempt to corrupt any man's wife, or forcibly take a married woman from her husband; for which reason those who have beautiful daughters give them in marriage very young, that they not be exposed to any violence. In the reign of Hussein, men of great distinction were wont to seize upon what women they pleased, whether married or single; but as Nadir himself was a strict observer of the law just mentioned, very few persons had the boldness to violate it in his time.[69]

Time and again in Nader's story we find him intervening to prevent or punish the abduction or rape of women (albeit with at least one glaring exception). The policy must have enhanced his popularity as a just ruler, and served to make another pointed distinction between the nature of his rule and that of the last Safavids, but it also reflected deeper, personal motives on Nader's part.

Nader also ended the practice of imprisoning royal heirs in the harem, as the Safavid Shahs had done. Instead he gave his sons military and regional commands to develop their abilities and fit them to inherit the right to rule. From the Moghan Nader sent Tahmasp Khan Jalayer with Reza Qoli Mirza to Mashhad, to act as his mentor there, and to supervise pacifications in Balkh and elsewhere. When Nader left the Moghan for Qazvin his other teenage son, Mortaza Qoli Mirza,† went

---

* *E'temad od-dowle.*
† Mortaza Qoli was Nader's son by Gowhar Shad, the younger daughter of Baba Ali Beg of Abivard. Nader married her in the early 1720s after his first wife, Baba Ali's elder daughter, the mother of Reza Qoli, died.

with his uncle Ebrahim Khan on a punitive expedition against a tribe in western Azerbaijan, from which the boy 'returned with the glory of a conqueror'[70]. At this time Reza Qoli was about 17 years old, and Mortaza Mirza at least two years younger. Like their father, they were learning their trade early.

The establishment of Mashhad instead of Isfahan as the new *de facto* capital of Persia, in the centre of Nader's power base in Khorasan, marked another important shift from Safavid practice. Yet it was important for Nader's dynastic plan that his grandson Shahrokh should have the added legitimacy of Safavid blood.

Nader, raised as a Shi'a and now to all appearances a convert to Sunnism, had little attachment to the precepts of either sect.[71] Some have speculated that he had little real religious faith at all, despite his pragmatic use of religious formulae in his public utterances. The French Jesuit who later became his personal physician said it was difficult to know what religion he followed, and that many who knew him best said he had none.[72] Russian diplomats must have reported something similar, because when speaking of the notorious atheism of Nader's Prussian contemporary Frederick the Great, the Empress Elizabeth apparently once said, 'He ridicules holy things; he never goes to church; he is the Nader Shah of Prussia.'[73]

Nader's shift toward Sunnism was purely political in its motives.[74] Beyond Persia, his conversion signified a bid for hegemony within Islam as a whole; an assertion of his wider political position that would have been impossible had he and his regime remained Shi'a. At the centre of Nader's motives there was no religious drive; rather an urge to dominate the world he knew, as Timur had done. One story says that a holy man was once talking to him about the religious idea of Paradise:

> After the holy man had described its wonders and
> delights, the Shah asked: 'Are there such things as war
> and the overcoming of one's enemy in Paradise?' On
> the holy man replying in the negative, Nadir remarked,
> 'How then can there be any delights there?'[75]

Nader was nonetheless curious about religion in general, as the account of his visit to Echmiadzin shows. Some years later he ordered a group of mullahs, Armenian priests and western missionaries to collaborate on a Persian translation of the Christian gospels, with Qur'anic glosses and annotations. But the hopes of the Christians that he might be converted by the revelation of Jesus were to be disappointed, and little came of this exercise in comparative religion. Some accounts say that when parts of the finished text were read to him he ridiculed the Christians, Jews, Mohammad and Ali equally, saying the translation showed that the Christian faith had absurd internal inconsistencies just as all the other faiths did. He boasted that he would devise a religion better than any that had yet been practised by mankind.[76] His French physician wrote that Nader believed himself to be as great as Mohammad or Ali because they were great only through having been great warriors, and because he had achieved as great a degree of military glory as they.[77]

This enquiry into Nader's religious attitudes indicates something else – a kind of naivety, blindness or autism. It suggests that, despite his extraordinary, relentless intelligence, there was something about religion he just could not grasp. Perhaps in his visits to Echmiadzin and Najaf there was wistfulness for something beyond reach. It may be that his early experience of the narrow, dogmatic Shi'ism that had been fashionable in the reign of Shah Soltan Hosein had left him unable to view the forms of religion with anything other than cynicism and contempt. But there are indications that he tried by decree to impose a tolerance between religions that reversed the intolerant Shi'ism of Shah Soltan Hosein's reign, and in at least one case he took action to reverse the forced conversion of Jews.[78]

At bottom, did Nader believe in God? He had been brought up in an atmosphere in which Islam was an essential and natural part of daily discourse – it is plain from his letters and speech, in which references to the Deity remain central. Islam is, famously, a religion whose central precepts are few and simple. It is unlikely that when Nader prayed before battle for example, he did so insincerely. He may have found that he started to pray for appearances' sake, for the benefit of his troops, but that as he prayed, he meant it. He would not be the first or last sceptic to find within himself a religious faith of surprising vigour in moments of crisis. However suspiciously we may view the judgement of some of his contemporaries that Nader was hostile to religion, his actions against traditional Shi'a practices and institutions speak for themselves. If he believed, it was with a strong admixture of harsh scepticism, contempt for superstition and hypocrisy, and a firm suspicion that no man-made religion had yet explained God properly.[79]

If Nader was indifferent to the religious observances of his subjects, he was pretty indifferent to their wishes and interests altogether. Within his little group of family, drinking companions and old bruisers, in his contempt for religious schismatics and hypocrites, pro-Safavid city-dwellers and other *Tajik* non-warriors, he was confident that it was enough to dominate with a strong army, use the army to extract the taxes necessary for its upkeep, and terrorise opposition into acquiescence. That was what Timur had done, after all;[80] when necessary Timur and his Mongol predecessors had massacred and destroyed whole cities, had devastated and depopulated regions and turned them over to pasture for horses and sheep – and by those methods Timur had conquered most of the Islamic world.

But here lay the error. Times had changed. Nader had been successful in war because his intelligent use of gunpowder weapons in large numbers had given him the edge over his enemies. Cannon and muskets were expensive, and were made in cities. Soldiers trained to use them properly had to be kept trained, drilled and paid. In Timur's time the loot and tribute from cities was of course welcome, but an army of nomads armed primarily with lances and bows could survive quite well without them. To defeat the Afghans and the Ottomans Nader could not do without the cannon and the jazayers made by Shi'a artisans in the cities. To pay for them and to pay the soldiers that wielded them he needed the wealth that could only come from the Shi'a merchants and their trade between cities. The wealth could only come from tax, and if the cities and their economies were to keep functioning, the tax would in the long run be paid only by consent. Consent under duress, consent with resentment, but consent nonetheless; and if the terror were carried too far, to the point where the artisans and merchants were forced deep into debt to pay the taxes, and could no longer feed their families, the flow of money, provisions, cannon and jazayers would slow and cease.

Timurid terror and urban consent were ultimately not compatible. Terror had its own appalling logic; like an addictive drug, more and more extreme doses of killing and destruction would be needed to achieve the same numbed effect. The wealth and tax revenue yielded by the urbanised economy would dwindle, and there would be revolt after revolt. Nader knew this, but he thought his conquests and the loot they supplied could keep him ahead of the economic consequences of terror, and that the money paid out to his soldiers and for their equipment would keep the economy of the cities going, or at least the parts of the economy he needed: the war industries.* But would that

---

* These must have expanded massively in the 1730s and 1740s.

work indefinitely, as the army, like an over-hungry parasite, inexorably turned Persia into a desert? Nader's prejudices inclined him to think that the devious city-dwellers could always be squeezed a little more, but he had realised by 1736 that he was close to the limit.

Before Nader left the Moghan, Nader revealed another aspect of his religious policy – perhaps one of the main drives behind it. Given the constant need for money to pay his troops, it was predictable; anyone familiar with the conduct of the princes of Europe in the protestant reformation might have seen it coming. Nader called together the mullahs that had come as delegates to the qoroltai, and asked them how they employed the vast revenues they had. They told him that they applied them to the religious purposes for which they had been intended by those who had given the endowments; salaries for mullahs who led prayers in the mosques, maintenance of theological colleges,* and upkeep of a great number of mosques, in which, they said, prayers were daily and hourly offered up for success to the arms of their prince, and prosperity to the empire of Persia.

Nader told them their prayers had obviously failed, since for fifty years the nation had been on the decline, and at last had been almost ruined by invasions and rebellions, until God's victorious instruments (meaning his army) had come to its relief, who were now ready to sacrifice their lives for the defence and glory of the realm. He said that these poor priests (pointing to his soldiers) were in want, and must be supplied by some means or other; therefore it was his royal wish that the greatest part of the religious lands and revenues should be confiscated and diverted towards paying the army. After the meeting he told the notables generally that if people wanted to support the mullahs, they would have to do so at their own expense in future.[81]

The apparent switch from Shi'ism to a form of Sunnism as the state religion need not have been accompanied by this expropriation, but it was logical. Nader had a number of different motives for abolishing the most extreme forms of Shi'ism, but the thought of the wealth he could grab from the humiliated Shi'a clerics must have been a powerful inducement. Politically, the change of doctrine made the expropriation easier, by undermining the legitimacy of the old institutions that had previously enjoyed this revenue; the expropriation weakened the power of the mullahs and made their opposition to his rule less effective.

The money yielded by the confiscations may not have been as much

* The *madrases*.

as Nader had hoped. Implementation was patchy and some of the property had already been plundered by the Afghans. The evidence is inadequate to make a final judgement, but one contemporary estimate of the value of the lands and revenues taken reckoned them at the equivalent of nearly three million pounds sterling;[82] a huge sum, as might be expected from the wealth of the Shi'a institutions previously.

In many respects, including the new emphasis on administrative efficiency, the secularising religious policy, the deliberate distancing from some of the forms of the Safavid monarchy, as well as his military practices, the regime inaugurated by Nader at the Moghan looks progressive to modern eyes – for all that his rule prefigured many of the less attractive features of nineteenth and twentieth century Statism.[83] The pattern of his accession to power, by sheer talent from obscurity in a period of chaos, appealing to popular yearnings for a strong, charismatic leader to deliver the country from its problems, also has modern rather than ancient resonances. Other modern-seeming features were to appear later – notably his development of a navy. But despite these progressive elements, Nader identified too little with the ordinary people of Persia truly to govern in their interest. If he had ever acted on the realisation that their interest was his interest, that tax revenue would only hold up in the long run if the people prospered, things might have been different. He knew that the harsh, destructive, Timurid cast of his rule would ultimately be unsustainable, and dangerous for the future of his dynasty. But at least for now, his solution was not to moderate the character of his government. Instead he sought new pastures on which to graze the war-horses.

From now on Nader's name appeared on the coinage and was read in the Friday prayers, as was customary for the sovereign in Muslim countries. As was usual, he had a poet devise a motto in Arabic, which also signified the date of his accession (AH 1148/AD 1736) in Arabic script. The poet came up with a motto which translates as 'That which has happened is for the best,'* which was stamped on the new coinage. Unfortunately, when switched around the first two letters produced a motto with the opposite meaning – 'That which has happened is not for the best.' Wits amused themselves with this and other plays with words around the motto. A new royal seal was also devised, with the inscription:

---

* *Al-khair fi ma waqa'a.*

> Since the jewel of State and Religion had vanished from
> its place
> God reinstated it in the name of the Iranian Nader* [84]

Festivities continued after the coronation, lasting to Nowruz and well beyond. Nader's next military objective was Kandahar, and he had lengthy talks with Afghan officers in the army about the lie of the land around that city, and the prospect of action against it. He finally left the camp on the Moghan plain on the 14 of April 1736, and went to Qazvin, where he stayed three months. From there he issued an edict that was sent throughout the country, enforcing the cessation of the traditional Shi'a practices that were most offensive to Sunni Muslims. [85]

Nader had achieved the goal he had aimed at, about which he had dreamed perhaps ever since he was a little boy playing in the dust of the Darra Gaz – the throne of Persia. He would not have been human if he had not given a thought to what the people who had sneered at him and his family in their poverty would be saying of him now. But often the things we most long for, once we have attained them, change and are found to be strangely unlike what we had imagined.

---

* *Negin-e dowlat o din rafte bud con az ja / benam-e Nader-e Iran qarar dad khoda.*

CHAPTER SEVEN
To the Gates
of Delhi

Unserm stärksten Triebe, dem tyrannen in uns, unterwirft sich
nicht nur unsre Vernunft, sondern auch unser Gewissen.

(To our strongest drive, the tyrant in us, not only our reason
but also our conscience submits.)

Nietzsche

As Nader savoured the untrammelled power of royalty in Qazvin in the early summer of 1736 he had two prime concerns: peace with the Turks, and the campaign against Kandahar. The two were of course connected. He could not undertake a major campaign in the east if he remained at war in the west. From the start, the new campaign was intended to reach further than just Kandahar. Shortly before he left the Moghan in early March, presumably having heard rumours around the camp, the Catholicos Abraham had exchanged words with Nader about his intentions. Nader said, 'Do you know caliph, that I plan to let you leave the day after tomorrow?' The Catholicos answered, 'May the life and rule of my Valine'mat be long. I put my hope in God, the Creator, that as I observe you today as the conqueror of Iran, I will with the help of God hope to see you as the conqueror of Kandahar and Hindustan.'* Pleased with this reply, Nader laughed and said, 'Well done, caliph, well done!'†

There had been rumours of Nader's intentions toward India as early as February 1734[1] and Nader may have had something of the sort in mind as early as 1730, when he had sent messages to the Moghul court

---

* i.e. Moghul India.
† *Barikallah, khalifay, barikallah* (CAC, p. 101).

demanding that the Moghul Emperor prevent fugitive Afghans from taking refuge there. Moghul inaction on the matter of Afghan fugitives was to be the eventual excuse for Nader's invasion of India. With the wider objective of India in mind, Nader issued orders for preparations to be made for the campaign against Kandahar. But there were a number of other problems to be sorted out first.

Nader had been in intermittent contact and negotiation with the Ottomans ever since his defeat of Abdollah Koprulu at Baghavard in June the previous year. The proposals agreed at the Moghan and presented by the Persians in Istanbul in August 1736 cannot have come as a complete surprise there. The war with the Russians was going badly for the Ottoman Sultan, and as the year went on war with Austria looked more and more certain. But although the Ottomans were keen to detach Persia from her alliance with Russia and make peace, and despite the welcome news of Nader's ban on anti-Sunni religious practices, the Ottomans could not accept Nader's proposal for a new Ja'fari mazhab.[2] The Persian demands for an exchange of ambassadors, and for prisoners to be freed on both sides, were rapidly agreed. In addition, the Ottomans made a major concession by agreeing the request for a Persian Amir ol-Hajj.

It was unusual for there to be an Amir ol-Hajj for pilgrims originating outside Ottoman territory (though the Ottoman Sultan had offered Ashraf Ghilzai something similar in 1728). The man's responsibilities would necessarily mean he took some authority in dealings with local Ottoman officials. This was a significant signal of religious goodwill; particularly given that, as the Ottomans must have known, many of the pilgrims would in their hearts be unreformed Shi'as, who would want to visit the traditional Shi'a shrines at Najaf and elsewhere in Ottoman Iraq as part of their journey.

But the innovation of a new column in the holy precincts in Mecca, and a new sect to join the four orthodox Sunni mazhabs, were impossible for the Ottoman side even to contemplate. Their regime was based on the principle of defending the norms of orthodox Sunnism, according to which any kind of innovation in religious doctrine, however politic or well intentioned, could only be unacceptably subversive. Nader's proposal, if even taken into serious consideration, would have created further ill will between the Ottoman Sultan and his subjects. One of the Ottoman negotiators insultingly contrasted the religious status of the two countries (by implication dismissing the idea that the Ottomans should make any concessions for the Persians), saying that whereas the Ottoman Empire had over the years killed more than ten million infidels and had based their dynasty on foundations of piety, the Persian dynasties had not engaged in such *jihad*. Instead they had behaved 'like a fickle woman… [or] like a towel, shifting from one hand to the other'.[3]

The chief Persian negotiator said Nader was even prepared to consider himself subordinate to the Ottoman Sultan, in a position like that of the Tartar Khan of the Crimea, if the Sultan would agree to the Ja'fari mazhab. To achieve lasting peace between the two countries, and permanent conversion of the previously heretical Persians to orthodox Sunnism, would it not be possible for the Ottomans to overlook their traditions? But the Ottomans were obdurate. They could not consider Nader's proposal until he had restored stability to all Persia's provinces. To prolong the process and avoid a breach, they suggested they should send an embassy to Nader's court, including two religious scholars, to look into the question of the Ja'fari mazhab in more detail.

In October 1736 the Ottomans and Persians signed a treaty in Istanbul that recognised Nader as Shah, and the old borders as they had been in the previous century, and formalised the other points of agreement from the negotiations, but left aside the religious issues. Nader never ratified it, and told the Russians, who were angry that he appeared to be breaking his obligations to them just as their war with the Ottomans was hotting up, that he would not make peace without Russia. Nevertheless a kind of truce held between the Ottoman Empire and Persia, and discussion of Nader's religious proposals continued, leaving open the possibility of continued war at a later stage. This suited Nader's purposes, and may have been his intention all along. It is quite possible that he had been cynical enough to insert the religious clauses into the proposed treaty as the most likely means by which an empty negotiation could be indefinitely protracted. Such an attitude would certainly have been congruent with the contemptuous view of theological matters he showed elsewhere.

Nader could have renewed war with the Ottomans in 1736. In some ways, the moment was propitious, given the Russian offensive that was going ahead on the northern shores of the Black Sea. The Russians were pressing him to join in. But he knew the military effort required would put too heavy a burden on the Persian people, already destitute from the effects of previous wars. And if he were to make a bid for supremacy over Islam as a whole, which was the underlying purpose of his religious policy, it would not do to push for it in open alliance with a Christian power. He needed a breathing space, for the country to recover, and a new source of cash to pay the army, before he renewed his attack on the Ottomans. That was the purpose of his expedition to India.

Some further news arrived at Qazvin while Nader was there. The island of Bahrain, off the southern shore of the Persian Gulf, had been restored to Persian rule. It had been lost to the Sultan of Oman in 1717/1718, in the midst of Shah Soltan Hosein's other tribulations. The revival of Persia's power in the Persian Gulf had been building since 1734, when Nader had appointed Latif Khan as his admiral, and had sent him to Bushire to commission a coastal fleet. The immediate purpose then had been to secure the capture of Mohammad Khan Baluch, who had taken refuge on the island of Qeys, but Nader's naval plans were not a passing whim.

Latif Khan had trouble obtaining ships, but after some unsuccessful adventures, including an expedition to Basra in 1735,[4] he sailed to Bahrain in 1736 in a borrowed vessel. There was little resistance and after a few skirmishes the island was back in Persian hands. Taqi Khan Shirazi, who regarded Latif Khan as his subordinate, sent the keys of the island's fort to Nader, and was rewarded with the attachment of Bahrain to his governorship of Fars.[5] This success encouraged Nader to consider wider naval enterprises. Given the great distances involved and the difficulty of travel overland, it was natural for him to connect these with his plans for India.

Other, less welcome news reached Nader in Qazvin. The Bakhtiari tribe had given him trouble in 1730, when some of them had refused to resettle at his orders. Since then, they had plundered travellers on the roads around Isfahan while Nader had been campaigning in Ottoman Iraq.[6] In the autumn of 1735 a full-scale revolt broke out, led by Ali Morad, a rash young chief of the Chahar Lang branch of the Bakhtiari. In a few months he had 20,000 men, including Lors and other tribesmen, and was boasting that he would destroy Nader and liberate Tahmasp from his confinement in Khorasan.

Nader could not pursue major new conquests in the east with a serious revolt unchecked behind him, any more than he could have left the Ottoman threat unresolved. He marched south from Qazvin, and ordered the governors of the area to attack the rebels. The Bakhtiari fought these troops hard, but were defeated eventually, and Ali Morad withdrew to forts in his native mountains, west of Isfahan. Nader came up and took the main Bakhtiari fortress of Liruk, and his men hunted down the fugitives in caves and ravines in the hills, capturing around 3,000 families.

Most of the rebels submitted to Nader, but Ali Morad could not be found, until a detachment of Nader's men caught a woman who had been spotted coming down from the hills for water. She resisted questioning bravely, but after having been deprived of sleep for 24 hours she admitted that she had been taking water to Ali Morad and his family. She showed Nader's men the cave where they were hiding. Ali Morad managed to hold out for several days, but eventually killed his wives and daughters rather than let them fall into Nader's hands, and gave himself up. He was taken to Nader in Shushtar.

Nader had suffered the rebellious Bakhtiaris long enough. The drawn-out hunt for Ali Morad had made him frustrated and angry. His earlier clemency had not been respected, so he decided now, bearing in mind his imminent departure for Kandahar and India, and the need for the country to stay quiet in his absence, to give a terrible example of his cruelty. Ali Morad was blinded, and his ears, nose, hands and feet were cut off. Two days later, in a pool of blood, the miserable young man asked for a drink of water, and died.[7] Several thousand Bakhtiaris were resettled to Khorasan, and large numbers of their fighting men were taken into Nader's army.

Nader marched on to Isfahan, where he arrived on 15 October with an army of 200,000 soldiers and camp followers, who 'devoured everything in their path, like a cloud of locusts'. There were celebrations and fireworks, but gloom descended when Nader doubled the taxes that were due. There were beatings and executions, estates were confiscated, 12,000 troops were billeted on the city and bodies appeared in the maidan outside the palace. The English reported that the city was 'near to ruin'. According to the Dutch a census by the town authorities before Nader's arrival had shown there were just 8,000 inhabited houses left in Isfahan, compared with 90,000 in the time of Shah Soltan Hosein, and 40,000 even in the reign of Ashraf Ghilzai.[8]

All over Persia Nader's officials were collecting money, provisions, animals and other supplies for the new campaign against Kandahar. In Kerman tax collectors beat up the merchants and other citizens, and stayed in their houses until they paid. The Banyans and merchants paid 1,500 tomans in silver, and so many draught animals were requisitioned that trade came to a standstill.[9] In Bandar Abbas such large quantities of food were seized that many traders were ruined. As ever, Nader gave careful thought to his preparations. Provisions for his men were sent ahead to dumps in the desert, along the line of his march. Large numbers of draught animals were commandeered, in at least one case so brusquely that caravans were stripped of their animals on the highway, and the merchants left with their goods by the roadside.

Following his usual practice, Nader gave money to his soldiers and coats of honour to his officers before the army set off on campaign. On 11 November Taqi Khan arrived from Shiraz with expensive presents for Nader, and a large contribution from Fars for the coming war. Nader rewarded his favourite with a fine horse and a khal'at.[10] Across the country, the huge demands for money, provisions and baggage animals inflicted great damage on livelihoods and on the economy.

While in Isfahan, the seat of the centralised bureaucracy under the Safavids, Nader set about changes to the administration of the country that were far-reaching, and would have represented a major modernisation if they had been completed. He had taken over the services of the old Safavid bureaucracy, but moulded his administration to a new form. Nader eroded the distinction between crown lands administered directly* and lands administered by provincial governors or others,† towards a system whereby provincial governors collected taxes locally and remitted the proceeds to the centre once they had made deductions for their own expenses. The openness of this system to abuse by governors and other officials was corrected by Nader's fearsome reputation, his employment of new officials to supervise provisional governors, and his use of spies. But while in Isfahan he also ordered a systematic assessment of landed property, beginning with the provinces of Fars, Isfahan and Azerbaijan, making no distinction between crown lands, religious properties or the properties of other protected groups. Taqi Khan Shirazi, in whose province the reforms went ahead first, was probably the architect of this innovation, and it is significant that he was summoned to Isfahan for its inauguration. Governors and officials were expected regularly to present detailed accounts of tax revenue and expenditure, and they were harshly punished if the accounts were found wanting. The purpose of all this was, of course, to maximise revenue to pay the army. Later rulers built on the definitive tax records that had been put together in Nader's time, and it is reasonable to see in these reforms the first impulse of his military revolution toward what could in time have been greater administrative and economic efficiency.[11]

The army left Isfahan on 21 November 1736, marching past the

---

* *Khassa.*
† *Mamalek.*

battlefield of Golnabad. Nader put on a new hat for the occasion, specially made with jewels and pearls set in gold. His army was 80,000 strong and mainly (perhaps wholly) mounted, the better to cope with the long distances and difficult terrain ahead. But as well as true cavalry, he took with him several thousand jazayerchi infantry mounted on ponies or camels, hundreds of zanburak camel guns, and some wheeled artillery. Tahmasp Khan Jalayer followed on later with 30,000 or more men from Khorasan. Another large body under Pir Mohammad Khan had gone separately on a punitive expedition against the Baluchis, and would rejoin the main force later, at Kandahar.[12]

Nader arrived in Kerman on 22 December and marched onward nine days later, after further depredations. Continuing eastward via Bam, the army reached Gereshk on 19 February 1737. The Afghan garrison there surrendered when Nader's cannon battered down their walls, but then the main advance toward Kandahar was slowed by want of fodder for the horses. Nader's largely or wholly mounted force had the advantages of speed and mobility, but there were many more animals than men, and they needed great quantities of grass, hay or other food every day if the army was to stay in the saddle. As they approached Kandahar the season was against them; the spring grass was yet to appear and Hosein Soltan's men had burned what fodder remained from the previous year. The army diverted north to get fodder from the Hazara tribes, and then went on toward Kandahar, camping on the west bank of the Arghandab river.

The night after their arrival there, the Ghilzais made what was intended as a surprise attack. But some of the Abdali Afghans in Nader's army had been warned, and by a ruse of their own intercepted one body of the Ghilzai horsemen as they made their approach. The Abdalis hailed the Ghilzais in Pashtun, pretending in the dark to be their comrades, but then attacked suddenly, taking the Ghilzais at a disadvantage. The Abdalis killed many of them, some drowned in the river as they fled, and the rest escaped. Another body of Ghilzais pushed further toward Nader's camp, but his guards fought them off and Hosein Soltan's men drew back to Kandahar.[13]

Despite the river being in full flood with spring meltwater from the mountains to the north, Nader forded it and moved up to the city, skirting to the south the high ridge against which it lay. The army camped on the eastern side, not far from the tomb of Mir Veis, the mastermind of the Ghilzai revolt of 1709. Nader celebrated Nowruz there on 21 March.[14]

Like Herat, Kandahar was strongly fortified. This was perhaps the most crucial siege of Nader's military career, but as usual, he did not have enough of the heavy siege artillery necessary to breach the thick mud walls that faced him, and was forced to adopt a blockade.* As at the siege of Baghdad, he erected a ring of towers to encircle Kandahar, interspersed with smaller turrets within musket-shot of each other. He sent bands of men out to subdue nearby forts and towns and secure his supply routes. On 9 April he gave orders for his men to move a little further off to the south-east, and to begin the construction of a complete new town, complete with markets, squares, bath-houses, stables, coffee-houses and mosques, to be called Naderabad. As at Baghdad, the construction of these buildings served both to occupy his own men during the long siege, and to dismay the besieged, to whom it made clear that the Persians meant to play the game to the finish. It was also important, in a long siege, to give the troops healthy living conditions; otherwise disease would spread and render the army more wretched and weak than the besieged. There were a number of skirmishes, but in general Hosein Soltan's men kept within the walls. He had been given plenty of warning of the Persian attack, and had laid in enough provisions for many months.

In the summer Hosein Soltan received the news that the fortress of Kalat-e Ghilzai had surrendered, along with one of his sons, and Mohammad Seidal Khan, who had commanded troops against the Persians under Mahmud and Ashraf, and against Nader in the Herat campaign of 1731. Nader treated Hosein Soltan's son kindly, but regarded Mohammad Seidal Khan as a dangerous troublemaker, and had him blinded.[15]

One account says that a poet from Khorasan made the journey to Kandahar to present a poem in praise of Nader. He read his verses at court, but Nader did not like them. He liked them so little that he had a court usher take the poet round the camp, offering him for sale as a slave, but there were no takers. Nader then asked him, 'How did you get here?' The poet replied, 'On a donkey.' Nader then had the donkey offered for sale. Immediately a good price was offered, and the donkey was sold. Nader gave the money to the usher, and had the poet run out of the camp, to general derision. Nader was not a great lover of the arts.[16]

---

* The mud walls of Indian and other eastern fortifications could, if solidly built, be more effective in absorbing the battering power of siege cannon than the stone or stone-faced walls of European artillery fortifications.

After ten months, the long siege was wearing down Nader's patience, and his frustration turned increasingly to suspicion and anger. He never liked being stuck in one place for any extended period, but it may also be that an early outbreak of his later illness, possibly malaria, appeared at this time. The Dutch in Isfahan had reported a rumour as early as the summer of 1736 that Nader had been taken ill in Qazvin and sometimes had trouble digesting his food. Digestive trouble was certainly one of his ailments later, which suggests the story may have been true. Nader would have tried to conceal any illness.[17]

In the summer and autumn of 1737 Nader's forces began to be augmented by the successful return of a number of subordinate commands; but some of their commanders suffered from Nader's frustration and bad temper. One was relieved of his command and suffered the bastinado as punishment for taking too long over the siege of a nearby town.

At the qoroltai on the Moghan, Nader had shown his trust in another of his commanders, Pir Mohammad Khan, by the praise with which he introduced him to the Catholicos Abraham. Having let Nader's troops into Mashhad to take the city in 1726, Pir Mohammad Khan had always proved a loyal and able subordinate. He had been Nader's first governor in Herat, and by the time of the siege at Kandahar was campaigning for him in Baluchistan. Perhaps he was too painstaking, or too scrupulous, and took too long over it. Malicious reports reached Nader that Pir Mohammad Khan was intending to revolt, and Nader sent orders for him to be beheaded. The campaign against the Baluchis having succeeded completely by that time, Pir Mohammad's troops arrived at the court in Naderabad with their former commander's head shortly afterwards.[18] Nader apparently came to regret Pir Mohammad Khan's execution. The incident was a forerunner of later, greater errors.

By the winter of 1737/1738 the Afghans in Kandahar were eating their horses, but still had significant quantities of basic provisions left. Nader fumed with impatience. Rumours went round that he intended to leave the siege at Kandahar in the hands of others, and take the main army on into India. Possibly with the idea that they would bolster the besieging forces and free up his veterans in accordance with this plan, in December he sent orders back to provincial governors to recruit 18,000 boys aged between 13 and 25, and send them to him in Kandahar. They were to march to join him via Mashhad and Herat by Nowruz. Isfahan and its surrounding villages had to supply 1,500 boys and young men toward this total, and there was much lamentation from their families as they were taken away. For the two months or so before they left, the boys had to drill every day with heavy matchlock muskets as tall as they were, that they could hardly carry, let alone handle properly. They were housed in caravanserais in the city, and madrases from which the mullahs had been expelled. By the time they left the Isfahanis were thoroughly glad to see them go, because they 'committed all kinds of violence in the city and had respect for nobody'.[19]

Before they arrived Nader decided it was time to change his tactics. At the end of January he ordered a general assault on the fortifications of Kandahar, and a detachment of bold troops succeeded in capturing a number of outlying towers. In particular, his soldiers took a tower on top of a hill, near the northern end of the ridge that ran behind the city on the western side. From this position, they were able to attack a further tower at the northern tip of the ridge, called the Chehel Zina or Borj-e Zangi, which was well garrisoned and furnished with artillery. They took that tower too, and with it gained an elevated position from which they could overlook the other fortifications of Kandahar. The soldiers toiled with great difficulty to drag cannon and mortars up there, enabling them to bombard other nearby walls and towers. The closest was a further tower, connected to the main circuit of fortifications, called the Borj-e Dede, and this is where the Persians concentrated their fire.[20] Step by step, tower by tower, the Persians were getting closer to the most vulnerable point of the walls of Kandahar.

The sustained cannonade on the Borj-e Dede may have done superficial damage, stripping away the parapets and exposing the defenders to the Persian musketry, but the Persian cannon were unable to demolish it or open a significant breach, and each night the Afghans worked furiously to make good the damage done during the day. On 13 March 900 men were assembled to attack the tower in a night assault, after a further preliminary cannonade. Three hundred of these were Bakhtiaris who, keen to redeem the reputation of their tribe after Ali Morad's revolt, had demanded the right to lead the attack. They were accompanied by equal numbers of Kurds and Abdalis: some of the most aggressive fighting troops in Nader's army. Nader selected them in this way to stimulate competition between the three parties.

Unfortunately the Afghans realised what the Persians were planning, and reinforced the troops in the tower. The attack went ahead, and the Persians lost 200 killed and wounded before they saw the impossibility of it. Nonetheless the men were undaunted, and began to prepare immediately for a second try.[21]

Nader and his commanders celebrated their second Nowruz outside Kandahar on 21 March 1738, with banquets and gifts as usual. On 23 March the Bakhtiaris and other troops made their final preparations for another attack on the Borj-e Deda. This time 3,000 men took part, each specially selected from a larger number of volunteers. They were carefully concealed in trenches, in caves and behind rocks within reach of their objective to keep the Afghans ignorant of the preparations, and Nader himself secretly spent the preceding night in the open with his troops. He promised them 1,000 rupees each if they were successful, plus the spoils of the city; but said that if they turned back they would be beheaded, and their bodies given over to flies and dogs. This caused some muttering among the soldiers, who resented his threats and lack of faith in them.

Nader saw that one member of the assault party was a mullah, a Bakhtiari called Adineh Mostafi. He wanted to take him out of the assault, saying that his life would be at risk and that as a scribe and a mullah, war and fighting were not for him. Mullah Adineh insisted he take part, saying, 'May I be your sacrifice. The affairs of the mortals of this world are truly the concern of mullahs and scribes. God willing, you will see my bravery.'[22]

One account says that Nader prepared the assault to coincide with Friday prayers, having been given information by a spy that the defenders of the tower would be reduced in number because many of them would be in the mosques.[23] After a final prayer at noon on 24 March for the success of the action, the signal was given from the Chehel Zina, and the Bakhtiaris surged forward with their scaling-ladders. Many of them were gunned down, but enough made it to the foot of the tower, erected the ladders and reached the top to engage the defenders. First to the top was Mullah Adineh. After a sharp struggle the Bakhtiaris took the tower and pressed on to the next one on the circuit of walls, supported by the remainder of the force, who moved forward behind them from their concealment.

Tower after tower fell, and the Persians' progress was marked by the flags they raised on the ramparts. The Afghans threw more and more troops into the fight but the Persian musketeers mowed them down with a torrent of bullets from the towers they had taken. Eventually Hosein Soltan saw it was hopeless and retreated to the citadel with a small number of Afghans, leaving the rest of the inhabitants to be killed or put in chains.[24]

Nader had the cannon of the city walls turned on the citadel, and aggravated the chagrin of Hosein Soltan with the thunder of a brisk bombardment. The following morning the Ghilzai leader sent out his elder daughter, Zeinab – 'a princess of rare prudence' – with a group of Afghan officers, to make the Afghan ritual of submission. Nader accepted gracefully. The next day Hosein Soltan himself prostrated himself before Nader, and was in return granted his life. He and his family were sent into captivity in Mazanderan.

In the prison of the citadel the Persians found the Abdali leader Zolfeqar and his brother, Nader's opponents in the siege of Herat in 1731/1732. They had fled then to Hosein Soltan in hope of finding refuge, but instead Hosein Soltan had thrown them in a dungeon. Nader sent them too to Mazanderan.[25] Nader's men also found a boy of about 15 in the prison; his name was Ahmad Khan Abdali, who was destined for great things. Nader took him into his army, where in time he rose to command the Abdali contingent.

The great fortress of Kandahar was razed, and its inhabitants were moved to occupy the new city of Naderabad, which became the capital of the province.* The Hotaki clan of the Ghilzai tribe, of which Hosein Soltan had been the leader, were resettled to Khorasan. They took there the lands around Nishapur and elsewhere previously occupied by the Abdali Afghans, after the siege of Herat; and the Abdalis were moved to lands around Kandahar. These great movements of people were all in train by mid-April. The other main clan of the Ghilzais were allowed to remain, and one of their chiefs, who had submitted to Nader early on in the siege of Kandahar, was made their overall head, and governor of the fortress of Kalat-e Ghilzai.[26] A large number of young Ghilzai warriors were taken into Nader's guard. The power of the Ghilzai Afghans was broken, the humiliation of the Ghilzai conquest of Isfahan was avenged, and the last piece of Persian territory lost by Shah Soltan Hosein had been regained.

Nader summoned Mullah Adineh and rewarded him with a large bag, which, as he walked away, the mullah realised was full of gold. He took the bag back, thinking there must have been some mistake. Nader said that even if it had been full of expensive jewels he would have considered it a cheap thing to give to him.[27] It was more normal for Nader to take money from mullahs than give it, but within a year Nader would

---

* Naderabad later reverted to the name of Kandahar, but below the modern city lie the foundations dug by Nader's soldiers in 1738. The old city below the ridge was not reoccupied.

owe Mullah Adineh a great deal more than he had given. The battered tower of the Borj-e Dede may not have looked it, but it proved to be the gateway to Delhi. Nader had now fully restored the old frontiers of Persia, but his ambition had not yet reached its high-water mark.

Nader stayed on for two months after the fall of Kandahar, and on 19 May 1738 welcomed an ambassador from Istanbul. The ambassador had taken over a year to make the journey via Isfahan and Kerman, accompanied by two advisers and a suite of 700 servants and hangers-on. He had been delayed in Isfahan, apparently because he contracted smallpox. When he arrived in Naderabad he presented some magnificent Arab horses, and a number of other precious gifts, which had been sent by the Ottoman Sultan to congratulate Nader on his coronation. But the message told Nader that the Sultan could not accept the Ja'fari mazhab, or the proposal for a fifth column in the Ka'ba.

Nader discussed these points politely with the Ottoman ambassador, explained that for him the religious questions were fundamental to the proposed treaty, gave him lavish presents, and sent him back to Istanbul with another Persian ambassador, so that the negotiations could be taken further.[28] Ambassadors travelled thousands of miles, delivered presents, and travelled back again, and so the charade went on.

In the previous year, after a skirmish near Kalat-e Ghilzai, some of Hosein Soltan's men had fled over the border of Kandahar province into Moghul territory, and it had become plain that, despite earlier messages to the Moghul court demanding that they should not harbour Afghan fugitives, the Moghul authorities were unable or unwilling to comply. Nader sent another ambassador to Delhi in May 1737[29] pressing the point, but no answer came. The ambassador had orders to stay only forty days, but time passed and there was no word from him. There was a rumour that he extended his stay because he was playing truant with a dancing-girl, but it is more plausible that Mohammad Shah and his courtiers just did not know what to do with him, and kept him on, in limbo.

On 21 May 1738 Nader marched out of Naderabad with his army, heading for Kabul. Shortly afterwards he crossed the traditional border between the Persian and Moghul empires* and reached Ghazni on 11 June. He was joined there by other detachments that had been on an expedition to subdue some of the Hazara tribes north of Kandahar. The Persians had killed many, and had carried off their women, but

---

* Near Moqor.

following his usual principle of gentle conduct toward females, Nader
had the Hazara women set free. He took trouble to subdue the Afghans
of the mountains around Ghazni also, before moving on to Kabul.[30] He
had much further to go, and it was essential to make his supply lines
as secure as possible. As usual, he showed benevolence to those that
submitted to him, but harshness to those who put up more than a token
resistance or broke their word.

Although he had received no despatches from his own ambassador,
many accounts say Nader had enjoyed a variety of other letters from
the Moghul court, to distract him from the frustrations of the siege of
Kandahar.[31] Prime among the alleged correspondents was the Nezam
ol-Molk, the regent or viceroy of the Deccan.* The Nezam ol-Molk was
the elder statesman of Moghul India, but after a failed bid to reform
the monarchy in the early 1720s, in the early years of Mohammad
Shah's reign, he had withdrawn from court life to rule in the Deccan.
The Nezam ol-Molk's family came from Samarkand in Central Asia,
and he was regarded as the head of the Turanian or Central Asian
faction among the nobility. Some accounts suggest that Sa'adat Khan,
the Subadar or governor of Awadh, also wrote to Nader at this time.
Sa'adat Khan came from Khorasan and was prominent in the Persian
faction. There was also a Hindustani faction, one of its leaders being the
head of the army, Khan Dowran.†

There was fierce rivalry between these factions and personalities,
and civil war had broken out several times in the preceding decades.
But the Moghul state suffered in addition from a variety of other related
problems. One was that these over-mighty nobles, and others, had
acquired tenure of large slices of Moghul territory by right of the offices
they held. They tended increasingly to govern in their own interests (a
prime example being the Nezam ol-Molk in the Deccan) and to turn
their territories into independent principalities. By 1738 Mohammad
Shah had only a relatively small piece of territory under his direct
control. With large slices of territory increasingly semi-detached from
the Moghul state in this way, *zamindar* landlords and other local leaders
were freer to aggrandise their own independence: sometimes in alliance
with the great nobles, sometimes against them, but always against the

---

* Also known as Chin Qilich Khan and Asaf Jah.
† My account of the complex state of faction politics and conditions generally
  in India is, for pressure of space, necessarily over-simplified. Alliances among
  the nobles shifted and changed over time, and composition of the factions by
  no means always corresponded to the nobles' origins.

interests of the Moghul monarchy.[32] Paradoxically, it seems that many of the zamindars had been strengthened by the very success of the Moghuls in the previous century in boosting the productivity of agriculture; for example through irrigation projects and the encouragement of more profitable cash crops. The process of decentralisation and disintegration of the Moghul structures of rule accelerated.

A prime beneficiary of the increasing weakness of the Moghul state were the Marathas, bands of militant Hindu warriors from the southwest, ruled by a confederacy of leading families, who expanded into areas where Moghul authority had weakened. In 1738 the Marathas even sacked the suburbs of Delhi itself, and forced Mohammad Shah to cede the province of Malwa. In the midst of these difficulties Mohammad Shah played one faction against another and maintained himself at court, but neither he nor his senior court officials addressed the deeper problems.[33] The Moghul regime reacted to events and immediate challenges, but failed to adapt to the more deep-seated changes in conditions that were undermining it.

The letters Nader received (if there was such a correspondence) were a manifestation of the weak condition of the Moghul state, and the divisions that were pushing it toward collapse.[34] Some accounts say that the Nezam ol-Molk and Sa'adat Khan directly invited Nader to invade, and in later years the story that the Nezam in particular had betrayed his master, was widespread. The couriers carrying otherwise rather nugatory letters from Nader to Mohammad Shah could easily have been carrying other messages. On the one hand, what could have been the point of a correspondence between Nader and the Nezam, unless it was in some way treasonable? On the other, it seems unlikely that the Nezam would have been so unsubtle as to make a direct invitation to Nader. Perhaps the letters merely assured Nader of the Nezam's goodwill, and offered his good offices to work to resolve the outstanding disputes between the two sovereigns to Nader's satisfaction. Yet given the Nezam's duty of loyalty to Mohammad Shah, even that would have been treasonable; and might well have been intended to suggest more than was written in black and white. Nader would have been gratified at the disunity revealed by the letters, but his intention to invade India was already fixed. The letters would not have made much difference, and if their authors had thought they could ingratiate themselves with him, they were mistaken.

As Nader approached Kabul, another delegation came to meet him. They were the nobles of the city, come to make their submission. The

Moghul governor of Kabul and Peshawar had earlier appealed to his masters in Delhi to send him at least one year of the five years' pay his troops were owed, so that he could defend Kabul against Nader. When the desperate message arrived with Khan Dowran in Delhi, he made light of it, saying that there was plenty of time and that the payments could wait until after the rainy season, when funds would have arrived from Bengal.[35] The governor got no answer to his pleas, and withdrew with most of his forces to Peshawar. Some diehards occupied the citadel, under its commander, and tried to hold out there.

Nader bombarded the citadel for several weeks, while the inhabitants of the city begged him not to make them suffer for the obduracy of a few. As the siege went on, according to one account, Nader ordered that 80 of his soldiers be executed by having their bellies torn open, for having been present when an Indian woman was raped, and for having done nothing to prevent it. Meanwhile, Nader's light cannon made little impression on the fortress, but his lack of heavy artillery was unexpectedly compensated for by the effect of one of the Moghuls' own big guns, the recoil of which apparently caused a tower and a section of wall to collapse.[36] The citadel and city made their final surrender shortly afterwards, at the end of June.

Nader sent a letter to Mohammad Shah, remonstrating with him for his failure to act against the Afghan fugitives. Nader explained his seizure of Kabul by saying that he had been forced to pursue the fugitives himself; but said he had been merciful to the Kabulis and had left them in possession of their property. Against all appearances, he protested his friendship toward Mohammad Shah. The message went with a Persian envoy toward Delhi, but the unlucky man never arrived; he was killed on the road near Jalalabad.[37]

From Kabul, Nader took his men north, to the Charikar district,* to rest in an area where fodder, water and other necessities were plentiful. Parties went out to reduce the surrounding Afghan tribes to obedience, and more recruits for the army came in, realising the opportunities for personal enrichment that might await Nader's army in India. The army moved on again early in September, heading for Gandamak, Jalalabad and Peshawar. The route was the same as that along which, a century later, the British army suffered one of its worst and most humiliating

---

* Close to the site of the modern airport at Bagram; important in the Russian/ Afghan war of the 1980s and again when US forces helped the Northern Alliance to defeat the Taliban in 2001.

defeats, at the hands of the Ghilzai Afghans.

While on the way Nader heard of the killing of his messenger, and at his orders an advance guard of mounted jazayerchis raced ahead to Jalalabad. They surprised the garrison, took the place by surprise, seized a large quantity of valuable grain, and perpetrated a punitive massacre. But the Afghan chief that had killed Nader's messenger escaped to his mountain stronghold nearby. The Persians went on and captured it, after some hard fighting through the trenches the Afghans had dug in the hillside. The men were all killed, and the women taken away in chains, including the chief's wives and sister.[38] Not far away, to the south of Jalalabad, is the site of another stronghold: the cave complex in the Tora Bora hills where US bombing and coalition forces failed to kill or capture Osama bin Laden in December 2001.

The main army stopped short of Jalalabad and camped at Bahar Sofla, a few miles to the south-west. While there on 7 November 1738, they were joined by Nader's eldest son, Reza Qoli Mirza, who had arrived at Nader's orders from Balkh. Nader liked to see his children and grandchildren, and as he got older, frequently ordered them to come to visit him. Nader had summoned Reza Qoli to make him viceroy of Persia in his absence.

Reza Qoli had been given responsibility for Khorasan just before Nader's coronation in 1736, and Nader had instructed him to act against rebels in Andkhui and Balkh, towns north of the Afghan mountains and south of the Oxus;* traditionally tributaries to the Persian monarchy. He had sent Tahmasp Khan Jalayer with him, to guide the young man and save him from any rash mistakes. The eager young man and the tough old bull advanced on Andkhui in the late spring of 1737. The place surrendered after six weeks. The rebels were another group of the fissiparous Afshars; some of them switched to the royal side at the start of the siege. This episode is a reminder of the fact that despite Nader's successes, many of his own Afshar relatives and fellow tribesmen, remembering old feuds from Nader's early days in Abivard, were still bitterly irreconcilable to him and his regime.

From Andkhui Reza Qoli's little army moved on to Balkh, which surrendered too after some fighting. But instead of stopping there, Reza Qoli wanted to press on over the Oxus, against Nader's orders; and rather than restraining him as he had been meant to do, Tahmasp Khan urged him to follow up their successes.[39] Reza Qoli crossed the Oxus in

* Otherwise known as the Amu Darya.

August with about 8,500 men. He then moved on to Qarshi, which was a significant town, subject to the Uzbek Khan Abo 'l-Feiz of Bokhara. The Persians settled down to a siege. Abo 'l-Feiz called up support from Khwarezm, Khojand, Tashkent, Samarkand and elsewhere, and marched to relieve Qarshi.

This was exactly the situation that Nader had feared, but Reza Qoli and Tahmasp Khan rose to the challenge. There was a battle, and initially the Uzbek charge pushed the Persians back, but the Persian artillery then came into play. The Uzbeks and their horses were unused to the noise and shock of artillery, and the cannon killed many of them. The rest retreated to the town. Reza Qoli must have been jubilant: this was heady stuff at the age of 19. But then orders arrived from Nader for him to return to the other side of the Oxus. These orders were given in no uncertain terms; Nader angrily accused Tahmasp Khan Jalayer of leading his son astray and reminded him that he had been ordered to go no further than Balkh. His letter addressed him 'O senile pimp...' and warned him that he would be beheaded.[40]

At the same time Nader wrote to Abo 'l-Feiz, assuring him of his respect for the Khan's sovereignty over Bokhara. By the winter the Persians were back on the southern side of the Oxus. But even then the bold pair would not lie still, campaigning into the Kunduz region north of the Hindu Kush, and even into the mountainous Badakhshan area even further east, until Nader again ordered them back to Balkh. When they were back there they were summoned to join him at Jalalabad, and went there quickly, via Kunduz and Kabul.

Nader did not rebuke Reza Qoli on his arrival. He felt a tender love for his son.[41] He was proud of his impulsiveness, and this early demonstration of military enthusiasm. He reviewed the troops from Balkh, gave them some of the fine Arab horses he was so fond of, and new weapons and armour. Most of them stayed with Nader's army. With Tahmasp Khan Jalayer he was more severe, and at first snubbed him, but Tahmasp Khan's obvious contrition eventually earned him forgiveness.

Nader had other concerns about the situation on the Oxus; he was getting word that Ilbars of Khwarezm was putting together a large body of Turkmen to attack Khorasan (where Nader's young nephew Ali Qoli was acting as governor). Nader intended after his venture in India to invade Transoxiana himself: he did not want anyone else, even his son, to take from him the glory of subduing the home territory of the great Timur. He made Reza Qoli viceroy of Persia in his absence, and gave him the right to wear the jiqe on the right side, to denote his royal status.* Nader gave him strict orders to stay on the defensive, even if Ilbars attacked, and to keep close guard on Tahmasp and the other members of the Safavid royal family in Sabzavar. He was to consult the officers and advisers Nader had given him. He was to take their advice, and not change them for other advisers, and should keep to these orders even if he heard nothing from Nader for six months. Reza Qoli left on 17 November and returned to Balkh.[42]

Nader loved and trusted his son. Many fathers overindulge their children, though few have as much scope to do so. Nader had faith in his family, that inner circle within his circle of trusted confederates. As time went on, he spent most of his spare time with his women and his family.[43] He had rejected the option of imprisoning his sons in the harem as the Safavids had done, in favour of giving them an active part in the running of the kingdom. Reza Qoli's rule as viceroy was a logical extension of that policy. But for all this looked the better, more sensible course if Nader's fledgling dynasty were to prosper, and for all that the other option was in every way repellent to him, there were risks involved. It was necessary for someone to rule Persia in his absence, and this division of responsibilities within the empire was less risky than other divisions of responsibility might have been. But it was a heavy burden to put on his young son. There were malicious people ready to exploit any divisions or misunderstandings. And as the frustrations of the siege of Kandahar had revealed, Nader himself was changing, under the pressures of rule, and perhaps the first symptoms of illness. He was showing a greater tendency to irascibility and suspiciousness.

Nader did not send Tahmasp Khan Jalayer back with Reza Qoli. He may have thought that, notwithstanding his impulsive behaviour already, his son was getting too old for a mentor. Back on the Oxus frontier, Reza Qoli was active and vigilant against the threat from Ilbars of Khwarizm, but the Turkmen horde was divided by rivalries and disagreements, and eventually faded away. Reza Qoli, who with his cousin Ali Qoli had made his headquarters at Abivard, went back to Mashhad.[44]

The day after Reza Qoli Mirza's departure, Nader's army moved on again, and camped on the eastern side of Jalalabad. While there, Nader was told that the Moghul governor of Kabul and Peshawar had finally nerved himself, despite the lack of support from his masters in Delhi, to

---

* Nader's second son, Mortaza, was honoured in the same way two days later.

stand and fight for his province. He was in the Khyber Pass with a force
of 20,000 Afghans, blocking the route to Peshawar. Although the Persian
army was much stronger, their numbers would make little difference in
the narrow valley of the Khyber. A frontal attack would be wasteful
of men Nader could not spare, and would risk a defeat which, in the
midst of the Afghan mountains, could be disastrous. If the Persians lost
face and looked vulnerable, tribes that were now friendly or submissive
might well switch over to hostility. As on previous occasions, Nader
decided to find a way round the obstacle. A local guide told him of a
difficult but passable route to the south, via the Tsatsobi pass, which
would allow the Persians to outflank the Moghul blocking force and
attack them from the rear.

On 26 November 1738 the Persians struck camp and moved to Barikab,
about 20 miles from the north-western end of the Khyber Pass. Nader
divided the army there, leaving most of his men with his son Mortaza
Mirza. Having made some payments to the chiefs of the local tribes to
secure their acquiescence, he sent 12,000 men toward the Khyber Pass
along the main road to screen his intentions, but he took the route to the
south with a force of 10,000 lightly equipped cavalry. He rested his men
in the evening for a while, and then pressed on in the moonlight, taking
several hours to get through the steepest, rockiest part of the pass in
the gloom. In the morning they emerged in the Bazar valley and turned
north. The Moghul commander had been told that the Persian army was
approaching the Khyber from Jalalabad and was arranging his men to
meet them when Nader's force, after an exhausting march of nearly 50
miles, suddenly appeared in his rear and attacked. The Moghul forces
were taken completely by surprise, but fought desperately for some
time, until their commander and several other chiefs were captured.
Then the rest fled, leaving many killed and wounded behind them. The
way lay open to Peshawar and the plain of the Punjab.[45]

The main army advanced through the Khyber Pass and after a pause
of three days Nader descended with it to Peshawar, which opened its
gates to him immediately. The Persians rested there until the beginning
of January 1739.

While in Peshawar Nader was given the bitter news that his brother
Ebrahim had been killed while fighting Lazgi rebels in the Caucasus.
Ebrahim, apparently stimulated by news of Reza Qoli's successes along
the Oxus (and perhaps by memories of an earlier occasion when the
boy had outshone his uncle), had decided to seek glory for himself in
the Caucasus mountains. The wrong place. He called up troops from

Georgia, Shirvan and elsewhere, and marched to attack the Lazgis in the mountains. He was successful in a major battle, but in the aftermath was ambushed in a wooded valley with his escort of jazayerchis. Caught at a disadvantage in the narrow valley and unable to manoeuvre, Ebrahim was wounded by several musket balls. Finally he was hit in the chest, and fell to the ground. One of his companions gave him some water as he lay there, but he died shortly afterwards. Few of his men escaped. The Lazgis initially treated Ebrahim's body with some respect, but later removed it from its coffin, hung it from a tree and burned it.

Nader took the news badly. He and his brother had lived through many hard times together, and Ebrahim had always been loyal, if not always prudent. This blow to his family would have to be avenged. Daghestan joined his list of targets for future campaigns, after India and Turkestan.[46]

Nader left Peshawar on 6 January 1739, heading for a crossing of the Indus, the first of the five rivers of the Punjab. A bridge of boats had been prepared at Attock for the army, and having crossed, they headed for Lahore, crossing the other rivers one by one and crushing all resistance. Nader's troops ranged widely through the Punjab, killing, plundering and seizing provisions. Many towns were burned.

Arriving at the river Ravi Nader found his route blocked by trenches and fortifications that the governor of Lahore had constructed. On 21 January he diverted round them and, from an unexpected direction, attacked the troops the governor had assembled to defend the city. The fighting continued the following day, but then the governor asked for terms. Some speculated that, at the prompting of the Nezam ol-Molk, he had made only token efforts to prevent Nader taking Lahore. But his capitulation saved the city from being plundered, and if his resistance to the Persians had been less than total, it was because he was more inclined to protect Lahore than to sacrifice it for the flaccid regime in Delhi. For his part, Nader was content to remove this obstacle from his path. He secured a contribution of 20 lakhs of rupees,* and confirmed the judicious governor in his post.[47]

Nader's conquest of Kabul had caused consternation in Delhi, and Mohammad Shah had recalled the Nezam ol-Molk to court. But Khan Dowran was in control there, and the Nezam's advice was little regarded. Letters were sent out all over northern India calling for

---

* One lakh was 100,000 rupees; 20 lakhs were equivalent to around £250,000 sterling at the time.

assistance, including to the Marathas. The Maratha leader Baji Rao, notwithstanding his many campaigns against Mohammad Shah, sent a significant force, but they never arrived. Nor did a promised force under the Nezam ol-Molk's son. But Sa'adat Khan responded from Awadh (Oudh), and promised to march quickly to Delhi with his troops. Subject again to discord and faction, progress in putting together an army and marching it over the great distances of northern India to confront the advancing Persians was slow.

The Moghul forces left Delhi on 13 December, and on the march were reported to cover an area two miles wide and 15 miles long. But the army went no further than the Shalimar gardens just to the north of the city until 12 January. Mohammad Shah himself joined them at the end of that month, but the army, encumbered with enormous numbers of servants and hangers-on, advanced no further toward the Persians than Karnal, only about 75 miles north of Delhi. There they ground altogether to a halt, and camped, around the middle of February.[48]

Nader learned in Lahore that the Moghul forces had emerged from their capital. He left there on 6 February and arrived at Sirhind on the 16th, and was told that Mohammad Shah was at Karnal with 300,000 men, 2,000 elephants and 3,000 cannon: but the real total of the Moghul host, including all the camp followers, may have been as high as a million.[49] Nader sent out an advance guard of 6,000 Kurds to investigate, and if possible to bring back prisoners that could tell him more about the Moghul positions. While they were away the Persians advanced further. Nader's harem and the army's baggage were left with a guard at Ambala. The main army moved on and camped at Shahabad on 19 February, only thirty-five miles from the Moghul camp at Karnal.

The same night the Kurds attacked the Moghul artillery guards at Karnal, taking some captives. They then retired to the north, sending the prisoners to Nader. He returned orders to the Kurds to explore further the terrain around the Moghul camp, and on the 22nd the main army moved on to Thanesar. Nader left his son Mortaza Mirza in command there and went on with a few men to Sarai Azimabad, only twelve miles from Karnal. There was some resistance at an old brick fort there, but the garrison gave up when Nader brought up cannon. Nader met the officers of his Kurdish scouting party, who had some more Moghul prisoners with them, and was able to get a clearer idea of the enemy positions.[50]

The huge, unwieldy Moghul assemblage occupied a large part of the plain of Karnal north of the town, and had surrounded itself with a mud wall 16 miles in circumference.* Huge cannon garnished the walls. A canal skirted the camp on the eastern side, and there were thick woods and jungle to the north, extending over a wide area either side of the road most of the way to where the Persians were at Sarai Azimabad. But within the Moghul camp there was a serious shortage of food, disease had broken out, and some of the troops were mutinous for want of pay.[51]

Nader was unwilling to attack such a strong position, and he did not like the sound of the approach toward it, which was why he had made his scouts look over the surrounding geography so carefully. Nader's scouting troops had free range for miles around, enabling Nader to form his plans carefully and get word quickly of enemy troop movements, which was the way he liked it. By contrast, the Moghuls seem to have done little scouting. Some of their people strayed out of the camp to look for forage from time to time, only to be cut off by the Persian skirmishers. The first time this happened the survivors, including some wounded, ran back to the camp in panic, and the cry went around – 'Nader has come! Nader has come!'[52]

According to one account, the mere appearance of the Persian light cavalry frightened the dispirited Moghul troops. The Persians wore the four-cornered *kulah-e Naderi* hat, eighteen inches high, with a goatskin or sheepskin wound round it; a woollen cloak on their shoulders, an open shirt that left the chest bare, short breeches, and leather boots. Each of them was armed with a sword, a matchlock musket, and an axe.[53] Nader's mounted infantry and foot soldiers wore similar clothing, though they would have worn a long red coat bound at the waist with a sash rather than a cloak. The heavy cavalry wore armour of mail and plate, and a steel helmet topped with a sharp spike to deflect downward sabre strokes.

Nader decided to approach the Moghul camp from the eastern side. On the morning of 23 February the Persian army moved further south-east, crossed the canal some way north of the Moghul positions, and camped north-east of Kunjpura, with the river Yamuna (Jumna) behind them. Nader galloped out in person, with a few picked troops as guards, to take a look at the plain of Karnal.[54]

---

* Fraser (pp. 152 and 20) says seven Coss, and gives one Coss as 4,000 yards. That gives a circumference just under 16 miles (Lockhart 1938, p. 133 says 14 miles). Mohammad Mohsen Siddiqi (p. 7) says five parasangs – a parasang was the distance a man could march in an hour and was usually calculated as between three and three and a half miles in length.

To the east of Karnal and Mohammad Shah's camp there were three or four miles of open plain before the village of Kunjpura. From the plain, Nader could see the Moghul banners floating in the breeze, and their artillery on the mud walls. He resolved to march past the camp on this side, and fight the Moghuls on the plain if they opposed him. Otherwise he would march on towards Panipat and Delhi to the south. But Nader believed the flanking movement would bring the Moghuls out to fight.

Nader returned to the Persian camp and called together his officers. Promising rewards for their bravery in the coming fight, he asked them what route they would take to save themselves, if they were beaten and forced to flee in the battle, being so far from home? It were better to fight gloriously together. He ordered them to remain in their armour while they rested and to stand ready through the night. That same evening the Persians received word that Sa'adat Khan had arrived at Panipat, about 20 miles south of Karnal.[55] He had covered the distance from Awadh quickly, despite suffering from an unhealed wound in his foot. Nader sent a force of cavalry to intercept him.

By this time the Persian army was around 160,000 strong, including camp followers and servants. Although many of these were armed, and all were mounted, only about 100,000 of the total were true fighting troops. One account says they included 40 Russians, and three Englishmen, but the latter must be very doubtful. The Russians, if present, would have been engineers, bridging experts, artillery specialists and other advisers. To add to the impression of numbers the women camp followers were dressed like the men, except that they were veiled. In addition to the men that had marched from Isfahan, and those that had joined them at Kandahar and Bahar Sofla, there were many Afghan tribesmen with the army. But others had stayed behind to garrison the places Nader had seized along the way.[56]

On the morning of 24 February,[57] Nader divided his army into three, giving the right wing to Tahmasp Khan Jalayer, the centre to his son Mortaza (attended by a group of experienced officers), and the left to Fath Ali Khan Kayani and an Afshar chief, Lotf' Ali Khan.[58] Mortaza's orders were to advance on a south-westerly axis and camp near Karnal. Tahmasp Khan and Lotf'Ali Khan were to guard his flanks, with the former positioned to oppose any intervention from the Moghul camp. As these dispositions went ahead Nader was told that Sa'adat Khan had evaded the Persians sent against him and, marching hard, had made his way through to the Moghul camp late the previous evening, arriving at about 10 pm. His arrival, long-awaited, had been celebrated with great rejoicing among the Moghul troops and camp followers.

But Sa'adat Khan's force of 20–30,000 men had become strung out along the line of march, and many of them were still straggling on toward the Moghul camp the following morning. The Persians from the intercepting force attacked this rearguard and pillaged the baggage. Sa'adat Khan presented himself to Mohammad Shah early on the morning of 24 February, and then retired to his tents;[59] but later he was told of the attack on the rearguard of his force, and that 500 laden camels were being taken away by the Persians. Immediately Sa'adat Khan roused himself again, calling his men to him, and left the camp on his elephant to rescue his people and retrieve his baggage. Exhausted as they were from their march, only about 1,000 horsemen and a similar number of infantry followed him, though another 4,000 answered a further summons a little later. The cannon were left behind.

Emerging from the camp at about noon, Sa'adat Khan attacked the first body of Persians he came across in the plain, probably some of the Kurds that had been serving as an advance guard over the previous days. After making a show of resistance, these men scattered and feigned flight as they were trained to do, drawing Sa'adat Khan and his men further eastwards away from the camp, shooting behind them as they went. The pounding of their horses' hooves would have thrown up clouds of dust, obscuring from the Moghuls the sight of the main Persian army drawn up ahead of them. Sa'adat Khan sent a message to the other Moghul commanders,[60] telling them that the Persians were retreating, and urging them to come out and fight in his support.

In the Moghul camp, Sa'adat Khan's message produced a disagreement. Mohammad Shah wanted his commanders to ride out in support of Sa'adat Khan, but the Nezam ol-Molk characteristically counselled caution, saying, 'Haste is of the devil.' The Moghul commanders had planned that the battle should not be fought that day but in two or three days' time. For once, Khan Dowran agreed with the Nezam: the troops were not prepared for battle, and it would not be possible to assemble the artillery to form the front line, as was customary. He accused Sa'adat Khan of having acted rashly, and declared that any troops sent to reinforce him would only make worse their defeat.

Mohammad Shah was unhappy already at Khan Dowran's handling of the campaign, and told Khan Dowran he was a 'conceited idler'. Stung by this rebuke, Khan Dowran armed himself, climbed onto his elephant, and prepared for battle. A large number of eager nobles and other horsemen joined him, including his brother and several of his sons. Amid a fanfare of trumpets and drums, they moved off, 8,000–9,000 strong, mainly cavalry with some matchlock-armed infantry, a few cannon and possibly a few brave men armed with gunpowder-propelled rockets. It is likely that larger numbers of Moghul troops left the camp to join Khan Dowran as the afternoon wore on. Nader himself later wrote, 'The ground was everywhere dark with their numbers.'[61]

The main Persian army had not advanced far, and Nader ordered them to halt when he saw Sa'adat Khan's men emerge from the Moghul camp. Nader was delighted to see them. He left his earlier dispositions as they were, and ordered his commanders not to move. His men brought forward the zanburak camel-guns, and unfurled his personal battle standards.[62] He armed himself with a helmet and body armour, and took personal command of 1,000 Afshar cavalry of his guard.

Nader selected three 1,000-man units of Kurdish, Qajar and Bakhtiari horsemen armed with heavy jazayer muskets, and a large number of zanburaks. He ordered them to dismount and take up concealed positions among the walls and trees in the gardens on the western edge of Kunjpura, as an ambush to await Khan Dowran's force. He ordered two 500-strong units of his trusted jazayerchis, mounted on horses, to take over the job of luring the enemy further eastwards; one to engage Khan Dowran's command and draw them toward Kunjpura, the other to engage Sa'adat Khan and fall back toward the Persian centre. These preparations made, Nader 'invoking the support of a bountiful creator' moved toward the enemy, his red-fringed banners floating overhead.

Sa'adat Khan delayed his advance so that Khan Dowran's men could come up, but the two commanders were too jealous of each other to coordinate their actions properly. The Persian jazayerchis lured them in diverging directions, and Khan Dowran moved rapidly onward without properly ordering his troops. Both commanders were by now too far from the Moghul camp to get any support from there.

As Sa'adat Khan advanced, Nader's jazayerchis fell back before him, toward the troops of the Persian centre, who were waiting for the Moghuls with camel-guns levelled and muskets trained. When the Moghul soldiers were within close range, the curvetting jazayerchis moved swiftly aside, and as the dust drifted away all the firearms of the Persian centre crashed out together. Thick powder smoke billowed between the lines of soldiers, and many of Sa'adat Khan's men fell from their saddles. The impetuous survivors surged forward to fight with their lances and sabres. There was bitter hand-to-hand fighting, and

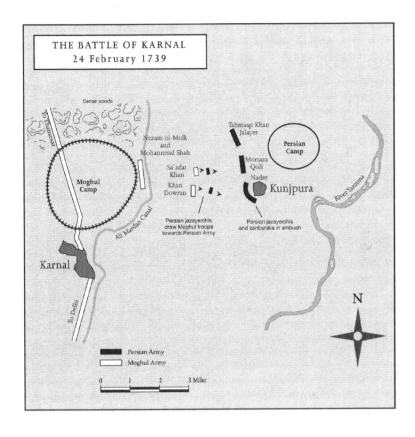

THE BATTLE OF KARNAL
24 February 1739

Dense woods

To Thanesar

Nezam ol-Molk
and
Mohammad Shah

Tahmasp Khan
Jalayer

Persian
Camp

Moghul
Camp

Sa'adat
Khan

Mortaza
Qoli

Nader

Kunjpura

River Yamuna

Khan
Dowran

Ali Mardan Canal

Persian jazayerchis
draw Moghul troops
towards Persian Army

Persian jazayerchis
and zanburaks in ambush

Karnal

To Delhi

N

Persian Army
Moghul Army

0   1   2   3 Miles

Mortaza Qoli's men were hard-pressed. Seeing this from his position
on the left, Nader sent a message to his son to dismount and pray for
victory.* Mortaza did so, and remounted. The Persians began to move
round the flanks of Sa'adat Khan's smaller force to encircle it.

As Khan Dowran drew near Kunjpura, the horsemen he had been
pursuing also melted away, and the Persian jazayerchis and camel-
gunners lying in ambush fired a punishing volley into his men. Khan
Dowran's troops were deafened and thrown into confusion by the
shock of the Persian shooting, which continued incessantly, the muzzle
flashes harsh pricks of light through thick banks of powder smoke.[63]
More and more of his men fell, and their firing in reply was ineffective.
Some of the survivors fled, and others tried to close with the Persians.
But most of Khan Dowran's men were gunned down before they could
get near. Nader waited immobile behind his jazayerchis and camel-
gunners, watching them working the hot guns; fire, reload rapidly and
fire again, as they had been trained to do.

In the Moghul camp, Mohammad Shah could hear the furious
Persian gunfire. He urged the Nezam ol-Molk to go to Khan Dowran's
assistance, but although the remaining Moghul troops marched out
and took up position behind the canal, they moved no further, and
the Nezam according to one account ignored all pleas for action, and
sat on the top of his elephant, sipping coffee. Perhaps he remembered
an incident at court a few years before, when Khan Dowran and his
hangers-on had jeered at him, saying, 'See how the Deccan monkey
dances.'[64] The Nezam left Khan Dowran and his men to their fate.

Standing high above the fighting, the Moghul elephants and their
howdahs naturally attracted fire from the Persian jazayerchis and
zanburak gunners. The big elephants of the nobles were protected
by metal armour, as were the howdahs; but the heavy ball from a
jazayer would punch straight through metal plate at close range.
Khan Dowran's brother, perhaps realising this, was killed jumping
down from his mount.[65] Khan Dowran's eldest son was also killed,
and another was captured. Khan Dowran himself was wounded more
than once, and then was hit in the face by the ball from a jazayer, and
fell senseless to the floor of his howdah, streaming blood. Many of
his men fled back towards the canal, but a thousand of the bravest
dismounted and fought to the death, bunched up with the skirts of

---

* BW says that Nader himself dismounted and pressed his face to the ground
  in prayer (p. 164).

their long coats tied together.[66] Some of Khan Dowran's most devoted retainers gathered around his elephant and led it back to safety through the smoke, the bodies and the confusion. Many of the Moghul nobles that had accompanied Khan Dowran were killed, and others were captured.

After nearly two hours, the fighting in the centre was still fierce. The commanders on their elephants made good targets here too. Sa'adat Khan's men, much depleted in number, were still fighting on grimly when the elephant that was carrying his nephew was wounded. Like an oversized, uncontrollable dodgem, the frantic animal charged Sa'adat Khan's elephant and both, entangled, careered in among the Persian troops, their distinguished occupants hanging on desperately in their howdahs. Sa'adat Khan continued to fight, shooting arrows down at the enemy below him, but eventually a fellow-Khorasani among the Persians hailed him, climbed up to him using a rope that was dangling down the elephant's flank, and persuaded him to surrender. The survivors of his command gave themselves up or fled if they could. For two and a half hours the Persians harried the defeated Moghul troops back to within cannon-shot of their camp, cutting down fugitives all the way.

As the day faded, Nader and his men faced the remaining Moghul forces behind their canal, at a safe distance. 10,000 Indians or more had been killed, perhaps 400 Persians, and a further 700 Persians had been wounded. It was enough – Nader forbore to attack the remaining Moghul force across the canal, under the guns of their artillery. He thanked God for the victory and gave his son Mortaza the new name Nasrollah ('Victory of Allah') to honour his part in it.[67] He sent out troops to surround the Moghul camp and put it under blockade, to prevent any provisions getting in and stop anyone escaping.

In the Moghul camp the news that Sa'adat Khan had been captured and Khan Dowran was believed killed spread great despondency, and order broke down. The tents, animals and other property of the dead and captured nobles were ransacked and carried off by the mob. When Khan Dowran was brought in, there was nowhere for him to lay his head.[68] He died shortly afterwards – but before he could die his enemy the Nezam ol-Molk visited, to mock him in revenge for earlier insults.

Nader had defeated only a part of the Moghul forces, but the ignominy of the defeat, the deaths of so many prominent nobles, and the capture of Sa'adat Khan, were a damaging blow to the prestige of the Moghul state. Worse was to come, but how had this disaster come about? Militarily, as in other ways, the Moghul empire had been living in an unreal world for some time. Elephants that made perfect target practice for artillery and huge cannon that took an age to reload and were almost immobile were symbols of this: they were for show – a male kind of thing, one suspects. They were more of a liability than an asset when dealing with any opponent experienced enough not to be in awe of them.[69] Few of the Moghul troops were trained to anything near the Persians' level of skill in musketry, and the overall proportion of soldiers in the army provided with firearms would have been much lower. Although both armies would have used heavy calibre weapons by comparison with those used in Europe, most of the Moghul firearms would have been matchlocks, while many of the Persians would have been armed with more sophisticated muskets or carbines with flintlock or miquelet-lock firing mechanisms. These were easier to use on horseback, and may have permitted a faster rate of fire. Many of the Moghul nobles that made up the cavalry disdained to fight with anything but the sword – 'l'arme blanche' as their aristocratic European contemporaries would have expressed it. A contemporary made his judgement on the superior military effectiveness of the Persians when he wrote that the Moghul troops fought bravely, but that 'the arrow from a bow cannot resist the ball of a jazayer'[70] – neatly summarising the effect of Nader's military reforms.

The Indian troops were also badly supplied. They had to find money for their food and equipment from their own pay, and their matchlock-men might typically only carry enough powder and ball to fire their weapons two or three times. Nader always took pains to prepare his campaigns, to supply his men with everything they needed, and keep them well equipped. They had the ammunition and training to win lengthy musketry duels.

The number of Persian casualties in the battle at Karnal was not low, showing that the Moghul troops had fought hard. They were brave and tough. But they were hopelessly badly led. The commanders failed to use their artillery, to coordinate their efforts, or to support each other; and in general were more interested in vindicating personal pride than in pursuing a common purpose. Added to which they placed themselves on the most vulnerable, unstable fighting platform that any enemy with a malicious sense of humour could have devised for them.[71]

Nader's conduct of the battle was typical, relying heavily on a small number of his most reliable troops, deployed in small, manoeuvrable units, many of them directly under his own hand.* In later years this battle came to be seen as the crowning glory of his military achievement. Some commentators have exaggerated the ease of his victory,† playing down the numbers of the Moghul force he fought and stressing their disarray. The mismanagement of the Moghul commanders certainly made it easier for Nader, but the victory was the fruit of his careful preparation, the discipline of his troops, and his calm resolve on the day. It was a decisive victory of the greatest magnitude.

On the evening of 24 February, Nader had Sa'adat Khan brought before him, and asked him how he could most easily collect a ransom from the Moghul Emperor and return to Persia. Sa'adat Khan recommended that he summon the Nezam ol-Molk and negotiate with him. Nader sent a man to Mohammad Shah, holding a copy of the Qur'an as a sign of peace. Mohammad Shah had considered fighting on, but his advisers persuaded him that the loss of so many senior nobles made this impossible, and the Persian blockade was turning the previous shortage of food into a famine in the Moghul camp. Nader's messenger asked the Emperor to send the Nezam to a meeting, and on the evening of the following day the Nezam ol-Molk left the camp with some other nobles for his discussion with Nader.

An eyewitness reported that as they went the Moghul delegates passed Persian soldiers on the battlefield, breaking into and ransacking baggage chests abandoned by the defeated Moghuls. By the time they arrived at the appointed place it was dark. The Nezam and other nobles were all mounted on armoured elephants, and were themselves covered in steel plate and chain mail from head to foot.[72]

According to another eyewitness account, Nader welcomed the Nezam warmly, and the two men had a lengthy discussion. This began with Nader asking why his ambassador had been detained, why he had been given no reply to his messages, and why he had been forced to march into India with his army, at great expense, to put these questions

---

* Nader destroyed the Moghul forces with similar tactics to those used by the Afghan Amanullah Khan against Ali Mardan Khan's Lors at Golnabad in 1722. In turn, the way the invading Afghans used mounted musketeers at the battle of Panipat in 1761 resembled Nader's use of his jazayerchis at the battle of Karnal. The military innovations of the Afghans examined by Gommans (Gommans 2001) owed a good deal to Nader Shah – after all their proponent, Ahmad Shah Durrani, had learned the military trade in Nader's army.

† Notably Sarkar and Lockhart.

in person. The Nezam answered that the Empire had not been able to comply with Nader's requests, but the reason for their silence had also partly been that they had wanted to see Nader in person, in order to have the honour of kissing his feet.

Nader smiled at this, and went through a series of Persian claims against the Moghul state. He said the Moghul Emperor still owed the Persian crown payment for a throne that Timur had sent to Delhi. He said that Mohammad Shah's grandfather had asked for, and received, military help from the Persians in the form of 10,000 horsemen, but had never paid for these troops. Finally, the Persians and the Moghuls had agreed a treaty of mutual assistance, that each would help the other if either were attacked; yet Persia had been ruined by various wars, and the Moghul empire had never sent the help it had promised. Nader was still paying interest on money he had borrowed to pay for wars to recover Persian provinces from the Ottoman Turks. Who would pay?

These claims were variously dubious, exaggerated, fictional and transparent; but the Nezam was not in a position to protest. He agreed they were just demands, and undertook to speak to the Emperor on Nader's behalf. He told Nader that his head was in Nader's hands, that he submitted himself to Nader's orders. Nader said that the Nezam had spoken well, and that therefore he would spare the lives of the Emperor and his troops. He told the Nezam to tell the Emperor that the two monarchs should meet in person the following day, between the two armies.[73] It was provisionally agreed that the Moghul Emperor would pay Nader a large tribute for him to return to Persia.

On 26 February Mohammad Shah came to meet Nader as arranged, carried on a splendid litter or palanquin. Tahmasp Khan Jalayer met him on the way with an escort, promising on the Qur'an that no harm would come to him. When they arrived at the Persian camp Nasrollah Mirza met them, and took Mohammad Shah inside, to where Nader was waiting outside his tent. Nader took him by the hand and led him inside. The two men sat together on a long couch, and they were served coffee. Nader passed Mohammad Shah the cup with his own hands, as a gesture of hospitality. They spoke in Turkic, as Nader had requested, to stress their common Turcoman origins. It was at this point that Mohammad Shah surrendered his Empire to Nader. Nader replied, 'I salute your throne and Empire, and, although I am master of it, I give it to you, if you will only satisfy my claims.'[74] Servants brought a meal, and Nader exchanged the dishes to show that nothing had been poisoned.

The meeting passed off in a friendly manner, and Mohammad Shah returned to his camp in the evening.

The defeat at Karnal had not convinced the Moghul nobles of the need for unity against the enemy. Back at the Moghul camp, a dispute arose over the redistribution of the appointments previously held by Khan Dowran; in particular over the office of Paymaster (*Bakhshi*). The Nezam ol-Molk secured the post for one of his sons, but this made some other junior nobles jealous, so Mohammad Shah tried to solve the problem by giving the job to the Nezam ol-Molk himself, along with the post of commander in chief of the army (*Amir ol-omara*). But this solution angered Sa'adat Khan. He told Nader that he could extract much more from Mohammad Shah than the sum discussed with the Nezam, if he went in person with his army to Delhi. The only obstacle was the Nezam ol-Molk; if Nader could snare him, everything would fall into his hands thereafter.[75] Nader thanked Sa'adat Khan for his advice, but probably did not need it; he had not come all this way to be fobbed off without the full plunder of Delhi. Sa'adat Khan moved his remaining possessions and followers to Nader's camp, symbolising his shift of allegiance.

Time went on, further visits were made between the nobles of the two sides, the inhabitants of the Moghul camp grew hungrier, and the tribute was not paid. The intrepid few that escaped from the camp were either killed or made captive by the Persians, or set upon by robbers on the roads. Eventually the food was all but exhausted and the people began to starve.[76] On 5 March Nader summoned the Nezam again, told him that Mohammad Shah must pay him another visit, and that he wanted much more than the amount previously discussed. The Nezam protested, and was detained in Nader's camp, but eventually agreed to write to Mohammad Shah, conveying the request for him to visit Nader a second time.

Mohammad Shah dutifully came again on 7 March, this time with his women, a large number of attendants and quantities of baggage, and 'found it advisable to stay', along with many of the other Moghul nobles. Nader kept Mohammad Shah waiting until dusk before he came to see him, and set nasaqchis to stand guard over him. From now on he was, in the politest possible way, Nader's prisoner.[77]

The next day Nader paid his soldiers, their servants and followers a gratuity of 3 months' pay in celebration. His troops went into the Moghul camp and removed the artillery, and such nobles and office-holders as were left. Starving and leaderless, the mass of troops and

others left in the Moghul camp were told they were free to go home. One
of Nader's officers pointed out that there were a great many animals
and valuable horses in the camp: the Moghul soldiers had been given
quarter and allowed to leave, but that need not apply to their horses.
Nader replied:

> I have given these people Quarter in all Respects; besides,
> the Bread of Soldiers depends on their Horses, most
> of them are in wretched and indigent Circumstances;
> should they lose their Horses, they and their Families
> would be reduced to Beggary and Starving. It would
> be far from Humanity to treat them ill, now they are at
> our Mercy; therefore don't molest or insult them on any
> Account.

The Moghul troops scattered.[78] Many of them were attacked, robbed
and killed along the way by roving bands of Persian foragers, bandits
or peasants from the villages.

On 12 March Nader left for Delhi, with Mohammad Shah and his
retinue trailing two miles behind. They reached the Shalimar gardens
on 18 March. Tahmasp Khan Jalayer and Sa'adat Khan had gone ahead
with 4,000 Persian troops and orders from both Nader and Mohammad
Shah for the *kotwal* to open the gates to them, so that they could secure
the fortress-palace of Shah Jahan. On 19 March Mohammad Shah was
sent into the city to prepare for Nader's reception. Sa'adat Khan went
back to the Shalimar gardens to accompany Nader into the city, and
Nader himself entered Delhi on 20 March 1739.[79]

7. Jazayer.

This fine eighteenth-century Persian musket, 24mm calibre and weighing 27.5 kg, with its forked rest (originally longer) and miquelet lock, fits descriptions of the kind of weapon used by Nader's specially-trained jazayerchis. It is a much heavier weapon than those in use in contemporary Europe, where a typical musket might weigh 5kg and and fire a 18mm diameter ball.

(Bern Historical Museum)

CHAPTER EIGHT
The Ruin
of Persia

*Perhaps there does exist a dark power that fastens on to us
and leads us off along a dangerous and ruinous path which we
would otherwise not have trodden; but if so, this power must
have assumed within us the form of ourself, indeed have become
ourself, for otherwise we would not listen to it, otherwise there
would be no space within us in which it could perform its
secret work.*

ETA Hoffmann

Nader stayed in Delhi for just under two months. While there, he
had ceremonial meetings with the captive emperor Mohammad
Shah and his nobles, he had his son Nasrollah married to a Moghul
princess, he may have enjoyed an asymmetrical flirtation with the
singer Nur Bai, and he took into his service the experienced and wise
physician Alavi Khan, to treat the increasingly troublesome symptoms
of his illness. But the main events* were the massacre that took place
the day after his arrival, and the collection of a huge tribute of gold,
silver, jewels and other valuables, worth as much as perhaps 700
million rupees. It is difficult to give a sense of scale for this sum. To put
it in some kind of context, it has been calculated that the total cost to
the French government of the Seven Years War (1756–1763), including
subsidies paid to the Austrian government as well as all the costs of
the fighting on land and sea, was about 1.8 billion livres tournois. This
was equivalent to about £90 million sterling at the time: close to the
rough estimate of £87.5 million sterling for the value of Nader's haul

* As narrated in the Prologue.

from Delhi.* At the other end of the scale, an ordinary working man in England at the time would be lucky to earn £20 sterling in a year.

The victory of Karnal and the conquest of Delhi made Nader an international figure on a wholly new scale. The news was carried all over the Muslim world by merchants and traders, and many thought a new epoch of Persian dominance was beginning. Representatives of the European companies in India and religious missionaries sent back reports of what had happened to their capitals, and were eagerly asked for more information on the Persian monarch and his achievements by return. The London newssheets reported his exploits. Nader himself, a few months later, sent magnificent gifts of jewels and elephants with ambassadors to the Ottoman and Russian courts,† to make manifest the splendour of his successes.[1] Within a few months books about Nader Shah were appearing in all the main European languages, and for a generation or more his name was familiar to educated people, if not a household word.‡ Delhi marked the zenith of Nader's successes.

Nader may well have intended, despite his reinstatement of Mohammad Shah before his departure from Delhi, that he or one of his sons would return to India at a later stage and establish permanent Persian rule there. His annexation of the former Moghul territories west of the Indus, confirmed before he left Delhi, would have facilitated this, as would his naval expansion in the Persian Gulf. A further indicator was the currency reform he ordained for all his territories at the end of 1739: all previous silver coinage was called in and reminted to be common currency with the Indian rupee.[2] In one way this monetary unification reflected the pre-existing pattern of trade between Persia and India; most Persian trade had for time immemorial gone eastwards, in the hands of Indian merchants. But the new coinage also presents powerfully the possibility of an Indo-Iranian empire, predating and pre-

---

* The insupportable debt resulting from this enormous war expenditure, augmented later by a similar or slightly larger amount to pay for French support to the American colonists in the War of Independence, brought about the fiscal crisis that precipitated the French revolution. £90 million in the eighteenth century might be equivalent to £5.4 billion today.

† The jewels sent to Russia, only a small part of the Moghul treasures, are today some of the most prized exhibits in the Hermitage collection in St Petersburg.

‡ In 1796 Arthur Wellesley, later the Duke of Wellington, took Jones's *Histoire de Nader Chah* with him to India. Nader's campaigns also featured in Napoleon's reading; and Byron mentioned him in *Don Juan*.

empting European colonial expansion in the Indian subcontinent.[3] That idea is perhaps big enough to tangle with already, without speculating too far about whether it would have been desirable, and for whom.

The massacre of perhaps 30,000 people perpetrated by Nader while he was in Delhi would hardly have been an auspicious curtain raiser for permanent Persian rule there. In the event, it was a foretaste of what was to follow not in India, but in Persia. Before the massacre, in contrast to many of his predecessors, Nader had used violence sparingly, as a last resort: later in his reign, atrocity piled upon atrocity. Giving the order for an act of that enormity must have made scruples of the kind Nader had sustained before seem absurd. The massacre at Delhi was not just shocking in itself: it presented Nader to himself in a new position, from which (particularly when out of temper with illness or frustration) previously unthinkable cruelties became possible, even normal. Unlike some of his later acts of political terror, Nader could have told himself that the massacre at Delhi was forced on him by necessity; and it is probably true that without it, he would have lost control of the city and the collection of the tribute would have become impossible. But it marked a turning point in his attitude to violence.

Nader Shah rode out of Delhi on 16 May 1739. He and his men paused overnight at the Shalimar gardens, and he repeated his orders for the return of the last female captives. As he rode away north on 17 May, Nader's preoccupations were with his soldiers, the heat, and getting his treasure safely back to Persia. The army took with it tens of thousands of camels and mules laden with treasure. There were also at least 300 elephants. Great quantities of gold and silver had been melted down into large ingots, each of which had a hole in the middle so that a rope could be passed through it. Two such ingots were carried by each camel, fastened to either side of the saddle.[4] There were also many chests of jewels, and thousands full of newly minted coin.

These burdens of gold and jewels were the main purpose of his Indian expedition. They had allowed Nader to declare a three-year remission of taxation in Persia, giving the people and the economy a pause for recovery, and enabling him to pay his army in the meantime. There was enough to pay for the preparations for more wars in addition – the campaigns in Turkestan and Daghestan – and for the eventual resumption of war with the Ottomans.

But first he had to get the treasures back to safety. The number of baggage animals was so great that it became difficult to protect them, and it was well known throughout the country that great riches were travelling with the Persian army. Peasants and bandits descended on the flanks and rear of the column at night, and carried off such animals as they could – as many as 1,000 by the time the Persians drew near Lahore. Nader in retaliation burned the nearby villages, adding to the devastation his army had caused on the outward journey.[5] Passing the battlefield of Karnal, he gave the headman of the town 5,000 rupees to set up a new village on the site of his former camp, to be called Fathabad – 'The place of victory'. For 5,000 rupees, it can never have been much of a village; but Nader needed his money for more victories.

After Nader's departure, the survivors in Delhi took stock. Mohammad Shah was still Emperor, but the prestige of the Moghul state had suffered a terrible blow. One could compare its effect with the damage done to the Spanish Empire by the capture of Havana by the British in 1762, or to the British by the loss of Singapore in 1942 to the Japanese.[6] But:

> 'Even this Blow, which is sufficient to give an Idea of the
> Trumpet of the Day of Judgement, could not in the least
> awaken out of the heavy Sleep of Security, and Lethargy
> of Indolence, those People, who were so much intoxi-
> cated with the Wine of Pride, and Self-conceit. They all
> agreed in a general Ill-will to each other, and their whole
> Talk and Conversation was full of Envy and Detraction.'[7]

In the struggle for supremacy at court, the Nezam ol-Molk had emerged on top. His two main rivals, Khan Dowran and Sa'adat Khan, were dead, and he had taken over the former's office as commander-in-chief of the army. His supremacy was unchallenged, for a time, and he may have felt that his intrigues and his letters to Nader had been crowned with success. Did he do a deal with Nader? We will probably never know. The Nezam does seem to have been given an easier ride in the collection of tribute than the other great nobles; Nader's warning to Mohammad Shah about the Nezam before he left could have been a dark joke, a double bluff.

But with Nader gone, Mohammad Shah liked the Nezam ol-Molk no more than before. Within a relatively short time the Nezam had to return to the Deccan to sort out disputes that had arisen between his sons, and others took his place of primacy at court. In his 80s, the wizened Nezam did not have long to live in any case. Within a few years he too was dead, cutting the last link back to the days of the great

Emperor Aurangzeb. Little was done to reverse the fortunes of the Moghul state, and its enemies no longer had any illusions about its strength, or its will to resist. Awadh, the Deccan and Bengal became effectively independent. Mohammad Shah fought off an Afghan attack in 1748, but then died. By then Nader too was dead, and in the following decade Delhi became a toy to be fought over between the Afghans and the Marathas. The Afghans eventually took Delhi, and decisively defeated the Marathas at the battle of Panipat in 1761.

On his return march from Delhi Nader diverted north of his previous route at Sirhind, in an attempt to escape the heat by climbing higher into the foothills of the Himalayas. This meant he bypassed Lahore, but the governor came out to him with a further tribute of a crore of rupees to forestall more devastation. By this time some of Nader's men were dying from heat exhaustion – 'The helmets on their heads were like blazing furnaces.'[8] Crossing the rivers was more difficult than on the outward journey, because they were in flood. While the troops were crossing the river Chenab, the iron cables parted under the strain and the water suddenly broke through the bridge of boats 'with a deafening roar'. The soldiers on the bridge were swept away, and many were drowned. It was necessary to move downstream, collect boats and rafts, and slowly ferry the men and animals over the river, which caused a long delay.

Nader lengthened the delay by ordering that his men and their baggage be searched. He declared that no-one should be allowed to take more than a limited value of money or valuables out of India, and that all jewels should be given up. Some men buried their plunder or threw it into the river rather than hand it over. Perhaps some of it is still there. Nader did this partly because he wanted to keep his men dependent on their pay. He must have feared that otherwise many of them would desert. But beyond this rationalisation, his motive was simple avarice: the urge to possess the wealth of Delhi entirely. With all his men finally on the western bank, somewhat the poorer, Nader himself crossed on 14 July. The event was signalled by cannon-fire.[9]

Now marching through heavy rain, Nader's army crossed the Jhelum and continued on through Rawalpindi towards the Indus, despite attacks by Yusufzai tribesmen. Nader, ever alert to new sources of military manpower, recruited some of them into the army. The elephants caused problems, because of the great quantities of forage they ate. Nader ordered that they should travel on ahead of the main column, to ease the shortage, but 75 of them died between Kabul and Herat.[10] From the Indus the army rode on through Peshawar and the Khyber Pass. They arrived at Kabul on 2 December 1739.

Kabul was going to be the administrative centre of the territories Nader had added to his empire west of the Indus. It was important to signal the change of sovereignty, and to make arrangements for the government of the new lands. To this end the chiefs of all the Afghan tribes came to do him homage in Kabul shortly after his arrival. They brought with them 40,000 tribesmen, no doubt encouraged by tales of Nader's successes in India to think that riches awaited them in his service. The recruits were enrolled in the army and forwarded to Herat, along with the treasures and valuables, and the large cannon brought out of India. Nader probably sent on a fair proportion of the main army too, to protect the valuables and to prepare for the coming campaign in Turkestan. He kept with him a smaller force. Nader confirmed in his post the former Moghul governor of Kabul and Peshawar, whom he had defeated in the Khyber Pass in November 1738.

But one important grandee had not obeyed Nader's summons to Kabul: Khodayar Khan, the governor of Sind. Despite cordial and even encouraging letters prior to Nader's invasion of India, Khodayar Khan had undergone a change of heart once he learned that his province had been given over to Nader by Mohammad Shah.[11] Nader was not yet done with India.

Khodayar Khan must have believed that Nader, safely back in Kabul, would not move through the mountains again in mid-winter to chastise him. After only six days, Nader left Kabul again to correct that optimistic calculation. Marching through the mountain passes,* his men descended through the treacherous Kurram valley in terrible cold, crossing the mountain torrent twenty-two times and losing many baggage animals.[12] On 5 January 1740 the Persians, having with relief reached the warmer climate of the foothills, arrived at Dera Esmail Khan on the Indus, after some fighting with local tribes. The local zamindars submitted to Nader there, and he descended the Indus by boat to Dera Ghazi Khan, but a further summons to Khodayar Khan again went unanswered.

Nader moved on downstream to Larkana, where he was told that Khodayar Khan had run away further to the south. In each place the

---

* The upper Kurram valley runs through the same remote hills where coalition aircraft and special forces attacked – with mixed results – the remnants of al-Qaeda and the Taliban in the Tora Bora caves, Zhawar Kili and the Shah-e Kot valley in December 2001 and the first few months of 2002.

local chiefs welcomed Nader and submitted to his authority. He left his baggage in Larkana with Nasrollah Mirza, and taking a selected force of cavalry, pressed on down the course of the Indus in pursuit. At Shahdadpur a messenger from Khodayar Khan gave him presents from his master and said that the fugitive had taken refuge in the isolated fort of Umarkot, inaccessible and surrounded by desert.

Undaunted, on 26 February, Nader ordered his men to gather forage, then led them through that day and the following night across the desert to Umarkot. Khodayar Khan had hidden his treasures and prepared for further flight, but when he saw the dust-cloud of Nader's approaching force his resolve faltered. Nader's implacable will had brought him from the ice and snow of the Afghan mountains to the burning desert of southern Sind, a journey of perhaps a thousand miles, in just two months. Khodayar Khan realised that Nader would never give up. Nader and his men quickly overtook him, put him in chains, and forced him to surrender the hidden treasures. These included some precious items that had belonged to Shah Soltan Hosein; looted from Isfahan by the Ghilzais, they had been sent out of Kandahar before Nader took the city, and bought up by Khodayar Khan. Nader returned to Larkana, accompanied by Khodayar Khan and the valuables.[13]

While at Larkana Nader received a visit from the governor of Lahore, who he had summoned – 'whereas between this powerful government and that of Hindustan there exists perfect concord'[14] – to support his action in Sind, and to prevent the flight of any fugitives. The governor brought his son, who was a favourite with Nader, and both behaved more like his vassals than subjects of the Moghul Emperor. But another expected visitor did not turn up.

Perhaps thinking of Alexander's campaigns by land and sea in the Makran and the Indus plain, and wanting to test the feasibility of sea communications with his new territories in India, Nader had ordered Taqi Khan Shirazi some months before to bring 25,000 troops from Fars to join him in Sind. Some of them were to go by land, and a fleet carrying more troops was to sail eastwards along the coast in support. The Dutch contributed one large ship, and a variety of others were requisitioned along the Persian Gulf coast. Taqi Khan was no Alexander, though he encountered some of the same difficulties. His men ran short of supplies and water, and were defeated by Baluchi tribesmen near Kish in the Makran desert. The expedition was an utter failure and by 16 April Taqi Khan was back at Bandar Abbas, with many dead.[15] When he found out what had happened, Nader sent a peremptory message ordering Taqi Khan to meet him in Naderabad (Kandahar).

Despite Taqi Khan's failure, Nader was in generous mood in Larkana. His prestige was high and the locals were gratifyingly submissive. He rested there for a while, celebrated Nowruz with great magnificence, and decided to reinstate Khodayar Khan, who had shown his contrition, renaming him Shah Qoli Khan to mark the occasion. He divided Sind into three, giving Khodayar Khan only the governorship of Thatta, the south-eastern part around the delta of the Indus. The part adjacent to Persian Baluchistan he allocated to the governor of that province, and gave the northern part to the chief of the Da'udputra tribe that had submitted to him at Dera Esmail Khan. Khodayar Khan was obliged to send Nader 10 lakhs of rupees annually and to contribute to Nader's army a body of 2,000 cavalry under the command of his son.[16] As ever, Nader was prepared to give defeated opponents a second chance in his service.

While in Larkana the governor of Balkh sent Nader a large quantity of melons. Nader was particularly fond of these melons, and a regular supply followed him on his travels, from Herat, Merv and Balkh, to be enjoyed by all his court. He received also some beautiful Arab horses from Reza Qoli Mirza, who knew well how his father prized a fine horse. A messenger with presents came also from Mohammad Shah, so Nader sent the man back to Delhi with some of the horses and two hundred camel-loads of melons as presents in return.[17] No doubt he kept the best of the horses: what would be the point of wasting them on a fool like Mohammad Shah... Rested after his exertions, enjoying the warmth of the south, perhaps with the symptoms of his illness in remission under the supervision of his new physician, Alavi Khan, with the sweet melons, the horses from his beloved son, the treasure from Umarkot and the respect of all around him as the conqueror of India, Nader was content.

Nader left Larkana in mid-April 'accompanied by the joy of good fortune, and the power of Solomon',[18] sending the newly minted Shah Qoli Khan home with another of the horses as a present. He sent ahead an order to Reza Qoli Mirza, who had gone to Tehran for Nowruz, to meet him in Herat. Nader had already named Herat as the base for his coming campaign across the Oxus, ordering that quantities of animals, supplies and troops should be sent there from all corners of his dominions. He arrived at Naderabad on 4 May 1740.

At some point before he arrived at Naderabad, Nader discovered that the former Shah Tahmasp and his sons Esmail and Abbas had been murdered at the orders of Reza Qoli Mirza. At Naderabad, Nader saw Taqi Khan, and took away his governorship of Shiraz in punishment for his failure of his naval expedition and his defeat in the Makran. But he may also have heard something from him about Reza Qoli's conduct of affairs as viceroy in his father's absence. Taqi Khan stayed at court.

Taqi Khan had come into conflict with Reza Qoli a number of times in the previous two years. Despite Reza Qoli's authority as viceroy over all Persia, Taqi Khan appears to have taken equivalent authority in Fars and the southern parts of the country, in uneasy rivalry. The two disliked each other, and there had been a number of disputes between them. On one occasion Reza Qoli had taken offence because Taqi Khan had sent his youngest son instead of his eldest as a representative to Reza Qoli's court. While the son was in Isfahan, en route, Reza Qoli had sent orders for his entourage to be stripped of their horses and valuables, and sent back to Bandar Abbas in disgrace.[19]

The report Taqi Khan gave to Nader would have been most unfavourable. Reza Qoli had dismissed some of the advisers Nader had given him, and had indulged in cruel and arbitrary punishments, having men beheaded for trivial offences. He had milked the Caspian silk trade for his own benefit, though to some extent this was a traditional royal prerogative. The silk trade through the Persian Gulf ports was not affected, because Taqi Khan was in control there. With his profits from silk, Reza Qoli had recruited and equipped a body of 12,000 jazayerchis and had dressed them in sumptuous uniforms of cloth of gold, with weapons decorated with gold and silver.

On the other hand, Reza Qoli had successfully kept Persia peaceful while Nader had been absent in India, which had been his prime responsibility. Some of the arguments between him and Taqi Khan had arisen because Reza Qoli had found out about and prevented some of Taqi Khan's acts of oppression or extortion. But Reza Qoli had made one major error in his father's absence. In the spring and again in the autumn of 1739 rumours had circulated in Persia that Nader was dead in India, and that an assembly was being called to the Moghan plain again, as for Nader's coronation in 1736, for Reza Qoli to make himself Shah. Reza Qoli had made a new jiqe for himself, studded with jewels; new dies for new coinage, and a new seal; all of which were taken as evidence that he intended to take the throne.[20]

According to the most authoritative account, the man responsible for keeping Tahmasp and his sons in custody in Sabzavar, Mohammad Hosein Khan Qajar,* had gone to Reza Qoli in Mashhad and asked for permission to kill them, saying that if the rumours about Nader's death proved true, the people of Sabzavar would rise in revolt, overpower the guards set over the Safavid princes, and make Tahmasp Shah again. Reza Qoli must have been relatively well informed about Nader's progress,[21] compared to the general populace, but there may have been a breakdown in communications in the spring of 1739, and again in the autumn, while Nader was struggling back through the Punjab. There were many hangers-on around Reza Qoli who were keen to make trouble. They may have told him that even if his father did return, he would not be sorry for Tahmasp and his sons to be dead.

Beginning to dream of himself as Shah, Reza Qoli hesitated, and then gave permission for the murders. Mohammad Hosein Khan returned to Sabzavar. Tahmasp was in the harem and sensed that something was wrong when the Qajar arrived: he refused to go out. The women clung to him and began to cry with fear. Having demanded repeatedly that Tahmasp come out, Mohammad Hosein eventually went into the harem, pushed the former Shah into a corner and strangled him there with a cord, despite the screams of the women. Mohammad Hosein then killed Tahmasp's nine-year-old son Abbas with a blow of his sword. Tahmasp's younger son Esmail tried to escape by jumping down a well, but was pulled out, screaming and asking after his father and brother. When he saw them 'lying like bloody tulips' he threw himself on his father's body, crying and wailing. Despite the pleas of the household, Mohammad Hosein Khan ordered one of his henchmen to kill Esmail too, and the boy's head was cut off. There is some uncertainty about the timing of these events, but new evidence suggests that the murders took place in May or early June 1739, just before Reza Qoli received the news about Karnal.[22]

Reza Qoli's wife, Fatima Begum, was Tahmasp's sister, but did not find out for some time what had befallen her brother and his children. One account says she saw her old nurse weeping at a banquet held to celebrate Nader's victory at Karnal, and only then learned what had happened. She committed suicide.[23]

---

* Mohammad Hosein Khan was the same Qajar chief that had kept the Qajar tribesmen of Tahmasp's army obedient after the death of Fath Ali Khan Qajar at the end of 1726.

Nader may have heard worrying reports of his son's behaviour while he was in India, but there was probably good mixed in with the bad, and there was certainly nothing so bad as the news of the murders. From Naderabad he went on to Herat, arriving there on 5 June. Nader erected a great tent ornamented with jewels and pearls from India, and put inside it many of the treasures, along with a newly made replica of the peacock throne. Since leaving India, he had ordered the adornment of an assortment of items, including horse-harnesses, quivers, shields and swords with the jewels taken from Mohammad Shah. These were now displayed in the tent too. Local people and travellers were allowed to pass through the tent and admire the contents. A few days later his third son, Emam Qoli, his grandson Shahrokh and his nephew Ali Qoli arrived there to welcome him, but there was no sign of Reza Qoli.

For several days Nader fêted the young princes, and gave them armlets and belts decorated with precious stones. Ali Qoli was now a young man, about the same age as Reza Qoli. Nader had already given him the governorship of Mashhad for a time, and had arranged for him to be married to a Georgian princess, the princess Kethewan, in the winter of 1736–1737. With his brother Ebrahim dead, Nader looked all the more fondly on his nephew, Ebrahim's son. He was bringing Ali Qoli on with military and administrative responsibilities, like one of his own sons; but Ali Qoli had shown less energy than Reza Qoli, and had amused himself in Mashhad rather than attending to the business of the province. Nader promised him that once the campaign in Turkestan was over, he would go to Daghestan and avenge Ebrahim's death. But there was still no sign of Reza Qoli. Finally, keeping Ali Qoli by him, Nader sent Nasrollah and the other princes back to Mashhad and prepared to leave Herat.[24]

By now Nader was thinking that some of the actions he had been prepared to overlook as youthful impulsiveness, were in fact signs that Reza Qoli was aiming to supplant him on the throne. This rumour had been flying around in Nader's absence, and once Nader began to show displeasure at his son's conduct, Taqi Khan and others would have been ready to whisper the thought of treason and strengthen his suspicions. The disobedience of Reza Qoli's campaign in Turkestan, when he knew his father intended to make war there himself, his extravagance, his removal of the men Nader had appointed to advise him, the murders, and finally this delay in coming to greet him, all seemed to point to the same thing.

On 20 June 1740 Nader left Herat with the army. Five days later he made camp about 60 miles north of Herat, and finally Reza Qoli arrived. Unfortunately, Nader's son did not present himself modestly, but arrived with a great fanfare, with his 12,000 brightly coloured jazayerchis in attendance. Nader reviewed them calmly, and in public made a show of welcoming his son, but the spectacle confirmed his impression that Reza Qoli's ideas were getting too grand. Nader did not like vainglory and magnificence[25] – it reminded him of Isfahan, Shah Soltan Hosein and Tahmasp.

After the review, Nader ordered the jazayerchis to be disbanded, dividing them out in small groups to his own commanders. Later, he spoke to Reza Qoli about his conduct as viceroy, and tried to mollify him over the loss of his soldiers. He explained that the empire could not support two armies and two courts – the people would not understand. He told Reza Qoli that grandeur and display did not suit him, and that he should conduct himself in a way that no-one could criticise. Growing more severe, Nader then reprimanded him for the killing of Tahmasp. He deposed Reza Qoli as viceroy and gave orders that Nasrollah be viceroy in Mashhad in his place. Reza Qoli would accompany him on the campaign in Turkestan. By nature proud and headstrong, Reza Qoli was bitterly humiliated.[26]

After three days Nader moved on via Andkhui toward Balkh, arriving there around the end of July. Nader had sent ahead teams of Indian craftsmen from Delhi to build boats to ferry his army across the river Oxus, and by the time he arrived in July there were over a thousand boats ready. Nader put an advance guard over the river at Kilif on 10 August, and loaded the boats with provisions and his cannon. The army then marched downstream to Kerki, where Nader sent Reza Qoli with 8,000 men two days ahead of the main army to Chaharju, with Ali Qoli keeping pace with him on the northern bank of the river. As when he sent competing units raised from rival tribes to attack a tough enemy, Nader was setting up a rivalry between the two cousins, to show Reza Qoli, with crude psychology, that his place was not of right, but had to be earned. When the main army reached Chaharju Nader's corps of veteran jazayerchis, 12,000 strong, joined the other troops on the northern bank to secure a bridgehead. His engineers then built a bridge of boats, with forts at either end to secure it, as was their usual practice in hostile territory. The rest of the army, with Nader's harem and guard, marched across on 6 September.

At this point Abo 'l-Feiz of Bokhara sent his vizier to Nader to try to avoid war. Nader heard him out but insisted that his master must do homage in person. Abo 'l-Feiz wanted to comply but had difficulty restraining his Uzbek vassals, who converged on Bokhara in large numbers to avenge the defeat Reza Qoli had inflicted on them three years earlier. Abo 'l-Feiz waited in some trepidation for the Persians with his forces near Qarakol, south-west of Bokhara. It seems some of his men attacked Nader's army on or around 11 September, but were beaten off by the fire of Nader's cannon and zanburaks. This was enough to subdue the ardent spirits among the Uzbeks, and Abo 'l-Feiz made his submission on 12 September, with his officials and vassal chiefs.[27]

Abo 'l-Feiz was permitted to keep his Khanate, as a Persian tributary. Nader had the *khutba* read in the mosques of Bokhara and coins struck in his name, but did not allow his soldiers to pillage there. He took many thousands of Uzbeks into his service, and sent them to Khorasan. He annexed all of Abo 'l-Feiz's territory south of the Oxus, but on 6 October he returned him his jiqe and seal and created him Shah. At the same time Nader sent men to Samarkand, where they took the great jade slab from over the tomb of Timur, and removed it to Mashhad. It broke in two in the process.[28]

Nader's health was again giving him trouble, and when Nader was unwell he was irritable, liable to morose melancholia and likely to fly into rages. His Indian physician, Alavi Khan, was able to treat the symptoms to some extent, and made recommendations for an altered diet. He would also have told him to drink less alcohol. Nader cannot have been an easy patient, but it seems Alavi Khan was up to the job – when Nader lost his temper Alavi Khan answered him back, reprimanded him and gave him wholesome advice that went beyond medical matters. When he had time to reflect, Nader respected the man's frankness, and the two got on. Alavi Khan was one of the few people able to restrain Nader. Between the dyspeptic father and the stroppy son, life at court would have been tense.[29]

The conquest of Turan (Turkestan) was of great symbolic importance to Nader, and to cement it he resolved on a marriage alliance, to bring the blood of Genghis into his family, as with Nasrollah's marriage he had brought in that of Timur. Abo 'l-Feiz had no choice but to obey. Two of Abo 'l-Feiz's daughters were selected, the elder for Reza Qoli, the younger for Ali Qoli. But Reza Qoli was told that the younger daughter was cleverer, more beautiful and generally to be preferred, so he asked Nader to let him have her instead. Nader refused, saying that this would be an insult to Abo 'l-Feiz. Reza Qoli was already resentful of Ali Qoli and the way he was being treated as his equal. He replied petulantly to the effect that if his wishes were so little regarded, he would not wed at all. Angry and frustrated with Reza Qoli, Nader married the elder girl himself and gave the younger to Ali Qoli as arranged.[30] The incident was a further twist in the downward spiral of ill will between father and son.

From Bokhara Nader sent messengers to Ilbars of Khwarezm, calling on him to come to his court and submit. Ilbars had the messengers killed. Nader made his preparations for a campaign towards Khiva. The hardships of his childhood and the long suffering of Khorasan under the raids of the Turkmen slavers were in his mind as he set out for Chaharju. On the way he heard that a body of Turkmen and Uzbeks were riding east at Ilbars' orders, with instructions to destroy the bridge of boats over the Oxus. Leaving his baggage behind, Nader left his camp in the middle of the night with a picked force of cavalry and rode hard for the bridge. Arriving early in the morning, he made sure all his men were safely over and then camped on the far side. His scouts the next day saw a column of black dust in the west, announcing the arrival of the Turkmen. Without hesitation Nader swiftly ordered his men and took them toward the approaching enemy. The two forces of horsemen closed rapidly and the Persians accelerated to a gallop, levelling their lances. 'Submerged by the waves of the victorious troops', the Turkmen scattered and fled.[31]

Nader and his men rested for a few days after this clash, and the rest of the army came up. While the army camped at Chaharju, Reza Qoli went to Nader and asked permission to return to Mashhad. Treading carefully, Nader's official historian recorded that this was because he desired ardently to see his brother Nasrollah – but it surely had more to do with Reza Qoli's unhappiness at his father's court. No doubt thinking good riddance, Nader let him go. At around this time Taqi Khan also left – having successfully secured from Nader his reinstatement as governor of Fars. Taqi Khan seems to have prospered in the poisonous atmosphere – his fortunes had revived as Reza Qoli's had sunk. No doubt he had dropped quips at Reza Qoli's expense into the uneasy flow of conversation. Taqi Khan was described as the Shah's first counsellor and favourite* – Nader would hear no criticism of him.

---

* 'Mignon'. There is no evidence to indicate a homosexual relationship between the two men (Nader was hostile to homosexuality according to Hanway, vol. 4, p. 269). It was an unusually close friendship, and in many ways an unlikely one. But then as now it was quite normal in Iran for male friends to show affection for each other in public without anyone drawing other conclusions.

Whether now or earlier, Ali Qoli also returned to Mashhad.[32] With his engaging new wife, his uncle's favour, and Reza Qoli humiliated, he too would have been content.

Around 19 October the army left Chaharju, with cannon and stores again loaded in the boats. The men marched downstream along the bank of the Oxus, surrounded by billowing dust, so thick that the soldiers could only distinguish their neighbours by their voices. Many developed eye trouble. To forestall raids and ambushes Nader divided the army into four divisions, which marched in front, behind and on the flanks of the baggage in long lines, making an extended hollow rectangle to protect it. If any man left the ranks, whatever the reason, the nasaqchis rode up and beat his head against his saddle as punishment. Nader also detached flying columns, to march outside the main formation, ready to ride to the assistance of any element of the army that might be attacked. Several times bands of Turkmen rode up, but withdrew when they saw that there were no weak points in the Persian order of march.[33]

When they reached the Deve Boyun Gorge, at the border of Khwarezm, Nader built a fortified depot for his stores and delayed there, hoping that Ilbars would come out to fight. There were some hard skirmishes with the Yomut Turkmen, but no pitched battle. Ilbars kept instead to his fortress at Hazarasp, and flooded the surrounding countryside to stop Nader bringing up his cannon. Nader arrived there on 6 November, but it became clear that Ilbars was going to sit tight. After a further delay, Nader was told that Ilbars' family and valuables were at Khangah, another of the five fortresses of Khwarezm, and he moved off in that direction in an attempt to draw Ilbars out.

The stratagem worked, and as Nader approached Khangah, he learned that Ilbars was on his way there too. An advance party of Yomut and Tekke Turkmen moved to threaten the Persians, and without delay Nader advanced rapidly and charged them in person with his guards. Many of the Turkmen were killed and others were taken captive. Ilbars regrouped his men at Khangah, then emerged again to give battle with a mixed force of Uzbeks and Turkmen, matchlock-armed infantry, and some cannon that had been captured from the Russians in 1716. Nader attacked, and Ilbars' force soon collapsed and fled. Ilbars took refuge in the fortress at Khangah, and Nader laid siege to it. The Persian cannon played on the walls for three days, and the Persian engineers exploded several mines under them.

As the Persians prepared for an assault on 14 November, most of the Uzbek garrison surrendered, and Ilbars himself was dragged out the following day. Nader might have shown him mercy, but the relatives of his murdered envoys protested, and Ilbars cravenly tried to avoid responsibility by saying the men had been killed without his knowledge. Nader said, 'If you have not abilities to govern the few subjects who inhabit your territories, you do not deserve to live.' He had Ilbars' throat cut, along with twenty or thirty of his followers, notorious raiders and slavers.[34]

With Ilbars dead, the other fortresses of Khwarezm surrendered; except Khiva, where the leading citizens trusted to their strong walls, and were reluctant to lose the large number of Persian slaves, abducted by the Turkmen, that cultivated the land around. Nader advanced to the city and began another siege. Within just four days the Persians had drained away the water in the ditch around the walls, and had made breaches in them by exploding mines, so that by 25 November they were ready to make an assault. Seeing the futility and danger of further resistance, the Khivans surrendered.

In the city and the surrounding region Nader found a large number of slaves, most of whom, like him, came from northern Khorasan. He gave them money, provisions and horses, and decreed the foundation of a new town for them south of Abivard, to be called Khivaqabad. There were also many Russians among the slaves, the survivors of Peter the Great's expedition to Khwarezm of 1716. Nader gave them money and horses also, and they eventually made it back to Russian territory. Nader took 4,000 young Uzbeks into his army, and appointed Taher Khan, a relative of Abo 'l-Feiz, as governor of Khwarezm. Among the foreigners that Nader found in Khiva there were two English traders, Mr Thompson and Mr Hogg. Nader gave them a passport and leave to trade in his territories, and told them they should appeal direct to him if they had any trouble. They recorded that even the lowliest of Nader's soldiers were well dressed in silk, and had plenty of Indian money.[35]

Despite his rapacity when extracting money from them to pay his troops, Nader was in favour of merchants and trade in principle. There are indications that he took the protection of trade more seriously after his return from India. He was active to ensure that the caravan routes were safe for merchants, which in his time they normally were. A number of incidents show that his openness to petitions from traders for redress against robbers or unfair treatment from officials was real, not just fair words.[36]

One story illustrates the reputation Nader gained for upholding security on the roads. A Persian merchant travelling from Kabul had been robbed near Nishapur in Khorasan, and complained to Nader, who asked whether anyone else had been nearby at the time of the robbery. The man replied there had been no-one. 'Were there no trees, or stones, or bushes?' asked Nader. The trader said, 'Yes, there was one large solitary tree, under whose shade I was reposing when I was attacked.' So Nader sent two of his executioners to flog the tree every morning, until it either restored the property that had been lost, or revealed the names of the thieves who had taken it. The punishment went ahead, and the tree was beaten every morning, but it had suffered less than a week when one morning all the stolen goods were found, carefully placed at its roots. The robbers had been so intimidated by the beatings inflicted on the tree, and the thought of what their punishment would be if they were ever discovered, that they had given up their plunder. When the outcome was reported to Nader, he smiled and said, 'I knew what the flogging of that tree would produce.'[37] The story may reflect the fact that Nader enforced the responsibility of village headmen for safety on the roads in their area.

On 29 November Nader issued an order stipulating that from now on he should be addressed in letters and in the *khutba* not as *Valinemat* (Lord of Beneficence) as formerly, but as King of Kings (*Shahanshah*) of the World, Rarity (*Nader*) of the Age, Command-giver of Persia, Throne-giver of Hindustan, and of Khwarezm, land of the Uzbeks.[38]

The King of Kings left Khiva on 9 December, marching for Mashhad via Chaharju and Merv. With typical care, he had given orders weeks before for wells to be sunk to provide water to supply the army along its route across the desert.[39] While at Merv he replaced the Afshar governor with a Qajar, and had several people put to death, including one, Rahim Soltan, who was said to have encouraged Reza Qoli Mirza to murder the Safavid princes and to make himself Shah.

From Merv Nader went on to visit his old home territory of Abivard, Kalat, the Darra Gaz, Kobkan and Khabushan. He ordered a monument to be erected at the place of his birth, surmounted by a dome topped with a golden sword – to show 'that the sword issued from hence'.[40] Apparently the workmen asked him the date of his birth, so that they could carve it on the building, but he told them to inscribe the present date instead, implying that he did not know the answer. While there, he made a speech to his officers, and told them how he had spent the early part of his life; the poverty of his family, the ass and the camel they had had, and how he had fed them. He said, 'You now see, to what a height it has pleased the Almighty to exalt me; from this you should learn not to despise men of low estate'.'[41]

At Kalat Nader gave orders to add new buildings to those already there, so that there would be squares, bath-houses and mosques inside the fortress as well as his treasury, where the treasures of India were kept, a mausoleum of black marble, and a palace. The water supply had been improved, and extensive gardens laid out. Nader also visited Khivaqabad, where he made gifts of food, money and clothes to the new arrivals. He entered Mashhad finally on 17 January 1741.

Nader's stay in Mashhad lasted just under two months. At the centre of Khorasan, his home territory and the main recruiting-ground in Persia for his army, Mashhad had become his capital.[42] He was more indulgent in Mashhad than in Isfahan. When told that his soldiers were being charged at a high rate for food and other necessities, he let it ride. While there he was reunited with his sons and his nephew, he made preparations for his next campaign, to Daghestan, and he examined the revenue accounts. One outcome of his audit was that a number of tax officials were executed.

Nader also, in accordance with vows he had made in India and in Turkestan, gave costly gifts to the shrine of Emam Reza, including lamps, carpets and an ornate lock studded with precious stones. The tombstone from Timur's tomb at Samarkand had arrived; it was taken to Nader and he mused on it for a while. Perhaps Nader was put off by the fact that the stone had been broken in transit; perhaps he saw an absurdity in stealing the great Timur's gravestone after all. It was not the first or last time that, having decided on some grandiose gesture, he later changed his mind. Nader was attracted to, but uneasy about grand demonstrations of kingly self-importance; it was one of the few things that ever made him vacillate. He announced that instead of that one, he would have a tombstone of gold encrusted with jewels, and the jade made its slow way back to Samarkand.[43]

Nader had erected a second tomb for himself in Mashhad, and some joker wrote graffiti on it to the effect that he was everywhere in the world, but his proper place was still empty. The writing was quickly removed for fear that Nader would find out about it and order many to be put to death as punishment – but it is likely that he was told, and forbore to punish anyone in his favoured capital.[44]

Nader was also giving thought at this time to his plans for a fleet in the Persian Gulf, but he was content to direct from a distance and allow others to implement his orders. His admiral in the Persian Gulf had been Latif Khan, who had retaken Bahrain for him in 1736.* In 1737 and 1738 Latif Khan made expeditions to Oman, ostensibly to support the Sultan of Oman against rebels there. The Persians were successful, but Taqi Khan, who accompanied the second adventure, quarrelled with both the Sultan and Latif Khan, and had the latter poisoned.

After Latif Khan's death the campaign went rapidly downhill. Taqi Khan was more talented at finance and court intrigue than naval logistics and military strategy. Some Persian garrisons were overwhelmed, and Arab seamen in the Persian fleet mutinied for want of provisions, going over to piracy. The mutineers were beaten in a sea battle in January 1739 but before the Persians could renew their efforts in Muscat, Nader ordered Taqi Khan to sail for Sind, on the expedition that ended disastrously in the Makran.†

After that debacle the Arab sailors mutinied again, prompted once more by Taqi Khan's failure properly to pay or provision them. The mutiny was serious, but in 1741 some of the mutineers came to terms. Nader had decided to put more effort into his Persian Gulf plans. Control of Muscat and the Straits of Hormuz was important if he were to communicate with his Indian territories by sea, and would enable him to milk revenue from all trade going in and out of the Persian Gulf – including trade with Ottoman-controlled ports. To those ends Nader decided to take up an offer from the English East India Company to build ships for him at Surat, where the Company's own ships were built, in the Gulf of Cambay on the west coast of India.[45]

The first of these ships arrived in 1741. They were excellent, but expensive. So Nader set about establishing his own shipbuilding yards at Bushire. One difficulty with this project was a lack of skilled shipbuilders. Another was that the Persian Gulf coast was completely devoid of timber; so Nader had it brought from the thick forests of Mazanderan, 600 miles to the north. Because the roads were poor or nonexistent, the timber had to be carried on the shoulders of porters for much of the way. Many died of exhaustion.[46]

There were further naval clashes with pirates and mutineers in 1741, but by the early months of 1742 the Persian fleet consisted of fifteen stout

* See above, Chapter 7.
* As described earlier in this chapter.

ships, most of them Surat-built. The keel of a large ship had been laid down in Nader's own shipyard in Bushire; and further disturbances in Oman again favoured a Persian intervention. The ensign that flew over the ships of the new Persian navy bore a red sword on a white field.[47]

The other projects absorbing Nader's attention in Mashhad early in 1741 were the forthcoming war in Daghestan, his revenge on the Lazgis for the killing of his brother Ebrahim;[48] and the resumption of war with the Ottomans, which was to follow. On 14 March 1741 he left Mashhad for Daghestan, having paid the army for a year in advance. He gave the government of Khorasan to Nasrollah in his absence, and took Reza Qoli and Emam Qoli with him. They celebrated Nowruz near Khabushan and marched on toward Astarabad. One account says that Nader wore a magnificent new crown at Nowruz, which in place of the usual black heron's feather denoting kingship, carried four, mounted together on a circular, jewelled band. The four jiqe symbolised not only the territories of Persia, India and Turkestan, which Nader had already conquered, but also the Ottoman Empire, which he had chosen as his next and culminating conquest (after the Lazgis had been crushed). But characteristically Nader, disliking the splendour of the crown, put it away and only ever wore it once.[49]

Nader's official historian says that the period of Nader's stay in Khorasan passed in constant celebrations,[50] but the dark antagonisms below the surface of court life had not gone away. Another account says that, while Reza Qoli was at Mashhad, he criticised Nader, saying:

> My father wants to conquer even the ends of the earth,
> and for that reason he oppresses us and all of Persia and
> does not stop fighting everywhere; but we have no means
> of freeing ourselves from him, neither we nor all of Persia
> nor the neighbouring states and monarchies either, unless
> he is overcome by death.

Of course, bystanders reported Reza Qoli's words to Nader.[51]

Before the army reached Astarabad the troops had a difficult time passing through the Gorgan valley in heavy rain. The troops had to cross the river repeatedly, and men and animals were drowned. Then one day, while the army was camped, a sudden flood swept down and carried off several thousand men and animals. Nader's treasury was also lost, worth about 500,000 tomans. The water continued to rise, and Nader himself, who had camped on a small hill and had refused to move to higher ground, was cut off. He sat on his portable throne and watched the waters rise. They rose further … and then fell. Nader crossed to safety on an elephant and moved on. His men went looking for the goods that had been swept away further down the valley. Some things were recovered, bodies were buried, and after two or three days the army moved on to Astarabad.[52]

While his men were resting in Astarabad, Nader discovered that a force of Abdalis he had sent against the Lazgis in Daghestan had achieved some successes, forcing the submission of several tribes – though many of the Abdalis had perished in the snow as they withdrew. He sent the Abdali commanders 200,000 rupees and coats of honour as a reward for them and their men.[53] Nader knew from previous experience that the campaign ahead of him in Daghestan would be difficult, but this was encouraging.

From Astarabad the army marched on to Sari, travelling through the thick forests of Mazanderan. The route ahead led through the Savad Kuh district, before crossing a pass over the Alborz mountains and descending to Tehran. As usual, Nader made his way in relative isolation, behind the main army. When he was travelling, he did not ride in company with courtiers or the senior officers of his army, but preferred the company of his women. Given that he was on the move most of the time, this meant that he preferred female company for much of his waking hours, as well as his sleeping hours. It seems that this preference became more pronounced in the latter part of his life.

As he rode with his women, protected only by the eunuchs, the watch-guards (keshıkchı) went a mile or more ahead to enforce the qoroq. The women rode on white horses. Female entertainers sang as they went along; there would have been perhaps 60 women (wives, concubines, maidservants, singers, dancing-girls) and 60 eunuchs altogether.[54] They were climbing through a narrow, wooded valley on 15 May 1741 when there was a loud bang from close by. A bullet grazed Nader's arm and hit his thumb where he was holding the horse's reins, then smacked into the neck of his horse, near the animal's spine. The animal, stunned, collapsed to the ground, taking Nader with it. An assassin had concealed himself twenty paces from the track, hidden well enough in the thick undergrowth of the forest to avoid being discovered by the guards combing the ground for the qoroq, and had fired at Nader as he passed.

According to one account Nader was able to describe his attacker, so he must have seen the man just before he fired. Either the assassin was

put off his aim when Nader's eyes locked with his, or Nader himself
pulled up, or was riding too fast – at any rate the man missed. By the
time Nader recovered and the harem guards came up, alerted by the
screams of the women, the assassin had gone. Reza Qoli was close at
hand too, and came to help, but he was the last person Nader wanted
to see as he struggled up from the ground – he snarled at him to get
away and stay out of his sight. Nader mounted another horse and rode
to the place from which the man had fired his shot, but there was no
sign of him. Reza Qoli and the guards searched, but after a while the
impenetrable thickets of the forest made any further pursuit pointless.

His injuries being minor, Nader rode on, after only a short delay
to bind up his thumb, to the place selected for that night's camp. But
the next day he stayed away from company, and did not come to the
divankhane as usual. After three days of this, he called his commanders
together and gave a description of his attacker – a tall, dark, thin-
bearded man. He asked them whether any of them had known of such
a man in the army. They said not. Their soldiers went through the
nearby villages, looking for suspects and dragging some people away.
Some tried to bribe the soldiers rather than be taken before Nader, and
the soldiers said to him that this was a sign of their guilt. But he replied
no, that they should be released: the man that had made such a daring
attempt on his life must have been a man of distinguished bravery, of a
courage equal to his own.

Painters were called from Isfahan to paint pictures of the man
according to the Shah's description, and these were circulated through
the empire. He gave orders that if found, the man should be brought
to him unharmed: he declared that he would spare the man if he gave
an honest account of the plot against his life. Two brothers, the sons of
Delavar Khan Teimani, told Nader that they had once had a servant
who answered his description of the assassin. He had been brave, and
was such a marksman that 'he could hit the neck-bone of a snake in the
dark': but he had disappeared some time before. Nader ordered the
brothers to find this marksman.[55]

Nader crossed the watershed of the Alborz mountains, and went
with the army on to Tehran. There he ordered Reza Qoli to stay,
allowing him freedom and the revenues of the province, but setting
guards to watch over him.[56] Reza Qoli was again in disgrace; Nader
already suspected his son of complicity in the assassination attempt.
In Tehran he met and spoke with the Russian envoy, Kalushkin. The
Russian reported that in their discussions Nader was determined to

keep his freedom of action, and could not be pinned down. He was much more difficult to talk to than previously. He was no more friendly toward the Ottomans than he had ever been, but Kalushkin could not be sure he would stay friends with Russia.[57] From Tehran Nader moved on to Qazvin, arriving around the beginning of June.

Nader had lost his brother Ebrahim in Daghestan, and was on his way to avenge him. But now he was losing or being separated from more and more of his oldest and closest relatives and companions. It seems that his mother, with whom he had suffered the poverty and humiliations of his youth, and whom he had loved tenderly, had died while he was in India. Nader's mother, hidden away in the women's quarters, appears very little in any of the contemporary accounts of Nader's life, and this obscurity is reflected by the fact that even the date of her death went unrecorded. The omission of this event even by Nader's official historian, suggests that Nader himself may have dictated that it did not belong in the account of his life, intended as a chronicle of stirring deeds and victories rather than a personal history. But another account suggests that the news of his mother's death affected Nader deeply, as one would expect from their closeness in his childhood and from the gentle influence she seems to have had on his attitude to women generally. Many people, however little it may appear in their outward conduct, experience disorientation and a sense of loneliness after the death of a parent, and this must have played a part in the changes that took place in Nader's inner life at this time. Apparently Nader wept when told the news, 'with true sadness' and after his return from India erected a mosque over his mother's tomb.[58]

Of those who had been companions and advisers in the past, Tahmasp Khan Jalayer, whose support had been so invaluable in his Daghestan campaigns of 1734, was now in Kabul and Sind, looking after Nader's Indian territories. Nasrollah, his right hand at the battle of Karnal, was in Mashhad. Reza Qoli, at one time his favourite son, was now in disgrace and under guard in Tehran. His favourite, the joker Taqi Khan, was in Shiraz.

And now in Qazvin Alavi Khan, the Indian physician who had done much to relieve his pain and restrain his furies since the army left Delhi, asked Nader's permission to leave for Mecca on the Hajj. Nader had promised him this pilgrimage in Delhi, and reluctantly let him go. Alavi Khan had done his best to alleviate Nader's bad temper as well as the symptoms of his illness, and had apparently been so successful that for a fortnight at a time Nader had not even ordered anyone to be beaten, let alone mutilations or executions. But from now on Nader governed increasingly without support, advice or restraint. While still in Qazvin, he learned that despite the success of his Abdalis against some of the Lazgi tribes, others had attacked and ravaged parts of Georgia. The news sent Nader into a rage, in which he again promised terrible vengeance on the tribes of Daghestan. He declared that he would make prostitutes of all the virgin daughters of their chiefs, and to avenge the death of his brother, he would behead five thousand Lazgis.[59] He sent another detachment of Afghans to restore order in Georgia.

When Nader arrived in Shirvan the memory of his previous campaign in the region and the size of the 150,000-strong army he brought this time* were enough to overawe many of the rebellious Lazgi chiefs. They came down from the mountains and kissed the foot of his throne, promising obedience. By mid-August Nader and his men were in Qumuq, where many more of the Lazgis made their submission to him. Among them was the obstinate Sorkhai, who had never submitted before. Nader received the chiefs graciously and gave them presents. He stayed in Qumuq a full month, perhaps thinking that he only had to wait, and all the Lazgis would come to make their peace.

While Nader was in Qumuq a courier arrived from Mashhad, to tell him that a band of Uzbeks had revolted in Khwarezm, taking Khiva; all the careful arrangements he had made for the government of that province at the end of the previous year had been overturned.† He sent orders for Nasrollah and his advisers to move against the rebels. In September he moved forward again along narrow mountain paths in difficult conditions, probing for the last centres of Lazgi resistance in the mountains of Avaria, around the fort of Khunzakh, in the furthest corner of Daghestan. There was hardly any flat ground, nor any path along which two foot soldiers could march abreast; even in the height of summer, snow covered much of the ground.[60]

Nearly all the Lazgi tribes were now reduced to obedience, and after the efforts of the Abdalis before his arrival, Nader had achieved their submission almost without a struggle. He was tantalisingly close to success. But Nader had lapsed from his own principles: he had taken too long over it. Suffering discomfort again from his ailments, perhaps

---

* The majority of the army was made up of Afghans, Uzbeks and Indians (Bazin, p. 289).

† In fact, within a year, the revolt in Khiva collapsed and the rebels were expelled. Representatives of the people of Khiva met Nasrollah at Merv in the summer of 1743 and submitted (JN, vol. 2, p. 136).

lulled into complacency by the apparent tractability of the rebel tribes, perhaps distracted by his suspicions and doubts about his son, he had not pressed forward vigorously enough, as he would have done five or ten years earlier. By the time the most crucial, clinching part of the campaign came, against the last fort in the most difficult terrain, in the highest hills, most exposed to the early advent of winter weather, it was getting too late. Maybe Nader could not face the effort of that last push, and wanted to get to more comfortable quarters. He may have thought, the campaign up to then having been so easy, that the last fort could be safely left to the next campaigning season. Around the end of September the slashing winds, snow and rain persuaded him to withdraw. The army pulled back eastwards for the winter, toward Darband and the lower ground by the Caspian.[61]

As Nader withdrew, the still-hostile Qaraqaitaq Lazgis demonstrated that they were far from a spent force, attacking some recruits that were marching through the mountain forests to join Nader at Darband, defeating them and carrying off some horses and baggage animals. These recruits were from tribes of Lazgis that had submitted; others of the same tribes had been ordered out of their valleys to resettle in Khorasan. Many villages had been burned. This treatment (marking a shift for the worse from Nader's earlier, successful policy of clemency to submissive peoples and individuals) dismayed and embittered the Lazgis as a whole, making them believe that Nader would show no mercy even when they submitted, and that they had nothing to lose by fighting on. It strengthened the will of the Qaraqaitaq and others that still held out against Nader to resist further.

The combination of cruelty to pacified tribes, and apparent weakness in the face of continued resistance in Avaria, was unfortunate. The memory of the defeats they had suffered six years before, along with the great prestige Nader had gained by the conquest of India, and his dire threats, had cowed the Lazgis initially. Now, as he withdrew, they began to wonder whether Nader was such a hard nut after all. As more of the Lazgis turned to resistance, their memory of Nader's tactics in his last campaign in the Caucasus made them more dangerous enemies. They would not try to defeat him by confrontation in open battle.

According to one account Nader's camp was raided in the night as he withdrew to Darband; the impudent Lazgis even broke into his harem compound, carrying off valuables and some of his women. Raiding and the abduction of women were the favourite sports of the young men of many of the tribes of the Caucasus. These events drove

Nader's anger to a new pitch – he had a number of his own officers and guards executed for their negligence, and he swore he would not turn aside until he had subdued the rebels. He camped at Darband on 16 October but marched out again on the 25th. He made his men build forts two or three hours' march apart all over the country, and returned to Darband on 19 November.[62]

From now on, as the opportunity of a quick punitive campaign faded, Nader's problems and frustrations in Daghestan grew and multiplied. Prime among them, after the gradual stiffening of the tribes' resistance, was the difficulty of supplying his troops with provisions. Daghestan was poor, rugged country and thinly populated, incapable of supplying Nader's large army even if the population had been friendly. The mountains, valleys and forests were also ideal for guerrilla warfare against his supply columns. The obvious solution was to bring in supplies to Darband by sea, but the Persians had no ships on the Caspian that were big enough.

Nader tried to get ships from the Russians, but the Russians refused, because they knew they would not get their ships back. They had in any case become uneasy at Nader's activity so close to their borders, and his increasingly suspicious and hostile attitude toward their envoys. Still allies in name at least, the Russians allowed their traders to bring in some supplies for the Persian army, but little more than a trickle, and at a high price. The Russian government took over the ships that had carried out this trade in order to control it more effectively. Nader managed, from the summer of 1742, to get Captain John Elton, an English trader, to carry rice from Gilan to Darband for him in a ship built for the English Russia Company in Kazan; but this only annoyed the Russians further.* At the recommendation of their ambassador, Kalushkin, they sent extra troops to guard the frontier on the Terek river, and the fort at Kizliar, and reinforced their garrison at Astrakhan.[63]

In January 1742 Ottoman ambassadors arrived at Nader's camp north of Darband with a reply to the messages Nader had sent to Istanbul from Naderabad in May 1738. The Ottoman position had not changed; the Sultan could not accept the Ja'fari mazhhab. Nader sent another letter in reply, but this time it took a more threatening tone. Phrased in

---

* Elton continued in Nader's service and successfully built up a little fleet for him on the Caspian, which by 1745 consisted of two frigates of about 18 guns, and four smaller vessels. But the Russians, who took a proprietorial attitude to everything to do with the Caspian Sea, grew angrier and angrier at Elton's activities. Elton was murdered in Gilan in 1751.

careful, precise diplomatic language the letter recalled that in former times the Persian Empire had included various provinces of Anatolia, Turkestan and India. Under the Safavids these provinces had been lost, but Nader, since his coronation, had made it his policy to restore them to Persian rule: except those ruled by the Ottoman Sultan. Nader still hoped that the Sultan would accept the proposal for a fifth mazhab, in order that friendship should be restored between the two empires, and causes of discord removed. If the Sultan would not agree, Nader would, in the most brotherly and friendly spirit, resolve to go himself into Turkey, in the hope that a conference between him and the Sultan could resolve these great matters 'to their mutual satisfaction'. Nader had in mind a conference like those he had enjoyed with Mohammad Shah and Abo 'l-Feiz.[64]

To back up his position in this dispute with the Ottoman Sultan, and to underline the importance of his religious policy, Nader called together the leading clerics of the empire again, and issued from Darband a further decree on religious observance. This was more strongly Sunni in tone than before, heaping praise on the first four caliphs, including the three normally cursed by Shi'as, and blaming Shah Esmail, the first Safavid Shah of Persia, for stirring up all the disputes that had divided Islam. It noted that all the assembled holy men and jurists had advised him of the correctness of this view of the matter. It called upon all his subjects to abandon the erroneous contrary doctrines, and always to give all four caliphs due reverence in their prayers – 'or risk the anger of heaven, and our own redoubtable resentment'.[65]

Before Nader could reopen hostilities with the Ottomans, the war with the Lazgis had to be brought to a conclusion. Nader did not show his usual energy in doing so; it seems likely that he was troubled by his ailments, and the unhealthy, damp climate. He moved against the rebels in Tabarsaran in May, but was stymied repeatedly by the hit-and-run tactics of the Lazgis. He was growing more and more frustrated.

In July, in order to make a secure base against constant raids, he established a new fortified camp a little inland from the coast, to the north-west of Darband. He bitterly named it Iran Kharab – the Ruin of Persia: hardly encouraging for the troops. The irony of this name was to take a terrible twist, and to prove truer than Nader could have imagined.

Slowly, Nader's soldiers gained the upper hand in the foothills of Tabarsaran, burning the rebel villages, and he moved on to make another attempt on Avaria. But 6,000 men of his advance guard were ambushed and defeated in a narrow valley in August, in a repeat of the debacle that had killed his brother. Furious, he executed several of the officers he held responsible. In September another force, this time under his personal command, led by 3,000 men chopping their way through the forests with axes, was also thrown back. At the same time another Persian force was more successful, capturing the Qaraqaitaq stronghold of Quraish, and forcing that tribe at last to make their submission. The fort of Quraish was demolished down to its foundations. Despite this last piece of good news, Avaria and the fort of Khunzakh were still unconquered. Nader was little further forward than he had been a year before. He withdrew to Iran Kharab in October in angry mood.[66]

At some point over the summer, Nader's people had brought to him a man called Nik Qadam, who had been arrested near Herat, and had confessed to the assassination attempt in the Savad Kuh. He was the man that the sons of Delavar Khan had identified from Nader's description after the shooting.

Nader promised Nik Qadam he would allow him to live if he told the truth; but if he heard one dishonest word, Nik Qadam would die immediately. The man told his story. He had been the friend of some of Reza Qoli's servants. Around the time Nader was returning from India, these people had told Reza Qoli of his marksmanship, and Nik Qadam had given him a demonstration. Reza Qoli asked the man if he would carry out a task for him, and he answered he would – 'even if it were to bring him the heads of his own children'. According to the story Reza Qoli asked the man, 'Can you kill the Shah while he is riding his horse?' He said that a number of others, including Mohammad Hosein Khan Qajar, had been present.

Nik Qadam had asked for an hour to think about it, then returned, and swore he could, and would. He had tried to find an opportunity to kill Nader before the start of the Turkestan campaign, but had failed. Then he had been ill. Finally, his chance had come in the thickets of the Savad Kuh – and he would have succeeded, but that God had decided that Nader's life was not to end yet.[67]

Nader told Nik Qadam that he would spare his life as he had promised. But his aim was too good: he would have to lose his eyes.[68] This done, Nader sent to Tehran for his son to be brought to Iran Kharab. To avoid arousing Reza Qoli's suspicions, he summoned Nasrollah, Emam Qoli and Shahrokh from Mashhad at the same time. The princes met in Tehran and travelled on to Daghestan together. They arrived at Darband in October 1742, but as they approached Nader's camp, they were met with an order for Reza Qoli to stay where he was overnight, while the other three princes went there directly.

Nader welcomed Nasrollah, Emam Qoli and Shahrokh with all the usual honours, but when Reza Qoli arrived the following day he was treated coldly. Before going into his father's tent, he set aside his sword, bow and quiver, as was normal; but when he entered Nader saw that he still had a dagger at his waist. Nader shouted 'Take that weapon from him!' Reza Qoli drew the dagger from its sheath angrily, and made to throw it on the ground, but one of the officers escorting him snatched it away. Nader cried that his son was out of his mind, and ordered that he be taken away, and guarded.[69]

Over the next few days[70] some of Nader's closest advisers and companions, including Mirza Zaki, Hasan Ali Khan and the chief mullah spoke with Reza Qoli, trying to get him to apologise and ask his father's forgiveness. But the prince was obdurate, and denied that he had done anything wrong. He said it was not true that he had sought his father's life; rather his father had sought to kill him. According to one account, he also criticised his father's war in Daghestan, saying that it was pointless, that the army were exhausted with marching and countermarching, and were suffering from lack of supplies: the people of Persia were the victims of his father's empty pride. By now, between Nik Qadam's confession and the stories his spies had told him, Nader was convinced his son was guilty. But he could not decide how to punish him – whether he should be killed, or blinded, or perhaps exiled or imprisoned, as Tahmasp had been. Even at this stage, he would have forgiven him, but Reza Qoli was too arrogant to ask forgiveness.

Nader tried to talk to his son again, but Reza Qoli still dismissed the accusation that he had wanted to kill his father and take the throne, saying that if he had wanted to, he could have made himself Shah while Nader was away in India. Why would he have waited to kill his father until he was back and in control again? Between anger and tenderness, Nader tried to persuade him to ask pardon and swear obedience, without success. The more harshly Nader questioned Reza Qoli, the more the prince declared his innocence. Both grew angry. Finally, Nader threatened to have his eyes cut out. One version says that Reza Qoli shouted back, 'Cut them out, and put them in your wife's cunt.'[71]

Nader's advisers kept trying to smooth the rift over, saying that perhaps malicious people had been spreading lies; that if Reza Qoli were blinded or executed it would be a terrible loss, since it was not possible he could have another heir of the same abilities. But in deference to Nader's fury they also had to say, on the other hand, that if the prince was guilty, then he should be punished. Unfortunately, there was no longer anyone at court with the force of personality of Alavi Khan, who could have steered the near-demented Shah down a wiser course. Finally, Nader gave the order that his son's eyes should be cut out and brought to him. When it was done, Nader looked at them, and began to weep.

As after the shooting in the Savad Kuh, Nader withdrew to the harem and did not emerge for three days. When he reappeared in the divankhane he berated the courtiers for not interceding to save the prince, saying, 'There is no compassion and fairness in Iranians.' Beside himself with grief, he cried, 'What is a father? And what is a son?'[72]

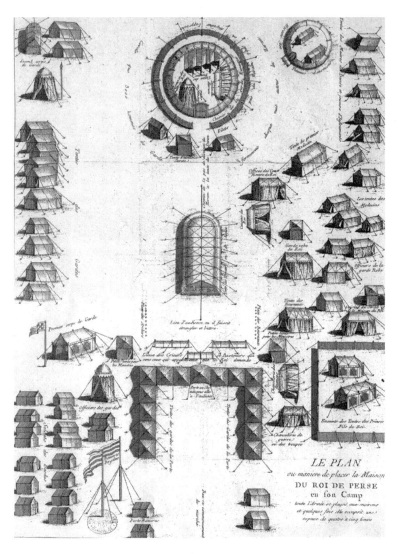

8. *Nader's camp.*

This plan accompanied the published version of Bazin's account of Nader's later years. In the centre is the great audience tent, the divankhane. At the top is the harem enclosure. At the bottom of the picture is the space for the camp market.

(Cambridge University Library)

CHAPTER NINE
Towers of Skulls

> *... but I am bound*
> *Upon a wheel of fire, that mine own tears*
> *Do scald like molten lead.*

> King Lear

Three days after the blinding, Nader went to see Reza Qoli. He put the prince's head on his chest, kissed him and broke down into tears. Many of the courtiers present wept too. At first Reza Qoli refused to speak, but finally he said, 'You should know that by taking my eyes out, you have blinded yourself and destroyed your own life.'[1]

On balance, it seems unlikely that Reza Qoli was guilty of deliberately planning his father's death.* The most unlikely aspect of the story that portrays him as guilty is the assertion that he planned his father's death even before Nader's return from India; before their meeting near Herat in June 1740. If Reza Qoli had been planning his father's death already, would he not have behaved more cautiously at that meeting? It was hardly sensible in those circumstances to appear before his father with such magnificence, and provoke his irritation. It is more plausible that Reza Qoli's real bitterness toward his father began then, with the peremptory end to his authority as viceroy, and the disbanding of his personal guard.

The likeliest explanation is that a group of courtiers that had formed around Reza Qoli during his period as regent decided, when the rumours of Nader's death in India proved false, that it would suit their

---

* This was the view of a number of contemporaries, including Mirza Mahdi and Pere Bazin, and later Sir John Malcolm.

purposes for Nader to die, and for Reza Qoli to replace him. Mohammad Hosein Khan Qajar (the murderer of Tahmasp and his family), and the sons of Delavar Khan Teimani were probably prominent within this group. Once they had selected Nik Qadam for the job and put the plan to him, he was in their hands; if he had refused, they would have killed him anyway. But after he failed, the conspirators must have panicked. Some of the Teimani tribesmen fled Nader's army after the failure of the assassination attempt, arousing Nader's suspicions. It would have seemed to the plotters that the only way to save themselves from Nader's wrath was to shift all the blame onto Reza Qoli. This was made easier for them by the souring of the mood between Nader and his son. So they delivered Nik Qadam up to Nader, having primed him with a story that would incriminate Reza Qoli. Nik Qadam had to play along, because otherwise his children's heads were forfeit. He was a brave man, and managed to convince Nader. The plan had the desired result – again made easier by Reza Qoli's headstrong and provocative attitude to his father.

But once his son had been blinded, and his anger had cooled, Nader realised that Reza Qoli must have been, if not innocent, then at least encouraged and helped by others. Some of the plotters were already dead, for their complicity in the killing of Tahmasp and his family. Nader had the rest killed, including the sons of Delavar Khan.[2] But he spared Mohammad Hosein Khan Qajar. This may have been to avoid trouble among the Qajars of Astarabad, but one suspects that if Nader's rage had turned on him, fear of a revolt would not have been any protection. The reason for Mohammad Hosein Khan's survival may have been that he did a deal with Nader after Tahmasp's murder, and that he acted as a spy for Nader within Reza Qoli's circle thereafter. There must have been at least one such informer. An eyewitness who met Mohammad Hosein Khan in May 1744 said he was 'in greatest confidence with the king, and honoured with the pompous title of "the high and mighty minister of ministers, partner of a kingdom, and nearest to the throne"'.*[3]

If Reza Qoli was not entirely guilty, maybe he was not entirely innocent either. In his anger and humiliation after his father's return from India, his thoughts had turned increasingly on his father's death. He must have had some idea of what his hangers-on had in mind

---

* Mohammad Hosein Khan was also the father of Chuki, one of Nader's favourites among the women of his harem. Nader and Chuki may even have been married.

– he certainly did not go to his father to denounce them, as he could have done. Reza Qoli was not stupid, and he would not have been the first prince to let his followers pursue dubious projects, of which he pretended, perhaps even to himself, to have no knowledge.

Some years later, after Nader had died, his court historian Mirza Mahdi was free to put down on paper his true opinions of his former master, as he had not been before. He wrote:

> From the beginning of Nader Shah's reign until his return
> from Khwarezm and his march into Daghestan, he was
> entirely occupied with the care of his empire and the ad-
> ministration of justice, in such a manner that the people
> of Iran would have given their lives for his preservation;*
> but after this time he changed his conduct entirely. At the
> instigation of some hostile spirit, this unhappy monarch
> gave his ear to ill-intentioned spies, and had the eyes of
> Reza Qoli, the best and the dearest of his sons, torn out.
> Remorse quickly followed this rash cruelty, and Nader
> Shah became like a madman. The reports of bad news
> that he received in succession thereafter of troubles in
> various parts of his dominion increased his rage.[4]

Some might say of Nader that the eventual failure of his reign was inevitable, given his insatiable desire for conquest, the inadequacy of Persia economically to support his grand plans, and his failure to add the qualities of a statesman and father of his country to his supreme military talents. But people change, and intelligent people like Nader look at circumstances and adapt to them. Although Nader was in some ways backward looking, in warfare in particular he had abandoned old ways for new in a strikingly original way, as a deliberate choice. It is not impossible that Nader could have adapted, altered his methods, had a long and successful reign and passed on a flourishing, extended empire to one of his sons or grandsons. His remission of taxes while he was in India shows he was at least aware of the tension between his methods and his aims.

In the rational pursuit of causes for the events of history we too easily forget the contingency and chance that pervade human existence,

* The citizens of Isfahan, for example, might not have agreed; but many others would, including members of many of the minority groups in the country.

and the chaotic nature of cause and effect, which can turn great matters on the smallest quirks.* We sometimes elevate those Causes too high, constructing a kind of iron determinism in our histories that belongs in fact to the mental process of history-making, not to the way events actually develop. Overly deterministic history risks failing to reproduce the true character of human experience, in which choice, chance, whim and coincidence are important, if not dominant, and alternative courses of events are always possible. It was open to Nader, prompted by the urgent need of his military machine for money and war materials, to pursue in Persia something like the modernising administrative and economic improvements that followed what has been called the military revolution in Europe. He had that choice; or to be more precise, the choices which, if taken, could have taken that process onward.

Although as we have seen, he made intriguing beginnings that started in that direction, he did not make those choices. One reason he did not was his illness; but Alavi Khan had been able to treat his illness, and moderate its effects on him and his conduct of government. If he had found another Alavi Khan to treat him, he might have come through the crisis of the early 1740s. This did not happen, because there was a deeper problem: his mental anguish over his son, Reza Qoli. The blinding of his son shook the certainties of Nader's psyche, the certainties that had underpinned his previous self-confidence and his successes. It shook them right down to their deepest root; and he was never the same man again.† Instead he went down a tortured path of bitterness, nihilism and anger, ending in something near madness.

Why did the blinding of Reza Qoli shake Nader so deeply? One might simply say that he loved his son. Or that his aim from the beginning had been to exalt his family and found a dynasty, and that he had now himself crippled that purpose. Or that he had defined

---

* If the bullet fired by Nik Qadam in the forests of Mazandaran had deflected an inch or two to one side and killed Nader, Reza Qoli would have taken the throne in the spring of 1741. Contemporaries rated Reza Qoli's abilities highly, and there is reason to believe that he would have combined his father's military abilities with a greater awareness of the importance of commercial and economic matters. Reza Qoli might well have taken the empire forward in a new, more constructive direction.

† Abd ol-Karim Kashmiri wrote that Nader, who previously had prayed devoutly in public in his earlier campaigns, ceased to do so in Daghestan; suggesting if not a loss of faith, then at least a new, misanthropic disgust at going through the religious motions (p. 164).

his project of monarchy and empire explicitly against the old Safavid model; only to repeat one of the most notorious cruelties of the Safavid monarchs – Shah Abbas' blinding of his sons.* One might more subtly link his blinding of his son with the death of his own father, suggesting the blow was all the greater for the fact that it destroyed his wish to give his sons the fatherly love that fate had snatched away from him as a child. Nader's sense of himself as an outsider had always strengthened his attachment to his family: a bulwark against a hostile world. Now he had shattered that bulwark, by his own actions.

These theories may bear some truth. All one can say for sure is that the blinding, coming as it did at a time when he was already frustrated and ill, destroyed something at his Nader's very centre, in such a way that he was never afterwards able to put it right. The psychiatrist and existentialist Viktor Frankl, in connection with his own experiences as a survivor of Auschwitz, used to quote Nietzsche's saying that he who has a *why* to live for can bear almost any *how*; but those that lost that central sense of purpose did not survive.[5] In blinding Reza Qoli Mirza at Iran Kharab, Nader poisoned the source of his own dynamism.

After the blinding, Reza Qoli's wounds were dressed so that they healed properly, and Nader sent him to be confined in the fortress at Kalat. Full of anguish and rancour as the winter of 1742/1743 closed in, Nader laid the blame for his troubles in Daghestan on the Russians. It is likely that the Russians did more to impede Nader's campaigns against the Lazgis than just restrict the flow of provisions to his troops. There was later a tradition in the Caucasus that the Russians had supplied the Lazgis with weapons and ammunition for their struggle against Nader.[6] At an earlier stage the Russians had been worried that Nader might advance into the area just to the south of the frontier on the river Terek. Now, angry, bitter and restless, Nader talked about taking Kizliar itself, the Russian border fortress, claiming that it had once belonged to Persia. There was speculation that he might carry on from there, perhaps with help from the Chechens, even towards the Crimea.

---

* There is a parallel with an even older archetype – the story of Rostam's killing of his son Sohrab, in Ferdowsi's *Shahname*:
> *From fishes in the sea to wild horses on*
> *The plain, all beasts can recognise their young.*
> *But man who's blinded by his wretched pride,*
> *Cannot distinguish son from foe.*

(trans. Jerome W. Clinton, *The Tragedy of Sohrab and Rostam*, p. 119).

In November 1742 Nader took his army northwards from Iran Kharab, towards the frontier with Russia. It is intriguing to speculate what might have happened if his army had encountered the Russians. Nader never fought a battle with any enemy trained and equipped to the norms of European warfare, and some would assume that his troops would inevitably have been overwhelmed by the western tactical system: the mid-eighteenth century system of elaborate drill and uniforms, linear tactics and formalised manoeuvre. But consider the battle of Jena in 1806. That was the decisive encounter in which the Prussian army, which epitomised the eighteenth-century system, was defeated by the modernised French system, which emphasised simplified drill and uniforms, speed of manoeuvre, large numbers, a rationalised and tightly integrated chain of command, a much greater emphasis on light troops and skirmishers (both mounted and foot), a strong artillery corps to wear down the enemy prior to the decisive tactical moment, and a powerful reserve of heavy cavalry to deliver the shock charge at that moment. That latter description is strikingly accurate also for Nader Shah's military system. In many ways the reforms that transformed the practice of war in Europe at the end of the eighteenth century brought western armies closer to an eastern model (albeit for independent reasons, little to do with conscious imitation). After their experiences in Daghestan Nader's troops were not at their best in November 1742. But who can say what would have happened if Nader's armies had fought the Russians.

Soon after he made his northward move Nader learned that the Ottomans were moving troops into the Caucasus. Two more Ottoman ambassadors arrived at his camp, with another message from the Sultan, again rejecting Nader's religious proposals. Nader sent a reply repeating his threat to go to the Sultan to resolve the matter in person. He also sent a message to Ahmad Pasha in Baghdad, ordering him to surrender that much-disputed city. The two men had old experience of each other by now. In reply to Nader's message Ahmad Pasha sent some fine Arab horses as a present, with a letter that did not reject Nader's request out of hand, but prevaricated.*

On 10 February 1743, realising at length the impracticality of

---

* Some pro-Ottoman contemporaries believed that Ahmad Pasha was altogether too friendly with Nader, and suggested he was scheming to surrender Baghdad. To impugn his loyalty, they nicknamed him Nezam ol-Molk; which shows how widely Asaf Jah Nezam ol-Molk's betrayal of Mohammad Shah was believed in at the time (Olson, p. 189).

attacking the Russians while the old Ottoman enemy armed in his rear, Nader moved southwards again, heading for the Moghan plain. He left a substantial garrison of Afghans behind in Darband. The previous good weather now turned bad, with snow and heavy rain. The many streams running down out of the mountains across the army's route turned into furious torrents, animals died of cold and exhaustion, supplies were short and some were lost in the mud and floods. Many men died too. It took forty days for the miserable remnants of the army to reach the river Kura, in the Moghan plain. If any of the soldiers were still wearing the silks of India by then, they were in tatters.[7]

The Nowruz celebration in Nader's camp must have been subdued that year; but at least there would have been relief among the troops that the Daghestan campaign was over. The Lazgis had not beaten the Persian army in battle, but the Persians were nonetheless defeated, and the centres of Lazgi resistance were still unconquered. Of all the tribes and peoples Nader fought in his life, the Lazgis were the only ones to force him to retreat, remaining themselves defiant: a lesson in guerrilla warfare that has been forgotten and relearned again and again in history, from Napoleon in Spain to the US in Vietnam.

Nader moved on again with the army in April, heading south. He bypassed Tabriz and camped at Marivan on 18 May, where he was met by Nasrollah, Emam Qoli and Shahrukh, who had again travelled to see him from Mashhad. With them was an ambassador from Delhi, with a large, intricately ornamented door made of sandalwood, and other presents. The whole ensemble travelled on together to Sanandaj. In preparation for the assault on Baghdad, Nader sent forward his powerful siege artillery, including hundreds of newly cast pieces, via Hamadan to Kermanshah.[8] This was to be the crucial, deciding campaign against the Ottomans, the culminating struggle to make Nader the prime monarch of the Islamic world. The preparations were on an appropriately apocalyptic scale.

An account from one of Nader's army pay clerks gives the numbers of troops under his command at the beginning of the campaign of 1743, divided up by the regions they originated from. Along with Hanway's description of the army a year later, it gives a picture of Nader's army at the peak of its power. The total drawn up by the pay clerk comes to a staggering 375,000 men, of whom as before only a minority were Shi'a Persians. They included 60,000 Turkmen and Uzbeks, 70,000 Afghans and Indians, 65,000 troops from Khorasan, 120,000 from western Persia (Kurdestan, Hamadan, Loristan, Fars and Khuzestan), and 60,000 from

Azerbaijan and the Caucasus. It is possible that the total included some servants or camp-followers, but other authorities say the soldiers had to pay their servants at their own expense; which would suggest that most if not all of this huge number, recorded for the purpose of keeping track of the soldiers' pay, were fighting troops.[9] The total does not include the large numbers of soldiers in provincial garrisons: the Afghans Nader had just left behind in Darband, for example, and the powerful new train of siege artillery at Kermanshah would also have been accounted for separately.

Nader knew that for a serious confrontation with the Ottomans he needed large numbers of trained infantry musketeers, as well as the light cavalry who would swarm forward and take control of the countryside and smaller towns of Ottoman Iraq, and the expensive siege guns for the bigger cities. Nader had been active in the preceding months to get provincial governors to send drafts of troops to the western provinces to replace those lost in Daghestan, and to prepare for the new campaign. An army of this size represented a huge effort. It was larger than the armies of Austria and Prussia, the main protagonists of the Seven Years' War that began in Europe in the following decade, put together.[10] But the cost was high.

There are indications that Nader's three-year remission of taxes, decreed while he was in Delhi and made possible by the riches he plundered there, along with the absence of the army from Persia from 1736 onwards, yielded a brief period of economic revival and even a modest prosperity in at least some parts of the country.[11] But although Nader may have paid some or all the expenses of the Turkestan campaign out of the plunder of India, the costs of his Daghestan campaign soon had his officials administering beatings to extract huge tax demands again. He must have known what the effect would be: perhaps he no longer cared. In some twisted way he may have wanted to punish the country as a whole for what he had done to his son.

The preparations for the campaign against Baghdad caused yet more suffering, which deepened further as the 1740s wore on. The tax collectors* forced people to sell their houses and goods, often at a fraction of their value, leaving them destitute. The economy stagnated for want of cash to exchange, many were ruined, and some fled into remote desert and mountain areas in the hope that the tax collectors would not find them. Large numbers emigrated, both westward to

* *Mohassil.*

Baghdad and Basra, and eastward to India. It has been estimated that the overall volume of trade had fallen to a fifth of its previous level in the 1740s by comparison with the period before 1722,[12] and that overall population size fell by a third or more. Persia had been relatively peaceful internally since Nader's departure for Kandahar in 1736, but the oppressive taxation, the discontent and despair soon led to new revolts, as had happened in the 1730s.

Nader appears to have justified his actions to himself on the basis of the precedents of Genghis Khan[13] and Timur, who had devastated Persia in the thirteenth and fourteenth centuries. One story says that an arrow was once shot into his tent with a note attached, accusing him of tyranny and irreligion, demanding of him whether he was a devil or a god, a tyrant, a king or a prophet. Nader answered 'I am neither god nor devil, tyrant nor prophet; but I am one sent from God, to punish an iniquitous generation of men'. He ordered that his words should be written out and displayed in the camp, along with the original note.[14]

Another piece of evidence that points in the same direction is Nader's choice of red for his clothing – the traditional colour of royal punishment, only worn by the Safavid Shahs when passing death sentences on wrongdoers. The fact that he chose red for the colour of his tents and his soldier's uniforms may have been meant as an extension of the idea, intended to inculcate awe, fear and obedience.[15]

To open the new campaign in Ottoman Iraq Nader sent detachments forward to occupy places around Baghdad and Basra, including Samarra, Najaf, Karbala, and the Shatt ol-Arab. Governors and provincial troops from the south-western provinces were instructed to besiege Basra. Nasrollah marched for Hamadan with the other princes, much of the baggage and supplies of ammunition on 1 July, and Nader followed a little later, having made arrangements for large quantities of grain to be sent forward to supply the army. Some of the Ottoman officials fled, but others, along with many Kurdish chiefs, submitted to the Persians. Ahmad Pasha knew better than to confront Nader in the open field, and stayed on the defensive. On 5 August Nader arrived at Kirkuk, where the garrison abandoned the town and retreated to the citadel. Nader's new siege cannon and mortars arrived a few days later, deployed and pounded the fortress from four sides from dawn to dusk, whereupon the Ottomans surrendered. Nader treated them mercifully. Shortly afterwards a Persian detachment also took Irbil, a little way to the north, controlling the way to Mosul.[16]

While still at Kirkuk Nader received a defiant message from the Ottoman Sultan, announcing a religious fatwa that permitted his Muslim subjects to kill Persians and make slaves of them, pronouncing that the new sect in Persia was contrary to true belief. Nader had been hoping that his contact with Ahmad Pasha, along with his occupation of most of Ottoman Iraq, might lead to a capitulation; but instead the Ottomans were defiant. This was a brave face: there was unrest and fear of revolt again in Istanbul after the fall of Kirkuk, and on 23 September the old grand vizier was replaced. Nader took his army on to Mosul, where he arrived and began a siege on 14 September, making camp a little way to the south-east, on the eastern bank of the Tigris river.[17]

As the Persians arrived, they fought a fierce battle with a force sent out from the Ottoman garrison of Mosul, defeated it and nearly cut off its retreat back over the river Tigris. Bridges were built above and below the city, and Nader ordered the construction of 14 protected batteries for artillery opposite the towers of the walls of Mosul. He had 390 pieces of artillery with him, including light cannon and 230 mortars. For once, there was no shortage of adequate siege guns. Once they were in position, the Persian gunners bombarded Mosul for eight days, the mortars starting fires and doing terrible damage in the interior of the city.* Many of the defenders were Christians, either natives of the city or refugees from nearby villages that Nader had sacked and burned. There were Muslim and Yazidi refugees too; all of them joined enthusiastically in the defence. As in Daghestan, Nader's harsh treatment of the general populace intensified the resistance against him. After the general bombardment, Nader concentrated his artillery against the north-western sector of the city walls, and their fire eventually succeeded in damaging a tower and making a breach. But the defenders, inspired by their commander, worked frantically and succeeded in repairing the damage with new bricks.

Under cover of the bombardment the Persians had also been digging mines under the walls of Mosul. When the Persians exploded the charges in these mines a lot of damage was done, but in one crucial sector the mine shaft was not properly back-filled after the charges had been laid, with the result that part of the force of the blast blew

---

* Unlike the ordinary cannon of this period, which fired solid iron shot on a relatively flat trajectory, mortars lobbed a hollow shell filled with gunpowder, designed to be exploded by a fuse once it reached its target, on a high trajectory. A modern mortar is a quite different weapon, though also firing on a high trajectory.

back along the shaft and into a trench where the Persian troops were gathered ready for an assault. Many of the Persians were killed or wounded. Even where the mining operations were more successful, the defenders quickly improvised new defences to fill sections of wall that had collapsed. In his frustration, Nader ordered a further series of massacres and burnings in the villages around Mosul, and the city itself was left alone for a few days. Then he ordered a further major assault, by thousands of soldiers, carrying 1,700 scaling-ladders. These men first used the ladders to get over the moat, then to climb the walls, but as fast as they could get to the top, the defenders cut them down. The assault failed and Nader lost over 5,000 men.

Nader tried at this stage to open negotiations, but the Ottoman commander was defiant and the defenders did their best to make the interior of the city look as normal as possible to Nader's messengers, so that when he asked them for their impressions of the state of the city and the will of its people to resist, the answers were disappointing. There were more negotiations and then, astoundingly, Nader asked the Ottoman side to present peace proposals. The Persian chief mullah conducted the discussions, and hinted that things might go well if the Ottoman commander presented Nader with some horses from his stable. The Ottoman did so, and agreed to forward peace terms to his masters in Istanbul. The Persians complimented the defenders of Mosul on their bravery. A letter arrived from the Ottoman Sultan saying that if Nader withdrew back to the Ottoman/Persian frontier, he could discuss peace terms with Ahmad Pasha. On 20 October 1743 Nader withdrew his army from Mosul. They marched back past Kirkuk and camped, still on Ottoman territory, but not far from the frontier. When the news reached Istanbul, there was great rejoicing.[18] But the siege of Basra continued, and the siege cannon from Mosul were sent on there.

What had happened? This was not the Nader that had laid siege to Kandahar for over a year, who had pursued Khodayar Khan the length of the Indus river and beyond. He had with him in Ottoman Iraq the largest force he had ever commanded, including the hard-bitten veterans of his Indian campaign. Around Mosul alone he had over 200,000 men. It is fair to say that this army, for size and quality, was probably the most powerful military force in the world at that time.* Nader's preparations for the campaign against the Ottomans had been

---

* Though the most advanced of the European states were probably better at siege warfare.

painstaking and very costly. This had been his campaign to throw reins around the neck of the Ottoman Sultan, to make him submit as the rulers of Delhi and Bokhara had done, fulfilling the promise he had made at the crowning of the infant Abbas III in 1732.[19] And yet after a mere 40 days of besieging Mosul, he had given up.

Some have explained this volte-face by citing the outbreak of revolts in Shirvan and Darband, where the Ottomans had inserted a false Safavid pretender to make trouble for Nader. He may also have heard worrying reports at this time about further problems brewing in Khwarezm, and the conduct of Taqi Khan in Oman.* But in October 1743 these troubles were potential or relatively minor. Nader did not think them so pressing that he returned to Persia immediately; he did not recross the frontier until the end of January 1744. Another explanation has been that he and his men were disheartened and defeated by the brave defence of Mosul;[20] but the same Persians had overcome worse setbacks, and had successfully seen through much longer sieges in the past.

Nader's men had suffered serious losses at Mosul, and the artillery had not produced the quick success he had hoped for there. After the expensive investment he had made in the artillery, this must have been disappointing. Nader was never at his best when conducting sieges, which above all demanded patience, and a willingness to make progress by slow increments. Patience was not his thing: he favoured boldness, movement and audacity. It is likely that his illnesses were again painful and troublesome. But these things had never before sapped his determination to follow through and finish what he had begun. The only adequate explanation is that after Iran Kharab he no longer had the heart for it. He no longer had the determination and focused will to apply the enormous military power he had assembled. It may not be a coincidence that he broke off the siege of Mosul at about the same time of year that he had blinded his son, one year earlier.

This was a major turning point, marking the effective end of Nader's long career of conquest: a whimper rather than a bang. It was his choice that ended the war, not any other factor. The sword he had forged, the great army he had assembled, equipped and fed, was there: fearsome in its size and efficiency, undefeated and ready to follow him anywhere. Most of Ottoman Iraq was in his hands, and he could expect

* Lockhart 1938 (p. 231) even suggested that Nader had been disturbed by a report that the Emperor of China was about to invade Transoxiana.

that its remaining cities would fall in due course. He knew that there was support for him among some of the inhabitants of Ottoman Iraq, and that the governor himself, Ahmad Pasha, was far from devotedly loyal to the Ottoman cause. The Ottoman government might send another army against him from Istanbul, but he had defeated those armies before (and would again). Shaken by many defeats and always vulnerable to unrest in the capital, the regime of Sultan Mahmud itself was in danger of falling if put under further sustained pressure. The prospect of a successful march on Istanbul was realistic; at least as realistic as the march on Delhi had been while the Persian army had been stuck in Kandahar in 1737–1738. In Istanbul further greatness awaited Nader: new treasures, new territorial gains, possibly the caliphate itself and supremacy over Islam as a whole. But he had destroyed the beloved son to whom he had intended to pass on that greatness. Broken in spirit, Nader turned aside from that final prize, allowing himself to be distracted from the gravity of the decision with horses and fripperies.

Nader left the camp and the army, and went with his women and just a small bodyguard of cavalry to visit the Shi'a shrines of Kazemein, Mo'azzam, Karbala and Najaf. His wives made generous donations to the shrines. Razia Begum, the daughter of Shah Soltan Hosein, gave a large sum for the repair of the shrine at Karbala. Gowhar Shad, the daughter of Baba Ali Khan, gave an even larger donation to gild the dome of the mosque at Najaf.*[21] These donations mark one of the few appearances that Nader's wives make in the contemporary accounts of his life. There is a suggestion of a rivalry between the two women, competing to make the more impressive gift. Rivalry between them would have been understandable. Gowhar Shad, the Afshar governor's daughter, the mother of Nasrollah, whose sister had been Nader's first wife before her, had known Nader since his earliest days as a musketeer and young lieutenant in Abivard. Razia Begum was the daughter of a Shah, but came from the court world of Isfahan that Nader had despised. And (as far as we know) she was childless.†

Gowhar Shad's donation of the greater gift indicates that she had the upper hand in the harem, but it is likely that younger women had become

---

* The same dome that is the centrepiece of the sacred precinct occupied by Moqtada al-Sadr's militia and besieged by US forces in the summer of 2004.

† The VOC records reported that she bore Nader a child in Mashhad in January 1731, but this child is otherwise unknown. The story may have been a false rumour, or perhaps the child died young.

Nader's favourites by this time. It is frustrating that we know so little of the lives of Nader's women, and his relationships with them. The record is distorted, distorting in turn what we know of Nader's personality. We know a lot about the tall, proud man with the loud voice, but when Nader drops the tent-flap and goes into the harem he disappears from our view just as he did for most of his contemporaries.* There are a few hints from which we can make conjecture, but little more. Some men might within their harems have behaved like the tyrants they admired but failed to be in the wider world of men. One suspects that with Nader the opposite was the case, that he relaxed, and perhaps laughed with the women about events and people he dealt with during the day, letting them soothe him with soft music and their quiet voices. Of course, their laughter would at times have had a brittle quality, and in this latter period the women must have found him as difficult to handle as everyone else did. Some of them at least may have been as much at ease in his company as he was in theirs. But we do not know.[22]

At Karbala Nader apparently performed the ritual walk around the shrine. He cannot have found the answers he might have looked for there. At Najaf Nader presided over an assembly of Muslim scholars and jurists from Iraq and all over his empire, both Sunnis and Shi'as. In a private audience with a delegate from Baghdad, who had been sent by Ahmad Pasha to observe and participate in the proceedings, he explained their purpose:

> [In] my realm there are two areas, Afghanistan and
> Turkestan, in which they call the Iranians infidels.
> Infidelity is loathsome and it is not fitting that there
> should be in my domains a people that calls another
> infidels. Now I make you my representative to go and
> remove all of the charges of infidelity and witness this in
> front of the three groups with whatever is required. You
> will report everything that you see and hear to me and
> relay your account to Ahmad Khan.[23]

The Ottoman delegate wrote later that although Nader was still a handsome man, his face showed the signs of age and senility; his eyes were yellowish, a number of his teeth were missing,† and he looked like

---

* With just one exception, at the end of his life, when we can follow him through the tent-flap.

a man of eighty.[24] Plainly his ailments and the strains of recent years
had marked him. At around this time he was treated by a French Jesuit,
Father Damien, apparently for a liver disorder. This description and his
later symptoms suggest that he was suffering from jaundice, probably
as a result of contracting malaria some years earlier.

The Council of Najaf had a number of overlapping purposes.
It served, as Nader said, to make explicit a religious reconciliation
between all the senior clerics of his empire, on the same basis as before:
abandonment of the most extreme anti-Sunni practices and outward
conformity with Sunnism. The removal of discord was important to
avoid trouble between the Sunni and Shi'a elements of his army, aside
from its effects among the peoples of his empire generally. It was also
intended to demonstrate to the Ottomans that Nader had brought the
Persian empire over to Sunni orthodoxy, and to get the recognition and
approval of the Ottoman authorities for it; overcoming the effect of the
earlier fatwa from Istanbul.

In the discussions, the chief mullah showed himself in full compliance
with Sunni orthodoxy. Some of the Sunni scholars present were sceptical,
and muttered under their breath that the Persians, having formerly
cursed the first three caliphs, could not be absolved by repentance now.
But the tacit pressure from Nader and the slick chairmanship of his
chief mullah were enough to produce at least a superficial consensus,
and a written document ratifying it, which all delegates signed. To
give the event a holier significance, the signature took place under a
canopy erected over the tomb of Ali itself. But the document contained
ambiguous phrases, including one well-known quotation from the
Emam Ali that could be taken to signify both that the first two caliphs
were righteous, and had lived and died in the true faith; and that they
were unjust and tyrannical, and had lived and died believing against
the true faith. After the signature ceremony, the Ottoman delegate
noticed that the chief mullah conducted prayers in an unfamiliar way.
When asked why, the chief mullah explained that the prayers were said
in accordance with the Ja'fari mazhab. This dismayed the man from
Baghdad; it seems that controversial subject had not previously been

† Other accounts also mention Nader's bad teeth (BW p 170), the condition of
which may have resulted partly from his partiality for sweets (in Bazin's plan
of his camp – plate 8, page 242 – the tent of the Shah's confectioner has a prominent
place between that of his chef and that of his physician). Abdol Karim
Kashmiri says he had lost all his molars, and swallowed his food without
chewing, which probably contributed to his digestive problems.

mentioned. He came to suspect that the apparent realignment of the Persians to Sunni orthodoxy in fact concealed as deep an adherence to their old beliefs and practices as ever.[25]

Nader got all the clerics together and got them to agree, superficially; but when they went home everything was as before. The Council changed nothing of any significance. The only thing that might have made it significant would have been a victorious military drive on Istanbul, where Nader could have forced the Ottoman Sultan to submit, and could have replaced him as the Shadow of God on Earth, as the caliph of Islam as a whole. But at Mosul he had turned aside from that project. Najaf was a wedding without a bride.

All this time Nader had been negotiating peace terms with Ahmad Pasha. The full details are not known, but they included Persian withdrawal from Ottoman Iraq, and one authority indicates that Nader may have retracted his insistence on a fifth pillar in the Ka'ba,[26] while maintaining his demand for recognition of the Ja'fari mazhab. The terms were agreed and the treaty was forwarded to the Ottoman Sultan for his approval. Nader sent orders for the siege of Basra to be lifted, and this was done on 8 December. Despite the arrival of heavy artillery at the end of November, heavy bombardments and many assaults, the Persians had been as unsuccessful there as at Mosul. Nader also withdrew his troops from Irbil, and settled down near the frontier, in his new, listless mode, to wait for a response to the peace proposals. He may have hoped that the Sultan would recognise the Ja'fari mazhab, and with that concession allow him to withdraw with honour. It was not to be. On 30 January 1744 he left for Kermanshah, irritated at reports of rebellions that were developing in various parts of Persia.[27] From there he travelled on to Hamadan, where he made camp a little to the north of the city and stayed for some time, receiving reports and issuing orders to deal with the revolts. He celebrated Nowruz there on 21 March 1744. The English merchant Jonas Hanway arrived at the camp on the 28 March, and stayed about ten days.* Hanway later described the camp

---

* The book Hanway wrote on his return to England, published in 1753, was for many years the standard account of Nader's reign in English, despite its deficiencies, plagiarisms and prejudices. A few years later Hanway wrote a book about his travels in England, and crossed swords with Samuel Johnson over the fashion for drinking tea (Hanway disapproved; Johnson drank great quantities). Johnson is supposed to have said that Hanway acquired some reputation by travelling abroad, but lost it all by travelling at home (Taylor

and the way life was ordered in it.

Nader's camp was always laid out on the same pattern.* At the centre stood the divankhane, the tent used for audiences, for delivering judgements and the rest of the Shah's official business. The Shah presided there from seven in the morning until ten at night, with only short breaks. By 1744 Nader had moderated his drinking;[28] perhaps a change brought about by Alavi Khan in his time as court physician. Given his increasing preference for the company of his women and children, it may be that he had given up the all-male drinking parties he had amused himself with earlier in his life, and now normally went from the divankhane straight to the harem at the end of the day. The divankhane was made of brownish-red cloth and was held up by three great poles, each of which had a large gilded ball on top. The front of it was always open, even in bad weather; the interior furnishings were simple and austere. It was approached through a large open space used for punishments and executions, on the other side of which there was a gate, watched over by guards who let through people called to the Shah's audience. On the other side of the gate was another large open space, surrounded on three sides by tents used by the guards. To one side of this open space, behind the tents of the guards, there was a compound for the tents of the royal princes. On the other side stood the two huge royal standards, made of silk, so high and heavy that it took more than twelve men to move them. The movement of these standards in the morning served as the signal to break camp, and the position in which they were planted at the end of a days' march showed where the new camp was to be pitched. Beyond the standards was the area set aside for the camp market, with rows of tents for sutlers and merchants.

Fifty paces beyond the divankhane, on the other side, lay the Shah's private quarters, guarded day and night by several thousand white-turbaned watch-guards *(keshikchi)*, in shifts. Here there was another, smaller tent, used by the Shah for secret audiences, and behind that was the gate to the harem. The harem was surrounded by a circular fence; inside it was a screen, also circular: a guard of Negro eunuchs patrolled between the two. There were about 60 eunuchs. Inside this double barrier was a day-tent for the Shah, a sleeping-tent for him, and

1985 p. 54). Hanway nonetheless retained to his death in 1786 a reputation as a good man and an energetic philanthropist (among other good works, he helped to set up the Foundling Hospital and the Magdalen Hospital for Penitent Prostitutes in London).

* See Bazin's plan of Nader's camp, plate 8, p.242.

several tents for the women, many of which were partitioned for several occupants. To one side of the harem compound was a similar, smaller compound for the Shah's dancing-girls, singers and female musicians. This whole complex of principal tents stood in the centre of the camp, and was surrounded by the tents of the officers, soldiers and camp followers. Hanway did not have an audience with Nader, but saw him one day walking from the harem to the divankhane. His clothes were plain and austere, but he wore many precious stones.[29]

Although he only saw a small part of Nader's army while he was at the camp, Hanway said it totalled around 200,000 men at this time. He described its composition and the equipment of the soldiers in some detail. Most of them were armed with a musket* and a sabre, but the Uzbeks and others, who served as light cavalry, might have only a lance, a bow, or a pistol, and a sabre. He tells us that the men paid for their own clothes, but they bought them from Nader, so he would have achieved some uniformity in their appearance by that means. We know from the records of the Dutch East India Company that he frequently ordered clothing for his soldiers in large batches. In general the Persians were proud of their marksmanship, taking care to weigh the powder when loading their muskets, except in the heat of battle. The Afghans were armed with lances, and Hanway makes a point of saying that they were very brave. There were 50,000 Afghans, 6,000 Uzbeks, 6,000 Turkmen and 6,000 Baluchis. The guard troops consisted of 1,000 'sons of elders', 2,000 'sons of gentlemen', and 10,000 gholams. These three elements were 'the genteelest of the soldiery' according to Hanway, and would have served as cavalry, as under the Safavids. The *keshikchi* on the other hand served on foot, guarding Nader in camp and on the march, and seem not to have taken part in battle.

Hanway lists the jazayerchis as foot soldiers.† There were 12,000 of them. He says Nader shaped the corps of jazayerchis carefully himself: they were well clothed, and carried very heavy muskets with wide bores; he says patronisingly that they had 'an imperfect resemblance to European infantry'. Hanway also lists 40,000 'kara-kashun' (black

---

* Hanway implies that most of the muskets were flintlocks or similar miquelet-locks by saying that some of the muskets were matchlocks. He is disparaging about the quality of the gun barrels, but other sources (and surviving examples) suggest the weapons were well made and reliable.

† We know from Nader's campaign in India that they sometimes served as mounted infantry, and even fought on horseback on occasion (see above, Chapter 5).

guards), also foot soldiers, whose appearance was 'indifferent' by comparison, and 20,000 Afshars, who would have been cavalry. The list is interesting, because it breaks the army down by troop type, unlike the pay clerk list of 1743 mentioned earlier. But it does not include the Bakhtiaris, Lors, Qajars or Kurds, among others, that we know from other sources to have been present in the army in significant numbers. Nor does it mention the important zanburaks and other artillery. Hanway accepted that the sum of the parts he listed fell short of the 200,000 total he had been given: the elements he does not mention would go some way to make up that shortfall.[30]

Hanway was curious about the contrast between the customs of Persia and Europe, and later wrote extensively on the subject. But he was strongly attached to the standards and norms of his own country; or rather, to a somewhat hidebound version of them. He commented at length on the status of women in Persia, and recorded a conversation he had with a mullah on the subject, who told him 'that though their law permitted a plurality of wives, and did not restrain men in their number of concubines; yet they always considered him as the most virtuous man, who confined himself to one wife, without any concubine...' Hanway described the way marriages were contracted, and wrote that 'hardly a single woman is to be found after the age of 16 or 18': but added '... marriage does not give them any liberty; for the women, to all appearance, are considered as little more than servile creatures formed for the pleasure and indulgence of their lord.'

But Hanway was none too happy with the greater freedoms he judged women in contemporary Europe to have, and himself believed women to be lesser creatures, made for domesticity and submission, with men set as guardians and protectors over them by Providence: 'Where an ABSURD EDUCATION [sic] does not make their vanity preponderate, love will ever prove the ruling passion in a woman's breast...' It is tempting to think that Hanway, himself a bit of a plodder, may have had some bruising encounters with the women that later became known as bluestockings in London. His conclusion was:

> Happy were it for the Christian world if women were
> more generally taught from the earliest time of life, that
> rebellion against husbands in Europe is at least as great
> a crime as Asiatic tyranny over wives; and the thoughts
> [sic] of the latter must necessarily make them shudder.[31]

By the time Nader had returned to Persian territory from Ottoman Iraq
and set up the military camp near Hamadan where Hanway saw him,
the rebels in Daghestan and Shirvan, who had begun their insurrection
under the Safavid pretender Sam Mirza early in the autumn of 1743, had
already been crushed. After some early successes they had assembled
an army of 20,000 men; but when Nasrollah Mirza arrived at Nader's
orders from Hamadan with reinforcements for the troops of the local
governors, the rebels' fate was sealed. The royal army met the rebels
in battle near Shamakhi on 20 December 1743 and defeated them. By
then another revolt had broken out in nearby Georgia, and Sam Mirza
fled to join that, but Georgians loyal to Nader defeated the rebels on 30
December, and Sam Mirza was captured shortly afterwards. He was
imprisoned, to await Nader's instructions.[32]

The news that had prompted Nader to return to Persia concerned
events in Astarabad and Shiraz, where revolts had broken out almost
simultaneously in mid-January 1744. The revolt in Astarabad had been
witnessed by Jonas Hanway, who unluckily arrived there by sea only a
few days before the rebels. He lost his goods and risked being killed or
made a captive, but managed to escape, and made his way to Nader's
camp to seek compensation for his loss.* The rebels were led by the
exiled son of Fath Ali Khan Qajar,† who had been supplanted by Nader
and executed by Tahmasp in 1726. They included 1,000 Yomut Turkmen
and 2,000 Qajars, mainly on foot. They took Astarabad on 28 January,
encouraged by letters from Sam Mirza. Nader sent orders that his old
command, the 1,500 cavalry based at Abivard, should go to put down
the revolt under their chief, Behbud Khan. When it came to a fight,
some of the Qajars changed sides, and the rebels were quickly beaten.
Fath Ali Khan's son escaped back into his desert exile, to emerge again
after Nader's death.

* Hanway noted on his journey that everyone, even within a few miles of his
  camp, complained about the devastation and poverty in the country caused
  by Nader's rapacious government. They called the Shah himself a 'rascal
  (*kurumsack)'* (vol. 1, p. 240). In fact *qorum saq* means 'a pimp to his own wife:
  a cuckold'. A merchant Hanway met in Qazvin complained to him that the
  country was destitute, and that Nader's great conquests had been achieved
  for him by an army of Persians, but he now ruled the Persians with a foreign
  army of Tartars.
† Mohammad Hasan Khan Qajar, not to be confused with his enemy
  Mohammad Hosein Khan. Mohammad Hasan Khan was the father of Agha
  Mohammad Shah, the founder of the Qajar dynasty.

Behbud Khan and Nader's governor, Mohammad Hosein Khan Qajar, who reappeared once the fighting was over, took a terrible revenge in Astarabad. Each of them erected a tall cone-shaped tower of whitened stone forty feet high, in which the heads of rebels and others were inserted in niches. This was a demonstration of ferocity that Timur had practised, which fact alone makes it likely that the towers of heads at Astarabad were erected at Nader's direct order. Mohammad Hosein Khan took advantage of the chaos to kill off large numbers of his Qajar rivals and enemies, and Behbud Khan was unable to restrain him. Executions were still going on when Hanway returned there towards the end of May. The country around Astarabad was a picture of desolation.[33]

There were further disturbances in Khwarezm at this time also, with war between the Uzbeks and the Yomut Turkmen, and more fighting between them and the Salor Turkmen tribe. Raids, plundering and destruction ravaged the whole territory. The client Khan Nader had appointed appealed to him for help, and Nader ordered his nephew Ali Qoli to go there from Mashhad.[34] Ali Qoli was not able to pacify Khwarezm properly until the following year.

But the most serious rebellion took place in Shiraz, led by Taqi Khan, Nader's former favourite. After his previous naval tribulations, Taqi Khan had finally secured a triumph in Muscat in 1743. The Sultan of Oman's subjects had rebelled again, and the Sultan had asked Taqi Khan for help, as before. He made a treaty with the Persians on the basis that they would restore him to power, in return for his recognition of Persian sovereignty over Oman. The campaign went forward successfully, and Taqi Khan himself crossed over to the southern shore of the Persian Gulf later in the year. Muscat itself had still been held by the Sultan's people, but the Persians moved in there and took control by a trick. The last rebels came to terms in July 1743 and Oman came under Persian control.

Unfortunately, Nader's difficulties thereafter meant that the fleet and the troops in Oman were neglected. After Taqi Khan returned to Bandar Abbas in November 1743, tribute payments from the former rebels that were to have kept the Persian troops in Oman paid, dried up. Eventually the Persian garrison of Muscat surrendered to the resurgent rebels. Their chief at length secured almost the whole of the territory of Oman, and got himself elected Sultan towards the end of 1744, founding the Al Bu Sa'id dynasty. An almost forgotten Persian garrison managed to hang on in Julfar until after Nader's death, but by that time the neglected ships of his fleet had been wrecked or were rotting away

in harbour.[35] By the summer of 1743 the construction of the one ship
that had been begun at the shipyards at Bushire had ground to a halt,
and was never resumed.*

Regardless of what was to happen in Oman later, Taqi Khan returned
to Bandar Abbas in November 1743 flushed with success. It is possible
that he had long intended to make a bid for power on his own account,
and that his efforts to sour the relationship between Nader and Reza
Qoli had been part of that. In December and January, with Shirvan,
Astarabad and Khwarezm in revolt, prospects must have looked
good. But Taqi Khan may have been prompted to revolt by Nader's
own actions – either an impossible demand for money or an order for
his arrest.[36] At any rate he had Nader's brother-in-law, Kalb Ali Khan,
murdered, and set off for Shiraz on 16 January 1744 in open rebellion,
with 6,000 troops. These were augmented along the way by tribesmen
who had killed Nader's tax officials, and by the time he reached Shiraz
Taqi Khan had a sizeable force with him. He occupied the city, but
before long Nader sent troops against him to join up with the local
forces that were still loyal.

The revolt of Shiraz was a serious matter; it was one of the most
important cities of Persia, the administrative centre of a rich province
at the heart of Nader's empire. The royal army that assembled to
retake Shiraz reflected the significance of the task – there were 40,000
soldiers. After four and a half months, in which the people of Shiraz
defended their city against the soldiers of their own Shah with great
vigour, the city fell and the besieging troops were allowed freely to sack
and plunder. Taqi Khan tried to escape in the confusion, but was soon
captured, and sent to Isfahan with his whole family. Shiraz, famous
as the city of the poets Sa'di and Hafez, had been embellished with
new gardens and thousands of trees at Nader's orders after he had
expelled the Afghans in 1730. Now great destruction was visited on the
city, hundreds and perhaps thousands of people were executed, and
the gardens were ruined. To replace the shady trees, two grisly towers
of human heads were erected, as at Astarabad. Once the sack was over,
plague broke out and 14,000 people died of disease.[37]

When Taqi Khan arrived in Isfahan he was humiliated by a mock
ceremony of welcome,† with crowds of people jeering him. In happier

---

* Its looming remains were still to be seen in Bushire as late as 1811; a sad
memorial to Nader's ambitions.
† *Esteqbal.*

days, when they had been close friends, Nader had apparently taken an oath never to kill Taqi Khan. Now he sent orders for a punishment that were as extreme as an unhinged mind could devise, save that proviso. Taqi Khan was castrated and one of his eyes was torn out: Nader had given strict orders that every care should be taken that he should not die of it. Taqi Khan was left the other eye in order that he should see what was to follow. Several of his relatives and friends were executed, including his brother and his three sons; then the most beloved of his wives was given to the soldiers and raped in front of him 'contrary to Nadir's usual regard to women'.[38]

That Nader ordered this act on the body of a woman to humiliate his former friend shows how far his personality and his former principles had degenerated into misanthropy and malice. It is likely that Nader blamed Taqi Khan not only for the rebellion, but also for his intrigues against Reza Qoli, and for his part in the events that led up to the prince's blinding. The remainder of Taqi Khan's family and dependents were sold into slavery, and he himself was then sent in chains to Nader's court.

When Taqi Khan arrived, Nader's anger seems to have cooled. Despite his misery Taqi Khan was a survivor, and had not lost his ability to get round his old master. Perhaps, despite the circumstances, he made a joke. Nader released from slavery those of Taqi Khan's family that had not been killed, and sent him to be governor of Kabul. Some historians have shown surprise at this apparent rehabilitation, after such cruelty, but if it was true that Nader had sworn to preserve Taqi Khan's life, Kabul was the safest place for him, far from the temptations and possibilities for intrigue that had seduced him from loyalty in his home province of Fars; and surrounded by Nader's toughest and most trustworthy allies, the Abdali Afghans. The attitude of the Afghan chiefs to a disgraced, one-eyed eunuch would for the most part have been contemptuous rather than compassionate.[39]

All this time, Nader had been waiting for a reply from Istanbul to the peace proposals he had negotiated with Ahmad Pasha of Baghdad. In fact, the Ottoman government informed Ahmad Pasha that they were unacceptable in February 1744, but neither they nor he thought it pressing to tell Nader. In March Nader became aware that the Ottomans were supporting another Safavid pretender, Safi Mirza. This man, like the previous one, pretended to be one of the sons of Shah Soltan Hosein, but was no more a sprig of the Safavid dynasty than Sam Mirza had been. Safi Mirza sent letters from Qars to potential supporters in the north-western provinces of Persia, encouraging them to revolt in his name. Some of these were passed on to Nader, reigniting his anger toward the Ottomans. He moved off again with the army, heading north-west. He gave orders that Sam Mirza, the other pretender, should be blinded in one eye and sent to Qars with a contemptuous message to the effect that, since the other pretender was already there, the two bogus brothers would be able to take a look at each other.[40]

As Nader headed north, a piece of good news reached him. Taimuraz and his son Erekle, princes of the old royal line of Georgia, had captured a large quantity of valuables being sent by the Ottomans to a variety of Lazgi chiefs as an inducement to them to revolt. Nader gave Taimuraz and Erekle the government of the Georgian territories of Kartli and Kakheti respectively as a reward. Having united his forces with those of Nasrollah Mirza, Nader left his baggage about 20 miles from the Arpa Chay river on 23 July and camped outside Qars. On 21 August the baggage and heavy war materials were brought up, and Nader built the usual forts and trenches encircling the town. The Persians settled down to another siege. Nader tried to deprive the Ottoman garrison of their water supply by diverting a stream (as he had done the last time he besieged the city), but this time the Ottomans managed to prevent him. On 9 October he broke off the siege, apparently because winter was approaching and Qars was notoriously cold.[41] One suspects that as before, at Mosul, the true cause had more to do with Nader's melancholia, persistent illness and listless discomfort. In earlier years he had prosecuted sieges and pursued campaigns right through the winter months in the most terrible conditions.

But having withdrawn to the east, Nader again became restless, and launched his men in four columns in a surprise winter campaign against the Lazgis. The Persians captured large numbers of their horses and other animals, and burned many villages. The tribes had not expected an attack, and the devastation inflicted by Nader's troops quickly brought most of their chiefs to submit. On 14 January 1745 he was back in Darband. From there he went back to the winter quarters that had been prepared south of the Kura; but within a few weeks, around the time of Nowruz, he moved back north of the river, where the pasture for his cavalry horses was better. He stayed there nearly three full months.[42] There was an empty aimlessness about all these movements, reflecting the loss of Nader's sense of purpose.

In June Nader moved back south-west with the army, but he fell seriously ill along the way and had to be carried in a litter. With some help from his doctors, he recovered, and the army camped near Yerevan.

While there he learned that two forces of Ottomans were advancing toward the Persian frontier; one directly toward him at Qars, the other further south, near Mosul. Nader sent Nasrollah against the latter enemy with a large body of troops, and prepared to face the former himself. Before breaking camp, he hosted marriage ceremonies for his son Emam Qoli and his nephew Ebrahim Khan, and despatched them to govern Khorasan and Hamadan respectively. Then he sent his baggage back eastwards, and left Yerevan on 7 August, heading west. His scouts told him that the Ottoman army had already left Qars. That night the Persian army camped on the old battlefield of Baghavard, where he had defeated the Ottomans ten years earlier. The following day the Ottoman army under Yegen Mohammad Pasha arrived seven or eight miles off, and began to construct a fortified camp.[43]

On 9 August,[44] the Ottomans came out of their camp, formed up and advanced to give battle to the Persians, with 100,000 cavalry and 40,000 janissary infantry. One account says that they ordered their battle formation and fought in European fashion.[45] No further details are given, but during his period of office as Ottoman grand vizier in the late 1730s Yegen Mohammad Pasha had worked closely with the colourful French renegade Bonneval, who had been taken into the Sultan's service to reform the Ottoman army. Bonneval had improved the artillery, had reorganised the janissaries into smaller tactical units, and had improved their musketry drill (it may have been partly thanks to these developments that the Ottoman forces in the Balkans had defeated the Austrian army decisively at the battle of Groczka in 1739, leading to the Austrians' later surrender of Belgrade). The Ottomans would have moved forward with their janissary infantry in the centre, in two or more lines, with artillery interspersed between the units (rather than in front as had been their traditional practice). The cavalry would have been positioned on the wings, to protect the flanks of the infantry.

This meant that Nader faced a potentially more formidable opponent than the last time he met the Ottomans on the field of Baghavard. But his own infantry training had also emphasised small manoeuvrable units and improved fire discipline. It remained to be seen whether he, or Bonneval and Yegen Pasha, had done a better job. As he prepared his men to meet the advancing Ottomans, Nader ordered his infantry to fire one volley only at the enemy, and then charge in with their sabres to fight hand-to-hand.* This would have negated any advantage the

---

* A tactic also favoured by Scots Highlanders in the seventeenth and eighteenth centuries.

janissaries might have gained in musketry.

The armies closed and engaged, but the cavalry of both sides held back. The infantry struggle went on for some time, each side attacking and counter-attacking; both commanders sending new reinforcements into the battle. One account says that, contrary to his usual practice, Nader in this campaign against the Ottomans had generally commanded the army from his throne within the camp, receiving word of developments and issuing commands to his troops by messengers. But by the early afternoon on this day his messengers were still telling him the fight was undecided, and he resolved to intervene personally.[46] Nader put on his armour, mounted up and led a reserve of 40,000 Abdali cavalry in a furious attack against the Ottoman flank. Even then the fighting was still fierce, and two of Nader's horses were killed under him, but his presence encouraged the Persians to new efforts. Ottoman resistance finally began to crumble, and 15,000 irregular troops from the provinces of Asia Minor fled. The main Ottoman body retreated in confusion to the safety of the entrenchments around their camp. Nader followed them up, but withdrew with his men to his own encampments at sunset.

In the following days Nader sent out detachments to cut off any supplies the Ottomans might try to bring through from Qars, and closed Yegen Pasha up in his camp with his men, who were growing mutinous. There were some skirmishes between the two armies, but the Ottomans failed to make any impression on the ring of steel Nader had thrown around them. One account says that there was an artillery duel in which the Persian guns showed themselves superior, firing both more rapidly and more accurately, until many of the Ottoman gunners lay dead, and the wheels and axles of the Ottoman gun carriages were shattered by the Persian fire, so that most of their cannon '... were silent, and of no more use than inert lumps of bronze, lying on the ground.'[47]

By now the Ottomans were close to mutiny and deserters were coming over to the Persians, telling them that the Ottoman army was about to withdraw. One night the Ottomans quietly pulled out, leaving tents pitched and lights and fires burning in their camp, but the Persians followed them and re-established the blockade.[48] At this point, on 19 August, Nader received letters from his son Nasrollah announcing that he had inflicted a serious defeat on an army of Ottomans and Kurds near Mosul. Nasrollah proudly offered to advance further into Ottoman territory and add it to Nader's conquests.

Nader sent the letters from Nasrollah to Yegen Pasha, to show him the futility of further fighting, but as the messenger arrived at the enemy camp a great tumult of shouting broke out among the Ottoman troops as riot and mutiny erupted. When the dust settled it was discovered that Yegen Pasha was dead, possibly by suicide but probably killed by his own soldiers. The leaderless and desperate Ottomans now fled en masse, the soldiers shouting to each other 'Go back, go back, people of Mohammad!'[49] The Persians pursued and cut down many of them; others were captured. Nader released the wounded prisoners and sent them to Qars; the others were sent to Tabriz and Tehran. In the battle and the later rout the Ottomans lost around 28,000 men, of whom as many as 12,000 were killed. The Persians lost about 8,000 men, mainly in the early stages of the first engagement.[50]

Nader had roused himself to lead the decisive charge of the Abdalis on 9 August, but this was almost the last outburst of his old energy. The superiority of the Persian artillery in particular shows the superb pitch to which the Persian army had been trained and equipped; one authority refers explicitly to a programme of re-equipment over the previous three years.[51] The Ottomans too had tried to bring their forces up to a new standard for this ultimate confrontation, but had failed. Nader had in truth by this time the world-beating army of which he had boasted: Nasrollah's offer to march into Ottoman Anatolia and conquer it was not empty braggadocio. But for once this battle had been fought defensively, reacting to an Ottoman invasion, rather than as part of a Persian campaign of aggression. Nader's will for continuing the struggle had gone.

Resting after his victory, Nader sent new peace proposals with the wounded Turks to Qars, afterwards sending an ambassador to discuss them in Istanbul. For the first time he declared himself ready to abandon the request for recognition of the Ja'fari mazhhab, and for the fifth column in the Ka'ba; but in return he demanded Baghdad, Basra, Najaf, Karbala, Ottoman Kurdistan and Van.[52] Although the Ottomans were initially inclined to rebuff Nader's latest proposals, the arrival of the Persian ambassador seems to have done something to change the Sultan's mind. Probably the envoy hinted that the territorial demands were flexible. As well as the religious proposals, Nader was abandoning his plans for the conquest of Ottoman territory and supremacy over Islam as a whole. After such a defeat, the Sultan can hardly have dared to hope that the years of war with Persia were about to end so favourably. An Ottoman ambassador was despatched to Nader's court. Meanwhile Nader slowly marched back via Hamadan to Isfahan, where he arrived on 28 December.[53]

Unfortunately Nader did not balance his new-found desire for peace with the Ottoman Sultan with a wish to relieve the pressure on his suffering subjects. By now his cruelty and avarice had become obsessive, and as soon as he arrived in Isfahan he set about beating the citizens to get their money. In a pattern that was to become familiar in each of the places he was to visit over the coming months, he laid a demand for 10,000 tomans on the governor of Isfahan, and set his men to apply the *falake* until the governor would name people from whom the money could be taken. One eyewitness who went to Isfahan at this time stood for a while outside the palace where Nader was holding audience. As he waited, attendants brought out a succession of people, some with noses and ears cut off, others with their brains knocked out and others strangled.[54]

On 2 February 1746 Nader left Isfahan, and arrived at Mashhad seven weeks later. Along the way he looked at accounts and interrogated officials in each place he stopped, and called others to him from other places further afield. To each his standard opening questions were: 'How much of my money have you eaten?* And who has it now?'[55] Many were tortured and mutilated. Some were beaten so badly about the head with sticks that their faces looked black 'like a wolf'. Nader's prodigious memory and intelligence had turned insanely irascible, enraged by the fear and petty evasions of one cringing clerk after another. His conduct was reaching a pitch at which no-one, not even those who had been most loyal, could feel safe.

In Mashhad, where previously Nader had been more lenient than elsewhere, he executed 100 officials and citizens, and demanded the city pay the enormous sum of 500,000 tomans† within one year. He ordered that the artillery kept in a large depot at Merv be prepared for another campaign in Turkestan. Nader celebrated Nowruz on 21 March and gave out large numbers of expensive khal'ats, but few of their recipients can have been easy in their minds.[56]

While he was in Mashhad a new revolt broke out in Sistan. It was led by the governor of Sistan, Fath Ali Khan Kayani; one of the sons of Malek Mahmud, from whom Nader had conquered Mashhad in 1726. He revolted after a summons to court and an outrageous tax demand for the province, like those levied in Isfahan and Mashhad. As well as many from his own province, large numbers of Baluchi tribesmen joined him.

* i.e. embezzled.
† The equivalent of £937,500 sterling at that time.

The governor of Kerman revolted too, for similar reasons, but some loyal troops hung on in the citadel of the city, making it relatively easy for reinforcements to suppress that rebellion shortly afterwards.[57]

On 12 April Nader went on from Mashhad to Kalat, Abivard and the Darra Gaz, as on previous visits. At Kalat he inspected the buildings and fortifications, and ordered some improvements. Apparently he passed his days there in celebrations and jollities, and deposited 4.5 million tomans in gold and silver coin in the treasure house. This was in addition to the jewels and other treasures of India that were already there. Kalat had become a speck of impossible wealth, at the centre of a great storm of poverty and misery across Nader's empire. He visited his completed birth-monument, and pronounced himself pleased with it. After another brief stop in Mashhad, Nader headed back westwards.[58]

At Kordan, about 40 miles west of Tehran on the way to Qazvin, Nader and his entourage met the Ottoman ambassador, advancing to meet him in the opposite direction. The Ottoman Sultan had given his ambassador instructions to seek a peace on the basis of the old frontiers first established in 1639, and an end to the Ja'fari mazhhab. After five meetings, the negotiators achieved a draft treaty on the basis the Sultan had wanted, and on 4 September 1746 the treaty was signed. At the ceremony Nader made one of his few shows of magnificence. He was seated on his reconstruction of the peacock throne, adorned with all the splendour of India: his hat, belt and clothes were all encrusted with diamonds.

The treaty incorporated mutual commitments to avoid activities that might endanger the peace, to free all prisoners, and to exchange ambassadors; a repetition of the Persian commitment to drop practices offensive to Sunni Muslims and show respect for the first three caliphs; and a commitment from the Ottomans to facilitate the free movement of Persian pilgrims to Mecca. It also expressed the hope that, now the commotions of war had died down, and the sword had returned to the scabbard, the blessing of God would fall on the two empires and the families of the two monarchs.[59]

Nader sent two of his most trusted officials to Istanbul with the treaty; one of them was his official historian Mirza Mahdi. They took with them as presents for the Sultan a golden throne covered with pearls, and two elephants that had been trained to dance when they heard music.[60] Perhaps Nader intended the throne to symbolise his generous restitution to the Sultan of secure authority over his territories, particularly the eastern ones. But it would be more apposite to say that the elephants were to dance on Nader's abandoned plans to defeat the Ottoman Sultan and make himself master of the Islamic world.

From Kordan Nader travelled south. As he went, reports reached him that the revolt in Sistan was spreading, and there were new signs of trouble in Khorasan. When he arrived in Isfahan at the beginning of December his suspicion and anger pushed him into a kind of driven frenzy. His soldiers pillaged the city and the surrounding villages without mercy or constraint. They drove groups of those that had been unable to pay through the streets with blows, 20 or 30 people at a time. Isfahan resounded with screams: it looked as if it had been taken by storm and sacked by a hostile army. Each day there were as many as 30 bodies outside the palace, of people either strangled at his orders or killed by his troops.[61]

Before he left Isfahan Nader had an inventory taken of the valuables in the palace, and discovered that a carpet was missing. He accused the man in whose trust the valuables had been left, but he denied any wrongdoing. Nader had the man beaten, upon which he said his predecessor had sold the carpet some years before. Nader asked who had been so impertinent as to purchase royal property. After more beatings, the man named eight merchants – two Indians, two Armenians and four Jews. The merchants were found, arrested, interrogated, and blinded in one eye. The brutal questioning yielded no significant information: the merchants were almost certainly innocent. They were chained together by the neck. The following day Nader had a large fire lit in the square of Isfahan, in front of the palace, and all eight were thrown into it to burn to death.[62]

9. *View from the West.*

This melodramatic engraving, showing towers of skulls, Justice trampled
underfoot and a bare-breasted female (Tragedy?) floating threateningly
through the air, formed the frontispiece to Jonas Hanway's account of Nader
Shah, giving a foretaste of Hanway's view of Nader. Published in 1753,
Hanway's version of events was central to most later accounts in English.
(London Library)

CHAPTER TEN
Full Circle

We can say that cruelty is used well (if it is permissible to talk in this way of what is evil) when it is employed once and for all… and then is not persisted in but as far as possible turned to the good of one's subjects. Cruelty badly used is that which, although infrequent to start with, as time goes on, rather than disappearing, grows in intensity. Those who use the first method can, with human and divine assistance, find some means of consolidating their position… the others cannot possibly stay in power.

Machiavelli

Nader's increasing mental instability in the last months of 1746 was made worse by his physical illness, which again became serious. In Isfahan he found a new chief physician, the French Jesuit Pere Bazin, who tended him until Nader died. According to Bazin, who took on the appointment reluctantly, Nader had always had a strong constitution, but was now suffering from a variety of disorders, primarily from a 'dropsical ailment' that made his body swell with fluid. He could not keep his food down, and regularly vomited an hour after eating. In addition he was badly constipated, had liver trouble, and persistent dryness of the mouth. It is likely that these symptoms resulted from a recurrence of Nader's liver trouble and jaundice, caused by an earlier malarial infection; possibly aggravated by excessive drinking in his younger years. Rather out of his depth, Bazin asked for and was granted a month to find and prepare medicines for the treatment. Notwithstanding his illness, Bazin described Nader as physically strong, tall, with an oval, tanned face, aquiline nose, well-formed mouth, the lower lip protruding slightly; small piercing eyes, a lively expression; and a loud, strong voice, which he nonetheless could moderate and sweeten when necessary.[1]

Problems of state shifted and sharpened along with Nader's physical disorders. Unrest and rebellion in the eastern provinces developed to an intensity that required his presence in person. He left Isfahan on 23 January 1747, heading east via Yazd and Kerman, toward Khorasan. There was mixed news from Sistan. Fath Ali Khan Kayani, the leader of the revolt there, had been captured and dealt with. But another of the rebels had escaped to the old fortress of Kuh-e Khwaje, and was defying Nader's forces from there. Nader sent his nephew Ali Qoli with 40,000 troops to deal with the problem, and later sent Tahmasp Khan Jalayer also.

Nader's demands for money grew ever more demented, and extended now even to his inner circle of old friends and family members. He had already confiscated the property of Ali Qoli's younger brother, and had laid impossibly high contributions on Taimuraz and Erekle, the Georgian princes. He had issued a long proscription list of people condemned to death, and his wildness was such that no-one knew who next would feel his wrath. He sent a demand for 100,000 tomans to Ali Qoli,* and a similar one for 50,000 to Tahmasp Khan. Growing suspicious when no response came from either, in his madness he sent new orders in quick succession for each to arrest the other, presumably on the crazy reasoning that one or the other would be loyal, and succeed, or kill or be killed in the attempt.

Rather than comply with Nader's clumsy manipulation, Ali Qoli and Tahmasp Khan Jalayer talked to each other about their predicament. They agreed the impossibility of their position, and resolved that they were safer together than if they remained separate. They delayed and evaded further enquiries from Nader's court, and it gradually became apparent that they had taken over leadership of the revolt in Sistan. This was much more serious than any previous revolt – these men were experienced captains, with veteran soldiers under their command. They also had long-standing friendships and kinship connections with many of Nader's closest officers and officials. Nader must have recalled with profound bitterness the favours and indulgences he had granted his nephew.

It seems Ali Qoli identified the loyalty of Nader's Afghan troops as

---

* To be raised from the inhabitants of Sistan, still in revolt.

the main obstacle to his revolt. In April 1747 he went to Herat to woo the Abdali chiefs there, with some success. Tahmasp Khan Jalayer, despite Nader's warrant for his arrest, was less at ease with the rebellion than Ali Qoli. He had been Nader's trusted lieutenant before Ali Qoli was even born, and had fought with him through many of his battles. Tahmasp Khan apparently showed signs of wanting to return to loyalty, and tried to persuade Ali Qoli to change his mind. Ali Qoli had no doubts; he knew there was no turning back. He had the old buffalo poisoned.[2]

As had become normal, Nader carried out further atrocities and cruelties along his road to Khorasan. At Kerman he celebrated Nowruz outside the city on 21 March 'with the usual marks of prosperity and good fortune', but within there were beatings and mutilations in search of wealth that was no longer there. Nader had a grudge against Kerman for the brief revolt the previous year, and there were mass executions. Two more grisly minarets adorned with severed heads were erected, and the army moved on at the end of March. Nader's health, according to his physician Bazin, was improving; but it is likely that the disease was episodic in any case, and that the remission was just one aspect of the illness, rather than the result of Bazin's medicines.[3]

At every turn, events now reminded Nader of his past mistakes. After a punishing march through the Dasht-e Lut desert, in the course of which a number of men and many animals died of thirst, Nader and his men arrived at Tabas in Khorasan, where he was met by 16 of his children and grandchildren. He stared at them for a long time, no doubt thinking of the other son whose life he had destroyed, and bitterly asking himself which of them would be the next to betray him. Nader asked the three eldest, Nasrollah, Emam Qoli and Shahrokh, one after the other, to take over the crown. All three excused themselves, on the basis of their youth, their incapacity, and their lack of experience, asking him to continue. Those who witnessed the scene thought it unlikely that Nader really wanted to give up the throne; rather that he made the offer in order to see whether the princes would be tempted, and that if any of them had shown a wish to rule, he would have had them arrested. He had always played with the idea of retiring to Kalat; perhaps by this time he was starting to think he really might do it. But letting go of the power he had won for himself was more than he could do. From Tabas Nader went on to Mashhad, arriving with his army and his thugs at the end of April. Once there, the same dismal round of extortion, flogging and mutilation began all over again.[4]

In Mashhad everything conspired to heighten Nader's anxiety and rage. Rebels intercepted his messengers, and the only news that reached him was bad. Many people, even among Nader's closest adherents and attendants, were hoping that Ali Qoli would be successful, and release the country from its ordeal. There were plots and the suspicion of plots everywhere; his spies reported to him at least part of what was said. Some of his officers exaggerated the gravity of the situation when they presented the news to Nader, for the malicious pleasure of depressing and enraging him further. By now the deterrent effects of the beatings and executions had dulled, producing a kind of fatalism mingled with savage resentment. The enemies he had gathered around him in his arrogance, reasoning that they would be less dangerous close to him, where he could keep his eye on them, now sensed his weakness. Unlike in his early days in Khorasan, Nader now had no brother Ebrahim or trustworthy lieutenant like Tahmasp Khan Jalayer to fall back on. Back in his home province, Nader was isolated, dangerously: an outsider once again.

For most people, Nader had now long outrun the stock of credit they had granted him as ruler when he had himself crowned over ten years before. According to traditional ideas of kingship, the prime duties of the Shah were to dispense justice, and maintain order.[5] At the beginning of Nader's reign, people were grateful for a prince with the military clout to eject the country's enemies, and keep rebellious provincial chiefs in line. Nader's justice was harsh, but many said that it had to be, and they felt he judged fairly. His military victories appeared almost miraculous, and people would have believed that they showed the approval of God. Nader was feared, but most felt that it was mainly wrongdoers and the country's enemies that had cause to fear him.

By the last years of his reign, all that had changed. Nader had undergone a terrible physical and mental decline, and had become a mere wreck of his former self. He was acting cruelly, out of all proportion to real or imagined crimes. The innocent were punished with the guilty,[6] and in such numbers that no-one felt safe. Instead of behaving like the godlike figure, above petty human concerns that a Shah was supposed to be, he pursued the wealth of his subjects obsessively, like a crazed thief. His armies were not protectors of the empire and the guardians of public order; instead they behaved like bandit gangs, driving into poverty, emigration and slavery the very people they were supposed to protect. In that atmosphere, and with the Shah alienating even his closest companions and relatives, it was impossible that he could reign much longer.

Aware of the danger that surrounded him, Nader sent Nasrollah and Shahrokh, the other princes and his harem to Kalat for safety. But this act was taken by some to signify the imprisonment of the princes, possibly prefiguring the sort of punishment that Reza Qoli had suffered, and caused further resentment.[7] Rebellion spread further. Nader's old enemies the Kurds of Khabushan declared themselves against him and for Ali Qoli, and raided his stud farm, between Mashhad and Khabushan. Since Nader's love of horses was well known, this may have been a deliberate ploy agreed with Ali Qoli to draw him out of Mashhad. Nader emerged with about 16,000 men to crush the Kurds. Some of the Kurds fled into the hills; others retreated to the citadel of Khabushan. On the evening of 19 June 1747 Nader camped on a small hill at Fathabad, seven or eight miles from the town.[8] Preparing again to attack and subdue the rebel Kurds of Khabushan, Nader had come full circle.

Aside from the Kurds, Nader had worries within his own camp. He distrusted the head of his household, Saleh Khan, but was more suspicious of the *keshikchi-bashi*, Mohammad Qoli Khan Qereqlu. The latter, an Afshar and another royal relative, was respected by the other officers of the army, and had distinguished himself by swift and decisive action in the past. He commanded a 1,000-man division of Nader's personal guard, made up of men from Nader's own Afshar tribe. Nader knew him to be discontented; one account says that Mohammad Qoli had been in communication with Ali Qoli by secret, coded letter.[9] It happened that Mohammad Qoli Khan's Afshar division was on duty that night. It is striking that the characters of this last drama, relatives, Khorasani Afshars and Kurds, so closely resembled those in the earliest episodes of his career, when he had been making his way in Abivard. The hatred he had earned from them in the savage feuds, betrayals and murders of those early days had never gone away; it had merely been suppressed. As his powers faded, and he became a lonely man in his own camp, the old scores came due.

Nader decided that evening to remove the threat posed by Mohammad Qoli Khan and the other officers of the guard. For years he had kept an uneasy balance in the army between Persians and non-Persians, Shi'a and Sunni Muslims, in order not to depend too heavily on any one tribe, sect or faction, and by competition to stimulate each group to greater zeal. Now he summoned Ahmad Khan Abdali, commander of the 4,000 Afghans in the army, to the tent set aside for his private audiences. Ahmad Khan came with some other Afghan officers.

Nader told the Afghans that he suspected his guard of treachery. He professed his trust in the Afghans, and said he wanted them to arrest the guard officers the next morning, killing any that resisted. Ahmad Khan Abdali was only about 24 years old, but a talented captain. He owed his position entirely to Nader, who had released him from a dungeon when the citadel of Kandahar fell to the Persians in 1738. He would have understood that Nader intended a massacre of the Persian officers. His men tended to be hostile to the Persians in the army, including the guard troops, and were loyal to the Shah. Ahmad Khan promised to obey Nader's orders, and the Afghans left.

At this point we should ask what really was happening here. Nader's actions show he was aware of the danger he was in. He was no longer fully rational, but self-preservation is normally a powerful inducement to clear thought. If, while the Afghans were with him, he had called in the officers he suspected, he could have dealt with the problem on the spot. Why did he not order the Afghans to arrest the officers of the guard immediately? The message of his whole life, of all his successes, was prompt action. Instead, in this crisis, he gave his enemies the whole night to pre-empt him. It is almost as if, with half his mind, even as he gave orders for the destruction of his enemies, he had decided with the other that this was the end of the road, and deliberately gave them the chance to kill him.

Someone had overheard the meeting between Nader and the Afghans, and told Mohammad Qoli Khan of it. He sought out Saleh Khan, and the two agreed to murder the Shah that night, before the Afghans could act. They put together a group of about 70 officers, nobles, guards and others they thought they could trust.

Nader slept that night not in his usual tent, but with Chuki, the daughter of Mohammad Hosein Khan Qajar, who had been one of his favourite women for some time. One account says he had been troubled all that day because of a dream, which repeated images he had first dreamed some years earlier, before he had become Shah. Then, he had dreamed that a group of nobles came to him. One of them had given him a sword, saying that with it he was being entrusted with the kingdom of Persia. Now he had dreamed of the same man again; but this time the man had said, 'Take the sword from the belt of this incompetent; he is not worthy of this task.' In the dream he had tried to hold on to the sword, but to no avail. In the morning Nader had told one of his ministers about it, and may even have considered flight to Kalat,[10] but the minister had reassured him that there was nothing to fear.

When he went to Chuki in the evening, she could see he was unsettled and anxious. He took off his hat and put it on the floor, revealing his white hair. The hair contrasted with his beard, which he kept dyed black.[11] Nader was drowsy, but would not undress to sleep. He lay down in his clothes. He told Chuki to let him doze, but to wake him if he fell into a heavy sleep.

When the conspirators got to the entrance of the harem compound, most of them refused to go any further. Only Saleh Khan, Mohammad Khan Qajar Erevani and one other had enough resolve to shoulder the others aside and go in, killing a Negro eunuch who tried to bar their way.

The noise woke Chuki, who shook Nader awake as Saleh Khan entered the tent. Nader leaped off the bed, drawing his sword and shouting abuse in his anger, but he tripped. As he lay on the ground, Saleh Khan cut at him with his sabre, striking between the neck and the shoulder and slicing off Nader's arm – but then went rigid with shock. Nader lay on the ground, bleeding profusely. He tried to get up, but failed. He asked them to spare his life. Mohammad Khan Qajar was more determined than Saleh Khan. He stepped forward with his sabre and struck off Nader's head with one blow.[12]

With Nader dead, chaos erupted. The murderers ransacked the women's quarters and the Shah's tents, robbing all they could find, and killing two of Nader's ministers.* The leaders of the assassins had intended to keep the affair quiet until the morning, but they could not restrain the looting. By the morning the Afghans were roused, and moved in a body toward the royal quarters with Ahmad Khan at their head, to find their way barred by more than double their number of guards. The Afghans refused to believe Nader was dead, and after a pitched battle they broke through to the tent and found the body lying in its own blood, with an old woman weeping over the head. The Afghans fought their way out of the camp and set off back to Kandahar. Not far from the camp they ran into a convoy of looted treasure that Mohammad Qoli Khan had sent to Mashhad. The Afghans plundered it, took the Kuh-e Nur diamond among other valuables, and went home.

Ahmad Khan Abdali knew that his former companions in arms would have plenty to keep them distracted from affairs in Herat and

* Chuki must have survived, because otherwise we would not have the detailed account of Nader's last night, which can only have come from her. Bazin says that the assassins left the women of Nader's harem alone, preferring to take the gold and jewels (p. 322).

Kandahar for some time to come. After he reached Kandahar, he called an assembly of the leading Afghan chiefs, and had himself made the first Shah of Afghanistan, taking the name Ahmad Shah Dorrani. He ruled successfully, establishing Afghanistan as an independent state, although his later conquests in northern India were short-lived.

Back at the camp at Fathabad, Mohammad Qoli Khan, who had kept himself out of harm's way during the assassination and the fighting that followed, sent Nader's head to Ali Qoli, to show that the task was accomplished. Before the ugly proof arrived, a body of Bakhtiari troops went to Kalat to secure the treasury and Nader's family. The Bakhtiaris surrounded the fortress. After some days a ladder was left against one of the towers by someone who had descended for water – possibly not by accident, and Ali Qoli's men made their way into the fortress. As they did so, Nasrollah, Emam Qoli and Shahrokh escaped on horseback, and rode furiously in the direction of Merv. Their enemies pursued them, and captured Emam Qoli and Shahrokh about 30 miles away. Nasrollah rode on, knocking one man off his horse with a blow from his sword, and made it through to Merv. But some soldiers from the garrison recognised him, arrested him and sent him back to Kalat. From there Nasrollah, Emam Qoli and Shahrokh were sent to Mashhad, and the two older princes were executed there. By then the former golden youth, poor, blind Reza Qoli, had already been murdered in Kalat.

Shahrokh, who was 13 years old, was spared and kept alive in secret because he was the son of a Safavid princess. Ali Qoli thought he might be useful if he should run into difficulties. All Nader's other male children and grandchildren (20 or more of them) were killed; even the youngest infants. Even two little boys, one three years old, the other no more than 18 months, named Chingiz or Genghis after Genghis Khan, were poisoned. But the killing did not stop there. To prevent Nader being followed by an heir as yet unborn, Ali Qoli had the bellies of the pregnant women of his harem torn open. Two weeks after Nader's assassination, Ali Qoli made himself Shah under a new title: Adil Shah, which means the just Shah.[13]

Persia's sufferings did not end with Nader's death. The greater part of the next 50 years was taken up by civil war as his empire split. Ali Qoli lasted little more than a year as Shah: he was more interested in enjoying himself than in consolidating his power. In the meantime the army rampaged through Khorasan, practising the habits of violent extortion their former master had taught them, and creating a famine around Mashhad.

Ali Qoli kept on Mohammad Qoli, the *keshikchi-bashi* who had organised the plot to murder Nader at Fathabad, as the captain of his own bodyguard. As the new Shah's rule grew unpopular, and the people of Mashhad began to starve, Mohammad Qoli again developed a plot to kill his master, but this time Ali Qoli was warned by a spy. He had Mohammad Qoli arrested, and blinded. Then, according to one account, Mohammad Qoli was pushed into the harem quarters where the survivors of Nader's women lived together. When they saw him they fell on him with scissors and the sharp little awls they used for needlework. He did not die until they grew tired of torturing him.[14]

Eventually Ali Qoli's own brother Ebrahim deposed and blinded him; both were later put to death by other contenders for power. The turmoil and violence continued: Shahrokh was crowned by a group of officers and nobles in October 1748, but then was deposed and blinded. Eventually he was put back on the throne and was allowed to continue as Shah of a truncated kingdom, under the influence of Ahmad Shah Dorrani of Afghanistan and his successors. Shahrokh ruled in this way, as a sad, blind puppet, until 1796. In the Caucasus another of Nader's protégés, Erekle, carved out an independent state in Georgia.

Within a few years many of the different elements of the army, along with most of the peoples Nader had resettled to Khorasan, had returned home. Among them were the small Zand tribe or clan from Loristan. One of their chiefs, Karim Khan Zand, eventually established himself as dominant in western Persia and ruled, for the most part peaceably, from 1765 to 1779. He never had himself made Shah, but ruled from Shiraz as *Vakil* (regent). After he died in 1779 there was civil war again, in which the Qajars of Astarabad eventually achieved supremacy. Agha Mohammad, grandson of the Fath Ali Khan Qajar that Tahmasp had executed in 1726, finally made himself Shah in 1796 and founded the Qajar dynasty, which reigned until 1925.

Unlike in 1722, foreign powers did not attempt to exploit the chaos in Persia to their advantage after Nader's death in 1747, instead leaving internal forces to resolve the struggle for supremacy. The Qajars eventually won that struggle, and under Agha Mohammad Khan set about re-establishing Persia's traditional boundaries. Agha Mohammad reconquered Georgia in September 1795, but this success proved short-lived. His brutality there stirred Russian interest again, and a Russian army annexed the territory in 1800. In a series of wars with the Russians in the early nineteenth century the Qajar monarchy lost many of Persia's other possessions in the Caucasus, and later, under British pressure, the

Qajars had to abandon their efforts to win back Herat too.

Nader's spirit lingered behind the Qajar dynasty, as a reproach. The Qajars accepted the loss of territory, they centralised and made some reforms, but they failed to maintain a strong, modern army and allowed energetic reformers to go to the wall.[15] Behind Persia's formidable natural boundaries, they reverted to something like the passive mode of rule of the last Safavids, abandoning the desire to contend on the world stage, for a quiet life. They presided, allowing the colonial powers to nibble away at Persia's sovereignty until the powers of the last Qajar Shahs were severely limited, and Britain and Russia declared zones of influence within the country itself.

Nader had pushed the country into war, and if his dynasty had endured and tempered military success with a little administrative wisdom (as some contemporaries believed they had reason to hope for from Reza Qoli, had he reigned), the growth of state structures, reform and modernisation would necessarily have accompanied military expansion, as they did in France and Prussia, and other European states in the seventeenth and eighteenth centuries. Much else might have followed: Persian dominance in the Islamic world, in the long term perhaps even removal of the Shi'a/Sunni schism and an uneasy parity of development with the West. In Europe, the expanded State, still competing militarily and culturally with its neighbours, was forced in the nineteenth century to co-opt a wider spread of social classes, leading to a more even spread of economic prosperity, stimulating rapid economic development and eventually, democratisation. Persia, with its long-established and powerful class of bazaari merchants and artisans (which, in alliance with the Shi'a ulema, eventually brought about the reforming revolution of 1905–1911)[16] was in theory better-placed for economic, social and political take-off than other countries in the region; there is no sound reason to believe that the developments that took place in Europe, or similar changes, could not have happened there too.

These might be thought big claims, but by 1743 Nader had achieved startling successes already. He had demonstrated his supremacy over the Moghul Empire, was close to achieving the same with the Ottoman Sultan, and controlled the most powerful army in Asia, if not the world. Like it or not, militarist absolutism was the usual precursor of economic, political and social development in this period. If Nader and his dynasty had succeeded, he might today be remembered as a figure in Iranian history to compare with Peter the Great in the history of Russia: as a ruthless, dynamic monarch who set his country on a new path.* But these things did not happen, because after 1742 Nader's rule faltered, grew impossibly oppressive, and failed. The grand vision of his reign was never fulfilled; the opportunities were lost, and the country fell back into chaos and torpor.

Ultimately rulers have to be judged on the actual outcomes of their rule, not on what might have happened. Sir John Malcolm wrote in the early nineteenth century that two generations later Persians spoke with pride of Nader's glorious deeds, and with more pity than horror of the cruelties of his latter years. Despite his crimes, they were grateful to him for reviving a sense of their ancient greatness among the Persians, and for restoring the country's independence.[17]

In the 20 years that elapsed between his capture of Mashhad at the end of 1726 and his death nearby in 1747 Nader ejected the Afghans, restored Persia's frontiers, and established his regime as the dominant power from Delhi to Baghdad. In doing so he rode over 20,000 miles[†] and fought 20 or more major battles; all but one of them victoriously. Taking into account his political successes in coming from complete obscurity to control this huge area and wield massive military power, his achievement was unequalled in Persian history, and has few equals in the history of the world. The wider possibilities opened up by his successes were tantalising, and his victories ensured the survival of Iran as a nation: the one enduring effect of his period of rule. But Nader's reign in the end was a failure and a disaster for his country, not just for the terrible suffering he inflicted on millions in his own lifetime and

---

* Nader would never have followed a self-conscious westernisation policy like Peter's, and Nader took less interest than Peter in economic development. But if Nader's regime had stayed on the rails through the crises of 1741–1742 and had endured longer this might have come. Peter had more time. He reigned from 1682 to 1725; 43 years to Nader's 11 (15 if you include the period of Nader's rule as regent after he deposed Tahmasp in 1732) – and most of Peter's more progressive reforms came in the latter part of his reign, after his visit to Germany, Holland, England and Austria in 1697/1698. There are other parallels between the two lives, notably the preoccupation of both men with military matters and their cruel treatment of their sons, on suspicion of treason. Peter's eldest son Alexis died under torture after being imprisoned in 1718.

† A rough and conservative estimate. Over his whole life Nader probably rode a distance equivalent to the circumference of the Earth, including over some of the roughest and most unforgiving terrain on Earth.

his own ignominious death, but also for the opportunities lost by the collapse of his regime, and the suffering that collapse brought about in later years. Reflecting the disorder and the national humiliations that followed Nader's death, the popular memory of later generations altered Reza Qoli's words after his blinding to have him say, 'It is not my eyes that you have put out, but those of Persia.'[18]

Notes

PREFACE
1. A point made by Jeremy Black in his *Warfare in the Eighteenth Century* (London 1999), p. 38.
2. For an important and thoughtful exploration of the counterfactual possibilities thrown up by Nader's invasion of India, see Subrahmanyam 2000 (notably, p. 365 for the East India Company's reaction to Nader's conquest of Delhi). See also below, Chapter 8, note 6.
3. See Bayly, pp. 1 and 13. A kind of lofty distaste may also have played a part – 'The eighteenth century is a horrible period in Iranian history – horrible to read about, horrible to disentangle, horrible to have tried to live in … I propose to treat this grisly epoch with the greatest possible brevity.' (Roger Stevens, *The Land of the Great Sophy*, London 1971, p. 30) This is fine Foreign Office prose, and some might agree with Stevens, after reading Nader's story. But we are obliged, if we want to try to understand history, to look at the darker as well as the lighter episodes.
4. There were though honourable exceptions, notably Sir John Malcolm, whose *History of Persia* did justice to Nader's record, correcting the relentlessly censorious account of Jonas Hanway – 'In describing eastern despots, there has often appeared to me a stronger desire to satisfy the public of the author's attachment to freedom and his abhorrence of tyranny, and despotic power under every shape, than to give a clear and just view of those characters whose history was the immediate object of his labours.' (Malcolm, *Two Letters*, p. 530).
5. This view persists in some modern histories, for example Spear 1990, Vol. 2, pp. 72–3.
6. Malcolm, *Two Letters*, p. 531.
7. See my forthcoming article, *Basile Vatatzes and his History of Nader Shah*.
8. Notably, Parker 1988, but also John A Hall 1986, p. 140 and passim.

9.   For example, Bernard Lewis, *What Went Wrong* (London 2002)
        – though Lewis' comment on pp. 20–1 about the 'wars between
        Turkey and Iran that ended in 1730 with a victory for the even less
        modernised Persians' is incorrect on a number of counts, and does
        not reflect well on Lewis' understanding of the events of the early
        eighteenth century in this region. The wars did not end then and,
        on any analysis that does not assume modernisation corresponds to
        proximity to the West, the Persians were not less modernised.

Prologue – ZENITH

1.   Hanway, p. 174, Fraser, p. 178; Sarkar, p. 60, Brosset, Vol. II, Part II,
        p. 360 – letter from Erekle II.
2.   I have called modern Iran Persia when I am writing about events
        prior to the twentieth century. But I call Persia Iran when I refer to
        modern times. It was the regime of the first Pahlavi Shah, Reza Shah,
        that insisted on the use of the name 'Iran' in the 1930s (the name
        Iranians have always used for their country in their own language).
        The name Persia derives from the province of Iran, Fars (Pars), from
        which the ancient Persian kings and the Persian language (*Farsi/*
        Persian) originated.
3.   Blake 1991, p. 68.
4.   Blake 1986, p. 171, JN, Vol. 2, p. 73.
5.   There are many descriptions of the Peacock throne. Mine follows
        Jean-Baptiste Tavernier, *Travels in India*, trans. V. Ball, Ed W. Crooke
        (London 1925), Vol. 1, pp. 303–5. The description in the AAN differs,
        but agrees on the quantity and size of the jewels, and names the
        diamond as the Kuh-e Nur (Vol. 2, p. 739n).
6.   JN, Vol. 2, p. 74.
7.   Hanway, p. 175; JS, p. 27; Fraser, pp. 179–80; Floor 1998, p. 307. There
        is a story that Sa'adat Khan died of a wound inflicted some months
        before (Lockhart 1938, p. 145n and, p. 135n) but it seems unlikely that
        a man dying a lingering death from gangrene in his foot would have
        ridden with Nader into Delhi a few bare hours before he finally died.
8.   Sarkar, p. 60.
9.   Fraser/Mirza Zaman, p. 120; Lockhart 1938, 145n; Hookham, p. 77.
        The title Sahebqeran was used by many other rulers after Timur.
10.   Abd ol-Karim Kashmiri (BW), fol. 83a.
11.   Fraser, p. 179.
12.   Sarkar, p. 7; Lockhart 1938, p. 122. Though many times invaded and
        conquered by foreigners, the Persians' literary and court culture

spread and influenced all the eastern part of the Islamic world, from Istanbul to Bokhara, Delhi and beyond. Truly an Empire of the Mind.

13. Malcolm, *History of Persia*, Vol. 2, p. 85 – I have regularised the names and titles in the quotation.
14. ARM, fol. 174a; JN, Vol. 2, p. 76.
15. ARM, fol. 174a; JS, pp. 27–8; Fraser, p. 181.
16. Fraser, pp. 181–2; Hazin, p. 298.
17. BW, fol. 81b – see also AAN, p. 745.
18. Fraser, p. 183.
19. ARM, fol. 174a; Fraser, p. 183.
20. Malcolm, *History*, Vol. 2, p. 83.
21. JN, Vol. 2, pp. 77–8; Sheikh Hazin, p. 299; Sarkar, p. 65; BW, fol. 82a.
22. ARM, fol. 174a; BW, fol. 82a; Fraser, pp. 186–7.
23. JN, Vol. 2, p. 79; Sarkar, pp. 66–7; Hanway, Vol. 4, p. 178.
24. Hanway, Vol. 4, p. 178; AAN, p. 747; in Floor 1998, pp. 307–8, a reporting letter from the VOC representative in Delhi says that the women were held longer and 'had to suffer the will of these butchers' – but the letter was sent shortly after the massacre ended, so could have been sent before the Dutch representative heard of the women's release.
25. BW, fol. 82b; ARM, fol. 175a.
26. Lockhart 1938, pp. 148 and 148n; Floor 1998, pp. 307–8. Different sources name different nobles, but the Nezam ol-Molk is more frequently named than any other. He may have been accompanied by Mohammad Shah's vizier, Qamar od-din Khan.
27. Avery, p. 40; BW, fols. 83a–83b; ARM, fol. 174b.
28. BW, fol. 83b; Floor 1998, p. 308 agrees the killing ended directly the order was received.
29. Sarkar, p. 66, Lockhart 1938, p. 149 and 149n, Subrahmanyam, p. 362, Floor 1998, p. 307.
30. Lockhart 1938, p. 147, Blake 1991, p. 162.
31. ARM, fol. 174b.
32. Fraser, pp. 186–9.
33. Hanway, Vol. 4, pp. 184–6 – Mirza Zaman says the Nezam eventually paid the one and a half *crore* demanded of him – Fraser 192–3.
34. Hanway, Vol. 4, p. 186.
35. Fraser, p. 200n.
36. JN, Vol. 2, p. 81, Fraser, pp. 189–90; Riazul Islam 1982, pp. 77–8.
37. ARM, fol. 176a, Lockhart 1938, p. 152.

38. Fraser, pp. 201–2.

39. Fraser, pp. 220–1; Lockhart 1938, pp. 152 and 152n. BW, fol. 84b says 80 crore. Some have suggested as high as 111 crore (Subrahmanyam, p. 362 quoting de Voulton). The VOC reported 100,000 crore, which suggests someone, understandably, got their orders of magnitude confused (Floor 1998, p. 308).

40. ARM, fol. 176b.

41. ARM, fol. 175b, JN, Vol. 2, p. 79, Fraser, p. 197.

42. Malcolm, *History*, Vol. 2, pp. 46/47 – one of Malcolm's quotations from otherwise unknown Persian manuscripts.

43. Fraser 198–9; Mohammad Bakhsh/Ashub, quoted by Lockhart 1938, p. 151.

44. In his compelling counterfactual exploration of this episode, Subrahmanyam chooses the moment Mohammad Shah and Nader first met, before Nader entered Delhi, as the point at which Nader could have decided to annex the Moghul territories. It seems to me more likely that he would have waited until Delhi and its riches were safely in his hands before reaching for the bigger prize; but the wider strategic considerations are much the same in either case (Subrahmanyam, p. 361).

45. JN, Vol. 2, pp. 81–82; Fraser, p. 207; Riazul Islam 1982, Vol. 2, pp. 79–83.

46. Fraser, p. 225.

47. Fraser, pp. 206–7, Sheykh Hazin, p. 301.

48. Fraser, p. 208, Brosset, p. 361.

49. Fraser, pp. 208–9.

50. Fraser, p. 221; BW, pp. 165–6 and, pp. 92–3; Lockhart 1938, p. 154n.

51. Fraser, pp. 209–10. The Gombroon diary (19/30 September 1739) confirms that Nader took away immense treasures from Delhi to Kabul, but not one Indian slave.

52. Hanway, Vol. 4, p. 196.

53. Cf. Stefan Zweig *Ungeduld des Herzens* – 'the heart's impatience to be rid as quickly as possible of the painful emotion aroused by the sight of another's unhappiness'. Hanway, Vol. 1, p. 250 states that the normal proportion of men to women in the Persian camp was ten to one.

54. BW, fol. 85a onward.

55. The Persian text translates literally 'my split itself' – ie her vulva. Abd ol-Karim Kashmiri treats this part of the story as a risqué joke.

56. Lockhart 1938, p. 154, quoting Mohammad Bakhsh ('Ashub').

Chapter 1 – THE FALL OF THE SAFAVID DYNASTY

1.   Lockhart 1938 (p. 18) favoured an earlier date for Nader's birth, 1688. But Avery (Peter Avery, *Nadir Shah and the Afsharid Legacy* in *The Cambridge History of Iran*, Vol. 7, p. 3) suggested that Lockhart was working from a copy of the *Jahangosha-ye Naderi* (JN) of Mirza Mahdi Khan Astarabadi that was misleading on this point. Avery found that the best manuscript versions of that central text gave the date 28 Muharram 1110, which corresponds to 6 August 1698; and the Moscow edition of one of the other most reliable contemporary sources, Mohammad Kazem Marvi, agreed with that date. Ernest Tucker, in his article *Explaining Nadir Shah: Kingship and Royal Legitimacy in Mohammad Kazim Marvi's Tarikh-i alam-ara-yi Nadiri*, in *Iranian Studies* 26: 11–12 (1993) cast doubt on this (p. 104n) *inter alia* pointing out that the more recent Riyahi edition of Mohammad Kazem favoured the earlier date. Doubt must remain, and (as Tucker urged) can only be resolved by further examination of the original manuscripts, but supporters of the earlier date need to explain Nader's apparent inactivity in the period 1705–1715, and the way Mirza Mahdi structured his account of Nader's early years (JN, pp. 3–4; Anvar edition, pp. 27–8; see also my forthcoming article, *Basile Vatatzes* – and also Chapter 10 below for Nader's age at the time of his death).

2.   Vatatzes, p. 12.

3.   JN, Vol. 1, p. 1.

4.   Or possibly Nazr Qoli – which may have meant 'slave of the votive promise' – suggesting that his father had prayed for a son, and named him in thanks (see Minorsky *Esquisse*, pp. 3–4, and Avery, p. 5–6); for simplicity I call him Nader from start to finish. The details of this paragraph are taken mainly from JN, Vol. 1, pp. 2–3. As Nader's official historian, Mirza Mahdi would have taken the details of Nader's birth from Nader himself, and close family members.

5.   *Cambridge History of Iran*, Vol. 7, pp. 580–1. I have followed the convention of using the term Turcoman for the Qezelbash and other Turkic tribes within Persia, and the term Turkmen for the Turkic steppe tribes like the Yomut, Tekke, the Salor and others, who lived on the northern borders of Khorasan. The latter group of tribes were Sunni Muslims and shared a distinctive, separate cultural identity.

6.   Vatatzes, p. 131; for his ability to read and write, see Rostam ol-Hokama, p. 344.

7.   Lambton, *Landlord and Peasant* (the classic text for understanding

Iranian rural life), p. lxv; Floor, *The Economy of Safavid Persia*, pp. 2, 8; and Tapper, *The Tribes in 18ᵗʰ and 19ᵗʰ Century Iran* in *The Cambridge History of Iran*, Vol. 7, p. 507. This picture of tribal life is necessarily simplified. The word itself conceals many complications; there are several different words for 'tribe' in Persian, with overlapping or parallel meanings. Tribes were split into sub-tribes and clans, and bonded together into confederations that sometimes became permanent. The complex problems of interpreting nomadic life are explored in the introduction to Tapper's *Frontier Nomads of Iran*. Beck 1986, pp. 42–59 gives a good account of the issues involved, in a description of the origins of the Qashqa'i; Gommans 1995 explains the economic sophistication of tribal life in this period.

8.   Lambton *Landlord and Peasant*, pp. 160–1.
9.   Reza Sha'bani has observed that although some have explained Nader's later cruelties to the Iranian people by the fact that he was not an Iranian, in most respects he appeared to be thoroughly Persianised (Reza Sha'bani 1986, pp. 116–22) – this view is supported by the seal inscription from the time of his coronation, on which he called himself 'the Iranian Nader'.
10.   AAN, p. 7. This story echoes with something similar recorded about the childhood games of Ayatollah Khomeini – see Baqer Moin, *Khomeini* (London 1999), p. 2 – 'Even as a youngster, my father always wanted to be the Shah in the games he played.'
11.   Hanway, Vol. 4, pp. 3–4 and notes thereto.
12.   *Cambridge History of Iran*, Vol. 7, pages 7–8.
13.   JN, Vol. 1, p. 3.
14.   Avery, p. 7.
15.   AAN, p. 12, Avery, p. 9; another version of the raid appears in Fraser, pp. 74–5.
16.   Vatatzes/Legrand, *Voyages*, pp. 205–6.
17.   AAN, p. 12.
18.   Arutin Effendi's account, set out by Ernest Tucker in his unpublished Ph.D. thesis *Religion and Politics in the Era of Nadir Shah: The Views of Six Contemporary Sources* (Chicago 1992), p. 83. Fraser (pp. 79–80) also reports that Nader was ill-treated by Shah Soltan Hosein's courtiers, though his version is rather different.
19.   Ibn Khaldun, *Muqaddimah*. Ibn Khaldun's analysis has been taken up more recently in Hall 1986, by the late, great Ernest Gellner, and by Jos Gommans (see Bibliography). But the idea of cycles in Islamic, and especially Persian history, has deep cultural resonances; notably

in Ferdowsi's *Shahname*, as presented by Kathryn Babayan (Babayan 2002, pp. 21–32).

20. Ibn Khaldun, *Muqaddimah*, Vol. 1, pp. 353–355. This summary of Ibn Khaldun's model relies on one of his more famous and lapidary passages, but does not do justice to its full complexity and subtlety.

21. Ibn Khaldun wrote that the cycle would typically take three generations, which may have been correct for the earlter dynasties he studied, but was too short for the later empires after his time, bolstered by loyal slave bureaucrats and slave soldiers, some of them armed with gunpowder weapons. The determinism of the cyclical process is less convincing for a period in which there is plain evidence for long-term, deep-seated change, under the influence of new technologies and trade patterns.

22. See Babayan 2002 for the complex cultural origins of the Qezelbash.

23. i.e. Persia, the Ottoman Empire and the Moghul Empire (Hodgson, *The Venture of Islam*, Vol. 3).

24. The details of the princes' life in the harem are found in Krusinski, Vol. 1, pp. 65–70. Krusinski takes pains not to sensationalise his account, which makes the case he makes for the debilitating effect of this kind of life on the princes all the more convincing.

25. See Gommans 1995, p. 2, p. 6 and *passim*.

26. Lambton 1977; Bayly 1989.

27. Mathee 1999, p. 241.

28. Mathee 1999; Gommans 1995, Floor 2000 and *Dutch Trade*: I have also drawn upon contributions from Rudi Matthee, Edmund Herzig, and Stephen Blake in the SOAS Conference *Iran and the World in the Safavid Age*, 4–7 September 2002, and advice from Willem Floor for this much simplified summary of the issues involved.

29. Bayly 1989, p. 23; Floor 2000, p. 2. The figures can only be estimates, but Floor suggests 9 million for the period before the Afghan invasion. Bayly's wider thesis that by eighteenth century the Ottoman, Safavid and Moghul empires were 'hollowed out' by economic and social changes with which they could not cope, is attractive but less convincingly argued for the Safavid case than the others (p 30). Foran presents a similar argument, in greater depth, but is heavily dependent on impressionistic non-Persian sources.

30. The *Tadhkirat al-muluk*, drawn up by court officials at the orders of the new Afghan overlords in 1726, in order to set out for them the operations of the State and its various bureaucratic organs (and the tax revenue to be expected) gives a good sense of the sophistication

(and resilience) of the Safavid system as the dynasty fell (ed and trans. V Minorsky, London 1943).

31.   The words come from Malcolm, *History of Persia*, Vol. 1, p. 594, but a number of Persian and other sources give the same story – cf. AAN, p. 18 and Krusinski, Vol. 1ps 62–64.

32.   '...the Shi'i clergy could now take part in the game of politics' (Babayan 2002, pp. 484–485 and note; also her forthcoming article *'In Spirit We Ate of Each Other's Sorrow:' Female Companionship in Seventeenth century Safavi Iran* quoting Mir Abu Talib Fendereski and the research of Rasul Ja'farian); also Arjomand 1984, p. 158; Bayly 1989, p. 45; Lockhart 1958, p. 38. See also note 61 here below. In fact, there is evidence that Shah Soltan Hosein continued some traditional patronage of the Sufis (Morton 1993, p. 243n). Arjomand (p 158) agrees that they were not fully suppressed.

33.   Krusinski, Vol. 1, p. 75. For contemporaries, the strong influence of a woman in government was in itself another sign of the monarchy's decadence. I looked again at the role of Maryam Begum after a comment made by Afsaneh Najmabadi at a Conference in Oxford in September 2004. Rudi Matthee's excellent *Pursuit of Pleasure* documents the long tradition of heavy drinking at the Safavid court.

34.   Rostam ol-Hokama, pp. 203–204 and 290. Perhaps surprisingly, the practice of marrying these women to great nobles, who had to present the children as their own heirs, is corroborated by Krusinski (vol 1 pp. 121-122). Temporary marriage (known nowadays as *sighe*) is a controversial Shi'a Muslim practice that has been used to legitimise what would otherwise be called concubinage or prostitution, and has never quite been suppressed.

35.   e.g. Krusinski, Vol. 1, pp. 119–122; as well as Rostam ol-Hokama quoted above.

36.   For example, in November 1739 the author of the Gombroon diary commented approvingly on Nader's 'superior sense and judgement' that he had discontinued the Safavid tradition of keeping the children of the monarch in the harem. For the preference of contemporary Persian mullahs for monogamy and disapproval of concubinage, see Hanway, Vol. 1, p. 265. These matters are contentious, but it is important to give an idea of the different voices involved, and the ways in which they may have interacted, without over-interpreting on the basis of some prior prejudice or theoretical system. See Matthee 2005 pp. 3-4, and Edward Said *Power, Politics and Culture*

(London 2005), pp. 113–115; also, pp. 57–59, p. 63 and, pp. 365–366.

37. Floor 1998 p19, p24.

38. Lockhart 1958, p. 42, quoting Mohammad Khalil Marashi. I have not used Marashi extensively, because he wrote many years after these events. But this story is the kind of genuine anecdote that gets remembered.

39. I am thinking here of Sartre (see *L'Être et le Néant*, Paris, Gallimard 1943, pp. 154–156) but although Sartre did argue this way, he went further in saying that, as radically contingent beings, it is an illusion for us to believe even at any given moment that we have a substantial identity or personality.

40. JN, p. 4 – AAN puts it earlier, but Mohammad Kazem's chronology is suspect.

41. Hanway's assertion that Nader murdered Baba Ali before marrying his daughter (vol. 4, p5) is not credible. Baba Ali's sons would not later have become Nader's devoted lieutenants if he had killed their father (see Lockhart 1938, p. 21).

42. Lockhart 1958, p46–47.

43. Krusinski, Vol. 1, p. 127.

44. Krusinski, Vol. 1, p. 123.

45. Chronicle of Sekhnia Cheikidze, in Brosset, Vol. 2, 2me Livraison, pp. 26–27.

46. Krusinski, Vol. 1, pp. 116–119; Floor 2000 gives a thorough overview of the decline in security on the roads;, pp. 33–35.

47. Krusinski vol. 1, p. 152 (there is a pagination error in this edition of Krusinski, and page numbers 149–152 are repeated); Avery, p. 12.

48. Krusinski vol. 1, p. 147–150.

49. Some sources indicate that Mir Veis actually rebelled at this stage, was captured and then sent to Isfahan, and Lockhart took that view (Lockhart 1958, p. 85 and note) – but Krusinski says not (vol. 1, pp. 153–154 and, p. 163), and it is doubtful that an unforgiving man like Gorgin would have let Mir Veis live in such circumstances.

50. Krusinski vol. 1, p. 158.

51. ZT fol. 203b; JN vol. 1, pp. ii-iii.

52. Krusinski vol. 1, p. 206.

53. AAN, p. 20.

54. AAN, p. 35 onwards; Avery, p. 13.

55. ZT fol. 205a; JN vol. 1, p. vii.

56. ZT fol. 205a; JN vol. 1, pp. vi-vii; *Cambridge History of Iran*, vol. 6, p. 317; Floor, 1998, p. 40.

57. ZT fol. 205a.

58. Krusinski vol. 2, pp. 44–46. For the persecution of the Jews see Moreen 1990, pp. 14 and 26–29.

59. Arjomand 1984, p. 158–159; Algar 1977, pp. 289–290; also Babayan 2002, pp. 484–485.

60. EG Browne *Persian Literature in Modern Times*, Cambridge 1924, p. 404; quoting the *Qesas ol-'Olama* of Mohammad Ibn Soleiman of Tonakabon who apparently described the story as 'widely current' in the nineteenth century (see also Lockhart 1958, p. 73n).

61. The best-known advocate of this position is the contemporary Iranian religious thinker Abdolkarim Soroush, who has suggested that whereas secularised politics permit popular religious belief to flourish, the enforcement of religious norms by a religious state tends to alienate and secularise society. Secularism in politics might paradoxically reflect ' the belief in the fundamental truth of religion coupled with concern over its contamination and profanation by political concerns' (quoted in Ali Ansari, *Iran, Islam and Democracy*, London 2000, p. 75). Ayatollah Hosein-Ali Montazeri, once Ayatollah Khomeini's designated successor and one of the most revered religious figures in Iran today, made similar points, albeit more guardedly, in an interview published in the Mideast Mirror on 20 January 2000, p. 15; and since elsewhere. Lambton 1977 believed the religious classes could have been discredited in the eighteenth century by their association with Shah Soltan Hosein's government (p 120).

62. Von Hammer, vol. 14, p. 87.

63. Lettre de Pere Bachoud, *Lettres Edifiantes et Curieuses Ecrites des Missions Etrangères*; vol. IV, Paris 1780, pp. 113–124; the text gives the date August 1722 for the sack of Shamakhi, but this is an editorial error, since the letter itself was written in September 1721 and the sack is known from other authorities to have taken place in 1721; Lockhart 1958, p. 127; Dickson, p. 504n.

64. Floor 1998, pp. 46–51.

65. This dislike is reflected in the attitude of some of the sources for this period, who are hostile to Fath Ali Khan – one example is Vatatzes, *Persica*, Book II passim.

66. (Lockhart 1958, p. 121); Clairac vol. 1, pp. 143–146; ZT fol. 205b.

67. ZT fol. 205a; Krusinski vol. 1, pp. 99–101. The way that these two reliable contemporary authorities agree on what went wrong with the Safavid state in these two passages is striking and important.

Other contemporaries like Mohammad Kazem (for example, p. 20) and Vatatzes (p 14) agreed a similar overall judgement. The chronicler closest to Nader, Mirza Mahdi, was relatively gentle on Shah Soltan Hosein, blaming instead his incompetent advisers and the malice of foreign invaders (see Tucker's assessment, Tucker 1992, pp. 141–142).

68. Floor 1998, pp. 57–60; ZT fol. 205b.
69. ZT fol. 207a; Lockhart 1958, pp. 134–136.
70. ZT fol. 205b.
71. Krusinski, vol. 2, p. 21.
72. Lockhart 1958, pp. 137–142; ZT fol. 207a.
73. Floor 1998, p. 88, Krusinski vol. 2, p. 22.
74. Zanburak camel guns had been around for a long time; it was the Afghans' use of them in large numbers in combination with the ancient feigned flight tactic that was novel. For an account of the Afghan military innovations of the later eighteenth century, see Jos Gommans, *Mughal Warfare* (London 2002).
75. See Matthee 1996 for the compelling argument that the Safavid state never was a 'gunpowder empire' in the fullest sense; never taking on completely the new mode of warfare according to which the mass of soldiers were armed with gunpowder weapons as a matter of course.
76. One of the more serious deficiencies of Lockhart's *Fall of the Safavi Dynasty* (which Dickson failed to notice) is his uncharacteristic failure to support his assertion (pp. 22, 27, 44, 130) that the Safavid army was in a serious state of decay (he made up the deficiency to some extent in his later article – Lockhart 1959 – though Haneda later dismissed that article as outdated – Haneda, p. 506). Lockhart argued that the army was in a poor state because of disunity between the 'traditional', tribal elements and the 'modern' standing elements: but earlier Safavid monarchs had managed to use those disparate elements successfully, as did Nader Shah later; turning multifarious tribal loyalties to his advantage by putting tribesmen in discrete units of their own and setting them in competition with each other.
77. Krusinski, Vol. 1, pp. 100–1.
78. Sheikh Hazin, pp. 118–19.
79. Floor 1998, p. 105; Krusinski, Vol. 2, pp. 49–50; Clairac, Vol. 1, pp. 276–7. Although Lockhart 1958 (pp. 152–3) does not refer to Krusinski in his footnote as he should have done, it is plain that he drew much of the detail from that account. Dickson (p. 506n), who criticised

Lockhart on this episode for 'lapses into generalities which are not
fully documented', was in error; as elsewhere, he could easily have
avoided his mistake by opening Krusinski, which, as is obvious from
the rest of Lockhart's narrative, was one of his main sources.

80.   Lockhart 1958, p. 118; Krusinski, Vol. 2, p. 75.
81.   Floor 1998, p. 125 (Lockhart 1958 has the date incorrectly as 6 May:
      p. 159n).
82.   ZT, fol. 210b; Krusinski, Vol. 2, p. 80.
83.   Krusinski Vol. 2, p. 90; Mohsen (fol. 207b), who also was there
      in person, confirms the grim conditions, the shortages and the
      cannibalism.
84.   Clairac Vol. 1, pp. 327–31.
85.   Krusinski, Vol. 2, p. 95–6.
86.   Lockhart 1958, p. 172, quoting the eyewitness Joseph Apisalaimian.
      Mohsen (fol. 208a), confirms the essentials of Shah Soltan Hosein's
      visit to Farahabad and his crowning of Mahmud.
87.   ZT, fol. 207b.
88.   The census figures are taken from Floor 2000, p. 3.

Chapter 2 – TAHMASP QOLI KHAN
1.   Precisely when is problematic; if Baba Ali died in 1716 as suggested
      in Chapter 1, on the strength of Mohammad Kazem's account, then
      Nader may have seized Kalat earlier. The chronology of these events
      in the AAN is difficult to unravel satisfactorily (cf. Avery, pp. 10–
      13).
2.   AAN, pp. 15–16; Tucker 1993, p. 104.
3.   AAN, p. 41.
4.   AAN, p. 44; Avery, p. 18. Vatatzes agrees that Nader initially allied
      himself with Malek Mahmud (pp. 70–71).
5.   He was described thus by the officers of the Dutch East India
      Company some time later – Floor, *Nader Shah*.
6.   BW, pp. 46–47.
7.   Vatatzes, pp. 74–75. According to Vatatzes, the governor was a
      Kurdish chief. Vatatzes' story is corroborated by part of Mirza
      Mahdi's account (JN, Vol. 1, pp. 8–9), which says that when a plot
      to assassinate Malek Mahmud failed, Nader murdered two of his
      allies while on a hunting trip, precipitating open war between the
      two rivals. See my forthcoming article, *Basile Vatatzes and his History
      of Nader Shah*, for a more detailed discussion of this episode.
8.   ZT, fol. 212a.

9. ZT, fol. 210b.
10. Lockhart 1958, p. 103 onwards (the Volynsky mission) and p. 123 (the Durri Efendi mission).
11. For an overview of diplomacy in Istanbul in this period, see Lavender Cassels, *The Struggle for the Ottoman Empire, 1717–1740*.
12. Vatatzes, pp. 52–53 and 57; Lockhart 1958, p. 188.
13. Lockhart 1958, p. 233.
14. Krusinski, Vol. II, pp. 101–2.
15. ZT, fol. 208a,.
16. ZT, fols. 210b and 211a.
17. ZT, fol. 209a; Krusinski, Vol. II, p. 108.
18. Krusinski, Vol. II, pp. 147–8.
19. Krusinski, Vol. II, p. 150; Krusinski's is the most detailed account of this event, but as usual Mohsen (fol. 209a) confirms the main facts.
20. Krusinski, Vol. II, p. 152; ZT, fol. 209a (Mohsen says that Mahmud ate his own excrement in his madness); see also Abraham of Erevan, p. 51.
21. ZT, fol. 209a.
22. ZT, fols. 212a and 212b; Avramov, p. 93 (Avramov suggests Nader had 'around 5000' men); Vatatzes, pp. 77–9. Vatatzes suggests that Nader exaggerated the number of his troops by appointing four min-bashis (commanders of a thousand), with subordinate commanders in proportion, despite the fact he had only 2,000–3,000 men. This could explain Avramov's inflated figure. The description of the meeting that follows is taken from Vatatzes, who places the event near Sabzavar rather than Khabushan.
23. ZT, fol. 211a.
24. Avramov, pp. 91–2.
25. ZT, fols. 212a and 212b.
26. Avramov, pp. 94 and 99; JN, Vol. 1, p. 39; ZT, fol. 223a; AAN, p. 66. Mirza Mahdi does not give the story of the letter presented by Avramov, but his account makes more sense with that additional element, which is hinted at also by Mohsen. Kazem implicates Nader directly in the killing of Fath Ali Khan, but Avramov's account in particular gives good reason to think this may be incorrect. See also Avery, pp. 25–7; and Lockhart 1958, pp. 309–10 and 513. As often, once the other factors cancel each other out, Mirza Mahdi emerges as convincing and plausible.
27. ZT, fol. 216a.
28. Fraser, p. 97n.

29. JN, Vol. 1, p. 40.

30. Avramov, pp. 96–7. The judgement by the courtier that follows is on p. 97.

31. The Greek Basile Vatatzes was one messenger; see my forthcoming article *Basile Vatatzes and his History of Nader Shah*. Russian involvement in Persia in this period is an important aspect of the story: see Lockhart 1958, pp. 345–50.

32. Avramov, p. 98; this exchange took place after the fall of Mashhad, in January 1727.

33. JN, Vol. 1, p. 40; the betrayal of Mashhad is confirmed by Mohsen, fols. 212b and 216a.

34. JN, Vol. 1, pp. 47, 50–1; Avramov, p. 95.

35. JN, Vol. 1, p. 42.

36. Vatatzes, p. 96.

37. Malcolm, *History of Persia*, Vol. 2, p. 106.

Chapter 3 – WAR WITH THE AFGHANS

1. JN, Vol. 1, p. 43.

2. JN, Vol. 1, p. 44.

3. Avramov, p. 99.

4. JN, Vol. 1, pp. 45–6.

5. Floor 1999, p. 277.

6. See Tucker 1992, in the Appendix: *Nadir's Concepts of Political Legitimation*); Layla Diba 1998, pp. 140 and 141; and Diba 1987, pp. 88 and 96. The fact that the hat was worn already at the time of Nader's coronation in 1736 (as reported by Abraham of Crete, p. 96), and was known then as the *Tahmasi*, suggests that its use originated in the period before Shah Tahmasp's deposition in 1732.

7. AAN, p. 23.

8. JN, Vol. 1, p. 47.

9. JN, Vol. 1, p. 52.

10. See Matthee 1996 for discussion of these issues, notably, p. 395.

11. JN, Vol. 1, p. 53.

12. JN, Vol. 1, p. 55.

13. Avramov, p. 101; Floor, *Nader Shah* confirms that Nader controlled the royal seal by the time Tahmasp reoccupied Isfahan in November 1729.

14. Avramov, pp. 101–2.

15. Avramov, p. 102.

16. JN, Vol. 1, p. 65; Avramov, p. 102.

17. Vatatzes, pp. 131–2. The description of the feigned flight tactic is particularly significant. Nader's troops used it to draw their Moghul opponents into a trap at the battle of Karnal in 1739. The Catholicos Abraham, who saw Nader's army in camp in 1735/1736, also noted the 'constant strict drills for both the cavalry and infantry' (p. 118).

18. Vatatzes, p. 133.

19. Vatatzes depicts Nader's army here, in 1728/1729, as divided between cavalry armed with traditional weapons and infantry armed with muskets, but it is clear from the Catholicos Abraham's later description that by 1736 the cavalry carried muskets too (p. 118).

20. JN, Vol. 1, p. 70.

21. JN, Vol. 1, p. 73.

22. Several of Nader's own letters describing his battles and announcing his victories survive, but though useful they do not go into great detail. Mohammad Kazem gives more detail than Mirza Mahdi about Nader's battles, but his accuracy is sometimes suspect.

23. Hanway, Vol. 4, p. 253.

24. Abraham of Crete, p. 118.

25. Gommans 2002. See also V. J. Parry, *La maniere de combattre*, in Parry and Yapp 1975.

26. Hanway, Vol. 4, p. 31n and, Vol. 2, p. 253. For what follows on the heavy weapons used by Ottomans and Persians, see Elgood 1995, pp. 49, 120–1. Some rifled weapons were made from an early date, but in small numbers and probably intended more for hunting (though the Marathas in India deployed small numbers of sharpshooters armed with rifled muskets in battle – see Cooper 2003); the majority of muskets were smooth-bored. To call musket-armed infantry of this period 'riflemen' is incorrect.

27. Parry and Yapp 1975, p. 18, and Matthee 1996, p. 389 and passim. As Nader rose to power in the 1720s, firearms were becoming common among the Lazgis in the Caucasus area (Bachoud, p. 118) but the Kurds and Afshars of Khorasan were still unused to firearms, and were armed only with lance and sabre for the most part (JN, Vol. 1, p. 12). Part of Matthee's thesis is that Safavid Persia lagged behind Ottoman Turkey and Russia in the introduction of large numbers of firearm troops. Murphey 2003 has adjusted previous ideas about so-called Ottoman militarism in the period up to 1700, but his notion that a military revolution took place in the years 1420–1440 with the corning of gunpowder, and that little changed for the next 300

years (pp. 107–108 and notes), is surprising, and does not inspire confidence. The military revolution, however one dates it, was not the outcome of one single technological change, but the result of the complex interplay over time of many different tactical, strategic, technological, cultural, social, economic and governmental factors. Changes in the technical preparation of black powder or flintlock firing mechanisms played a relatively small part: it took time for commanders to realise the potential of new weapons and techniques, and changes in the use of weaponry were generally more important than changes in the weapons themselves.

28.   See Parker 1988, and Parry and Yapp 1975, p. 24.

29.   Krusinski, Vol. 2, p. 170.

30.   Lockhart 1958, p. 286. The position taken by the Ottomans was also consistent with the Russian/Turkish treaty of partition, which recognised Tahmasp as the legitimate ruler of Persia, if he would accept the partition.

31.   JN, Vol. 1, p. xxvi; ZT, fols. 209a–209b.

32.   Clairac, Vol. 2, p. 331.

33.   Clairac, Vol. 2, pp. 333–340; von Hammer, Vol. 14, p. 153; JN, Vol. 1, p. xxvi; ZT, fol. 209b.

34.   JN, Vol. 1, p. xxvi; ZT, fol. 209b.

35.   Ashraf also made a treaty with the Russians at this time. See the *Cambridge History of Iran*, Vol. 7, p. 322.

36.   Krusinski, Vol. 2, pp. 196–198; Lockhart 1958, pp. 298–299; Dickson, p. 511. Dickson took Ashraf's notion of a hierarchy of races and presented a similar list – with little or no evidence – as a crass caricature of what he imagined were Lockhart's racial attitudes.

37.   I have taken this idea from a contribution by Bill Beeman to an exchange of emails in the Gulf 2000 internet forum – the theory was explored further in his 1986 book *Language, Status and Power in Iran*. Popular resistance to foreign invasion also emerged as a phenomenon in the Mongol period – see Jürgen Paul *L'invasion Mongole comme revelateur de la societe Iranienne* (pp. 46–47 and passim) in Denise Aigle ed *L'Iran face a la domination Mongole* Tehran 1997. Hamadan was prominent in the resistance then too.

38.   JN, Vol. 1, p. 75, Adle, p. 240.

39.   Hanway, Vol. 4, p. 27; AAN (p. 108) suggests 44,000, but this seems too high. Sheikh Hazin says the Afghans were more than double the number of the Persians (p. 193); Fraser that there were 30,000 Afghans and 16,000 Persians (p. 95).

40. AAN, p. 110.
41. For a classic account of the near-universality of war in human history, see Michael Howard, *The Invention of Peace* (London 2000), p. 1 and passim. Also Tim Blanning's quite brilliant Introduction (on the origins of wars generally) in *The Origins of the French Revolutionary Wars* (London 1986)
42. Hanway, Vol. 4, p. 28.
43. AAN, p. 111.
44. JN, Vol. 1, p. 76; AAN, pp. 110–113; Hanway, Vol. 4, pp. 28–29; Sheikh Hazin, p. 193; Adle *passim*; Lockhart 1958, pp. 330–331. Mirza Mahdi's suggestion (omitted in the Jones translation) that there were European gunners (*tupchian-e farangi-nezhad*) with the Persian artillery is not impossible; they could have been supplied by the Russians (see Adle, p. 239 and Lockhart 1938, p. 36n). But it seems unlikely that they could have been French.
45. Richard Holmes, *Redcoat* (London 2001), p. 254: quoting Lt. George Gleig.
46. JN, Vol. 1, p. 77; the cause of the quarrel appears in Sheikh Hazin, pp. 193–194.
47. Sheikh Hazin, p. 194.
48. Sheikh Hazin, pp. 196–197.
49. Cf. Hanway, Vol. 4, p. 30.
50. AAN, pp. 113–115; JN, Vol. 1, p. 79–80.
51. JN, Vol. 1, p. 81; Mohammad Kazem (p. 117) also makes a point of the way Nader used banners and music to encourage his men at the start of this battle.
52. Ibn Khaldun *Muqaddimah*, Vol. 2, pp. 48–49.
53. Lockhart (1958, p. 333 and 1938, p. 38) believed that Ashraf was drawn out of his positions, but it is not clear on what authority. Mirza Mahdi is quite explicit that the Afghans stayed in their trenches (JN, Vol. 1, p. 82), and this is consistent with the other sources.
54. JN, Vol. 1, pp. 81–83; AAN, pp. 116–118; Hazin, p. 197; Hanway, p. 31; GD, 24 Dec/4 Jan; Floor *Afghan Occupation*, pp. 161–162. There has been a muddle over the dates of this sequence of events. Lockhart 1958 (p. 333n) wrote that the Gombroon diary's statement that Ashraf left Isfahan on 13 November was to be preferred, because the EIC representatives were on the spot (in his *Nadir Shah* Lockhart wrote that Ashraf's departure from Isfahan on 13 November was three days after the battle). But in fact the GD says 15 November (after correction to the Gregorian calendar), not 13 November, and

there is good reason to think that the GD was wrong anyway. The VOC Isfahan diary, which is more painstaking over dates, agrees with Mirza Mahdi that Ashraf left within a few hours of returning to Isfahan after the battle, which took place on 13 November.

55.   On this date, most of the authorities, including the Gombroon Diary (entry for 1/12 January) are agreed.

56.   Hanway, Vol. 4, p. 34; the incident is corroborated by Mohammad Kazem (p. 119).

57.   Hanway, Vol. 4, p. 35. Mohammad Kazem's account is again similar (p. 120).

Chapter 4 – WAR WITH THE OTTOMANS

1.   GD, 14/25 February and 5/16 July; drawing on letters from the EIC representatives in Isfahan.

2.   Hanway, Vol. 4, p. 270.

3.   Floor, *1998*, p. 262 and *Nader Shah*; GD, 24 December/4 January, 14/25 February and passim.

4.   AAN, pp. 120–1. Hanway says wrongly that Nader was to marry Tahmasp's aunt – Vol. 4, p. 36. Rumours circulated later that Nader married Tahmasp's sister without his consent – GD 30 April/11 May 1730.

5.   Sheikh Hazin, p. 198; JN, Vol. 1, p. 86; Hanway, Vol. 4, p. 36; Fraser, pp. 99–101.

6.   Rostam ol-Hokama, Vol. 1, p. 382.

7.   I am grateful to Kathryn Babayan for showing me her article '"In Spirit We Ate of Each Other's Sorrow": Female Companionship in Seventeenth-century Safavi Iran' ahead of publication. Her article gives an account both of the satire (Aqa Jamal Khwansari *Aqa'ed on-nisa*, ed. Mahmud Katira'i, Tehran 1970) and the Hajj poem (*Safarname-ye Manzum-e hajj*, ed. Rasul Jafarian, Qom, 1995).

8.   JN, Vol. 1, p. 88; ZT, fol. 215a.

9.   JN, Vol. 1, pp. 90–1 – an allusion to the Qur'an, 80:34–8.

10.   JN, Vol. 1, p. 90; Sheikh Hazin, pp. 199–200; Nader's demands that the EIC help to block the Afghans' escape by sea are reported in the Gombroon diary for 24 December/4 January; he made similar demands of the Dutch.

11.   Sheikh Hazin, pp. 200–2.

12.   JN, Vol. 1, pp. 102–3; Lockhart 1958, p. 338n.

13.   JN, Vol. 1, p. 92; see Riazul Islam 1970, p. 139 and 1982 (Vol. 2), pp. 37–8 for a summary of the letter carried to the Moghul emperor by

the envoy.

14. Nader's stay in Shiraz is described in JN, Vol. 1, pp. 91–93. As usual, the dates in Jones's translation of Mirza Mahdi have to be corrected. Hafez was often used for divination in this way, before Nader's time and since. It would have been fairly simple to make sure the book fell open at the right place. The story of the petitioners comes from AAN, p. 126.

15. JN, Vol. 1, p. 96; Mirza Mahdi says the formal instrument ceding the provinces was delivered to Nader at Borujerd. For contemporary gossip (probably garbled) in Isfahan about Nader's intentions and the jiqe, see Floor, *Nader Shah*. The VOC reports are an excellent source for what happened in Isfahan. But one has to aim off for a certain prejudice against Nader (unsurprising given his demands for money with menaces) and they are less reliable for events further afield, for which it better in general to rely on Mohsen, Mirza Mahdi and Mohammad Kazem, one or more of whom were travelling with Nader most of the time.

16. Clairac, Vol. 3, pp. 105–9 (Gardane's *Relation*).

17. JN, Vol. 1, p. 95.

18. JN, Vol. 1, p. 98; AAN, p. 134; Tucker 1992, p. 210.

19. JN, Vol. 1, p. 99; Abraham of Erevan, p. 59.

20. JN, Vol. 1, pp. 104–6.

21. Olson 1975 discusses the various causes of the Patrona Khalil revolt.

22. JN, Vol. 1, p. 109.

23. JN, Vol. 1, p. 111.

24. Avery, p. 29; AAN, p. 161.

25. JN, Vol. 1, p. 114.

26. Abraham of Crete, pp. 48–9; Floor, *Nader Shah*; and Perry 1975 for a full discussion of forced migration.

27. JN, Vol. 1, p. 100.

28. JN, Vol. 1, p. 117.

29. JN, Vol. 1, p. 120.

30. JN, Vol. 1, p. 124.

31. JN, Vol. 1, p. 135; Abraham of Erevan, p. 64.

32. ZT, fol. 215b.

33. ZT, fol. 215a.

34. JN, Vol. 1, p. 138.

35. JN, Vol. 1, pp. 139–40; ZT, fol. 215b; Hazin, p. 218; Horne letter of 15/26 March 1732, in the Persia Factory Records, India Office Collection,

British Library, G/29/16 Part 1, fol. 50, para 21; von Hammer, Vol. 14, pp. 253–4.

36. ZT, fol. 215b; Horne letter para 22; AAN, p. 224.

Chapter 5 – COUP D'ETAT

1. JN, Vol. 1, p. 142.
2. JN, Vol. 1, pp. 143–5. Mirza Mahdi probably drafted the manifesto himself, as Nader's secretary at this time.
3. Malcolm, *Two Letters*, p. 533.
4. Ibid.
5. Ibid.
6. Fraser, pp. 227–8 and 230–1. The Turkic and Persian tradition of '*razm o bazm*' (fighting and boozing) is given its full due in Matthee 2005 (notably pp. 48-49)
7. Floor, *Nader Shah*.
8. JN, Vol. 1, pp. 140–1; Floor, *Nader Shah*.
9. Floor, *Nader Shah*.
10. JN, Vol. 1, p. 151, though Floor (*Nader Shah*), has him arriving on 26 August; AAN, p. 185 for the story of Tahmasp considering flight.
11. Fraser, p. 106 (the package of letters is mentioned on, p. 105); Hanway, Vol. 4, p. 71.
12. Floor, *Nader Shah*; JN, Vol. 1, p. 152; AAN, pp. 231–3; Hanway, Vol. 4, p. 71; ZT, fols. 215b and 223b; GD 17/28 September 1732. Accounts of Tahmasp's deposition differ over details; Mirza Mahdi, as usual putting Nader in the best light, mentions the drinking, but presents the event as if Nader used the occasion to try to persuade Tahmasp to change his mind about the treaty with the Ottomans. He says Nader only decided to depose the Shah when it became clear he was intransigent. The other sources agree that the coup was planned and that Nader got Tahmasp drunk deliberately. There is no agreement about exactly when the events took place, nor on the duration of the drinking-party (Mohsen, who is generally reliable, says three full days) but it was either in the last days of August or the earliest of September 1732.
13. Arutin Effendi, quoted in Tucker 1992, p. 86.
14. JN (Vol. 1, p. 153) has 7 September (17 Rabi I); Floor has 8 September (*Nader Shah*).
15. Floor, *Nader Shah*; ZT, fol. 216b.
16. AAN, p. 234.
17. GD 3/14 October 1732.

18. Floor, *Nader Shah*.
19. Bazin, p. 317.
20. Fraser, pp. 227–30. Cockell, who wrote this description on the strength of his meetings with Nader and his companions, was an employee of the East India Company like James Fraser. By 1742, when Fraser's book was published, Nader was buying ships from the East India Company, and this may have lent a rosier hue to Cockell's and Fraser's descriptions of Nader than might otherwise have been the case.
21. Hanway, Vol. 4, p. 268; for Nader's reputation for sexual continence, see Malcolm, *History*, Vol. 2, p. 85n.
22. Floor, *Nader Shah*; there were rumours circulating as early as Spring 1730 that Nader wanted Tahmasp to remove himself and the court from Isfahan to Qazvin (GD 30 April/11 May).
23. Floor, *Nader Shah*.
24. AAN, pp. 143–5 (see also Tucker 1992, pp. 211–12).
25. Vatatzes, p. 97.
26. JN, Vol. 1, pp. 155–6.
27. JN, Vol. 1, pp. 157–8.
28. JN, Vol. 1, p. 162. Mirza Mahdi says the engineer was sent by a German king, but it is more likely that he was a German supplied by the Russian government. Peter the Great had encouraged large numbers of Germans skilled in technical trades to emigrate to Russia.
29. Mirza Mahdi (Vol. 1, p. 163) says 30,000 but this seems on the high side and exceeds by 10,000 the total for the whole garrison of Baghdad given by Hanway (Vol. 4, p. 81).
30. JN, Vol. 1, p. 164.
31. Abraham of Erevan, pp. 77–8.
32. Floor, *Nader Shah*; the more moderate VOC estimate is probably to be preferred to the 110,000 suggested by Mirza Mahdi in the *Durre-ye Naderi* (given by Lockhart 1938, p. 71). The figure quoted earlier for the total number of people in the Persian camp also comes from Floor. Emin (p. 5) and Mohsen (fol. 216b) confirm the sufferings of the population of Baghdad.
33. Hanway, Vol. 4, pp. 83–4.
34. Eyewitness account of Jean Nicodeme, in von Hammer, pp. 517–18.
35. VOC sources suggest Mohammad Khan Baluch was left with 4,000 horse and 12,000 foot (Floor 1983, p. 80).
36. Von Hammer, p. 521.

37. Von Hammer, pp. 522–3. Mirza Mahdi claims that the Ottomans fought from the entrenchments round their camp, but Nicodeme's version is more plausible. Eyewitness accounts from the Ottoman side presented by Clairac (Vol. 3, pp. 288–99 and 307–11) and Hanway's account, drawing partially on them (Hanway, Vol. 4, p. 85), say specifically that Topal Osman had the option of fighting a defensive battle along the line of a gully formed by the old course of the Tigris river, but instead advanced over it to attack the Persians. There is more confusion about what actually happened in battles than about any other kind of historical event. Descriptions of them that try too hard to remove the sense of confusion risk giving a less accurate picture.
38. JN, Vol. 1, p. 169.
39. Fraser, p. 234.
40. Eyewitness account of Jean Nicodeme, in von Hammer, p. 524; also Topal Osman's own report, Clairac, Vol. 3, pp. 307–11. Mohsen says 23,000 Persians were killed (fol. 216b).
41. Hanway, Vol. 4, p. 91.

Chapter 6 – NADER SHAH
1. Hanway pp. 93–4; JN, Vol. 1, p. 170.
2. JN, Vol. 1, pp. 171–2.
3. Floor, *Nader Shah*.
4. Floor, *Nader Shah*.
5. *Cambridge History of Iran*, Vol. 7, p. 303.
6. See Floor 1983. The grumpy VOC reports from Isfahan said the Isfahanis were unlikely to join the revolt, because 'The Isfahanis are smarter than women and great cowards, who are only capable of swallowing their pilauw and to dress up themselves to please their whoring women' (ibid., p. 82). The VOC representative van Leijpsigh sometimes let his frustrations boil over. He had many friends in Isfahan, particularly among the merchants (see Floor, *Dutch Trade in Afsharid Persia*) but disliked the bureaucrats he had to deal with. He should have been given a holiday.
7. JN, Vol. 1, p. 173; also Floor, *Nader Shah*.
8. Fraser, p. 231 Fraser mentions in connection with this anecdote that Nader's mother was still alive in 1737, but does not say directly that the incident took place in that year. It makes more sense to place it before Nader's coronation.
9. JN, Vol. 1, p. 181; Hanway, Vol. 4, p. 99; and Nader's own letter to the

Count of Hesse-Homburg (then commander of Russian forces in the Caucasus) in PRO State Papers 91/16, fol. 30 onwards.

10. PRO State Papers 91/16; Emin, p. 6 confirms Ahmad Pasha was close to surrender.

11. JN, Vol. 1, p. 183.

12. JN, Vol. 1, pp. 186–7; GD 3/14 February 1734 (based on a letter from Tahmasp Khan Jalayer, who was there); Fraser, pp. 112–13; Hanway, Vol. 4, p. 111 (Hanway's account is based largely on Fraser's). The VOC records suggest there was no battle at all (Floor 1983, pp. 84, 85 and 85n) but their account is probably consistent with the precipitate flight indicated by the other sources. The rebels did not put up much of a fight.

13. JN, Vol. 1, p. 193; Floor 1983, pp. 90–1; GD 8/19 May 1734. Fraser says he hanged himself in prison (p. 113).

14. Floor, *Nader Shah*.

15. JN, p. 191; Lockhart 1938, p. 81 (quoting a letter from Geekie, the British East India Company representative in Isfahan); Floor, p. 45.

16. *The Koran*, Penguin Classics, trans. N. J. Dawood (1990), p. 236.

17. Abdollah Mostowfi, *The Social and Administrative History of the Qajar Era*, 2nd edition, Vol. 1, pp. 13–14. I am very grateful to Peter Avery for this story and his translation of it.

18. Malcolm, *History of Persia*, Vol. 2, pp. 290–1.

19. JN, Vol. 1, pp. 193–4; Floor, *Nader Shah*; Lockhart 1938, p. 83 and 83n; Cambridge History of Iran, Vol. 7, p. 324 (for discussions with the Russians).

20. JN, Vol. 1, p. 195; Nader's capture of Shamakhi and siege of Ganja was reported to St Petersburg, where the Russian government passed the report on to representatives of other governments. The British mission reported the information onward to London on 24 December 1734 (despatch from Rondeau to Harrington, in the Public Records Office, State Papers 91, Vol. 17, fol. 183). A translation of Nader's own account of the Battle of Baghavard was later passed back to London in the same way (see below).

21. JN, Vol. 1, pp. 196–7.

22. Lockhart 1938, p. 86.

23. JN, Vol. 1, pp. 202–3; Mirza Mahdi may have adjusted the numbers killed in favour of the Persians.

24. See Nader's own account in State Papers 91/18 fols. 237–8; JN, Vol. 1, p. 211; and Abraham of Crete (CAC), p. 28.

25. CAC, p. 30.

26. CAC, p. 32.
27. CAC, p. 102.
28. CAC, pp. 34–5.
29. JN, Vol. 1, p. 211; the Ottoman numbers following come from Nader's own account in State Papers 91/18 fols. 237–8.
30. CAC, p. 35.
31. CAC, p. 38.
32. CAC, pp. 37–41; for the Ottoman casualties, see State Papers 91/18 fols. 237–8; JN, Vol. 1, pp. 213–14; Hanway made a lower estimate of 20,000 Turks killed; but he was not there (Vol. 4, p. 120). Nader's officials passed an estimate of 30,000 to the VOC (Floor, *Nader Shah*).
33. Public Records Office, State Papers 91/18, fol. 238. The earlier quotations are also from this letter.
34. CAC, p. 118.
35. JN, Vol. 1, p. 221.
36. JN, Vol. 1, p. 224. Before he departed, the Tartar Khan Qaplan Girai appointed Ahmad Khan governor of Darband and Sorkhai governor of Shirvan (JN, Vol. 1, p. 222); but the Lazgis were in control in neither place, even before Nader began his campaign against them.
37. JN, Vol. 2, p. 2.
38. ZT, fol. 217b; Lockhart 1938, pp. 96ff.
39. CAC, p. 77.
40. CAC, pp. 56–7 and 57n; JN, Vol. 2, pp. 2–3; ZT, fol. 217b. Mirza Mahdi suggests there were 100,000 delegates at the qoroltai, but Mohsen's figure of 20,000 is more reasonable.
41. Morgan, *The Mongols*, pp. 61–2.
42. CAC, p. 60.
43. CAC, p. 62–3.
44. CAC, p. 64.
45. Fraser, pp. 228, 229 and 233; Floor, *Nader Shah*. The practice of issuing several different streams of written dictation and oral orders simultaneously (reported by Fraser on the authority of Cockell) is reminiscent of Caesar and Napoleon.
46. CAC, pp. 130–3.
47. Avery, pp. 34–5; AAN, p. 446–7.
48. CAC, pp. 70–2.
49. Floor, *Nader Shah*.
50. The sources broadly concur on Nader's message (JN, Vol. 2, pp. 3–4; AAN, p. 453; Fraser, p. 115). The Catholicos Abraham (pp.

88–9) leaves out mention of the Safavid princes (and the killing of the chief mullah later – subjects that were perhaps too sensitive for him) but gives a more detailed and precise idea of the way the discussions were handled and the timing of them. In what follows I have followed the Catholicos' account for the most part.

51. Floor, *Nader Shah*.
52. AAN, p. 455. Riyahi, Mohammad Kazem's editor, suggests in a footnote that there may be some doubt that Abol-Hasan is the correct name. Fraser's account – p. 118 – has the chief mullah making a principled stand against Nader's religious innovations at a later stage of the qoroltai, and paying the price for it, but Mohammad Kazem's account is more authoritative.
53. I have made a composite version of Nader's three conditions, drawing upon the accounts of CAC (pp. 90–1) and JN (Vol. 2, p. 5), who agree on the essentials.
54. CAC, p. 92; Mohsen gives a similar account of the delegates' views (fol. 217b).
55. CAC, p. 92.
56. CAC, p. 144.
57. The text of the five proposals is taken from Lockhart's (*Nadir Shah*, p. 101) translation of Mirza Mahdi (JN, Vol. 2, p. 6), with some amendments. The gist of the proposals, which were later presented to the Ottoman government in Istanbul, is corroborated in sources from the Ottoman side – see Tucker 1996, p. 24.
58. CAC, p. 110. The remainder of the Catholicos' account was reported by another priest, who stayed on in his place.
59. CAC, pp. 110–11.
60. CAC, pp. 112–15.
61. Sheikh Hazin, p. 272; for the rumours, see Vatatzes, p. 237 and Hanway, Vol. 4, p. 123 (both believed it).
62. Though Lockhart 1938 (p. 279n) mentions a story that a theologian, Seyyed Mortaza, of the Buyid period, suggested to the caliph a solution to the schism in Islam whereby the Shi'as should be allowed a fifth mazhab, to be called the Ja'fari. There is no indication that Nader or any of his advisers were aware of this story, or that the idea was common currency. The VOC records suggest that Nader may have begun some anti-Shia measures as early as the spring of 1734, when it seems he banned the Ashura ceremonies in Isfahan (Floor, *Nader Shah*).
63. Darling, p. 3; Tucker 1993, pp. 109–10; see also Lambton 1980. Among

the contemporary authorities, this theme is particularly strong in Mirza Mahdi's account.

64. The source for this is a document cited in Mohammad Hosein Quddusi's *Nadernama*; quoted in Tucker 1992, pp. 26–7.

65. Tucker 1994, pp. 174–5. My interpretation of the significance of the Ja'fari mazhab proposal owes much to Tucker's careful analysis. Mohammad Kazem says that people continued in private to perform the traditional *ta'zieh* re-enactments of the martyrdoms of Karbala despite Nader's ban on them (p. 982). See also Algar's (1977) discussion of the significance of these developments for Shi'ism more widely.

66. CAC, pp. 143–4; Bazin, pp. 285–6; Floor, *Nader Shah*. Most of the coin and seal inscriptions from the early part of Nader's reign also seem to avoid using the title 'Nader Shah' directly. The VOC records suggest the title *Valine'mat* was used until the end of the Turkestan campaign in 1740 (see below), though this is not corroborated by the Persian sources. There are many examples of the title of 'Shah' being used earlier, and Sheikh Hazin explicitly says Nader assumed it at the Moghan (p. 270). It may be that Nader forbore to use the title officially, but that it was generally used of him outside court and administrative circles.

67. Krusinski, Vol. 1, p. 106.

68. Lambton 1977, pp. 123–7. See also Chapter 7 below, note 13.

69. Hanway, Vol. 1, p. 271.

70. JN, Vol. 2, p. 14.

71. Hanway, Vol. 4, p. 276.

72. Bazin, p. 318.

73. Rambaud, *Histoire de la Russie* (Paris 1900), p. 442 (the reference in Lockhart 1938, p. 281n is incorrect).

74. Reza Sha'bani, quoted in Tucker 1994, p. 165.

75. Mohammad Mahdi ibn Mohammad Reza; quoted in Lockhart 1938, p. 281. It is impossible to know whether stories like this are strictly true, but by reporting ideas that contemporaries exchanged and found credible, they can still tell us important things about their subject.

76. Hanway, Vol. 4, pp. 218–19. Napoleon in his own delusions of grandeur said something similar – see the memoirs of Mme de Remusat, quoted by David Chandler in his *Campaigns of Napoleon* (London 1998), p. 248. The VOC records confirm the story of the translation of the gospels (Floor, *Nader Shah*).

77. Bazin, p. 318.
78. Tucker 1994, pp. 176–7; Moreen 1990, p. 52.
79. Some of the sources that portray Nader's religious scepticism most starkly are western (Bazin, Malcolm, Hanway, VOC) which might make one suspicious; but the Persian authorities would be naturally reluctant to speak openly about the religious shortcomings of a great King. As on other matters, the western writers would have been dependent for information on their Persian contacts, and for the most part probably only repeated what they had been told by them in confidence. One of the most trustworthy and thoughtful Muslim sources, Abd ol-Karim Kashmiri, says that Nader ceased to pray and show respect for God from the time of the beginning of his campaign in Daghestan (p. 164). Even aside from other evidence, Nader's annexation of religious endowments was an exceptional action, requiring an explanation.
80. Morgan, *The Mongols* (Oxford 1990), pp. 201–3 – 'Timur's career was really a series of plundering expeditions on a massive scale.'
81. Fraser, pp. 121–2.
82. Fraser, p. 122: Sefatgol, p. 229; Lambton *Landlord and Peasant*, pp. 131–2.
83. Subrahmanyam 2000, p. 368 and elsewhere makes a case for Nader as a forward-looking, charismatic, Napoleon-like leader rather than a backward-looking figure.
84. CAC, p. 145 (translation slightly amended).
85. Fraser, pp. 126–7.

Chapter 7 – TO THE GATES OF DELHI
1. Floor 1998, p. 198.
2. Tucker 1996. This article, drawing heavily on Ottoman sources, gives an excellent account of the negotiations and their significance. See also the *Cambridge History of Iran*, Vol. 7, p. 308.
3. Ibid., p. 26.
4. GD, 18/29 June 1735; Floor 1987, pp. 39–40.
5. JN, Vol. 2, p. 14; Floor 1987, pp. 41–2.
6. Floor, *Nader Shah*.
7. JN, Vol. 2, pp. 20–1; AAN, p. 475.
8. Floor, *Nader Shah*; GD 23 August/3 September 1736.
9. Floor, *Nader Shah*; GD 23 August/3 September 1736.
10. Floor, *Nader Shah*; the account of the situation in Bandar Abbas and the seizure of merchants' animals on the road comes from the GD,

18/29 August 1736.

11.   Lambton 1977, pp. 123–7; drawing on Rostam ol-Hokama (pp. 557–8) and the *Fars-Nama* of Hajji Mirza Hasan Fasa'i. Nader's administration must have involved a major bureaucratic effort.

12.   JN, Vol. 2, p. 21; Floor, *Nader Shah*; Fraser, p. 128; Hanway, Vol. 4, p. 146. The VOC in Isfahan estimated the total size of the army at 200,000 plus 20,000 women, but their man in Kerman confirmed Hanway's and Fraser's figure of 80,000 (plus 900 sutlers). Hanway drew on Fraser's account but may have had other sources; he gives 30,000 men for Tahmasp Khan Jalayer's corps where Fraser gives 40,000. Hanway and the VOC representative in Isfahan doubted that such a large force could have taken the desert route to Kerman; but they did.

13.   JN, Vol. 2, pp. 23–4; AAN, pp. 486–8. As elsewhere, Mohammad Kazem's account is more detailed, but one suspects that Mirza Mahdi may have confined himself to facts of which he was certain. The latter says that Hosein Soltan led the attack personally; the former names other commanders.

14.   JN, Vol. 2, pp. 25–6.

15.   JN, Vol. 2, p. 31; Floor, *Nader Shah*.

16.   Floor, *Nader Shah*.

17.   Ibid.

18.   JN, Vol. 2, p. 33; AAN, p. 536.

19.   Floor, *Nader Shah*.

20.   JN, Vol. 2, pp. 39–40; Floor, *Nader Shah*.

21.   JN, Vol. 2, p. 40. The Jones translation of Mirza Mahdi gets the date of this attack wrong, and the total number of Persian troops involved.

22.   JN, Vol. 2, pp. 42–3; AAN, p. 544.

23.   AAN, p. 542.

24.   JN, Vol. 2, p. 44; Floor, *Nader Shah*; AAN, pp. 544–8. Lockhart (*Nadir Shah*, p. 119) has the final assault taking place on 23 March (2 Dhu'l-Hejja), but Mirza Mahdi seems to say the preparations took place on that day, and the assault on the day following. The VOC records (Floor) agree the successful attack took place on 24 March (3 Dhu'l-Hejja). Anand Ram, like AAN, says that Kandahar fell through treachery (though he says a traitor actually opened a gate to the Persians – ARM, fol. 163a).

25.   JN, Vol. 2, p. 44; AAN, p. 549.

26.   JN, Vol. 2, p. 45.

27.   AAN, p. 550.

28.   JN, Vol. 2, pp. 46–8; Bazin, p. 287; Floor, *Nader Shah*.

29.   Riazul Islam, Vol. 2, pp. 49–50 summarises the letter carried by Nader's ambassador, and gives the earlier correspondence in which Nader urged action against the Afghan fugitives.

30.   JN, Vol. 2, pp. 50–1.

31.   Two of the more authoritative sources for this are JS (p. 2), and Fraser (p. 129): though the former strongly favoured Khan Dowran and the Hindustani faction and was therefore hostile to the Nezam ol-Molk. There is no mention of the letters in the main Persian sources, and it is just possible that the whole story was fabricated by the Hindustani faction to discredit their rivals. But Chandra (p. 249) thought the story plausible. Tucker (1998) also explores some of the intricacies of Moghul court politics, and of the authors who wrote to aggrandize the interests of the main courtiers.

32.   Chandra, pp. 266–7; Gommans *Mughal Warfare*, pp. 68–9; Subrahmanyam, p. 350; Alam, pp. 303–7 and passim.

33.   This is of necessity an over-simplified overview of complex and contentious issues. For the state of India at this time, see Chandra, Subrahmanyam, Sarkar, Alam, Bayly and Spear.

34.   Floor, *Nader Shah*.

35.   ARM fols. 164a–164b (Lockhart *Nadir Shah*, p. 125n has, fol. 163b incorrectly).

36.   ARM fols. 163b–164a; Hanway, Vol. 4, p. 151. It might sound improbable that the recoil of a single gun could have done such damage, but the structure could have been weakened by several discharges, it is likely that the fortifications were in poor repair, and the tower could well have served as a buttress to a section of wall. The Moghuls had a penchant for huge cannon, which had a weighty recoil. The soldiers' punishment appears in Fraser, p. 151.

37.   JN, Vol. 2, pp. 52–5; a letter appears in Fraser, pp. 138–9 and is discussed by Riazul Islam 1982, Vol. 2, pp. 60–2.

38.   JN, Vol. 2, p. 57.

39.   AAN, pp. 584–585; Lockhart *Nadir Shah*, p. 164; The *Cambridge History of Iran* (Vol. 7, p. 42) seems to be in error on this point.

40.   AAN, p. 603.

41.   See for example Bratishchev, pp. 479 and 475.

42.   JN, Vol. 2, p. 59; AAN, pp. 624–5. Lockhart doubted (p. 168n) that Mohammad Kazem could have known of private instructions given by Nader to his son, but it is likely that he told his sons' advisers what the instructions were.

43.   Bratishchev, p. 483.

44. Lockhart *Nadir Shah*, p. 169; JN vol2, pp. 85–6.
45. JN, Vol. 2, p. 61; Sheikh Hazin, p. 290; Fraser, pp. 134–6; Floor 1998, p. 208; the 10,000 figure for the cavalry force that Nader attacked with comes from Fraser. See Bellamy 1990 for the analysis of this clash by the Russian General Kishmishev – '…a masterpiece in the History of War' (p. 214).
46. JN, Vol. 2, pp. 61–2; AAN, p. 676.
47. ARM fols. 167b–168a; Sheikh Hazin, pp. 293–4; JS, p. 2, JN, Vol. 2, pp. 63–4.
48. ARM fols. 168b–169a.
49. The 300,000 figure comes from Mirza Mahdi, and corresponds with a report from the VOC in Delhi in mid-December (Floor 1998, p. 205n). Mirza Zaman gave a total of 200,000 fighting troops (Fraser, p. 153). ARM gave more than 50,000 horsemen, but there would have been a large number of footsoldiers in addition. Sarkar (p. 38) suggests there may have been as many as a million in the camp all told. 200,000 fighting troops and one million total is enormous, but reasonable. The VOC estimate of 500 battle-trained elephants (as opposed to animals used to move guns and baggage) and 1200 cannon is plausible.
50. JN, Vol. 2, pp. 65–7.
51. JS, p. 7; Tieffenthaler, p. 49; Sarkar, pp. 40–2; the account of conditions in the camp comes from Floor 1998, p. 306.
52. Sarkar, quoting Gholam Hosein.
53. The description of the Persian light cavalry comes from De Voulton, quoted in Subrahmanyam, p. 358 and Lockhart 1926 p. 234; and from the letter of Père Saignes, which seems to derive from the same source. There are some discrepancies between the various versions; in particular Subrahmanyam and Père Saignes have the musket as a *fusil à meiche* (matchlock), while Lockhart says a flintlock. The accuracy of the French texts is probably better. A cavalryman would always have preferred a flintlock or miquelet-lock weapon to a cumbersome matchlock. But at this period the more expensive weapons would have gone to elite troops like Nader's gholam cavalry and jazayerchis; it is quite plausible that light cavalry skirmishers would have had cheaper matchlock weapons (see Gommans 2001, p. 376). De Voulton describes the cloak as 'a cloth garment in the style of the *Heyduque*' – the Hungarian light cavalry of the period, whose long cloak (sometimes hooded, and worn loosely over the shoulders) later evolved into the hussars' pelisse. Saignes' version

gives the horsemen a shield in addition, and says their coats were green, yellow or red. We know from other descriptions and pictorial evidence that Nader also had armoured heavy cavalry (notably Abraham of Crete, p. 118).

54. JN, Vol. 2, pp. 66–8; Tieffenthaler, p. 49.

55. JN, Vol. 2, p. 68; the speech is from Brosset, Vol. 2, 2me Livraison, p. 358.

56. Fraser, pp. 154–5; Hanway, Vol. 4, p. 164. Hanway largely repeats Mirza Zaman's estimate, as reported by Fraser, but adds some details. Others give lower numbers for the Persian army – Floor 1998 says 50,000 (p. 307). The version of De Voulton's reports in the French archives (Subrahmanyam, p. 358) gives an army of 80,000 horsemen and 20,000 infantry, which with the addition of camp-followers would be about right. But the Portuguese version translated by Lockhart (Lockhart 1926, p. 230) gives 60,000 total, of which only half were fighting troops. It is likely that the discrepancy arose in the translation and retranslation that led to the Portuguese text. This is the version which mentions the Europeans; De Voulton may have mentioned the Englishmen to prejudice French readers further against Nader.

57. For my account of the battle I have drawn upon JN, Vol. 2, pp. 68–72; Fraser, pp. 155–9; ARM fols. 169b–170b; JS, pp. 9–23; Hanway, Vol. 4, pp. 165–7; BW, fols. 76a–79a; Brosset, Vol. 2, 2me Livraison, pp. 358–60 (Erekle II's letter to his sister); Tieffenthaler, pp. 49–51; Sarkar 42–52; and Lockhart *Nadir Shah*, pp. 135–40. Most of the main authorities give a similar account of events, but they differ on important details, creating some confusion. My interpretation differs from Lockhart's. Of the main contemporary sources for the battle, only two were soldiers and eyewitnesses present on the battlefield – the Georgian prince Erekle, and Nader himself (Malcolm, *Two Letters*; Riazul Islam 1982, Vol. 2, pp. 74–6 summarises the same letter, but without the detail of the battle). The remainder got their accounts of the fighting at second hand. Reading those two accounts carefully, along with Tieffenthaler (who gives more detail on the positions of the various bodies of troops than most, and places the Persian camp further east, which is important), Abd ol-Karim Kashmiri's, and Mirza Mahdi's, led me to revise the previous interpretation of events. The new interpretation does not seriously conflict with the other contemporary accounts (Anand Ram, Siddiqi, Harcharan Das, Hanway, Fraser), which are important for individual incidents. Several writers are

clear that Mortaza Mirza commanded in the Persian centre. Erekle and Tieffenthaler agree that Sa'adat Khan attacked there, and that Khan Dowran attacked toward Kunjpura (plausible anyway for the fact that Nader posted himself and his best troops there, where the larger body of enemy troops were heading). Erekle, who was in the Persian centre with Mortaza Mirza, says directly that Sa'adat Khan fought on after Khan Dowran's command had been defeated. This too is plausible, given the weight of firepower directed at Khan Dowran's men. I have followed Anand Ram's account (supported according to Sarkar by Gholam Hosein Tabatabai) in suggesting that Sa'adat Khan left the Indian camp without conferring with the other commanders. I have discounted the suggestion in Hanway (repeated by Lockhart and Sarkar) that Nader, like Timur, used platforms of burning materials slung between camels to scare the Moghul elephants. No other source corroborates it, Hanway was not there, and it sounds very like a fable some mischievous veteran thought amusing to repeat to a credulous Englishman.

58. BW, fol. 77b.
59. ARM fol. 169b.
60. JS, p. 11.
61. Malcolm *Two Letters*, p. 543.
62. JN, Vol. 2, p. 70; Brosset, Vol. 2, 2me Livraison, p. 359.
63. JS, p. 12.
64. Fraser, p. 68. Other Moghul sources give a similar story – cf. Tucker 1998, p. 216. See also JS, p. 19.
65. Fraser, p. 158n.
66. BW, fols. 78a–78b.
67. AAN, pp. 14, 729. Lockhart (*Nadir Shah*, p. 140n) was sceptical that Mortaza was renamed on this occasion, saying that no other account gives him that name previously – but the Catholicos Abraham calls him Mortaza Qoli (eg, pp. 84, 114), though he seems initially to have confused him with Nader's nephew Ali Qoli (p. 78). The figure for the Indian casualties is taken from de Voulton, (Lockhart 1926, p. 230) (Nader himself, probably exaggerating, put the numbers higher; and said an even larger number were taken prisoner) and those for the Persians from Fraser, p. 168; on p. 158 Fraser mentions higher numbers, but these were probably exaggerated.
68. Sarkar, pp. 51–2.
69. Tieffenthaler, p. 50.
70. BW, fol. 77b.

71. For an intelligent discussion of the state of Moghul warfare in the eighteenth century, see Gommans 2001, pp. 366–73. See also the quotations from De Voulton in Subrahmanyam, p. 358.
72. Tieffenthaler, p. 52; Sarkar, pp. 56–62; Mohammad Bakhsh ('Ashub') in Elliot and Dowson, Vol. 8, pp. 233–34.
73. The account of the meeting with the Nezam was reported by the Frenchman de Voulton, who was in the Nezam's entourage. It is known in several versions. There is Lockhart's translation of a version in Portuguese (Lockhart 1926), there is a version in the French national archives, from the records of the French colonial company (quoted extensively by Subrahmanyam), and a version in Hanway (Vol. 4, pp. 168–9). Although both Lockhart and Subrahmanyam have their doubts about de Voulton, at this point he reports detail about discussions the outline of which many of the other sources agree. Being so close to the Nezam's interest, De Voulton would not have reported any allusion to the previous correspondence between Nader and the Nezam. See also Sir J Sarkar's account (pp. 56–60), based largely on Harcharan Das. Hanway (Vol. 4, p. 171n) gives the amount agreed for the tribute as 20 crore, Tieffenthaler 2 crore. Sir J. Sarkar favoured the lower figure of 50 lakhs.
74. Lockhart 1926, p. 233; BW, fol. 80a; JN, Vol. 2, p. 72.
75. Lockhart *Nadir Shah*, p. 142, citing Harcharan Das; JS, p. 24.
76. JS, p. 26.
77. ARM fol. 173a; Fraser, p. 175, Sarkar, pp. 62–3.
78. JS, p. 26; ARM fol. 173b; the quotation comes from Fraser, p. 218.
79. ARM 172b; JN, Vol. 2, p. 73; BW fols. 80b–81a

Chapter 8 – THE RUIN OF PERSIA
1. BW, pp. 8–10.
2. GD, 5/16 February 1740; Floor, *Dutch Trade*.
3. See Subrahmanyam 2000. For the currency reform, see GD for 5/16 February 1740.
4. Lockhart 1926, p. 237.
5. Fraser, pp. 211–12.
6. Chandra, p. 237 and Riazul Islam 1970, p. 185 agree the important effect of the Persian invasion.
7. Fraser, pp. 215–16.
8. JN, Vol. 2, p. 83; BW, p. 2.
9. JN, Vol. 2, p. 83; ARM fols. 179a–180b; BW, pp. 3–5; Hanway, Vol. 4, pp. 201–2; Floor *Nader Shah*; GD 22 Feb/5 March 1740; Malcolm, Vol.

2, p. 86. JN and ARM disagree on the timing of Nader's arrival at the Chenab, but agree on the date the crossing was completed.

10. BW, pp. 10–11.

11. JN, Vol. 2, pp. 84–8; Hanway, Vol. 4, pp. 200–1.

12. BW, pp. 15–16; JN, Vol. 2, pp. 88–9. Lockhart 1938 (p. 159) follows BW in saying that a quarter of the spoils of India were lost with these animals, but Mirza Mahdi says the treasures were on their way to Herat.

13. JN, Vol. 2, pp. 90–2; ARM fols. 182b–183a; BW, p. 21.

14. The text of the letter requesting the governor's support appears in ARMfol 181a and in Riazul Islam 1982, Vol. 2, pp. 87–9.

15. Floor 1987, pp. 46–7; GD entries for October and November 1739; Lockhart 1936, p. 11.

16. ARM fol. 184a; BW, pp. 21–2.

17. JN, Vol. 2, pp. 94–6. Given that Mirza Mahdi, as Nader's court historian, ignores or obscures most of the tragic events that were about to overtake Nader, I suspect that he indirectly alluded to the disasters to come by rose-tinting this episode.

18. JN, Vol. 2, p. 97.

19. GD, entries for November 1739; Lockhart 1938, p. 176.

20. GD 23 December 1739/3 January 1740; Bratishchev, pp. 471–2. The beheadings appear in the VOC reports, on the authority of Reza Qoli's Dutch physician (Floor, *Nader Shah*).

21. The VOC record indicates a gap between 23 June, when news of the victory at Karnal reached Isfahan, and 12 December, when a courier arrived there from Peshawar (Floor *Nader Shah*). The GD also reports a reappearance of the rumours of Nader's death in October/ November 1739.

22. The AAN (pp. 766–77) suggests that the murders happened shortly before Reza Qoli received word of Nader's victory at Karnal. Lockhart believed that there was a long hiatus in communications that meant Reza Qoli did not get the news of Karnal until late February or early March 1740 (though even Lockhart – p. 178n – said it was astonishing the news should have taken so long to reach Mashhad). Lockhart may have been led astray by Bratishchev, who says that the murders took place in the first half of 1740 (p. 467). But Bratishchev's chronology is confused; he too links the murders to the hiatus in communications in spring 1739, but says explicitly that this hiatus only lasted three months, from Nader's conquest of Lahore. That makes it possible that the 1740 date in Bratishchev's text was a

simple editorial error, and should have read 'the first half of 1739'. Newly available evidence from the VOC archives backs up the view that the murders took place in May or June 1739. That authority says that the news of the victory at Karnal reached Isfahan on 23 June 1739; on 30 June the Dutch reported a rumour that Tahmasp had fled (his flight features as part of the story of the murders in Hanway also – Vol. 4, p. 209); on 3 July that Tahmasp had been killed, and on 18 August 1739 that Mohammad Hosein Khan had been the murderer (Floor *Nader Shah* and correspondence with Willem Floor). Sheikh Hazin says directly (pp. 301–2) that Tahmasp was put to death on 7 Safar 1152 (16 May 1739) – the same day that Nader left Delhi. The Wakhusht Chronicle also dates the murders to 1739, not 1740 (Brosset, Vol. 2, 1e livraison, p. 404). There is a gap in the Gombroon diary from July 1738 to August 1739.

23. AAN, pp. 766–71. Bratischev's suggestion (p. 468) that Reza Qoli murdered Fatima Begum is less plausible.
24. JN, pp. 99–100; BW, pp. 26–7; AAN, pp. 626, 654–6.
25. Bratishchev, p. 480.
26. AAN, p. 785; BW, p. 29; Bratishchev, pp. 478–9.
27. JN, Vol. 2, p. 83, pp. 101–3; AAN, pp. 788–93; BW, pp. 34–9. Mirza Mahdi and BW record no battle at Qarakol. Mohammad Kazem describes it in some detail, and Lockhart follows his account (*Nadir Shah*, pp. 187–8), but all three historians were with the army at this point, and Mirza Mahdi is normally more reliable. It is possible there was some kind of skirmish. There are other discrepancies between the historians' coverage of the Turkestan campaign (notably on the movements of the princes). I have tended to follow Mirza Mahdi and Abd ol-Karim Kashmiri.
28. BW, p. 44.
29. BW, pp. 165–6 and, pp. 92–3.
30. AAN, pp. 800–1; Lockhart 1938, pp. 189–90. As far as is known, Reza Qoli remained unmarried after Fatima Begum committed suicide – but the family tree Lockhart put together on the basis of Mohammad Kazem's account (*Nadir Shah*, p. 291) suggests she gave him three more sons after her death. Either there was another marriage that went unrecorded, or they were the children of concubines.
31. JN, Vol. 2, pp. 107–8; BW, pp. 50–1; BW makes the battle more close-fought, saying the Persians were weakened by thirst and wavering until Nader brought up water and rallied them.
32. JN, Vol. 2, pp. 108–9; Floor *Nader Shah* (on Taqi Khan). Bratishchev

(p. 479) says that Reza Qoli left Nader at Chaharju because he was ill, but this seems unlikely.

33.   BW, pp. 57–60; AAN has a battle at Fetnak, between Deve Boyun and Hazarasp, but again neither Mirza Mahdi nor BW mention it.

34.   JN, Vol. 2, pp. 109–12; Floor, *Nader Shah* (the VOC record is based on a victory declaration – *Fathname* – sent from Nader to Reza Qoli); Hanway, Vol. 4, p. 206 (the quote is from Hanway).

35.   JN, Vol. 2, pp. 113–14; Hanway, Vol. 4, p. 207.

36.   Floor, *Dutch Trade*; Bazin, p. 294; Hanway, Vol. 1, p. 245.

37.   Malcolm *History of Persia*, Vol. 2, p. 103n – Malcolm says the story was taken from 'a Persian MS in my possession'. See also Lambton *Landlord and Peasant*, p. 132; for the system of security on the roads under the Safavids see Floor 2000, pp. 33–5.

38.   Floor, *Nader Shah*.

39.   BW, pp. 51–2.

40.   BW, pp. 71–2.

41.   Hanway, Vol. 4, pp. 3–4.

42.   Hanway, Vol. 4, p. 245 says that Mashhad was considered as the capital by 1744, but no authority seems to have knowledge of any decree to this effect, or to know from what date Mashhad became the capital.

43.   BW, p. 74; AAN, p. 827. For other examples of his vacillation over and ultimate rejection of royal self-importance, see Floor, *Nader Shah* for his rejection of the palace built for him in Qazvin, and note 49 below.

44.   JN, Vol. 2, p. 115; BW, pp. 75–6; Sheikh Hazin, p. 272; Hanway, Vol. 4, p. 270. Hanway is the only one of these authorities to say there were executions on this occasion.

45.   GD, 7/18 May 1734.

46.   Lockhart 1936, p. 12 (quoting the Gombroon diary); Bazin, p. 319.

47.   For the preceding paragraphs see Lockhart 1938, pp. 182–4 and 212–16; and Lockhart 1936; and Floor 1987, pp. 43–9 (though there seems to be a misprint in Floor's article for the date of the naval battle of January 1739). These accounts give a more detailed version of events.

48.   AAN, p. 832.

49.   Bratischev, p. 480.

50.   JN, Vol. 2, p. 118.

51.   Vatatzes, p. 277. Cf. Bratishchev, pp. 474–77; especially, p. 475. In Vatatzes' narrative this treasonous statement led directly to the

blinding of Reza Qoli, and took place later, while Nader was in the Caucasus. But despite Vatatzes' imprecision on the sequence of events, this account is close to the sort of thing Reza Qoli (and others) would have been saying at this time. Mohammad Kazem (p. 837) agrees that Nader was warned about Reza Qoli before the assassination attempt in the Savad Kuh.

52. AAN, pp. 833–4; BW, pp. 80–1.
53. JN, Vol. 2, pp. 120–2.
54. Hanway, Vol. 1, p. 249.
55. AAN, pp. 834–5; JN, Vol. 2, pp. 122–3; BW, pp. 85–6; Hanway, Vol. 4, p. 210; Bratishchev, pp. 483–6.
56. Bratischev, p. 487; JN, Vol. 2, p. 123.
57. Lockhart 1938, p. 200 (quoting Soloviev).
58. Bazin, p. 319.
59. BW, pp. 163, 165–6.
60. JN, Vol. 2, pp. 123–5.
61. JN, Vol. 2, p. 125.
62. JN, Vol. 2, p. 126; Bazin, p. 290; Hanway, Vol. 4, p. 224.
63. Han way, Vol. 1, pp. 126–7 and, Vol. 4, pp. 225–6; Lockhart 1938, pp. 204–6.
64. JN, Vol. 2, pp. 127–8.
65. JN, Vol. 2, pp. 129–32.
66. JN, Vol. 2, pp. 133–5; Lockhart 1938, pp. 206–7.
67. AAN, pp. 835–7; Bratishchev, p. 490. I have followed Mohammad Kazem's account for the most part.
68. Hanway, Vol. 4, p. 210n.
69. Bratishchev, pp. 495–6.
70. What follows is put together from AAN, pp. 851–3; Bratishchev, pp. 497–503; and Hanway, Vol. 4, pp. 210–11. Mirza Mahdi omits mention of the blinding of Reza Qoli in his main narrative, which was written in Nader's lifetime. He only wrote openly about the blinding in the final chapter of his book, written after Nader's death.
71. Hanway, Vol. 4, pp. 211, 211n.
72. Bratishchev, p. 503. Bazin says Nader had 50 courtiers strangled, who had stood by when Reza Qoli was blinded, because they had not offered themselves in his place (p. 294) but Bazin appears to exaggerate Nader's frightfulnesses at a number of points and these killings are not mentioned by the other authorities.

Chapter 9 – TOWERS OF SKULLS

1.   AAN, p. 853.
2.   JN, Vol. 2, p. 127.
3.   Hanway, Vol. 1, p. 300.
4.   JN, Vol. 2, p. 187.
5.   Viktor E Frankl, *Man's Search for Meaning* (New York 1959), p. 126.
6.   Emin, p. 266.
7.   JN, Vol. 2, p. 139; Lockhart, *Nadir Shah*, pp. 209–11.
8.   JN, Vol. 2, pp. 140–1. The gifts from Mohammad Shah appear likely to be those for which Nader gave thanks in a letter recorded by Riazul Islam 1982, Vol. 2, p. 108.
9.   AAN, pp. 887–8; Hanway, Vol. 1, p. 253.
10.   Christopher Duffy, *The Army of Frederick the Great* Newton Abbot 1974. The Austrian army was 177,500 strong in 1756; the Prussian 143,000 strong.
11.   Emin, pp. 7–8 (for Hamadan); Lockhart, *Nadir Shah*, p. 197 (Mashhad). The Gombroon diary for 19/30 September 1739 suggests a similar effect. See also Floor, *Dutch Trade*. It seems Isfahan did not share in the revival; trade there was at such a low level that the VOC decided in March 1740 to close their factory; and Kerman took more than half a decade to recover from the depredations of 1736. According to VOC records, interest rates were at two per cent per month in Isfahan in March 1738 (Floor, *Nader Shah*); this does not sound low, but it rose to a ruinous 15 per cent per month *minimum* in Bandar Abbas in early 1747 (Lockhart, *Nadir Shah*, p. 286) because the Shah's extortions were so severe and unpredictable that few lenders would take the risk that a borrower would be bankrupted and forced to default before the debt could be repaid. For the suffering and destitution from 1743 onwards, see Hanway, Vol. 1, pp. 223, 233–4, 242–3 and *passim*; Lerch, p. 417 and *passim*; Lambton, *Landlord and Peasant*, p. 133 (quoting from the Chronicle of the Carmelites); Floor, *Dutch Trade*; and Emin, p. 8. Lockhart does not support his claim that the three–year remission of taxes was actually revoked (*Nadir Shah*, p. 238; repeated by Lambton 1977, p. 128 but not substantiated by the reference she cites there); the remission would have expired anyway in the spring of 1742, and it is evident from accounts of his son's viceroyalty that officials in many places continued to collect tax before then anyway.
12.   Floor, *Dutch Trade*.
13.   AAN, p. 914.

14. Hanway, Vol. 4, p. 275; Malcolm (*History of Persia*, Vol. 2, p. 107) gives the same story, taken 'from a Persian MSS'. Compare also Nader's self-justification quoted in Chapter 6 (note 4).

15. See Chapter 6, note 66; also Lockhart, *Nadir Shah*, p. 159 for an example from Nader's campaign in India of a case where the red colour indeed did inspire terror in the way intended.

16. JN, Vol. 2, pp. 142–3.

17. JN, Vol. 2, pp. 144–5; AAN, pp. 899–905; For events in Istanbul, see Olson, pp. 154–6.

18. For the siege of Mosul I have followed JN, Vol. 2, pp. 145–6; Olson 1975, pp. 170–7 and Lockhart, *Nadir Shah*, pp. 229–32. Olson's dates differ slightly at one or two points from those given by Mirza Mahdi; I have followed the latter.

19. The French reported, after Nader's departure from Delhi in 1739, on the strength of Persian sources, that Nader intended to besiege Istanbul and subject the Ottoman Turks (Subrahmanyam, p. 365).

20. Olson 1975, pp. 174–5, 186–7. Olson somewhat over-dramatises the importance of the siege of Mosul, and almost avoids mentioning the later Ottoman defeat at the second battle of Baghavard altogether. See also Lockhart *Nadir Shah*, p. 231.

21. JN, Vol. 2, p. 155.

22. When I wrote this I was thinking of John Winkler's words about the laughter of women in classical Greece ('The Laughter of the Oppressed', in *The Constraints of Desire*, London and New York, 1990, pp. 206–9), but on consulting his text I found that Winkler himself referred back to the researches of Kaveh Safa-Isfahani into mimes and word-play at women's parties in modern Iran.

23. Abdollah al-Suwaydi, quoted in Tucker 1994, p. 171.

24. Abdollah al-Suwaydi, quoted in Lockhart *Nadir Shah*, p. 272.

25. Tucker 1994, pp. 173–5. My account of the council of Najaf follows Tucker's analysis.

26. William Aspinwell, the British diplomatic representative in Istanbul; cited in Olson 1975, p. 186.

27. JN, Vol. 2, p. 161.

28. Hanway, Vol. 4, p. 268; for his attitude to his wife and children, see Bratishchev, p. 483.

29. The description of the Nader's camp is taken from Hanway, Vol. 1, pp. 243–51 and Bazin's plan (p. 242). Bazin gives 3,000 *keshikchi*; Hanway 4,000 and the Catholicos Abraham 6,000 (p. 79); the numbers probably fluctuated at different times.

30.   Hanway, Vol. 1, pp. 251–3.
31.   Hanway, Vol. 1, pp. 265–76.
32.   JN, Vol. 2, pp. 157–9, 164.
33.   Hanway, Vol. 1, pp. 192–4, 296–303; JN, pp. 161–2.
34.   JN, Vol. 2, p. 162.
35.   Lockhart 1936, pp. 12–14; Floor 1987, pp. 51–3.
36.   Floor, *Nader Shah*; Bazin, pp. 196–7; JN, Vol. 2, p. 160–1.
37.   JN, Vol. 2, p. 161; Hanway, Vol. 2, p. 243; Floor, *Nader Shah*; Lockhart, *Nadir Shah*, p. 242.
38.   Hanway, Vol. 4, p. 243.
39.   Hanway, Vol. 4, p. 243; Bazin, p. 197; JN, Vol. 2, p. 161; Lockhart, *Nadir Shah*, pp. 242–3.
40.   JN, Vol. 2, p. 164.
41.   JN, Vol. 2, pp. 165–7. For these events and their chronology, I have followed Mirza Mahdi's account; Lockhart follows von Hammer in placing Nader's arrival at Qars rather earlier, but the later date fits the flow of events better. Mirza Mahdi does not suggest that Nader withdrew from Qars deliberately to attack the Lazgis; in his subtle, indirect way he seems to imply that by this time no-one, Nader included, quite knew what the Shah was going to do from one day to the next.
42.   JN, Vol. 2, pp. 167–8.
43.   JN, Vol. 2, pp. 169–71; AAN, p. 1057. Bazin's account of the marriages is garbled; he seems to date them to 1743 (p. 293). It may be that his editor messed up or misunderstood his dates: a few pages later he jumps from September 1744 to December 1746 (pp. 299–302).
44.   11th Rajab; Lockhart (*Nadir Shah*, p. 250) appears to have confused Mirza Mahdi's dates, giving 11 August. Vatatzes confirms 9 August 1745 as the date (p. 284).
45.   AAN, pp. 1058, 1072. It is doubtful whether Mohammad Kazem would have had a clear idea what this meant; he was probably passing on something told him by one of Nader's officers. There is an echo of this in Vatatzes, who seems at one point to describe the efforts of the Ottoman soldiers to keep to linear formations: 'some curving, some twisted and some straight' (p. 283).
46.   Vatatzes, whose account (pp. 282–3) gives colour to what was previously known of this battle, is the source that says the cavalry of both sides were initially kept back. He says the Persian cavalry were superior and the Ottoman cavalry feared to attack them (one of the sources presented by Sha'bani also says the Ottomans did not have

the will for a cavalry fight – Sha'bani 1977, pp. 34–7). By contrast, Ottoman sources suggest that their troops came close to beating the Persians (*Cambridge History of Iran*, Vol. 7, p. 309).

47. Vatatzes, pp. 283–4; Hanway, p. 252.
48. JN, Vol. 2, p. 172: Sha'bani 1977, pp. 34–7.
49. Vatatzes, p. 284.
50. JN, Vol. 2, pp. 171–4; Hanway, Vol. 4, pp. 252–3; AAN, pp. 1071–2; von Hammer, Vol. XV, pp. 96–7; Vatatzes, pp. 280–5; Sha'bani 1977, pp. 34–7; Lockhart *Nadir Shah*, p. 250. I have used Vatatzes for his vivid details rather than the overall structure of events.
51. AAN, p. 1072.
52. Von Hammer, Vol. XV, p. 98.
53. JN, Vol. 2, p. 176.
54. Emin, p. 12 (the chronology of Emin's time in Isfahan is wrong, but this is the only time that his path could have crossed Nader's).
55. Hanway, Vol. 4, p. 272; the quote following, about the beatings, comes from AAN, p. 1084.
56. AAN, pp. 1084–8.
57. AAN, pp. 1183–5.
58. JN, Vol. 2, p. 178.
59. JN, Vol. 2, pp. 180–4; von Hammer, Vol. XV, pp. 117–8.
60. JN, Vol. 2, p. 179.
61. Bazin, pp. 300–1.
62. Bazin, pp. 300–2; JN, Vol. 2, p. 189; Emin, p. 12.

Chapter 10 – FULL CIRCLE

1. Bazin, p. 304 (physical description, pp. 315–16).
2. JN, Vol. 2, pp. 179, 189; Hanway, Vol. 4, pp. 259–60; Vatatzes, pp. 295–7.
3. JN, Vol. 2, p. 186 (including Nowruz quote); Hanway, Vol. 4, p. 259; Lockhart 1938, p. 259; Bazin, p. 307.
4. Bazin, pp. 307–10.
5. See particularly Lambton 1980 and Darling 2002.
6. JN, Vol. 2, pp. 186, 188.
7. Golestane, p. 13.
8. Bazin, pp. 310–11; JN, Vol. 2, p. 190.
9. Vatatzes, pp. 297–8.
10. Bazin says that Nader had kept a horse saddled in the harem compound for several days, in order to be able to escape in an emergency. Both Bazin and Golestane say he considered flight, or

even left the camp, but was persuaded to return. Nader was plainly not fully rational at this time, and this behaviour is possible, but stories of attempted flight are a stock feature of dramatic narratives in this period.

11.   Bazin, p. 315.

12.   Golestane, pp. 15–19; Bazin, pp. 314–15; BW, pp. 166–7; Hanway, pp. 261–2; JN, Vol. 2, p. 190; Vatatzes, pp. 297–301; Lerch, pp. 443–4. Golestane and Bazin have the most detailed accounts of Nader's murder. According to Bazin, Nader was 65 or 66 when he died; but it is clear that his illness had aged him and even a man with some medical experience could have underestimated the effect of that. Al-Suwaidi exaggerated his aged appearance even further, saying that he looked 80 years of age when he saw him in late 1743 (see Chapter 7). By contrast Abdol Karim Kashmiri, who was a close friend of Nader's physician Alavi Khan (who had much more medical experience than Bazin), believed that he was no more than 50 years old when he died, despite knowing that some people put his birth as early as 1687 or 1691. He said the date of Nader's birth was not known, because no-one had his horoscope (p. 170). The Chevalier Gardane (Clairac, Vol. 3, p. 105) put his age at 'about 40' in 1730, but the VOC reported (with some scepticism) in 1736 a story that Nader was 'over 60', that he was ill and that he was going to retire (Floor, *Nader Shah*). This version, which would produce an impossible birth-date of 1676 or earlier, prompts the theory that rumourmongers hostile to Nader exaggerated his age and infirmity in order to sap confidence in his rule. It is possible that western authors like Hanway were taken in by this, and repeated an earlier date for Nader's birth than was actually the case, creating in time a false orthodoxy about the birth date. See also the first note in Chapter 1.

13.   JN, Vol. 2, pp. 191–2; Bazin, pp. 328–30; Golestane, pp. 22–5.

14.   Bazin, pp. 331–2.

15.   Keddie, *Qajar Iran*, pp. 37, 87, 89.

16.   Keddie, *Qajar Iran*, p. 91.

17.   Malcolm, *History*, Vol. 2, pp. 107–8.

18.   Malcolm, *History*, Vol. 2, p. 97; and Lockhart 1938, p. 209. For the more plausible, contemporary version of Reza Qoli's words, reported by Mohammad Kazem, see Chapter 7.

Select Bibliography

Some of the entries below include brief comments, but for extended discussion of some of the most important contemporary sources, see Tucker 1992, 1993 and 1998; and the appendices of Lockhart's *The Fall of the Safavi Dynasty* and *Nadir Shah*.

Abd ol-Karim Kashmiri *Bayan-e-Waqe'* (BW), trans. H. G. Pritchard, BM MS Add 30782, fols. 64–112; also trans. Francis Gladwin *The Memoirs of Khojeh Abdul-Kurreem*, Calcutta 1788 (Pritchard translated the first half of the text, Gladwin the second; references to the former translation are denoted by folio numbers, to the latter by page numbers). Original Persian text BM MS Add 8909; modern edition ed. K. B. Nasim, Lahore 1970

Abraham of Erevan *History of the Wars (1721–1738)*, ed. and trans. G. A. Bournoutian, Costa Mesa 1999

Abraham of Crete *The Chronicle of Abraham of Crete* (CAC), ed. and trans. G. A. Bournoutian, Costa Mesa 1999

Abo 'l-Hasan ibn Amin Golestane *Mojmal ol-tavarikh*, published as *Mujmil et-Tarikh-e Badnaderije*, Leiden 1891 (Modern edition ed. Mudarris Rezavi, Tehran 1965)

Adle, Chahryar, 'La bataille de Mehmandust (1142/1729)', in *Studia Iranica* 2, Fascicle 2, 1973, pp. 235–41

Alam, Muzaffar, *The Crisis of Empire in Mughal North India: Awadh and the Punjab, 1707–48*, Delhi 1986

Algar, Hamid, 'Shi'ism and Iran in the Eighteenth Century', in *Studies in 18th Century Islamic History*, ed. Thomas Naff and Roger Owen, Carbondale and Edwardsville 1977, pp. 288–302

Anand Ram Mokhles, 'Tadhkere' (ARM), trans. Lt. Perkins, BM MS Add 30780, fols. 162a–184a; printed in Eliot and Dowson, *The History of India as told by its own Historians*, London 1867, Vol. VIII, pp. 76–98

Arjomand, Said Amir, *The Shadow of God and the Hidden Imam*, Chicago 1984

Arunova, M. R., and K. Z. Ashrafyan, *Gosudarstvo Nadir-Shaka Afshara*, Moscow 1958

Astarabadi, Mirza Mohammad Mahdi, *(Tarikh-e) Jahangosha-ye Naderi* (JN), translated into French by Sir William Jones as the *Histoire de Nader Chah*, London 1770; original Persian text ed. Abdollah Anvar, Tehran 1377 (1998) The Jones translation contains many errors, particularly with dates and names, but is an accessible version for those who cannot read Persian of this indispensible history of Nader Shah's life and times. Some of the discrepancies between Jones' translation and modern Persian editions reflect differences between the original Persian manuscripts, rather than inaccuracies in Jones' translation. Mirza Mahdi was Nader's official historian, and understandably avoided including anything critical of Nader in his work. There are also indications that by the time the work was finished (about a decade after Nader's death), Mirza Mahdi needed to avoid offending some of the leading personalities of the Qajar tribe. Nevertheless, Mirza Mahdi's painstaking, detailed account is the single most important source for the life of Nader Shah, and even where it initially looks doubtful he often turns out to be the most accurate source.

Axworthy, Michael, 'Basile Vatatzes and his History of Nader Shah' (article, forthcoming)

Babayan, Kathryn, *Mystics, Monarchs and Messiahs: Cultural Landscapes of Early Modern Iran*, Cambridge (Massachusetts) 2002

Babayan, Kathryn, '"In Spirit We Ate of Each Other's Sorrow": Female Companionship in Seventeenth-Century Safavi Iran' (article, forthcoming)

Bachoud, Pere Louis, 'Lettre du Père Bachoud, Missionaire de la Compagnie de Jésus en Perse, Ecrite de Chamakie le 25 Septembre 1721', in *Lettres Edifiantes et Curieuses Ecrites des Missions Etrangères*, Paris 1780, Vol. IV, pp. 113–124

Bayly, C. A., *Imperial Meridian: The British Empire and the World 1780–1830*, Longman 1989

Bazin, Père Louis, 'Mémoires sur les dernières années du règne de Thamas Kouli-Kan et sa mort tragique, contenus dans un lettre du Frère Bazin' (1751), in *Lettres Edifiantes et Curieuses Ecrites des Missions Etrangères*,

Paris 1780, vol. IV, pp. 277–321 (a second letter by Bazin follows, pages 322–64)

Beck, Lois *The Qashqa'i of Iran*, Yale 1986

Bellamy, Christopher, *The Evolution of Modern Land Warfare: Theory and Practice*, London 1990

Blake, Stephen P., *Shahjahanabad: The Sovereign City in Mughal India, 1639–1739*; Cambridge 1991

Bratishchev, V., *Nachricht von denen traurigen Begebenheiten, die sich zwischen dem Persischen Schache Nadir und dessen Sohne Resa Kuli Mirsa in den Jahren 1741 und 1742 zugetragen haben*, in G. F. Mueller. *Sammlung Russischer Geschichte*, St Petersburg 1763, pp. 459–503

Brosset, M.-F. (ed.), *Histoire de la Géorgie*, St Petersburg 1856–1857, Vol. 2, Parts 1 and 2, (contains *inter alia* the chronicles of Vakhusht and Sekhnia Chkheidze)

de Bruyn, Cornelis, *Voyages*, Amsterdam 1718

Cambridge History of Iran, Cambridge 1961–1991, Vols. 6 and 7 (various editors) – particularly the account by Peter Avery in Vol. 7 of Nader Shah's reign (pp. 3–51)

Cassels, Lavender, *The Struggle for the Ottoman Empire, 1717–1740*, London 1966

Chandra, Satish, *Parties and Politics at the Mughal Court 1707–1740*, second edition, Delhi 1972

Clairac, Louis André de la Mamye, *Histoire de Perse*, Paris 1750

Cooper, Randolf G. S., *The Maratha Campaigns and the Contest for India*, Cambridge 2003

Curzon, Lord G. N., *Persia and the Persian Question*, London 1966

Darling, Linda T., '"Do Justice, Do Justice, for That Is Paradise": Middle Eastern Advice for Indian Muslim Rulers', in *Comparative Studies of South Asia, Africa and the Middle East*, Vol. XXII, Nos. 1 and 2(2002), pp. 3–19

Diba, Layla S., 'Visual and Written Sources: Dating Eighteenth-Century Silks', in Carol Bier (ed.), *Woven from the Soul, Spun from the Heart*, Washington 1987, pp. 84–96

Diba, Layla S., *Royal Persian Paintings*, London and Brooklyn 1998

Dickson, Martin B., 'The Fall of the Safavi Dynasty', in the *Journal of the American Oriental Society*, vol. 82 (1962), pp. 503–17. Dickson's attack on Lockhart in this article is ungenerous and immoderate, notwithstanding his identification of genuine errors on Lockhart's part. The wilder parts of the article are quite groundless and amount to little more than an extended sneer (see above, Chapter 3, note 36). Dickson criticised Lockhart (p. 515 onwards) for ignoring social, economic and other developments in favour of a strictly political account. Compare with Dickson's introduction to his own *Shah Tahmasb and the Uzbeks* (his doctoral thesis); in which he describes the parameters of the study saying 'A further limitation set has been the emphasis on the political aspect of these relations. It is hoped that the necessary background will emerge here to make subsequent cultural, economic and institutional studies more meaningful' (p. 1). Marshall G Hodgson once drew attention to Dickson's failure to publish (*Venture of Islam*, vol. 3, p. 29n): Lockhart's achievement in print was huge by comparison. Since Dickson's death, the publications of his pupils have demonstrated his achievement as a teacher.

Elgood, Robert, *Firearms of the Islamic World*, London 1995

Emin, Joseph, *The Life and Adventures of Joseph Emin*, ed. Amy Apcar, Calcutta 1918

Ferdowsi, *The Tragedy of Sohrab and Rostam*, trans. Jerome W Clinton, Washington 1987, revised edition 1996

Floor, Willem, 'The Revolt of Shaikh Ahmad Madani in Laristan and the Garmsirat (1730–1733)', in *Studia Iranica*, 12 (1983), pp. 63–93

Floor, Willem, 'The Iranian Navy in the Gulf during the Eighteenth Century', in *Iranian Studies*, 20 (1987), pp. 31–53

Floor, Willem, *The Afghan Occupation of Safavid Persia 1721–1729*, Paris 1998

Floor, Willem, 'New Facts on Nadir Shah's Campaign in India', in *Iran and Iranian Studies: Essays in Honour of Iraj Afshar*, ed. Kambiz Eslami, Princeton 1998, pp. 198–219

Floor, Willem, *The Persian Textile Industry*, Paris 1999

Floor, Willem, *The Economy of Safavid Persia*, Wiesbaden 2000

Floor, Willem, *Nader Shah: God's Wrath and Punishment* (forthcoming – based on an earlier version published in Persian in Tehran in 1989). Invaluable like many of Willem Floor's earlier publications, this quotes Dutch East India Company (VOC) source material extensively. As well as providing accurate dating for a number of important events, it gives a lot of rumour and gossip (often with the warning that time would tell whether it was accurate) that adds an extra layer to the range of contemporary source material available.

Floor, Willem, 'Dutch Trade in Afsharid Persia (1730–1753)' (article, forthcoming)

Foran, John, 'The Long Fall of the Safavid Dynasty: Moving Beyond the Standard Views', in *The International Journal of Middle East Studies*, No. 24 (1992), pp. 281–304

Fraser, James, *The History of Nadir Shah*, London 1742. This important early work includes a translation of Mirza Zaman's journal for the period of Nader Shah's invasion of India (Mirza Zaman was an eyewitness to those events), and some eyewitness impressions by the British East India Company's representative in Isfahan, Cockell.

Gellner, Ernest, 'The Tribal Society and its Enemies', in *The Conflict of Tribe and State in Iran and Afghanistan*, ed. R. Tapper, London 1983, pp. 436–48

Gombroon diary (GD) – the records of the British East India Company (EIC) at Bandar Abbas, drawing on letters from their traders in Isfahan, Kerman and elsewhere – held in the India Office Collection of the British Library, classmark G/29/ vols. 3–6 and 16

Gommans, Jos, *Rise of the Indo-Afghan Empire 1710–1780*, Leiden 1995

Gommans, Jos, 'Indian Warfare and Afghan Innovation During the Eighteenth Century', in J. L. Gommans and D. H. A. Kolff (eds.), *Warfare and Weaponry in South Asia 1000–1800*, India 2001, pp. 365–95

Gommans, Jos, *Mughal Warfare*, London 2002

Hall, John A., *Powers and Liberties*, Harmondsworth 1986

von Hammer-Purgstall, J., *Histoire de l'Empire Ottoman* (French translation by J. J. Hellert), Paris 1835–1843

Haneda, M., 'Army III – Safavid', in *Encyclopaedia Iranica*, ed. Ehsan Yarshater, London and New York 1987, Vol. II, pp. 503–06

Hanway, Jonas, *An Historical Account of the British Trade over the Caspian Sea...to which are added The Revolutions of Persia during the present Century, with the particular History of the great Usurper Nadir Kouli* (4 vols.), London 1753. Hanway is a good source for the period when he was an eyewitness in Persia in the early 1740s, but must be used with caution for the remainder of his narrative, which often draws heavily on Clairac, Fraser and others. He sometimes takes an offensively condescending tone when speaking of the Persians, and was criticised by Malcolm (see Introduction, note 4)

Harcharan Das, *Chahar Guldhar Shuja'i*, partly translated by Munshi Sadasukh Lal, BM MS Add 30782, fols. 113–205

Hodgson, Marshall G. S., *The Venture of Islam*, Chicago 1974 (especially Vol. 3: *The Gunpowder Empires and Modern Times*)

Hookham, Hilda, *Tamburlaine the Conqueror*, London 1962

Islam, Riazul, *Indo-Persian Relations*, Tehran 1970

Islam, Riazul, *A Calendar of Documents on Indo-Persian Relations*, Tehran and Karachi 1979/1982

Keddie, Nikki R., *Qajar Iran and the Rise of Reza Khan 1796–1925*, Costa Mesa 1999

Krusinski, Fr Judasz Tadeusz, *The History of the late Revolutions of Persia*,
    London 1740; facsimile edition, New York 1973

Lambton, Ann K. S., *Landlord and Peasant in Persia*, London 1991

Lambton, Ann K. S., 'The Tribal Resurgence and the Decline of the
    Bureaucracy in the Eighteenth Century', in Thomas Naff and Roger
    Owen (eds.), *Studies in 18th Century Islamic History*, Carbondale
    and Edwardsville 1977, pp. 108–29. This important article makes
    compelling use of Rostam al-hukuma in particular, and although some
    have recently questioned Lambton's main thesis, it still repays careful
    study

Lambton, Ann K. S., *Theory and Practice in Medieval Persian Government*,
    London 1980

Lerch, Johann Jacob, '*Nachricht von der zweiten Reise nach Persien von 1745 bis
    1747*', in *Büsching's Magazin*, Vol. 10, Halle 1776

Lockhart, Laurence, 'De Voulton's Noticia', in *Bulletin of the School of Oriental
    Studies*, Vol. 4, Part 2 (1926), pp. 233–45

Lockhart, Laurence, 'The Navy of Nadir Shah', in *Proceedings of the Iran
    Society*, Vol. 1, Part 1, London 1936, pp. 3–18

Lockhart, Laurence, *Nadir Shah*, London 1938

Lockhart, Laurence, *The Fall of the Safavi Dynasty and the Afghan Occupation
    of Persia*, Cambridge 1958. This book, for all the faults identified by
    Martin Dickson (see Dickson 1962), is still the best guide in a single
    volume to the facts of these events in English, as is his *Nadir Shah* for
    the later period; even though Lockhart's idiom is old-fashioned and
    interpretation of events and their causes has moved on. Lockhart
    made errors in his references, as do many scholars, but was careful
    to discriminate between his sources, always giving greater emphasis
    to contemporaries and eyewitnesses. The generous bibliographical
    appendices of both books will still be of value to serious students of the
    period for many years to come.

Lockhart, Laurence, 'The Persian Army in the Safavid Period', in *Der Islam*,
    34 (1959), pp. 89–98

Malcolm, Sir John, 'Translations of Two Letters of Nadir Shah, with
    Introductory Observations in a Letter to the President', in *Asiatick
    Researches*, 1808, Vol. 10, pp. 526–47

Malcolm, Sir John, *History of Persia*, London 1815

Marvi Yazdi, Mohammad Kazem, *Alam Ara-ye Naderi* (3 vols.) (AAN) ed.
    Mohammad Amin Riyahi, Tehran (Third edition) 1374/1995. Mohammad
    Kazem's history of Nader is frustrating, anecdotal, lacking in dates and
    precision, but gives a lot of detail and many lively stories not found in

any other account. He was a traditionalist and though an admirer of Nader's military successes, he did not approve of Nader's usurpation of the throne, and saw Nader's later troubles as divine punishment.

Matthee, Rudi, 'Unwalled Cities and Restless Nomads: Firearms and Artillery in Safavid Iran', in Charles Melville (ed.), *Safavid Persia: The History and Politics of an Islamic Society*, London 1996, pp. 389–416

Matthee, Rudi, *The Politics of Trade in Safavid Iran*; Cambridge 1999

Matthee, Rudi, *The Pursuit of Pleasure: Drugs and Stimulants in Iranian History 1500–1900*, Princeton 2005

Miklukho-Maklai, N. D., '*Zapiski S Avramova ob Irane kak istoricheskii Istochnik'*, in *Uchenye Zapiski Leningradskogo gosudarstvennogo universiteta. Seriia vostokovedcheskikh nauk*, Part 3 (128), Leningrad 1952, pp. 88–103

Minasian, Caro A., (ed. and trans.), *The Chronicle of Petros Gilanents*, Lisbon 1959

Minorsky, V., '*Esquisse d'une Histoire de Nadir-chah'*, in *Publications de la Société des Etudes Iraniennes et de l'Art Persan*, No. 10, Paris 1934, pp. 1–46

Minorsky, V. (ed. and trans.), *Tadhkirat al-Muluk*, Cambridge 1943

Mohsen, Mohammad, *Zobdat ot-Tavarikh* (ZT); Browne MS. G. 15 (13), Cambridge (modern edition ed. Behruz Gudarzi, Tehran 1375/1996). Mohsen was one of Nader's tax officials. Nader commissioned this history for his son, Reza Quli, and it was written in 1741/1742. Mohsen is an important source, particularly for the reigns of Shah Sultan Hosein and his son Tahmasp, but his account ends in 1736. Unlike Mirza Mahdi, who was relatively gentle with Nader's predecessors, Mohsen was an Isfahani, had been present at the siege of Isfahan and was naturally rather more critical.

Mohsen Siddiqi, Mohammad, *Jowhar-e Samsam* (JS), trans. A. R. Fuller BM MS Add 30784

Moreen, Vera B. (ed.), *Iranian Jewry During the Afghan Invasion* Stuttgart 1990

Morgan, David, *The Mongols*, Oxford 1990

Morton, A. H., 'The chub-i tariq and Qizilbash ritual in Safavid Persia', in J. Calmard (ed.), *Etudes Safavides*, Paris and Tehran 1993

Murphey, Rhoads, *Ottoman Warfare 1500–1700*, London 2003

Olson, Robert W., *The Siege of Mosul and Ottoman-Persian Relations 1718–1743*, Indiana/Bloomington 1975

Parker, Geoffrey, *The Military Revolution*, Cambridge 1988

Parry, V. J., and M. E. Yapp (eds.), *War, Technology and Society in the Middle East*, London 1975

Perry, J. R., 'The Last Safavids', in *Iran* IX (1971)

Perry, J. R., 'Forced Migration in Iran During the Seventeenth and Eighteenth centuries', in *Iranian Studies*, Vol. 8, Part 4 (1975), pp. 199–215

Perry, J. R., *Karim Khan Zand*, Chicago 1979

Perry, J. R., 'Army IV – Afshar and Zand', in Ehsan Yarshater (ed.), *Encyclopaedia Iranica* London and New York 1987, Vol. II, pp. 506–8

Quddusi, Mohammad Hosein, *Nadernama*, Mashhad 1960

Rostam ol-Hokama, trans. and ed. Birgitt Hoffmann, in *Persische Geschichte 1694–1835 erlebt, erinnert und erfunden – das Rustam at-Tawarikh in deutscher Bearbeitung* (2 vols.), Bamberg 1986. If Mohammad Kazem represents the muse of history *en deshabille* (as Sir J Sarkar once wrote), then Rostam ol-Hokama presents her *in flagrante*. This book reveals a whole world of scurrilous rumour and storytelling, of contemporary bazaar gossip, that we might not otherwise have known to exist. With it, we can guess at what may lie behind some of the half-understandings and misunderstandings of contemporary western authors, and the silences of the more orthodox Persian chronicles.

Saignes, Père, 'Lettre du Père Saignes de Chandernagore, 10 Février 1740', in *Lettres Edifiantes et Curieuses Ecrites des Missions Etrangères*; vol. IV, Paris 1780

Sarkar, J. N., *Nadir Shah in India*, Calcutta 1973 (reprint; first published 1925; condensed from a series of lectures given by Sir J Sarkar at Patna University in 1922). An important and painstaking summary of the Indian and Persian sources, but omits some others, notably Erekle IIs letter (in Brosset), Nader's own account of the battle of Karnal (in Malcolm, *2 Letters*) and Tieffenthaler

Sekhnia Chkheidze *Chronique*, in M.-F. Brosset (ed.), *Histoire de la Géorgie*, Vol. 2, 2me Livraison, St Petersburg 1856–1857

Sefatgol, Mansur, 'The Question of Awqaf Under the Afsharids', in Rika Gyselen and Maria Szuppe (eds.), *Studia Iranica: Cahiers vol. 21 / Materiaux pour l'Histoire Economique du Monde Iranien*, Paris 1999, pp. 209–29

Sha'bani, Reza, *Tarikh-e Ejtema'i-ye Iran dar 'asr-e Afshariye*, Tehran 1986

Sha'bani, Reza (ed.), *Hadis-e Nadershahi*, Tehran 1977

Spear, Percival, *History of India* (2 vols.), London 1990

Subrahmanyam, S., '*Un Grand Dérangement*: Dreaming an Indo-Persian Empire in South Asia, 1740–1800', in *Journal of Early Modern History*, Leiden 2000, Vol. IV, pp. 337–79

Tapper, R., *Frontier Nomads of Iran*, Cambridge 1997

Taylor, James S., *Jonas Hanway: Founder of the Marine Society*, London and Berkeley 1985

Tieffenthaler, Father J., '*Beschreibung des Feldzuges Thamas Kulikhan*', in J. Bernoulli (ed.), *Historisch-Geographische Beschreibung von Hindustan*, Berlin 1785–1787, Vol. 2, Part 2, p. 49f.

Tucker, Ernest, *Religion and Politics in the Era of Nadir Shah: The Views of Six Contemporary Sources* (unpublished Doctoral dissertation, University of Chicago, 1992)

Tucker, Ernest, 'Explaining Nadir Shah: Kingship and Royal Legitimacy in Mohammad Kazim Marvi's Tarikh-i alam-ara-yi Nadiri', in *Iranian Studies*, Vol. 26, 1–2 (1993), pp. 95–117

Tucker, Ernest, 'Nadir Shah and the Ja'fari Madhhab Reconsidered', in *Iranian Studies* vol. 27, 1–4 (1994), pp. 163–79

Tucker, Ernest, 'The Peace Negotiations of 1736: A Conceptual Turning Point in Ottoman-Iranian Relations', in *Turkish Studies Association Bulletin*, 20/1 (Spring 1996), pp. 16–37

Tucker, Ernest, '1739: History, Self and Other in Afsharid Iran and Mughal India', in *Iranian Studies*, Vol. 31, No. 2 (Spring 1998), pp. 207–17

Vatatzes Basile, *Voyages de Basile Vatace en Europe et en Asie*, ed. E Legrand, Paris 1886

Vatatzes, Basile, *Persica: Histoire de Chah-Nadir*, ed. N Iorga, Bucharest 1939. Vatatzes' history of Nader was once believed lost, and has been under-exploited, partly because of the difficulty and obscurity of the Greek in which it is written. To my knowledge, mine is the first account of Nader's life that has used Vatatzes' material to any extent; and I have only been able to make a start on it. Vatatzes is repetitive, inexact, frequently inaccurate and untrustworthy, but he was an eyewitness to some events and heard directly from other eyewitnesses about others. Used carefully, he can yield useful information (see my article, forthcoming, above).

Zeller, R., and E. F. Rohrer (eds.), *Orientalische Sammlung Henri Moser-Charlottenfels*, Bern 1955

Index